D1559597

The Lowenfeld Lectures

The Lowenfeld Lectures

Viktor Lowenfeld
on
Art Education and Therapy

EDITED BY JOHN A. MICHAEL
FOREWORD BY LAURA H. CHAPMAN

THE PENNSYLVANIA STATE UNIVERSITY PRESS
UNIVERSITY PARK AND LONDON

The illustrations in this book are from Viktor Lowenfeld, *Creative and Mental Growth,* 3rd ed. (New York: Macmillan, 1957), and have been reproduced by permission, as follows:

Fig. 1: Courtesy Dr. Irene Russell, *Research Bulletin,* The Eastern Arts Association, Vol. 3, No. 1 (1952). Figs. 2–8, 12–14, 16–28, 31, 34–36; Viktor Lowenfeld, *Creative and Mental Growth,* 3rd ed. Figs. 9–11, 29–30, 32–33: Courtesy Educational Project, Museum of Modern Art, New York, N.Y. Fig. 15: *National Geographic Magazine,* Vol. 111, No. 3 (March 1957), p. 379. All charts and the graph: Viktor Lowenfeld, *Creative and Mental Growth,* 3rd ed.

Frontispiece: Dr. Viktor Lowenfeld working with a handicapped child.

Library of Congress Cataloging in Publication Data
Lowenfeld, Viktor.
The Lowenfeld Lectures, Viktor Lowenfeld on Art Education
and Therapy.
Includes bibliography.
1. Art—Study and teaching. I. Michael, John Arthur,
1921–   II. Title.
N85.L65   707   80–29265
ISBN 0–271–00283–2

Contents

CONTENTS

Section II
Art and the Adolescent

Section III
Art Education Therapy

CONTENTS

Foreword by Laura H. Chapman

Viktor Lowenfeld is widely acknowledged as the most influential art educator of this century. His research on children's drawings, paintings, and sculpture is known to an international community of educators, as well as to scholars in developmental and clinical psychology. His investigations of children's art were motivated by a desire to understand how the creative and mental growth of children is mediated by art activity. His studies of the typical developmental stages of children's growth in art were enhanced by his early research into the artistic activity of the blind and partially sighted, the mentally retarded, and the emotionally disturbed. Lowenfeld's research was extensive and rich in information for teachers, but it is not alone for his research that he became so influential. From the testimony of his students and colleagues, Viktor Lowenfeld was also a great teacher and humanitarian.

For those of us who were not privileged to study with Viktor Lowenfeld, this book provides a rare and wonderful opportunity to distinguish the facts from the mythology which now permeates many discussions of his research and teaching. This volume is a compendium of Lowenfeld's class lectures recorded while he was teaching at The Pennsylvania State University in 1958, less than two years before his death. Diligently transcribed and edited by Dr. John A. Michael, and appropriately published by the Penn State Press, the lectures show that Lowenfeld was a man of compassion and flair, of wit and wisdom, of firm beliefs and extraordinary knowledge of human nature. In addition, the transcripts present important extensions of Lowenfeld's thought which have not previously been published, including invaluable commentaries on his most widely read book, *Creative and Mental Growth.*

This record of Lowenfeld's class lectures is a welcome addition to the literature of art education, but it is not just a document of historical interest, for the content of the lectures and the model of educational leadership presented here are relevant today.

Leaders in education have much to learn from the model offered by Viktor Lowenfeld, whose influence continues to be felt more than twenty years following his death. He was a man gifted in the arts of persuasion, and a man of deep convictions; but he was cautious in using these talents and careful to reveal to others the basis of his beliefs. Indeed, throughout these class lectures we find evidence of his concern for the ethical principles which guide educational practice. Having witnessed Hitler's rise to power in Germany and the indoctrination of youth into the Nazi movement, Lowenfeld was acutely aware of the power invested in the role of "teacher" and the potential for the abuse of power by anyone in a position of leadership. As his own reputation grew, he was confronted with the task of exercising leadership without misusing the power others had invested in him through their admiration. He was able to meet this challenge with grace and generosity because his actions were congruent with the humanistic values that he espoused. Through these class lectures, we can more fully appreciate why he became a legend in his own time.

Many topics of current interest in the field of education are treated in these lectures. A few may be cited to suggest the scope and depth of Lowenfeld's thought:

☐ the multi-dimensional nature of learning and "talent";

☐ the manner in which children create and express meaning through art activity;

☐ the concept of "learning by discovery" and methods of teaching which forward active, personal knowledge;

☐ the function of rote mastery and imitation in learning;

☐ the relationship of student attention to the student's emotional and imaginative identification with a subject;

☐ the effect of teaching methods employed in one subject upon learning in another subject;

☐ the relationship between mastery of skills and creative performance in various fields of endeavor;

☐ the contradictions in American culture and their bearing on education in art.

Several class lectures will be of special interest to the growing number of professionals in art therapy and other educators who work with the blind and partially sighted, emotionally disturbed, and mentally retarded. Because Lowenfeld viewed art therapy as a heightened or intensified form of art education, the lectures devoted to case studies of "art as therapy" should be seen as an extension of his more general discussions of children's growth. The case studies are not only valuable demonstrations of the process of interaction which Lowenfeld employed as an educator-therapist, but also reveal the criteria he used in order to judge how effective he had been in this role.

In addition to his pioneering work in art therapy, Lowenfeld was at the forefront of several other directions in education which today are regarded as innovative. Three are particularly important: the interest in qualitative evaluation and research, the active involvement of teachers in the research process, and the use of art criticism as a means of disclosing the educational significance of children's involvement in art.

Viktor Lowenfeld established the first major center for doctoral study and research in art education when he joined the faculty at The Pennsylvania State University. In this program, he encouraged his students to engage in quantitative research and to use the most sophisticated statistical techniques then available to scholars in the behavioral sciences. Nevertheless, what made a lasting impression on many of the researchers he trained was his own sensitivity to the unique, dynamic "wholes" which are the central phenomena in studying children and their art. It is no accident that the first and most fully developed rationale for qualitative research in art education was offered by one of Lowenfeld's students and colleagues, Kenneth R. Beittel, who cites Lowenfeld as a paradigm of the responsive researcher—a researcher who is immersed in specifics and who gains an understanding of contexts and processes through personal engagement with the research situation.*

In these class lectures, we see that one of Viktor Lowenfeld's major aims was to cultivate the teacher's interest and skills in research so the teacher would bring a research orientation into the classroom. The teaching process is portrayed to his students as a responsibility that should be intellectually grasped, inquired into, reflected upon, modified in the light of new understanding. He introduces his students to research as a tool for them to become more sensitive teachers, more conscious of their actions and how children respond to them.

In addition to cultivating this research orientation to teaching and introducing the findings of current research, Lowenfeld developed his students' skill in a form of research that we now would call "art criticism." His intent was to train teachers who would be able to discern the educational significance of children's art activity. Toward this end, Lowenfeld teaches his students to analyze the subject matter in a child's art work and the interpretation the child has given to it, based on the visual "evidence" in the work. His students are called upon to analyze the function of various formal devices—line, color, shape, texture, size, proportion, placement—as carriers of expressive meaning. In the same systematic way, he teaches his students to examine the medium and technique, the function of detail, the role of imitative and invented forms within the art of children. He cautions against making unwarranted inferences when little is actually known about the child or the context in which the work was created. These general procedures are employed so the meaning of the child's work is disclosed as fully as possible. Today, art educators recognize that children, too, can learn to decipher the expressive meaning in visual forms if they are introduced to these and related tools for understanding art.

*Kenneth R. Beittel, *Alternatives for Research in Art Education: Inquiry into the Making of Art* (Dubuque, Iowa: Wm. C. Brown Co., 1973).

In these lectures we see that Lowenfeld, who achieved fame for his analysis of children's growth in art into "stages" and who is known for his distinction between visual and haptic orientations to art, is deeply resentful of categories, pigeonholes, and labels which prevent people from seeing larger patterns and details. In a discussion of the well-known visual-haptic distinction, for example, Lowenfeld says: "Why should you detect visual and haptic? They are only a fraction of our personality. . . . I don't give a damn really whether you can . . . detect visual and haptic tendencies." He then emphasizes the larger point: In teaching the adolescent, there is an alternative path to motivation than the traditional "visual" emphasis on seeing nature, learning perspective, and employing conventional representation. The alternative is to encourage students to sense they are actively and personally involved in an experience and to discover ways of expressing that personal relationship. In the end, Lowenfeld asks: "Do you see, then, the meaning? . . . We have enough cubbyholes—I. Q.'s and I don't know what all—by which we are classified. So let's forget this kind of evaluation, and let's only think of ways that we can reach people."

In the light of his own resentment of labels, I doubt that Lowenfeld would feel comfortable with the fact that he is often regarded as the best representative of the "child-centered" philosophy of art education. His recommendations for teachers were framed with a deep commitment to democracy as the social foundation for education. For Lowenfeld, the freedom to become an individual was a political premise for education, not merely a psychological guidepost. Intellectual growth was clearly important to him, but he did not regard it as independent of other aspects of human development— the social, emotional, creative, aesthetic, and physical dimensions of learning. He was against the mindless development of skills and the exclusive attention given to subject-matter learning which he saw in many schools and which, unfortunately, have been exacerbated by the back-to-basics, minimum-competency movement of the last decade.

That we continue to speak of various educational philosophies as "child-centered," "subject-centered," or "society-centered" betrays one of the most fundamental failures in American education. It is the failure to see that the social and developmental aims of education need not be opposed to the historic mission of the school as an agency for transmitting knowledge from one generation to the next. The teaching of all subjects—the arts, sciences, and humanities—might be improved dramatically if educators were to employ the rich legacy of theory and practice which Lowenfeld has bequeathed to us. It was his hope that the insights gained through the study of artistic activity might inform the work of all educators, not just art educators.

For those educators who want a fresh look at the teaching of subject matter and so-called basic skills, these class lectures will, I believe, suggest why these general aims of education cannot be achieved without giving equal attention to other dimensions of learning too often neglected in schools, particularly the creative and aesthetic dimensions. For art educators who may wish to give greater attention to the study of art as a subject matter—with content to be mastered and skills to be learned—the lectures offer guidance in how this might be accomplished so that learning is meaningful, based on discovery, deeply felt, and long cherished in memory.

I am confident that I speak for many others in education, particularly those in the arts, in expressing my appreciation to those who have made this publication available, especially Dr. John A. Michael, who studied with Lowenfeld and undertook this project as a tribute to him, little knowing how difficult it would be. Through his efforts, we have the rare privilege of turning back the clock and vicariously entering the classroom of a person whose fame has made it difficult to separate fact from fiction. I hope *The Lowenfeld Lectures* will be widely read, not only for their historical importance, but also for their utility in understanding contemporary theory, research, and practice in teaching.

Laura H. Chapman

Cincinnati, Ohio

Editor's Introduction

Viktor Lowenfeld arrived in New York in December of 1938, having escaped with his family via England from the German invasion of Austria. After a brief period of lecturing at Columbia and then at Harvard, he served as Chairman of the Art Department at Hampton Institute, Hampton, Virginia, and also worked at various institutions as an art therapist and psychologist for emotionally and mentally disturbed children. In 1945, while still at Hampton Institute, Dr. Lowenfeld wrote his famous text, *Creative and Mental growth,* which was first published in 1947. In the meantime, he had joined the faculty of The Pennsylvania State University in 1946. The second edition of *Creative and Mental Growth* was published in 1952, and the third edition appeared in 1957. Since Dr. Lowenfeld's death in 1960, other editions have been published, being coauthored by W. Lambert Brittain. Another important book by Dr. Lowenfeld, *Your Child and His Art,* was published in 1954. Books by Lowenfeld have been translated into German, Hebrew, Swedish, Norwegian, Japanese, Arabic, Italian, Spanish, Danish, and Chinese.

In 1957, Lowenfeld was named "Art Educator of the Year" by the National Art Education Association, and his book *Creative and Mental Growth* was used as a text in more colleges and universities than any other book in the field of art education.

As a result of his teaching, research, writing, and speaking engagements, Dr. Lowenfeld became the most significant and influential voice in the field of art education. Many people call the 1950's "The Lowenfeld Era," a fact borne out by the following remarks about his work:

> The significance of Lowenfeld's work for aesthetics or the science of art is fundamental and should cause something like a sensation in the learned world. (Herbert Read)

> In Lowenfeld's work a fine sense of understanding, systematic spirit, and unprejudiced research are combined. (Albert Einstein)

> Lowenfeld does for the drawing of children what Piaget has done for their thinking. *(The Harvard Educational Review)*

The distinctions between impressionism and expressionism have been endlessly discussed and one theory has followed another. The real solutions to such problems entail experimental evidence—the type of data which Dr. Lowenfeld presents. *(The New York Times)*

Lowenfeld's analysis has great importance for general psychology as well as the psychology of art. This serious and fundamental research on a basic aspect of art is one which deserves careful study not only by aestheticians and psychologists, but also by teachers of drawing, painting, and sculpture. *(Parnassus)*

Professor Lowenfeld has made a contribution of the utmost importance to the psychology of the arts and the field of child creativity. *(The Teacher's Forum)*

Dr. Lowenfeld's research, knowledge and insights in the field of art education, and his teaching ability attracted hundreds of students to his classes at Penn State University, where, under his leadership, one of the largest graduate programs in the United States developed. Among the students who came to study with him as a result of his eminent reputation were Mrs. Ellen D. Abell and the writer. Mrs. Abell, who recorded the class lectures of Dr. Lowenfeld which appear in this volume, tells her own story:

In 1956, having read the second edition of Viktor Lowenfeld's book, *Creative and Mental Growth,* I was eager to become more fully acquainted with this book and its author. In no time I was in Dr. Lowenfeld's class at The Pennsylvania State University where the revelations of Dr. Lowenfeld's personality and teaching changed his book from words on the printed page to a dynamic, living source of inspiration and practicality. I had gone to Penn State with no thought of using a tape recorder. Then Dr. Lowenfeld, who had known Cizek personally, read verbatim words which Cizek had used for classes of children as he taught them, and for groups of parents as he presented his ideas of teaching. The dramatic and surely authentic reading made Cizek newly alive for everyone who listened. This led to another idea: how fine it would be to record the qualities of Dr. Lowenfeld's own voice and words—not only his impersonation of Cizek! Yes, as much as possible of Dr. Lowenfeld's voice, and words should be recorded. It was time to approach Dr. Lowenfeld about this. As characteristic of him, he gave me his generous and helpful permission to make the recordings. I liquidated my emergency fund to procure a recorder and tapes. After a little practice, I began recording early in the summer session in 1958. The plan had begun!
   When the tapes and time were ended, I tried to give the recordings to Dr. Lowenfeld (all I had wanted was for them to exist), but he would not accept them, saying that they were mine and that he did not wish them to belong to anyone else.

The taping by Mrs. Abell of the voice of Dr. Lowenfeld when he was doing what he truly loved—talking with his students about children/adolescents and art experiences—was in many ways an act of providence, since his voice was soon to be stilled. These lectures, recorded at the height of his career and less than two years before his death, are indeed remarkable treasures for the field of art education. Dr. Lowenfeld was to teach only one summer (1959) after these tapes were made; he died in May of the following year. To have the recorded voice, in daily lectures, of a great teacher and leader is rare for any discipline. We in art education should "rejoice and be exceedingly glad" that through these taped lectures we and future generations may know Dr. Lowenfeld and his work firsthand.

The responsibility of the Lowenfeld tapes weighed heavily upon Mrs. Abell. She very much wanted the tapes to be transcribed, edited, published, and made available for everyone, but this was a formidable task for her and she seemed unable to accomplish it. Finally, after years of inactivity with the tapes and in failing health, Mrs. Abell gave the tapes to me in 1973, with a request that her original desire be carried out. At this point, I approached Mrs. Lowenfeld and found that she strongly felt the tapes should be made available to the field, both as tapes and in written form. She encouraged me to work with them.

I soon realized that the magnitude of the task was too great for me without the help of other professionally dedicated persons. These were found among the graduate students in art education at Miami University. One of these students, Linda Stevens, copied (with her own advanced audio equipment) all thirty-one tapes in such a way as to screen out much of the background noise and deterioration. Linda also transcribed all of the tapes in longhand, a tedious task that required an average of twenty hours per week for more than a school year. I then listened to all of the tapes while viewing the longhand copy, checking for accuracy. During the next year, the longhand copy of the thirty-one tapes was typed by Nancy Carter. Using the typed lectures, Virginia Shewalter, an English language specialist, put the lectures in correct paragraph form and worked with the punctuation. I again reviewed all of the tapes, comparing the spoken word on the tapes with the text and the intent of Dr. Lowenfeld. At last, the lectures were ready for the final typing. This was done by the following graduate students in art education, who volunteered their services: Linda Barnes, Terry Boone, Ellen Donaldson, Patricia Finn, Cynthia Ford, Phoebe Gallagher, Janean Gille, William Griffith, Pam Hall, Huston Henry, Timothy Kemp, Arlene Klafter, Rebecca Kull, Marti Lampe, Brandon McFadden, Ruth Montelius, Deborah Platter, Mary Louise Shuba, Rosemary Stimson, Bobbie Walker, and Margaret Williams. I listened once more to all of the tapes as I proofread the typed lectures, correcting where necessary.

The verbatim manuscript of the thirty-one lectures was submitted to The Pennsylvania State University Press. I believed that it would be most fitting for the institution where the lectures took place to publish them, since it was during the time Dr. Lowenfeld was at Penn State that he developed such a profound impact upon the field, both here and abroad. Under Dr. Lowenfeld's leadership the Penn State Art Education Department became, to many persons, the center of art education in the United States. Scholars came to study there from all over the world. The doctoral program in art education, which was initiated by Dr. Lowenfeld, still ranks as one of the top programs in the country. Publication of these lectures was approved by The Pennsylvania State University Press with the provision that the written lectures be edited further for flow of thought and readability. Working with the Press's editors, I carefully edited all of the lectures into the form presented herein, retaining as much of the original transcription as possible.

When Dr. Lowenfeld came to the United States at the age of thirty-five (he was born March 21, 1903, at Linz, Austria), he was already a recognized scholar in the field of art education in his own country and beyond, having published two important books, *Die Entstehung der Plastik (The Genesis of Sculpturing)* and *Plastische Arbeiten Blinder (Sculptures by the Blind),* with a third, *The Nature of Creative Activity,* having just been published in England. As a result of his experimental work when teaching in the Realgymnasium in Vienna (1924–38) and having been in charge of "creative teaching" at the Hohe Warte Institution for the Blind (1926–38), he became known for his research in creativity and art expression. Dr. Lowenfeld had graduated from the Kunstgewerbeschule (1925) and the Art Academy of Vienna (1926), as well as the University of Vienna (1928). This rich educational and experiential background resulted in his possession of a sensitivity to the arts and a knowledge of the European Child Study Movement, with a research and psychological orientation to the field of art education. Lowenfeld's artistic sensitivity, versatility, and expertise had been demonstrated in other areas, as well—he had been a child prodigy on the violin and, later, had designed and executed the stained-glass windows for the concert building at the 1925 World's Fair of Paris on the Decorative Arts.

By 1938, before coming to the United States, Lowenfeld's life had already directly touched many people of greatness. Among these were: Gustaf Minikin (reformer and educator), Siegfried Bernfeld (educator and psychologist), Martin Buber (religious philosopher), Karl Kraus (poet), Rabindrinath Tagore (philosopher and educator), Eugene Steinberg (sculptor), Oskar Kokoschka (painter), Karl Liebknecht (social thinker), Franz Cizek (teacher), Ludwig Munz (art historian), Sigmund Freud (psychologist), Herbert Read (philosopher/aesthetician), and Karl Buhler (psychologist). The effect of these early contacts is clearly seen in the depth and understanding of Dr. Lowenfeld's lectures.

The first twenty-five lectures which appear in this book were given in the summer of 1958 at Penn State. These include all of the lectures which Dr. Lowenfeld gave in a course concerned with child art. The text for the course was his book *Creative and Mental Growth*. Child art was his favorite interest and teaching area, and it was the level at which he had most of his experience and conducted most of his research. The reader will note that many of the lectures begin with Dr. Lowenfeld answering written questions from his students, a method he frequently used with large classes. Many times it is in his answers to these questions that one gains a deeper insight into his approach to art education and his own approach to teaching.

Lectures 26 and 27 were given to a class involved with secondary art education. Students invited Dr. Lowenfeld to speak during the last two class periods of the course.

Lectures 28 through 31 were given in a class concerned with using art experiences with handicapped persons for therapeutic purposes. Dr. Lowenfeld called this "art education therapy." In these lectures, he presents three case studies: a neurotic child, a mongoloid adult, and a deaf-blind child. Dr. Lowenfeld did a great deal of work with handicapped persons, finding that he could learn much which was applicable to the normal/average child.

Viktor Lowenfeld was one of the first, if not *the* first, to teach a course which involved both European and American development of art education. In a famous lecture—the one that inspired Ellen Abell to record his other lectures—he imitated Franz Cizek as Cizek taught his juvenile art classes in Vienna. This lecture, being mainly of historical interest, does not appear in this book. Dr. Lowenfeld had worked with Cizek and was well acquainted with his theory, methodology, and personality. In his lecture Dr. Lowenfeld acknowledged that the discovery of child art found its "culmination in the work of Cizek" but went on to deplore Cizek's emphasis on the purely aesthetic and visual aspects. This emphasis, Dr. Lowenfeld said, "is much against our philosophy, and I believe also against the needs of our time." The goal of art education, in Dr. Lowenfeld's words, is "not the art itself or the aesthetic product or the aesthetic experience, but rather the child who grows up more creatively and sensitively and applies his experience in the arts to whatever life situations may be applicable."

The reader/listener should note that Dr. Lowenfeld, as a native of Austria, spoke German before coming to the United States. At that time (1938), he spoke very little English. Although he later became fluent in the English language, he retained some unusual phrases and sentence structures as a result of his foreign background. I have tried to preserve these qualities as much as the demands of clarity permit, in order to give the reader a feeling for the character and personality of Dr. Lowenfeld. My paramount aim has been to present a readable statement, eliminating redundancies and superfluous material and, I trust, presenting Dr. Lowenfeld's thoughts with maximum clarity.

In many of these lectures, Dr. Lowenfeld referred to examples of child/

adolescent art work and charts which appeared primarily in the third edition of *Creative and Mental Growth*. Without these examples, much of the discussion in these lectures would be meaningless to the reader or listener. I am thankful and greatly appreciative for permission granted by the following to use these illustrations: The Macmillan Publishing Company, Inc.; the National Art Education Association; and the *National Geographic Magazine*. Any omissions of acknowledgments result from the difficulty in finding sources.

Tapes of the thirty-one lectures presented here are available for listening as a part of the Viktor Lowenfeld Memorial Collection in the History of Art Education at King Library, Miami University, Oxford, Ohio. Ellen D. Abell initiated this collection with a gift of a significant number of volumes, in addition to the tapes, in 1976. Mrs. Lowenfeld augmented the collection by giving a number of volumes from Dr. Lowenfeld's own bookshelves. Others have also made contributions.

Concerning this book of lectures, I extend sincere thanks for the great effort put forth by the following dedicated people:

To Mrs. Ellen D. Abell for recording the voice and words of Dr. Lowenfeld.

To Mrs. Viktor Lowenfeld for giving permission and encouragement.

To Miss Linda Stevens for retaping and transcribing the original tapes.

To Miss Virginia Shewalter for the basic styling of the transcribed lectures.

To Mrs. Nancy Carter for typing the first draft from the handwritten copy.

To the graduate students in art education at Miami University who typed the final manuscript.

To Dean Spiro Peterson of the Miami University Graduate School and Research Office for making funds available to copy the illustrations.

To Dr. Laura H. Chapman, outstanding, young, internationally known art educator, for her tremendously insightful and perceptive evaluation of these lectures in her Foreword.

To Chris Kentera, Director of the Penn State Press, his staff, and the faculty press committee, for realizing publication.

To all my colleagues in the field of art education for their support and encouragement.

To my family for encouraging me and enduring compassionately my dedication during the long and tedious process of having the spoken words of Dr. Lowenfeld transcribed into an organized and readable form.

SECTION I
Art and the Child

LECTURE 1

Introduction to Art Education:
The Individual and the Creative Art Process

Time and again we have people in this course who have never engaged in the creative process, in fact, who have been brought up with the concept — very much in contrast to our concept—that there are people who can create and people who cannot create. Now, this is not true, because one of the great differences between man and animal is that man creates and an animal does not. If you have a spark of human feeling and thinking in you, then you indeed are a creative person.

But your creativeness may be buried; you may have been frustrated, usually at a time when you lost confidence in your own creativeness. And this is generally at the time of puberty. Probably imposed upon by foreign standards, you were asked to perform rather than to create; and in this striving for exactness, you lost the feeling that what you create is important to yourself. From then on, you stopped expressing yourself adequately in the visual arts and probably moved on to other forms of expression. But these forms of expression, such as appreciation, or looking at things, or making your household beautiful, or dressing, or whatever means you apply in your daily lives which touch upon creativeness—all these means lack something which participation in the visual arts has. And that is, they do not confront you with your most inner self. When you dress yourself, you enjoy it. Indeed, you select; and in the selection—if you don't make your own dresses—you proceed according to multiple choices. Do you understand? You have certain dresses at your disposal, and from these you select. This selection, or this bringing into relationship of a dress to your own personality, is a creative act. But it differs from starting from scratch and developing something out of nothing and including into this something your innermost relationships. Now this is what working in the visual arts can do for you.

As I said, in the beginning, we always have students who come here and think they cannot create because they have never actually engaged in the creative process. Then, the creative process becomes most significant to them after they leave. For instance, just now, during this last semester, I

1

was most fortunate in having in my mural-painting course students who have never done anything before. One special education teacher came here. Oh, if I could only demonstrate to you how timid she was in the beginning—how she scarcely was able to draw a line because she was afraid. You could only slightly see the pencil strokes because she didn't dare put on pressure! I will show you occasionally what she produced. And then we had two others who were elementary school teachers and who also had never done anything in the visual arts to express themselves. For the first time, they approached their own ego, faced their own selves creatively in the visual arts. And then we had one from the psychology department who asked me very cautiously in the beginning, "Do you think this course would be of any value? I would like to try it because I've heard that people do find some of their—that it may be of some clinical importance." And so, as he was in clinical psychology, he came here and tried it out on himself. The result—amazing! When these people left, altered, they had an intense feeling that these murals which they had created were a part of themselves. As a matter of fact, I can tell you that I have received letters from these people in which they told me that they have never gone through any experience in their lives that compared with it. A woman left in tears because she felt she left something behind in her mural which was so important to her that she couldn't part with it. It's like leaving your children and probably never seeing them again. This was the content of a letter which I received from one of these students. So, may I say at this point that it is this relative significance which counts. Do you see? The Sistine Chapel may have been to Michelangelo no more significant than the mural here has been to one of these students.

Regardless of the final product, then, we are thinking of art education as a process and not as a final product. We think of it as a means to an end, and the end is always the individual. So, how we can influence the individual through art will be the subject matter of this course. We begin with the baby and go right up into kindergarten and elementary school. We shall not include adolescence, only touch upon it. It would be too much to cover in these six weeks.

We will be interested in the effect that art has on people. And it is needless to say that, with the development of greater sensitivities and greater understandings of the importance which the creative process has for individuals, the aesthetic product grows, too. So, we are not neglecting the aesthetic product by any means. But it is only of secondary significance. For to me, it was most important that this woman had this great experience in which, probably for the first time, something of herself was revealed to her that helped her into greater human perfection, if we can talk of human perfection. This is on a continuum, as you can see; but we are most interested—indeed, all of us—in living in a better world and, first of all, in being happy in the deepest sense and not in the superficial meaning which we attach to it in this era of materialistic gains. You know I do not have to emphasize that our present happiness is almost determined by the set of values created by our "high standard of living." And this certainly is a set of values which only leads to emotional and mental breakdowns, because material goods will never replace the inner equilibrium that we are seeking throughout our lives. If we can do something, we have to do it in the most formative stages of childhood because during this time the foundation is laid for developing sensitivity to our environment and ourselves; and if we do not gain it in childhood, it is very difficult to conquer it later on—if not almost impossible.

So, then, we will mainly deal with the question: What role does creative art activity play in influencing the child at the elementary level toward becoming more happy in the deepest sense and toward becoming more sensitive toward himself and toward his environment? Only through this sensitivity toward himself and his environment will an individual become a useful member of a society. As we go through all the stages of growth, we have no other possibility than that of going chronologically. But before we begin, we have to clarify certain issues. We cannot fall into the subject matter and discuss how children react to their environment unless we clarify a certain necessary attribute of art processes, the creative process, and know what we are talking about.

How far should we go in our interpretation of children's drawings? When do we do injustice to ourselves and the child in interpreting the use of drawings? We will have to talk about some of the therapeutical aspects, inasmuch as I believe that we all are interested, of course—all the time in our classes—in getting our children more organized in themselves. Whenever such organization takes place and whenever a child moves from a somewhat lesser chaos to a better organization inside of himself, in my opinion, therapy takes place. So we cannot separate art education and therapy. I think it's intimately bound up with the nature of art education; and, therefore, we will occasionally discuss some of the effects on children which we have in our classrooms and to which we react in various fashions.

In this course we will have tests, because it will be most interesting to me to see how much you nodded your heads and how much you really understood what we were talking about. But I do not believe in any curve grading, because I hope that you will all understand everything. I believe that, when you come to such a course out of your own desire, you have the intention of gaining as much as you can. I hope that this course will be so meaningful to you that you will understand everything. And when you don't, I will feel very bad if you do not raise your voice or write your questions down on a little piece of note paper so that we can discuss in more detail those concerns which you have not been able to grasp. May I say that I do not expect anyone not to understand the course; but if it should be so, then it is probably your fault when you do not come out with your questions.

Now, in the very beginning, I would like for us all to get a basic understanding so that, when we speak of creative activity and children, we think basically that every child should express himself according to his own individual potentialities. That means that we exclude the thought from the very beginning that there are children who cannot express themselves. May I say this is not true to the facts, because there are children who express themselves easily and there are those who have great difficulty. There are lots of children who say, "I can't draw," you see, but basically, within our own selves, we believe that all children have the potential ability to create. And if they say, "I can't draw," it is only a sign that they have become, at some point in their lives, inhibited and we will not stay quiet until we have brought out the creative potentiality of each child.

How we shall do that will be the subject matter of this course. We will hear what we should do with children who continuously say, "I can't draw." But may I say, right in the beginning, that "I can't draw" is as much a generality as it is when you go to a physician and say, "Doctor, I have pain." The physician also would not be satisfied with such a statement. What would he do? He would ask you, "Where does it hurt?" And then if you were to say, "I don't know"—that means, if you were insensitive toward your own body and would not be able to locate your pain—he would start pinching you. At some point you would say, "Ouch," and he would stop. But then he would even pinch more and would say, "Does this hurt? Does this hurt more, or does this hurt more?" Then he would be able to locate your pain, and he would be happy because he can at least make a diagnosis and say, "Well, I believe your pain is caused by an upset stomach"—or your kidneys or whatever it may be. You see, this is exactly the same approach we should use as teachers. So when a child says, "I can't draw," don't leave him with the generality—just as a physician would not leave you with a generality when you say, "I have pain." What would be the logical question? "What do you want to draw?" "What do you want to draw?/Where does it hurt?" Do you see?

So we presume, of course, that the child who says, "I can't draw," has some desire for drawing. Therefore, we ask him, "What do you want to draw?" Soon we will hear that some of the children have no such desire, and Johnny may step from one foot to the other and say, "Mmm, anything." Don't we hear that? "Anything." Well, this is equivalent to the patient who says, "I don't know where it hurts." That means he has not yet located the area of his sensitivity which promotes his desire to express himself—just like a child who has all his speech apparatus at his disposal and remains mute. Such a child apparently has no desire to communicate. Something, then, is wrong with this child who does not want to speak and who doesn't want to use all his faculties which were given him by God. So, what we would like to create in the child now is a desire to express himself, or a readiness. Other-

4

wise, the child will remain mute in his expression. If we ask the child, "What do you want to draw?" and the child says, "Hmm, just anything," then we have to pinch him to search for his sensitivities which lead to expression. It is the task of the teacher to do this. It is a great misunderstanding of teachers to think that every child expresses himself and the teacher just watches. As we all know, it is true in some cases—probably in many cases—in which the child in his early formative stages hasn't been disturbed by some of the influences which are detrimental to his freedom of expression. And, indeed, children who are mute and have no desire to express themselves are not healthy children, for they accumulate all the bitterness, aggressiveness, and joy within themselves and never have the opportunity to embrace others in their joy, in their sadness, or in their excitedness. So it is very important that we not be satisfied with the child who steps from one toe to the other and says, "Hmm, just anything."

So what will we do? How do we pinch the child? The physician—well, he has it easy. He uses his hands and pinches wherever you feel pain, wherever he can touch you. He deals with material things, the body, while we deal with the body and the mind—a combination of them. This is more difficult but not as difficult as we believe, for we can easily learn to understand the experiences which are meaningful to children. Yet we are still left in the dark when we try to pinch him. We say, "What do you want to draw?" And he says, "I don't know, anything." Then we say, "What did you do yesterday? Why I just saw you playing tag outside with Mary. Weren't you?" "Yes." And now we inquire about his sensitivities.

This probing is the great contribution of art—of art in education in general, not only in elementary education. I think this is the great contribution of art to man: art embraces not only physical skills and abilities, not only the mind, but also the emotions and many aspects of growth which we otherwise would leave untouched even in our present educational system. I would like to become more poignant and clear about this so that we all understand it.

If Johnny goes through the creative process—that means, when he wants to document himself by means of a crayon, or pencil, or brush—he first must think of something. He must base what he draws on a basic experience, and this is the crux of the whole of teaching. We forget that some of the children don't have basic experiences which become so important to them that they want to express themselves. What is a basic experience?

A basic experience is any experience in which the whole individual participates. That means his thinking, in which he discovers something; his feelings, in which he feels what he has discovered; and his perceiving, in which he has become sensitively aware through his senses so that what he has discovered has meaning to him. This is a basic experience. But whenever you separate the one from the other, you will not arrive at a basic experience. For example, whenever you separate what you see from your feelings, you have become a photographic camera. You may record what you see, but it has no meaning to you; so this is not a basic experience. In a basic experience, feeling, thinking, and perceiving unite. It does not necessarily need to be a deep, philosophical experience. Oh, no, a basic experience may be playing ball under certain circumstances or seeing a drop of dew on a flower at a certain time when it has become meaningful to you. A basic experience presumes sensitivity on the part of the one who experiences it. "Refined sensitivity" we call those relationships which are experienced not in total, but in details. In every refined experience, we discover the nature of things. When we, for instance, see a total tree, the tree, as such, is not a basic experience unless the tree has become meaningful to us, meaningful in its lights and its shadows. Then it is a visual experience, meaningful in its coolness, meaningful in its motions, meaningful in some phase of its details. Do we understand each other? Any generalization, then, which we experience only in its total effect and which does not open itself up for inquiry or for individual emotional relationships will not be or become a basic experience.

Sensitivity, then, becomes one of the major issues in teaching art. And may I say right in the beginning that our most basic concern is that we teachers have to become sensitive. Unless we are sensitive, our children will not become sensitive through us. As it is with love, it is with sensitivity. One who has never experienced these sensitive relationships in one's own work or in one's own environment, including our neighbors, will never be able to experience and develop sensitivity in others. But in a time like ours, when sensitive relationships have been replaced by mass experiences and when the television set becomes the center of a family, almost replacing family relationships, to remain sensitive to one's own self becomes almost a lost art, especially if we include in that the satisfaction which we expect for every one of us from his own work. Today a job is usually regarded only as the means by which we may accumulate money rather than as a means of satisfaction. The odds are against us in our era of materially minded people. But this is, again, a challenging situation. You see, if everything were wonderful or perfect, art education might be superfluous. But because we are living in a time in which mass production, mass education, mass seeing, and mass experiencing have somewhat suppressed sensitive feelings toward our own individual relationships, we believe that art education has a special mission to bring out of the individual his own creative potentialities and combine in him the experiences which otherwise remain separated. We should learn to know what children experience at different levels in their development so that we will not make the mistake of imposing our own senses on children but rather be very happy with a drawing which shows the deep experience of the child—a heightened sensitivity, not a generality. You see, for as long as the child says, "An elephant," and cannot break it down according to what the elephant meant to him, the child will not be able to express it. This is your basic feeling as an adult, too. It's not only the child's. You cannot express yourself either unless you can break the experience down into the components which have become meaningful to you.

I can give you a little example right now, an example which I repeatedly have given to audiences: You remember a traffic light? Do you know a traffic light? Do you know the shape of a traffic light? You see, here you have question marks. A traffic light consists of what? A yellow light, green light, red light? Which is in the center?

Student: Yellow.

Lowenfeld: Yellow. Which one is on top?

Student: Red.

Lowenfeld: Is it?

Student: Most of the time.

Lowenfeld: Yes, it is. Always.

Some of you may already be questioning whether the red is on top or the green is on top. Those who question it have had only a general impression of a traffic light. But you know who would be most certain? The colorblind individual, because for him the location means stop and go. He cannot differentiate between red and green. They both have the same meaning. So he has to know where the one is located. Therefore, to him, this differentiation in a traffic light is meaningful, more meaningful than it is to you. Do you see? Now, when Johnny draws a traffic light, he cannot draw it unless he knows the differences in location, or he will question himself concerning his relationship to the traffic light. The same is true—that he has to question himself—concerning his relationship to a tree, or to an elephant, or to whatever he does on every level. Sure, we have to accept the child on the level at which he is; but it is our task to help him to become more sensitive, to enrich his concepts, and to establish more sensitive relationships. And it is in these tasks that teachers mainly fail because they think they should be happy with everything the child does. This is not true.

So when Johnny comes home from the circus with a general experience and is not ready to express himself, a deeper inquiry into details—that means, a breaking down of generalized experiences into more meaningful experiences—will establish greater sensitivity to details. And this will make it more tangible. It is this lack of tangibility to sensitive experiences, when things remain nebulous or when things remain as generalities, which prohibits creative expression. But may I say at this point that we are not doing this mainly for the purpose that the child should draw an elephant—of course not. Our end is to make the child more sensitive, not just to the elephant, but to the whole world which surrounds him. Out of such sensitivity, then, grows a deeper understanding of his relationships; for if he learns to identify with an elephant in his drawings, he will learn to identify with Mother as she goes shopping and carries the bag and selects and pays, or whatever she does. In this identification, self-identification, the child grows; for without this, no cooperation is possible. You see, active cooperation only results from the fact that we identify ourselves with the needs of others. And that begins with the elephant, the tree, Mother, or whatever the child draws. So there are great implications in those creative processes, as we shall see, and we will talk about them so that we learn to understand how the child changes as he goes through creative processes on all levels.

LECTURE 2

The Creative Art Process: Extending the Frame of Reference via Self-Expression

One misunderstanding is that people do not understand the meaning of contemporary education—I do not want to call it progressive education. I just say that what we do now is to let the child grow and we simply watch. Now, this is not right. On the contrary, we should be very sensitive to the needs of the child. Actually, this sensitivity toward the child's needs is one of the most difficult things that teachers have to achieve. Why? To be sensitive to the child's needs means to understand the child. And, for an adult, there is nothing more difficult than that, because we always feel we are human beings and the child is a human being. We transfer, then, our feelings to the child instead of learning to know the child's feelings, translating them, and putting ourselves into the child's position.

Growth is something which makes us forget what we have gone through when we were children. For instance, who of you would think of the fact that even your own baby, when you bring it up, will not be able to focus and see the world as you do? A two-year-old child physically has entirely different abilities than we have. First of all, when he looks around, his eyes do not adjust as quickly as our eyes do to distance and near objects. On the contrary, the child, when he looks around, sees the world as we do when we look in a relaxed manner, without focusing, at things. You see, if you look blankly—well, you see everything, but it's a kind of hazy way you see it. And this is the usual way a child up to two years looks at things. We forget these differences. We also forget very easily that we are looking at the world from a different perspective. Differences in height give us an entirely different feeling. A square which may have looked large to you when you were a child, you know, all of a sudden has shrunk to a little square. This may happen to you at any time. When you haven't been to your hometown, and you remember your hometown far back in childhood, and you go back to your hometown, everything now has diminished in size because the relationship between you and your environment has changed. Even the angle of view has changed. Now that implies that if we put ourselves into the place of

9

the child and learn the needs of the child, then we will know the child's thinking, the child's feelings, the child's imagination, and how the child accumulates knowledge, how he learns. It also means that we will know how the child sees, hears, and touches—in other words, how the child takes in the world. I don't have to stress this to you—that it has always been the longing of many great artists, authors, and musicians alike to look at the world again with the eyes of children. And only a few have conquered this longing. Even the late Brahms, in one of his later songs, writes or sings or gives expression to this longing in saying, "O wüsst' ich doch den Weg zurück, Den lieben Weg zum Kinderland!" "Oh, that I know my way back to the children's land!" is the translation. And this has deep meaning. Children look at things differently from the way we do. Almost everything is new to them. Everything must be investigated, explored, and found out for themselves. If we could reconquer this freshness toward experience, if we all of a sudden could see as we did when we were children—this is a light, you squint, you play with the light, you move around, the light flickers. You remember that game? And you remember many things which we today take for granted and no longer see with the eyes of children. Well, if we could reconquer this feeling, teaching would be much easier because we would understand children much better.

Now, this question, "Should we be happy with everything the child does?" suggests that we should just be bystanders in education and just look at what the child produces.[1] Rather, we should start with our motivation where the child's ends. Then teaching would have the meaning of expanding, extending the child's frame of reference, rather than being satisfied with where he is. And that extension óf the frame of reference, which is a very important principle not only in art education but in education in general, means that we have to know the level of the child's thinking, feeling, and perceiving for expression in general. As soon as we know the child's level, we can extend it and not impose our new knowledge, our own knowledge, adult knowledge, upon children. I'll give you an example. Many parents and teachers alike have come to me and have asked me, "What should I do? My child always draws the same thing. He always draws airplanes." Another mother says, "My child always draws guns." Well, we're living in a time, of course, in which those things play an important role. But as soon as the child repeats the same thing again and again, it is a sign that the child's imagination does not work flexibly. He only has one vocabulary which he repeats again and again. Why? Why does he repeat it? Well, there may be two reasons. The one reason may be that he repeats the same thing because he is very much interested in this one thing: in this case, guns or airplanes. And the second reason may be that he repeats it because he seeks security.

---

1. Lowenfeld started classes by answering questions written by students.

He doesn't want to be exposed to anything else and thus escapes into this one pattern which he knows, a gun, and repeats the same thing again and again—something like a self-assurance. He wouldn't say it, but if I think aloud for the child, he would say, "I can draw a gun. I can draw a gun. I can draw a gun. I can draw a gun, another gun, another gun." You know, in other words, he is no longer open for new experiences. He has closed himself up.

For us in education as elementary school teachers and also as art teachers, it is a wonderful thing that we gain entrance into the child's thinking through his drawing and into his feelings merely by looking at his drawing. And now, knowing that a child repeats the same thing for these two reasons gives us another feeling about the child. Now we'll ask ourselves, "Is this a strong interest, or is it a stereotyped repetition which the child did merely out of some feeling for a sense of self-assurance?" We can easily detect that. If the child repeats the same thing because he is interested in guns or he is interested in planes, then his interest will be shown in his drawings. How, do you think?

Student: Differences in details?

Lowenfeld: The differences of details. He will show different kinds of guns; he will show us different kinds of airplanes. He will show commercial planes and war planes and jet planes; he will show us a variety of them. He will even show us different views, on the ground and in the air and in different situations. Therefore, we would see a certain flexibility in his subject matter although the subject matter is the same.

Now, may I say that there is nothing wrong if a child for a certain period becomes interested in only one thing. But if this period lasts for too long a time, then specialization has started too soon in childhood and may be in the way of giving the child more flexible experiences with his environment and with his own self. And this is, of course, the thing which we should not accept.

So, I would not be happy with everything the child does. You understand? For instance, if he were to repeat, even out of interest, the same thing over too long a period, I would try to extend his frame of reference. How do we do it? Well, very simply. You would say, "Well, have you ever thought to which lands a plane can go?" You start always where the child is with his interest. "Where can it land? It can land where? Oh, in foreign lands? Well, do you know anything of foreign lands? Oh, let's take an airplane trip. Let's take an airplane trip from here to—I don't know where." And now you have already started to extend the frame of reference. "Let's get out of the plane now, and let's find how the land looks. Could you make me a picture of what you see when you get out of the plane?" Even a drawing of the airfield would be an extension of the frame of reference. Now do you see? This would be quite easy for someone who is interested in planes.

How would you know if the child is not interested in planes but merely draws a plane as a stereotype, as an escape mechanism, just like a child who goes into a tantrum when he cannot meet a new situation? This is what we call an escape mechanism. An escape mechanism in art, or in a drawing, is a drawing which does not meet the child's own needs; that means, a drawing which does not express the flexible relationships which a child should have with his environment. For instance, if Mary is tired in the evening but wants to go ahead playing with her dolls and all of a sudden you feel the child should go to sleep, you tell her, "Mary, now it's time to go to bed. Put the doll away." Now the child, unprepared for this change, may not be able to meet it, and thus escapes into a behavior pattern such as a tantrum. The child may start crying, "I don't want to go to bed. I don't want to go to bed," and so forth. Now this does not meet the new situation, but it is repeated every time when the child cannot really accept a change. And such a tantrum, of course, we call an escape mechanism. In art, an escape mechanism may be the repetition of the same thing; only it is not as violent. But the thinking is the same. It means the child cannot adjust to a new environment and, therefore, repeats the same pattern again and again. Now if this happens, we are not happy with everything the child does. Is this clear? We would, of course, be unhappy because we would feel that the child is in a trap and cannot meet new situations.

The inability to meet new situations will be in the way of the child's growth. Without meeting new situations, the child will grow inflexibly, stiffly, and rigidly, and, therefore, will suffer in his adjustment. What should we do? We do the very same thing in principle as we have done with the child who is restricted in his interests. We would extend the frame of reference of the child; that is, if a child draws guns—only guns, you know—and has a stereotyped pattern of guns and fills the page with this repetition of guns, well, we would ask him, "What kinds of guns do you know?" And even the difference between the sizes of various guns may be the first departure from a stereotype. He will have discovered that there are large guns and there are small guns. This little difference to which we have to be sensitive may already be indicative of the first departure from a stereotyped escape mechanism. But later on we may ask the child, "What do you do with guns? Shoot? At whom do you shoot? Oh, kill anything? Rabbits?" and so forth. "Oh, wouldn't it be fun to find out what you do with a gun? Now you think hard what you can do with a gun. How do you hold it? And what do you do? Here, let me see what you do." The first thing may be that the child makes from the gun a few dotted lines, and at the end of the dotted lines there may be a circle with two ears which may be a rabbit. This may be, again, a new departure from a stereotype. We have to accept it as a new step to freedom because, at first, the child was a prisoner of his own escape mechanism and now the child gradually has been freed from this prison and extends into a larger environment. This is important for us to know. The principle is that we always start on the level of the child and try to move from this level. It would be entirely wrong, of course, if we were to go to the child and say, "Don't draw these silly guns! Don't you know anything else?" This would inhibit the child even more because, for the time being, the gun, or the repetition of guns, has been a means of security for the child and, all of a sudden, you deprive the child of a necessary security. If poor Johnny didn't need it, he wouldn't do it. It's not a voluntary thing. On the contrary, we should have feeling and sympathy for the child and see that the poor child is just inflexible, and we should help him move away from his inflexibility.

Now, may I throw in here a word, a very important word. You may have heard of some controversy concerning therapy in our art classes. I would like to clarify this right at the beginning, because it is very important to me. I have found, on my tours across the nation, many classrooms in which teachers engage in diagnosing children's drawings, saying, "This child is maladjusted because he is using black colors." Or "This child is sexually inhibited because he always emphasizes all protruding things, and protruding things are symbols for phalli, I know." This is definitely not our business. We must not engage in any diagnosis of children's drawings which is drawn from inferences. Yet, in art education, we have to make a very important contribution, such as we have just now discovered—a contribution which does not diagnose the child's drawings or the child's personality through symbol inferences or all kinds of things about which we only guess and for which we do not have the background. I do not say that such diagnosis is wrong, please; but we should leave it to those who have the proper background, to psychoanalytically trained individuals.

Psychiatrists may be able to read from drawings other things than we do. But our force or strength is in another direction. Everything is legitimate which is visually conceivable to you, that which you can see in the child's drawings. We then do not draw any psychoanalytical inferences. That means, if we see a repetition of the same thing, then for us this is a repetition of the same thing and shows the child's inflexibility. Do I make myself clear? We, therefore, should not say if a child draws an elongated nose, "This nose is most probably a phallic symbol, a hidden one, and the child is oversexed, or masturbating, or something," which may be true, don't misunderstand, as an interpretation. But it is absolutely out of our field! For us, a long nose, an elongated nose, is a nose and nothing else. And in art, with our background, we know if a child elongates a part—that means, exaggerates this part—for us this only means that this part has been given more emphasis. You see, we do not draw any inferences from symbols, but rather we simply read what we see and take it and accept it. A child who has drawn a long nose apparently has been occupied with his nose and has been—well, we can draw from that probably some physical inferences. Maybe the nose has been important to him. For what reason? Well, we'll leave that to the psychologist or psychiatrist. Have I been clear about this matter?

We will, however, see that there are many points which introduce to us a new knowledge about the child. And if we are going to find out what we can see in children's drawings, then we shall never do it for diagnostic, psychoanalytical purposes but for the purpose of becoming more sensitive to children and their needs. As long as we see only the generalized child, the total child, without becoming sensitive to individual differences, we commit a form of discrimination, the same form of discrimination which we commit if we speak of Jews, of Negroes, or in general terms, of Catholics, or whatever you would like to say. We only know individuals. As long as we do not break down a generalization into details, we have not become sensitized to the details. And, as Gordon Allport—one of the fine, outstanding psychologists in the country—says, "Any generalization bears the germ of discrimination." Do you see?

The same is true if you say, "I don't like contemporary art!" You are discriminatory in your attitude. And we have proved that discrimination in one part of our thinking refers to discrimination in others. Such studies have been made, as you may know. So, in questionnaires in which people engage in such generalizations as, "I don't like contemporary art; I don't like Jews," you see, these are very much related to each other because both are generalizations. Before seeing a generalization, you look at yourself in a mirror and give yourself a hard push and say, "Have I made the effort to find out the details within this generalization so I can say, 'Do I really embrace all the details in making such a statement?'" And then you will change your opinion, because you never can embrace all the details since all the details of a race consist of all the individuals of the race and all the details of a belief in religion consist of all the individuals who believe in it. And there are good Catholics and good Jews and bad Catholics and bad Jews; and there are good whites and bad whites and bad Negroes and good Negroes, according to individual differences. So, please—there are wonderful works of contemporary art if you look for them, so you should never say, "I don't like contemporary furniture," because it is all different. Don't make such generalized statements; because, as soon as you do, you commit yourself to a discriminatory attitude. I hope you realize that you can never be a good teacher unless you see the individual child. It is one of the deep ethical beliefs that we should regard human beings according to their individual attributes.

This brings up another question, a question which is very commonly accepted here in this great country. The question is this: If individuals are mentally retarded or if they are not on the level of the average child, are they perhaps *not* able to do creative work? Should they do some copying

14

because copying gives them self-assurance? Well, I would only like to answer that it has not created self-assurance in a parrot to repeat the same thing. Ethically, we should always keep in mind that, as long as there is a spark in a human being which can be kindled to a flame, we should never give up trying to kindle the spark. This is a very, very important issue. And then we have the answer, of course. One of the greatest distinctions or differences between man and animal is that man creates and an animal does not; we have no right to degrade any human being on any level to an animal-like situation. We have responsibility to kindle the spark of creativeness whenever there is still breath in an individual.

May I say that I'm not saying this only theoretically, because I have worked in institutions of mentally and emotionally disturbed individuals. I have worked in institutions for the blind and the deaf. My experiences have told me that it is one of the most rewarding feelings if you can bring out an individual from an animal existence to a human communication. I have had such an experience with a deaf-blind child who was completely cut off from her environment and could not communicate at all.[2] For the first time, through her creative work, she discovered that she and I were thinking of the same thing. She was modeling, and all of a sudden she realized that I knew what she was modeling. Such great feelings should be fostered and not thwarted. It is very important, whenever we are in contact with any human being, that we try to foster creativeness; that means, the ability to imagine and explore and invent in whatever medium we use.

So I have answered, I hope, the question, "Should we be happy with anything the child does?" We should always have the intention of bringing the child to a higher level of sensitivity, of sensitive relationships. Sensitivity, of course, would not let us remain only with generalities. We will not go into details of what sensitive relationships mean. But as we go and as we develop our understanding of the child, we will hear that sensitivity means something different on various levels of development. Sensitivity for a scribbling child means something different than sensitivity for a child who is eight or ten or twelve years old. So we shall discuss the meaning of sensitivity in great detail as we move in our discussions through the various developmental stages.

There is another question here: "As stated in our discussion, it is the teacher's job to create sensitivity in the individual. If it's the teacher's job to create sensitivity in the individual's thinking in these days of mass education along with mass experiences, is it possible to instill this individual sensitivity in a large group situation? If it is possible, how is it done?" Teaching is a question of conviction. The first thing of which you have to be convinced is your own power to convince. If you have this power, you can move moun-

2. See Lecture 31, A Case Study of Camilla.

tains. Yes, indeed, I believe that. And if I did not believe it, I would resign today from what I do. I believe firmly that, wherever I go, my feeling and thinking and perceiving will be felt. I even feel that it will be felt if I don't open my mouth, if I'm just here, so strongly do I believe in our ability to influence people. A strong conviction, an ethical and almost—why do I say almost?—a religious conviction that all things which we do are never wasted is a primary concern in education. And you know, we have proof of that through history.

None of our great religious philosophers, thinkers, or leaders—Christ or Moses or Gandhi—needed to be put on a pedestal or work in a specific place. As you know, Jesus worked in a very narrow, geographically narrow, circumstance. He was born somewhere in a stable in a very unknown little place on the earth, if you consider this vast world. If you are convinced of the importance of what you do as a teacher, you may work somewhere in the mountains in a one-room school, and you may move the world. And strong convictions through sincerity are the most contagious things on earth and are more powerful, as you know, than any material values. For example, we do not know anything of the rich merchandise and merchants of the Renaissance, but we do know of Michelangelo.

There are things of which you have to be convinced. So you ask, in a period of mass education, "Can we convey something of our sensitivity?" Oh, yes, indeed, because also sensitivity is contagious. At the very moment in which I speak to you about my sensitive relationships, you may discover in yourselves some of these, too. Wherever you go from this time on, you may be seeking them. And this search also will be felt in your children. So when you motivate your children, even if you have sixty in your class, your sixty children will feel it when it is part of yourself. But they also will feel it if you are only superficial and if the sensitivity is not part of yourself. So, as you shall see during this course, we will go deeply into our own selves in all things which we do. Continuously will I ask myself when I do things—and you will ask yourself, secretly, too—and this will be part of an inquiry which we shall see is the most important part of the course: "Do I think this way with my children?" Oh, some of you will discover: "I have not done that. Oh, really, I've taken a child and overpowered him. This really was not ethical. But I had to do it at that moment, so I can be excused." Yes, indeed, you can be excused, because we all are human beings and at particular moments certain things only can be done and our power doesn't go further. But we will have something of a new conscience in the back of our mind, and this is very important. So I may say, yes, I firmly believe that sensitivity is contagious just as any other strong motivation is contagious.

As a matter of fact, we have made experiments with regard to that. There's one doctoral dissertation done by Lawrence McVitty, now at Indiana State Teachers College. His doctoral dissertation was "An Experiment on the Effect of Various Art Motivations on Children." And there is another study which has also been done here as a doctoral dissertation in which Dr. Lansing, now at the University of Illinois, wanted to find out whether classroom motivations have different effects upon different classroom sizes and class numbers (room sizes and class sizes). And the two studies together now give us a deep insight as to what actually happens. The finding of these studies is that it is *not* best to motivate a small group of children. For instance, a motivation with a small group of children is not as effective as a motivation with a middle-sized class. There is an optimum and a minimum. If you have a class of fifteen, according to the study of Lansing, the class is not as effectively motivated as if you have a class of twenty-five. Thirty is the optimum, and any number over thirty is already on the negative side. Let us say, thirty-five is not as good as thirty; but thirty is better than fifteen or twenty. Probably the reason for it—of which we are not entirely sure and which we only got by inferences—is that, in a small group, one diversion causes the whole class to deviate from what you're doing. For instance, in a class of fifteen, if a child starts coughing, it diverts the rest of the class much more than if he is coughing in a class of thirty. There is another thing which we know from practice, of course. Have you ever been at the "best" football game where there are only a few spectators around? It won't affect you as much—it won't motivate you as much—as if the bleachers are filled. Why? Because mass motivation is contagious, as I said. So if you motivate a class, let us say, of thirty or thirty-five, don't be unhappy. Your sensitivity will be felt probably even more than if you have a class of fifteen. I hope that what I say now is meaningful to each of you even in this class of seventy. And it may be even more meaningful than if I had three here, because any diversion in thinking might also cause me to be distracted in my motivation. Yes, I believe that sensitivity, if it is genuine and part of the person, is felt.

But there is a comment at the end of the question which I think we should discuss: "If it is possible, how is it done to improve sensitivity?" May I say that if you have not been brought up sensitively, if you have not been sensitized to yourself so that what you do is meaningful to yourself, and if you only regard what you do as something of a "must," then please look into yourself and discover the meaningfulness to others of what you do, and you will be amply rewarded. If you haven't been sensitized to what surrounds you with regard to your sensibilities (that is, sensitive sensory experiences) so that you use your eyes, not just for seeing but for observing and becoming emotionally involved in what you see, and your ears, not just for hearing but for listening and becoming emotionally involved in what you listen to—if you have not experienced that, you have missed a great thing in life and in religion, too, because you have not listened to Him, nor have you seen the Creator anywhere in the world. So there are things which go much

17

deeper than a discussion of art with regard to children, as you can see. Only if you become sensitive to your own self and your environment (which includes your neighbors), will you be rich in your life, even without a new car. You see, in our striving for material wealth at this time, often we cannot afford to look at the wealth which we gain unless it means money in our pockets.

Now, may I end this by saying that sensitivity consists of a daily, hourly, constant inquiry into your own self and your relationship to your environment. And in this, I believe, the breaking down of generalizations into details will always help us. If we try to see the little things, if we try to hear the intricate differences, if we try to put ourselves into our neighbors' place regardless of where they are and what status they have, then we come closer to this inquiry which results in sensitive relationships.

"Is psychological projection similar to a sensitivity?" It is part of it, as I have just now said. Empathy—or putting ourselves into the place of another, which means psychological projection—is a part of sensitivity; yes, that part which deals with human beings. But we also should become sensitive to things other than human beings, especially because in the awareness towards those things which do not breathe and do not laugh and do not eat is sensitivity developed concerning those things which surround us. And in those things we shall discover, too, the Creator. Even in our actions and our decisions, we should be guided by sensitivity. This is more difficult because we do not see immediate reactions.

"Can negative basic experiences stifle creative expression?" No, I do not believe that. There may be a stumbling block, but a stumbling block is often a thing by which we learn. I believe that if life is too smooth, we don't gain much by it. We overlook all things because everything is readymade and presents itself without hindrances. Here I agree with the great philosopher, Maeterlinck, who says, "Only through suffering you grow." When things come too easily, man too easily deteriorates because he takes things for granted. This is not conducive to sensitivity. So may I say, and this is what is meant here by negative basic experiences, an unhappy love may result in one of the greatest works of art—Munch's *Jealousy,* for example. And a happy love may not necessarily outdo the basic negative experience of not finding the expected echo in one's love. So I would not say that [negative basic experiences stifle creative expression]. On the contrary, I would say that, also with regard to this, we suffer. Our children suffer very greatly, very greatly, by being surrounded by a wealth of toys—so much so that nothing is left for them and for their imaginations to act upon. Who has not seen those cases filled with toys in every one of our families with children? This is one of the downfalls of our high standard of living. For, through such filled toy boxes, we only deprive the child of his own inventions and, thus, of this flexible relationship with his own imagination. Stum-

bling blocks, desires which we cannot immediately reach, may be conducive as long as they are not too strong and, therefore, frustrating. It is up
to our sensitive relationships as parents and as teachers to provide the
child with enough stumbling blocks which may help him, because the overcoming of them may bring about the expansion of his exploratory and
inventive attitude.

This statement puzzles me. It says: "Self-expression, as a term, is often
misunderstood. Is it wrong to think that self-expression means the expression of thoughts and ideas in general terms of content? This is a great
mistake because thoughts and ideas can be expressed imitatively (see page
four in your book[3]). Self-expression seems to me to be the reaction of any
individual to a situation that excites his senses or sensibilities. Self-
expression is visual reaction to such a situation—therefore, the content of
his reaction." I shall answer this next time, because we will go into greater
detail concerning this question. We are not yet that far into our subject
matter. We will differentiate between subject matter of a literary content
and subject matter which deals with such experiences as expressed here—
the excitability of sensitive experiences, you know. That is a difference I
have put in my book, and I will deal with it next time.

"Where does imagination fit into the creative process? Is it part of the
thinking, feeling, and perceiving act or something quite different? Does it
stem from the intellect or emotions? And does environment affect its outcome?" Imagination is a result not only of thinking, not only of feeling, and
not only of perceiving, but, as we all know, of thinking, feeling, and perceiving combined into a unity. That which we imagine is filled with our relationships to what we imagine. Of course, we could not imagine it in an abstract
form; therefore, it must relate to things which have been perceived, even if
perception has not really taken place. That means, we perceive something
which we only know by association or in which we combine various
aspects—such as an angel, if you want me to give you an example. You see,
an angel does not exist; but we have some associative thinking with regard
to an angel. We know it's by association when a child thinks of an angel as
probably some kind of a human being with wings attached.

3. *Creative and Mental Growth,* 3rd edition (New York: The Macmillan Company, 1957).

LECTURE 3
Growth Components and Art Education

When a child displays stereotyped repetitions in drawings, we should try to make the stereotype alive and meaningful to the child, regardless of what the stereotype is. If the stereotype is a gun, we will make the gun meaningful. We will not divert the child from his stereotype. This is against our educational principles, because it will neither satisfy the child nor will it help the child to become less frustrated and drop a means in which he has found security, the repetition of one item. If the stereotype is an airplane, we will extend the frame of reference of airplanes and will make the airplane meaningful. If the stereotype is a cowboy and it is the stereotyped repetition of one and the same figure, we will make the figure meaningful. If the stereotype is a fashion figure and a girl has become so bound up with copying a fashion figure that she repeats it again and again, we will make the fashion figure meaningful. We will go to a party, and so forth, you know. We extend the frame of reference so that the figure becomes alive. But the school psychologist, whose attention we also have drawn toward the child, may use entirely different means. He will not use visually conceivable means which are specific to art education therapy, but he will use means which touch the child's behavior, probably methods with which we are less acquainted because of our background—unless we have also studied clinical psychology.

I would then say, if we continuously see such stereotyped repetition, it is our responsibility to do remedial work within the framework of art education. It is needless to say that, in art education therapy, the motivation is nothing but an intensified motivation which we usually give in classrooms. So it is not different in nature. It is the same in kind as that which we usually would give when we make things meaningful to children concerning details, but in remedial matters—let us say in therapeutical situations—this would be more intensified. Am I clear in this?

I have another note here: "I have students who have been copying for a long time. They seem to derive satisfaction and recognition from it, and my attempts to 'wean' them away from it have been unsuccessful. Is there any

20

way to do it?" May I say that there is only patience. If children have become dependent on coloring books and they love them too well, it is a matter of continuous motivation towards sensitive experiences which will gradually give the child more satisfaction and encourage him to do something on his own rather than to fill in those patterns which are drawn for him. And the same is true when students copy. Indeed, there is some satisfaction derived from it, especially if it is later rewarded. But the first thing which I would do is to stop rewarding them for it, for the coloring in. Also, get in touch with the parents who do the rewarding; because, if the reward afterwards does not take place, one of the important stimuli is no longer there. We will talk about the meaning of coloring books and workbooks and what we should do with them and how we can "wean" children away from them later, probably today, when we discuss the influence of coloring books and copying methods on children.

But may I say this—our common understanding is that not everything is good that children enjoy nor is everything good for students that students enjoy. It's a somewhat peculiar attitude which many teachers take, and also parents, that everything that children enjoy must be good for them. Now this is not true at all, as you know. They all enjoy sweets, candy, and so forth; and it would never come to our minds to adjust their diet to sweets and to candy because they love them and drop all vitamins and vegetables and whatever we would give them in a balanced diet. So, what children love is not necessarily good for them; and indeed we will see that the filling in of preconceived, predetermined lines is certainly very hard on their creativeness.

Now the "weaning" can only take place by presenting children with stimulation which excites their sensibilities and their emotions; and if the stimulation is strong enough, their minds, their imaginations, will become active and they will push aside coloring books by themselves. Well, this also involves a principle. You see, we accept the coloring book as part of the child as long as the child is bound up with it, and to use force would be just as bad as to use force in other matters. I told you last time it would not be good to tell a child who engages in the repetition of guns, "Don't draw these silly guns," and take away the drawing and frustrate the child by not allowing him to engage in it. It would be just as bad to take a coloring book from the child and to say, "Oh, throw away these silly coloring books," if the child is really engaged in doing it and has the desire to do it. These are not educational methods, and they do not even agree with our ethics because we would never include force in our educational principles. To take something away by force would not alter the child's behavior. We can only offer as a balance our conviction that our stimulations and motivations in making the child more sensitive to other things will be so strong that the child will drop the coloring book.

Student: I've had that experience —when children become so taken up by the creative that they soon don't want to do the coloring book.

Lowenfeld: Right, we have had the same experience in our children's art classes. We have had numerous children who come in with coloring books, and so forth, and soon, without any effort, drop them, throw them away. The parents come and say their children don't want to use them any longer. So this is not uncommon.

Since children love to explore and investigate and do their own thing, it is only natural that they do it if they become motivated and also receive some reward afterwards from the teacher for their successful conclusion of a motivation. But if a parent would like to get rid of a child by keeping him busy and giving him coloring books, of course the parent is happy that the child is busy and colors; and when the child comes and says, "Look what I've done," and the parent says, "Beautiful, beautiful, Johnny, do the next one," the child is rewarded and the parent is rid of the child. And this is, of course, one thing which favors the coloring book in the view of many parents, because they are too busy to spend their time with their children. This is one of the diseases of our time, too, you see. We have lost the feeling even for our own children and the patience and the enjoyment of being with them.

Now I come to our subject matter, still keeping on the table this one note which I received with regard to self-expression so that we can discuss it a little bit later. We have made big strides in art education during the last few years, inasmuch as we have experimentally proved that certain relationships exist between the personality development of children and their creative expression. We were relying before merely on subjective statements. Now we can rely upon experimentation—those things which we have received by continuously engaging in research which determine relationships that exist between the personality of children and their creative work. We have further made inquiry into the nature of creative processes. And in the realm of this inquiry, we have found something very important—important not only for art education, but, I believe, for education in general. We have not yet become aware of the great implications which these studies have for education in general.

You know as well as I do that the educational system in which we still find ourselves, in spite of all the progress which we have made (especially on the elementary level) in moving from a subject-matter-centered institution to a child-centered institution, emphasizes a narrow phase of learning, that learning which deals with the accumulation of knowledge. We are still concentrating, in our elementary schools, mainly on the accumulation of a better knowledge, especially in the three R's—in that, we have not changed very much. That means we are anxious to have our children read and write and do arithmetic, and, of course, we are anxious that they achieve the goal which we place before them. Yet in this, we concentrate too soon on specialization, on subject matter, on the accumulation of that kind of knowledge which deals mainly with the intellect. And in this, we neglect some very important phases that deal with other components of growth which do not emphasize the intellect in particular, but which emphasize the relationship of various phases of growth in the child. These components include our ability for emotional growth, our ability to use our senses (perceptual growth), our ability to organize things harmoniously (aesthetic growth), and our ability to cooperate and live in a society so that we can make our contributions and recognize the needs of others (social growth). We have also failed in our ability to promote creative growth. I believe that these components—or an emphasis on all of these components of growth—are vital for the growth of any personality. I also believe that the lack of emphasis in our educational system on these other components of growth is largely responsible for the many mental and emotional ills in this nation. As you know, percentage-wise, we have the largest number of emotional and mental ills of any nation, in spite of our high living standard. Because I believe that this is so vital for our growth and for our society, I think that art education will make a special contribution to the educational system for all these components of growth are part and parcel of any creative process, as I shall demonstrate to you in this course.

Now, I'll give you a practical example of this. Johnny creates something—to be more concrete, I will say Johnny tries to paint a picture. We could demonstrate this with any other creative process in any medium, whether it is creative writing or some creative composing of music or dancing or creative activities with crafts or materials. But I will use creative activity as it refers to making pictures because that is the content of this course. When Johnny starts to paint a picture, let us say, he wants to paint how his father digs a hole in the yard for planting a tree. Well, now, what actually happens to Johnny? First of all, he will only draw or paint if the underlying experience which he has had in the backyard with his dad, who planted a tree, was strong enough to motivate him to express what he has seen, what he has felt, or what he has experienced when planting a tree or when watching someone else planting a tree. So a basic experience preceded the creation of the drawing of how Dad planted a tree. If this experience were not strong enough, he would not draw it; but it would then be our task to make the child recall it in greater detail. We would, for instance, ask:

"Johnny, what did you do yesterday?"

"I was in the yard."

"Why were you in the yard?"

"Dad planted a tree."

"How did Dad plant a tree? What kind of tree was it? Was it a big tree? Was it a heavy tree? How did Dad hold the tree? Did he have difficulty?

Did you help him? Where was the tree before it was planted? Where did you get this tree? Did you carry it in your car? It wasn't a big tree, then? How tall was the tree? Could you hold it?"

Creating a very definite relationship to the tree would then excite the sensitivities of the child. His feelings of holding it, touching it, feeling the texture of it, seeing it, lifting it, feeling the weight of it—it would then be our responsibility to motivate all this so that the child would better recall the incident. "When Dad dug the hole, how did he do it? Did he do it first with a pick? Or with a shovel? Was the ground hard? Was it soft? Did he get big clumps of soil out of the yard? Were there many rocks?"

You see, all this recalling means breaking down a generalization into its details. You remember, we said that sensitizing individuals means breaking down general experiences into details. But let us say Johnny was sensitive to begin with. He would not need such a motivation, and he would go right ahead. But, you see, this is the difference which we see in children when we motivate them. There are some who are immediately ready to go ahead who have been sensitized in the past, and there are others who need sensitization in the classroom. So you have quite a different range of children, from those who are apparently rather dull to those who aren't, coming to class already in a somewhat excited condition.

What happens, then, to the child when he recalls? Well, when he re-calls, he recalls in terms of what? In terms of what he could think of; how much he could remember or keep in his memory of what he has seen. He recalls, then, a knowledge—a knowledge which he has at his disposal. We call this knowledge the "active knowledge" because he has it at his disposal. We all have two kinds of knowledge with us: an active knowledge, the knowledge which we can readily use when we recall things; and a passive knowledge, the knowledge which we know but cannot use. Now, I'll give you an example. The example is best understood when we go into another realm of expression—language. We all have an active knowledge about certain words. That knowledge, or that vocabulary, you would then call the active vocabulary. The active vocabulary is the words which we use in our daily lives. The average college graduate has about five thousands words in his vocabulary. Yet we know, for instance, that Shakespeare used about fifteen to twenty thousand words, so many more words than we use in our daily-life vocabularies. According to arithmetic, then, this would mean that we only understand every fourth word in a Shakespearean play. This is not true at all when reading Shakespeare. Indeed, we understand Shakespeare fluently, although now and then we find a word which we have to look up in the dictionary or only get its meaning out of the general context. But, indeed, our passive vocabulary, the vocabulary which we know but do not use, is much larger than the active vocabulary, the vocabulary which we know and use. Do you understand that?

In a good language lesson, you should come out with a larger active vocabulary than you went in with; because many words have become meaningful to you and, therefore, you have incorporated them into your active vocabulary. You see, even after this course, you will leave and many words will have become activated so that you will be able to use them in your daily life. You will speak of, oh, probably a child's "schema," which now is not even anything which resounds any feeling in you as something—as if it were a word that you have never used in your whole life because it has not become a meaningful part of yourself. And there will be many other words which you, from now on or after this course, will have incorporated into your active vocabulary. Thus, your words which you now will use, or later will use, in your daily language may not be four thousand five hundred, but probably four thousand five hundred and fifty, just to give you an example of this. Thus, we have activated some of your passive vocabulary. Now, did I make myself clear in this distinction between active knowledge and passive knowledge?

When Johnny recalled his experience of planting a tree, only his active knowledge about the tree and what happened will be at his disposal. He will remember whatever he has actively at his disposal: What kind of a tree was it? Did it have buds? Were the buds already out? If he did observe it, he will incorporate it; if he did not observe it, he will omit it. So Johnny's drawing will give us a good account of his active knowledge of the world around him. The active knowledge, as I said before, depends very greatly on what has become meaningful to individuals, and this is true for words as well as for forms and shapes and everything that surrounds us. Therefore, our emotional relationships will be very important in enlarging our active understanding of the world which surrounds us; because if things become important to us, we will incorporate them into our active knowledge. So if Johnny was a tree climber and was looking forward to climbing this tree sometime in the future, he may have thought of a different way in which the branches fork out from the tree. But if he got stuck by the stickiness of the buds when he was holding the tree and he recalls this sticky material which is on the buds, then he has become emotionally attached to the sticky consistency of the substance which usually surrounds early buds and he will include the buds, do you see? Anything of emotional significance which may have become important to him will be included. If he has seen that Dad was rather annoyed by the many rocks in the ground and asked him to help him carry away or clean out the hole of rocks, the rocks will be included because they have become part of his knowledge, his active knowledge. Why? Because they have impressed him emotionally and have become meaningful to him.

So immediately you see that Johnny not only uses his intellect but he also uses his emotional relationship to the event which he tries to depict. Therefore, he immediately differentiates between meaningful and meaningless things in his drawings, although this may be done subconsciously. As he differentiates, of course, he has to think of it. And as he thinks of various situations—when digging the hole, when putting the tree into it—in his mind, he goes through continuous adjustments to new situations almost in the sequence that he draws them, you see. He first may draw the yard. Then he may put the fence around it, and then he thinks: "Well, is Daddy now leaning the tree against the fence? Let's draw the tree against the fence. Or should Daddy hold it while I put the soil into the hole?" You see, in his thinking, he adjusts continuously to new situations. This adjustment to new situations is one of the most outstanding factors in any emotional growth. And since an adjustment to new situations takes place in every second of a creative process, emotional growth plays an important part.

This adjustment to new situations not only takes place with regard to the recalling of an experience, but it even takes place when Johnny uses his materials because, here also, he is confronted with new situations. Let us say he uses a paint brush and poster paint; and as he paints, the paint material reacts in certain ways. Let us say, two colors may merge, or a color may be too dry, or the paint brush may be too dry and leave spots—so he has to continuously adjust to the reactions of the material. This, as a whole then, is an important factor in the creative process, because the child continuously uses his emotional responses to whatever takes place, both in his imagination and in his actual painting experience.

Now, I have perceived that we use not only our intellect (our active knowledge), but also our relationships and our ability to adjust to new situations in the creative process. But how could we ever recall a thing if we had not observed it? So, indeed, our sensory experiences play an important part in any creative process. Do you see? If I observe—that means, if I see things in details—I will better be able to recall things than if I only see a generalization of them. So this becomes a very important part—we all know that psychologists agree about the fundamental fact that no learning is possible without perception. You all know that. We all know it from those unfortunate human beings who are deprived of their senses—who cannot see, who cannot hear, and who cannot move.

Well, I only have to recall a recent experience at the cerebral palsy institution. You see there how difficult it is for people with severe cases of cerebral palsy in which experiences of movement and motor coordination are completely disturbed, in which the ability to speak is disturbed, in which the ability to react to things is lessened and children or grownups can scarcely respond. The director of this institution several years ago was a wonderful woman, who unfortunately was stricken herself by cerebral palsy and since has died; but she was a marvelous woman. She needed to be wheeled around in a wheel chair; and when I greeted her, when she saw me, she could scarcely speak because her motor coordinations were disturbed.

She said, "How do you dooooo," you know, and this took all her effort. But people said, and still say, that she was a great philosopher. She was working on a book, but she could only dictate probably twenty words a day with great effort and was exhausted afterwards.

Indeed, we do learn by perception, and if our perceptions are disturbed, the severity of the disturbance affects our learning. The logical conclusion from this would be, for all our educational systems, that we should refine our senses in order to learn better. Isn't that quite logical? Yet our educational systems completely neglect and disregard this very important issue. If it were not for art education, we would have no organized curriculum or course of study which includes the refinement of our sensory experiences or what I shall call in the future "sensibilities." May I give you this definition, because many do not understand the distinction. Refined sensitivity in sensory experiences we call "sensibilities." Now, how much do we deal with sensibilities in our educational system on the elementary level or even further up? Almost not at all, depending on the individual teacher. You see, there are wonderful individual teachers who make special efforts, even subconsciously, with regard to this, because they are so taken themselves by these sensitivities or sensitive experiences of their sensory mechanisms. Yes, but this is only haphazardly done and accidently a part of their classroom activities. Yet it should become a planned activity of growth, or to promote growth—the type of growth which we call "perceptual growth." Perceptual growth is the growth which takes place in the refined use of our sensory experiences, you see: it is the growth of our sensibilities, the refined use of our sensory experiences.

Now, what is a refined use of our sensory experiences? You should know by now. What is it?

Student: Sensibilities.

Lowenfeld: Sensibility? What is sensibility? Now, don't answer the refined use of our sensory experiences because I would like to know what it is. What would you like to motivate or stimulate? The breaking down of a general sensory experience into its details; that's always sensitivity. Do you remember that?

We are not satisfied with generalizations—with the whole tree, and then leave it at that. We would like to know what it is that makes the leaves— but, first, what does a tree consist of? And that we can only see if we depart from and break down the generalization. Then we discover the tree has branches, twigs, leaves, and so forth. And what makes the leaves wiggle? Well, then we will see that various trees have different lengths of—what do you call them—stems on the leaves, and some are very, very short stems. They don't wiggle so much—others are longer, you see? And through such breaking down of our total sensory experiences, we refine them. We refine them also when we see different distinctions in color. As long as we say,

27

"This blouse is red," we have just recognized the red of the blouse. But if we become more sensitively aware of the kind of red it is, then we are going into greater detail with regard to red; and the same is true for tactile experiences and for hearing, you know. To become more sensitive to musical experiences means to hear the intricate details of harmony and counterpoint, do you see? This is to become more sensitive toward auditory experiences. To refine our sensory experiences means to break them down into their details. Now, this is extremely important. For as long as we cannot do it, we will only see generalizations and our learning will be affected by it, because our knowledge depends on this breaking down, on this refined ability to use our sensory experiences. If we cannot do it because we are disturbed in our mechanisms, then it is hard to introduce substitutes.

For instance, how hard it was for Helen Keller to get a picture of this world! You know Helen Keller, the great deaf and blind person? She even mastered several languages. When I saw her, she greeted me in German— imagine!—just to show that she understands German. Of course, her pronunciation and her ability to speak is not like that of a common person, like one of us. She still speaks, "Howw doo youu dooo," you know, very distinct in the formation of her language and speech apparatus; but you can understand her, especially if you have become used to the kind of language which she uses. But, indeed, for her, this was an introduction of all kinds of substitutes. Have you ever read some of her stories or even her poems? She speaks of the blue sky. She even speaks of the moon and the stars, although she never has the understanding that we have of the moon and stars. She would be very surprised, probably even disappointed, if one day she would be able to see the moon and the stars; because, in her mind, she has introduced some substitute images which are only, well, let's say, some kind of mixtures of associations which she has with her tactile world and they probably never even come close to what the real images are in the visual world. For instance, the dark blue sky for her may mean silence—do you see?—but not the dark blue skies we see as blue. So learning becomes very, very difficult without perceptual growth.

Yet Johnny, when he painted his tree, when he painted the fence, when he painted the whole yard, could only paint what he could visually recall. And the more he can recall in details, the richer is his concept in his painting; and this we have to remember, because much of our learning about motivating creative expression will consist of motivating for richer concepts. Do you see? If we were to see that a child only draws a man with two eyes and omits the nose and the mouth, we would not be satisfied with the child's drawing. We would try to activate in the child the feeling which he has concerning his mouth. We would probably give him an experience with regard to his mouth, and then all of a sudden he would feel his mouth, and he would include it in his drawing as an enriched concept, as an activated experience; and this activation takes place both through emotional experiences and also through perceptual experiences. So perceptual experiences are very important in any growth—including creative growth—and in any creative process.

But this is not the only experience which the child has. When he sits down and paints Daddy, he not only recalls it but he closely identifies with Daddy. "How did he hold the shovel? The tree— that was a heavy tree, I couldn't even lift it, but Daddy could just hold it. He had big hands so he could hold it." In other words, while he is drawing or painting, while he is going through the creative process, he closely identifies with the subject matter. He puts himself into the place of Daddy. How strong he must be; how he was standing. He couldn't draw Daddy unless he recalled how Daddy was standing; and the more intensely he can identify himself with the experience of holding the tree, the richer will be his drawing. So to identify one's self with the experience, to put one's self into the place of it, is also identical with, or a part of, any creative process.

To put one's self into the place of another is one of the most basic presumptions for cooperation. If I do not put myself into your place, I will not understand your needs and I will not be able to actively cooperate with you. So, from the very beginning of any creative process, Johnny engages in social growth. Social growth begins with identifying first with one's own work and then by putting one's self into the place of another and recognizing the needs of others. So you see what is included in any creative process—much more than we ever would have thought. As the child is putting himself into the place of Dad and how he is digging the hole and how difficult it is and how big his hands must be in order to be able to hold the tree, he is thinking; "Now where should I put Dad? Where should I put the tree? Where should I put the fence? Where should I put the shovel? Where should I be?" In other words, he organizes all these different matters which he wants to represent.

Now, may I say, this organization and all of this process in children's drawings is unconsciously done and not consciously produced. But it is, indeed, part and parcel of any creative process and is not less important because it is unconsciously done. On the contrary, it may even be more important because it becomes an unconscious part, a subconscious part, of the total child and his personality. So, you will see, as the child now organizes these things and brings them into a harmonious relationship, he engages in one important thing—he brings his thinking, his feeling, and his seeing into some relationship as he draws. Now he says: "Dad is a big man. Well, I must start him here so that I can get him on the paper. The hole should be there, and I'll put myself here. Well, the fence is here; it goes across." Now, you can see that there are children who do not organize things immediately in their minds, but start and then say, "I don't have enough space at my disposal." They run out of space. Then the question is, "Where should I put this? I have no space there," and they mean they have no drawing area. But there are other children who draw so small, you know, that they have plenty of space left, and they are disappointed when they are through and their drawing just looks so empty.

To bring back what they produce into a harmonious relationship to the area of the paper and in relationship to the subject matter which they represent is also an important factor in the creative process. We call the growth component which relates to this harmonious relationship "aesthetic growth." Aesthetic growth takes place always when we move from chaos to a better organization. Whenever we improve organization, we engage in aesthetic growth, but especially when we bring into relationship not just one part of our personality, but our total personality; that is, our thinking, the intellect; our feeling, the emotions; and our perceiving, whatever it may be—touching, seeing, or moving; that means also, moving the pencil on the paper, you see. This is establishing a coordination, and any coordination leads toward better and more harmonious relationships. The more sensitive we become to details in movement or in coordination, the more we will control our creative medium, do you see? This is also part of an aesthetic growth. Because whenever we move from generalizations to greater sensitivities toward organization, we engage in aesthetic growth. May I say that here is the greatest contribution of art education to therapy. Do you see? Why? Because whenever we move from chaos to a better organization in our thinking, feeling, and perceiving, we have become a better organized individual. And this, indeed, is the common goal of any therapy. Therefore, aesthetic experiences are greatly related to this harmonious feeling within our own selves.

As we have seen, the child engages in almost every component of growth and, last but not least, also in thinking and exploring for himself and inventing things, using materials in his own way, and expressing this independently—the type of growth which we call "creative growth." You can see now that art education introduces not only the advancement of the intellect—learning, or the accumulation of knowledge—but also introduces all the components of growth which make the child a whole individual. You may have heard the term "whole individual" so many times during the last few years that it has almost become an educational stereotype. But I hope this "whole individual" has now become meaningful to you because we have not left it with a generalization, do you see? We have tried to break it down into its details, and we have now become sensitive to the term "whole individual." This is always important when we try to relate things meaningfully to our own life.

LECTURE 4

Imitation, Workbooks, Coloring Books, Standards, Self-Expression, and Subject Matter

In the creative process, children are often interfered with by means which are extrinsic to the bringing into play of the various components of growth. As we learn to understand these interferences, we learn to understand the motivating power of those experiences which are conducive to developing creative growth. As we have said before, basic to any creative experience is the fact that individuals must become sensitive to themselves and to their environments. You may have recognized last time that all of these components of growth will not come into play unless the individual is sensitive to his own experiences and to his environment. You see, if Johnny repeats his stereotypes and cannot adjust to new situations, he will not be open to bringing into play his past associations, his intellect, as he thinks and brings into his active knowledge those things which he can recall. Do you remember when we said that? Of course, if he is stiff and rigid, he can't use these past associations; he will only think in terms of repetitions, and he won't even go out. He won't bring into play his own emotions and evaluate what is more important and what is less important. He won't be able to adjust to new situations as the experience unfolds. He will only be able to think of the same things. He will not be able to recall sensitive sensory experiences. "What did I see when Dad worked in the yard? How did he dig the hole?" Those fine or refined sensitivities will not come into play if a child is not flexible in his thinking. Nor will his ability to identify with the needs of others be of help to him. We shall see that there are methods that we use even on the elementary level which are detrimental to developing this interplay of all these components of growth.

Basically, there are two methods which we usually use in our classrooms. One is the method of imitation, which may be conducive but which, in most instances, is detrimental to the interplay of the components of growth. Let's look at the nature of imitation, and let's find out when imitation is conducive and when it is detrimental to the child's growth. May I say that we cannot draw a really distinct line between them, because one

31

method may gradually change into the other method as we shall see. To begin with, we cannot flatly speak of imitation when we speak of education because there are different kinds of imitation. Can you think of different kinds of imitation which have different meanings to your own life and to your own ability to see and experience the world? I'll give you an example. Let us say you go abroad. You go on a trip to Europe—you go to France. What would be necessary in order to make your life rich in France, in addition to your own sensibilities?

Student: Language?

Lowenfeld: Language. You would have to learn the language. And language, of course, to a great extent, can only be learned by imitation. Do you see?

So imitation is very conducive to your growth if you go to France and would like to communicate with the people there and would like to feel at home. Unless you speak French, you will not feel at home in France because, well, you will be filled with all kinds of complexes, even when you go into a store to buy something. You would hesitate at first to go into the store; you would think it over. "Do you think they will understand me?" and so forth. So you would probably only select the largest stores, and you would look for where it says, "English," you know. And you would go only where the language you use was spoken. So, indeed, to learn a language is one of the best examples of good methods of imitation. But look, if you learn a language—let us say you learn French by imitation—you learn the word, the symbol, as well as the pronunciation. Even the inflections of the language you can learn to master to a certain degree by imitation, depending on when you start to learn, what your talent is for language, and so forth. But, imagine that you learn the language but you do not grasp the words' meanings. You still learn by imitation, but the words are not meaningful to you. So is it purely imitation which is involved in the learning of a language?

What kind of imitation do we use? This is the question that we should answer today in order to understand methods of imitation which are detrimental to one's own growth. So what kinds of imitation do we use? Could we put them all under the same denominator, or could we group them? When we learn a language by imitation, as well as many other things, what is our ultimate aim?

Student: Communication.

Lowenfeld: Communication—to express ourselves and communicate with others.

So, is the aim identical with the learning process? No, if it were, then we would go down to the level of a parrot and repeat the same word again and again without understanding the word's meaning or its relationship to one's desires, fulfillment, and emotional needs. So it is important, when imitation is used, that we distinguish between imitation which is used for another end and imitation which is used for imitation's sake. I told you there is no clear line. But, indeed, when we learn a language by imitation, we learn the language in order to express ourselves, to communicate. That is, we learn language, and we use imitation only as a means to an end and not as an end in itself. So, whenever this distinction is clearly seen, imitation assumes educational significance.

Whenever imitation is done as an end in itself, then we sink to the level of a parrot. The individual then has no choice to say what he wants to say or to apply those seven components of growth which we mentioned last time. There are methods in our educational system which are not concerned with using imitation educationally, that is, as a means to an end. I'm sorry to say that, in our school system, we still have the idea that we can use one subject detrimentally to promote another one. I'll give you an example. If you are teaching in an elementary classroom, you may have used workbooks, time and again, as a help to teach children a better number concept, to teach them arithmetic, and to give them an idea of what numbers are and how numbers relate even to things. Add five birds to three birds. How many birds do you have? Well, in this process, of course, the whole child is involved. How could it be different? Because in all of what we do, we do not do only with one segment of our own self. The child, especially, always becomes involved as a whole. So, if in this workbook you have a symbol which looks like this bird, and it says, "Add six birds to this bird," then the child will start adding six birds to this bird and will, in this way, get used to a stereotyped representation of a bird. This, for him, is now a bird, a bird which is accepted by the teacher. I had a conversation not long ago with the man who is the author of this workbook of which I am speaking, one that is very much in circulation in our schools. I asked him: "Did it not occur to you that you are using here, in order to promote a number concept, something which is foreign to the number concept—namely, the drawing of birds or kites or stick figures or rabbits? How many rabbits do you have, you know? And these rabbits are, of course, stereotyped rabbits—or cats, and so forth. In this way, the child only picks out and has no choice in using his own imagination but must use the kind of symbol which you have dictated." The answer was: "Oh, I did not want to interfere with art. I was interested in promoting the relationship between numbers and things so that the number becomes a reality to the child, so that he thinks of six birds and not six because six may not be meaningful to him." You see, in this approach, the author has engaged in compartmentalized thinking. He thinks that the child is divided into number concepts and art and whatever makes up the various segments of life. He does not think that, when the child engages in one imitation for the imitation's sake, the child may become conditioned to depending on those concepts which are represented to him.

33

Now, may I say that we have used this in making some experiments so that we should not rely upon opinions only. Dr. Irene Russell and Dr. Waugaman—at that time, they were at New York State Teacher's College—and Dr. Heilman, at Kutztown, engaged in an experiment. But Dr. Waugaman, especially, made this study with these stereotyped work-book drawings. What she did was this. She presented to the children a motivation which should make the children sensitive—she sensitized the children to birds. For this she used a story about how hungry birds get in winter. It is in winter, when they are looking for food. Well, she tried to make the children really identify with the birds. She said: "Have you ever felt aches in your stomach when you were hungry? Or thirsty? Oh, some-time, I know, when you were on a trip or on a hike, you were so, so thirsty you started crying. Didn't you? Who started crying when you were so thirsty?" So she tried to relate an experience to the children's own experi-ences, and she said: "Now you know, in winter, sometimes birds are flying around and can't find any food because everything's covered with snow. They fly around for a long time looking out, looking out, but not finding anything. They are really so hungry, it aches. And they get weaker and weaker and more tired and more tired. And then they can no longer flap their wings. All of a sudden they get so tired and drop and die. Yes, if you can't eat, you know, you get very weak." This was the motivation.

Then she said: "You see, now we are trying to get food for our birds. Have you ever spread some crumbs on a place where the birds can reach it? Let's spread some crumbs and let's watch the birds; see how they come and pick the crumbs. Did you watch the birds? Next time when you come, you will tell me what you have seen. Look at the birds; see how they come and land. What do they do? They flap their wings, and then what do they do? Yes, they spread their legs and then gently land. And then they start picking the crumbs. You can hear them. The crumbs are hard, and the beak is strong. Did you hear them? Look how they look around. They have tiny little eyes. Yes, well, next time when you come, you will have looked at birds." And then, after this motivation, she asked the children to draw how birds come and pick the crumbs. In their drawings, you could scarcely see birds which did not show the experience.

Of course, the strength of the motivation is always responsible, along with the inherent sensitivity of children. The environment, the parents, the home—these are all responsible for how sensitive children relate themselves to such motivation. You must understand that the motivation of a group of children is like a collection of vases of different shapes. Some are open, and others are narrow and deep; some are tenderly shaped, and others are bold; some have a very thick wall and others have a very thin wall and break easily. Those who have done some pottery know what I mean. So you have such a great variety of shapes and forms; and when you give a motivation to children, the responses are equally different. You may have some children who are wide open; they see the whole motivation immediately. Others, well, you don't see them respond to the motivation. They are deep and narrow, and you have to look way down, and then you see how they apply themselves. Some children are bold in their drawings, you know, and cannot be easily disturbed. Others are fragile, and any slight diversion will disturb them. A class that is given a motivation is as different and varied in its reactions as you may see in the shapes of vases—different in form, in exterior, but also in weight, and in all various matters.

So, you should not expect all children to react in the same way. On the contrary, every child reacts in his own individual way to show in his drawings the individual experience that he has had when he thought of the birds and how they were picking the crumbs. So, of course, in a class of thirty, you get thirty different kinds of reactions. If the children have been sensitized, well, they all will draw birds according to their individual relationships. This may be the thought of a child—a bird; a bird has wings; he flaps them. So he may even draw four wings to show the flapping. It has a neck and beak. In the head, it has a tiny little eye. Look at the beak. It has a crumb in between. Look how it spreads the legs. Depending on the active knowledge, the knowledge which was of importance to the child, the drawings will now differ. But of importance is that each child relates himself, individually, to his own work.

Now, after the children had been given this motivation, they were divided into two groups. The one group kept on being motivated creatively in their sensitivity; the other group was exposed from then on to workbooks, and the children were also given a chance to express themselves. At the end of—I believe it was six weeks, if I am correct—it was found that the children who used workbooks no longer could express themselves freely when given a motivation. Again, they were all given a motivation—also with birds, but a different one—and the children drew again. Those children who were exposed to workbooks repeated stereotyped patterns or figures, such as you have in Figure [1], where you will find the experience illustrated of which I am speaking. The children became, then, dependent on a certain symbol. Some even misunderstood the symbol as I have illustrated it and drew birds like this, a clearly misunderstood stereotype imitation. Now, what conclusions can we draw from this experiment? You will note in the book that about sixty-five percent of the children were affected by the stereotypes. The rest still had established some individual relationships.1

What we can learn from this is very important. First, we learn that whatever we do in arithmetic also has some meaning in art. And whatever we do in art also has some meaning for arithmetic. In other words, wherever we influence the child, it will be felt in the child. We no longer can speak of subject matter, as such, but we have to relate subject matter always to the

Fig. 1. Effect of coloring books on a child's creative expression.
(*a*) A child's expression before he was exposed to coloring books.
(*b*) Coloring book illustration which the child had to copy.
(*c*) After copying from coloring book, the child lost his sensitivity, as shown in drawing.

child. And this is an educational principle which we have to keep in mind, because it is very important. The other thing that we learn is that, apparently, concepts which are not the child's own concepts cannot be used flexibly but only rigidly. The teaching aspect which we can draw from this is that, apparently, such means as workbooks—and I count into the same category of methods coloring books—regiment children into a sameness of expression and disregard one of the most important principles of democratic teaching, that is, to give the child an opportunity for individual differences, an opportunity to express himself as an individual. We have to remember this at all times. May I say that there may be teachers and parents alike who would say, "Well, didn't the child draw the birds or imitate the birds only as a means to an end, the end being the number concept?" Do you see? Yes, indeed; yes, indeed. This was the argument which the author of the workbook used. But one end must not destroy the other end. This is another principle. The end of developing a number concept should not destroy the end for children to become creative. In promoting the number concept, the child's creative concept and/or flexibility may have been destroyed. So it is not always good if we say that imitation is good if we only use it as a means to an end; because if the end is detrimental to the child, it's bad, too.

You see, in the same way, we may say, "All my children love coloring books." Well, the end may be that they enjoy. Yes, but is this enjoyment good for the child? So, if the end is detrimental to the child, we will not accept it either. And we call detrimental any ends which do not serve the child's individual desires and need for growth. Here we have seen that children become dependent on adult concepts. And this dependency on adult concepts destroys the child's own sensitivity to his relationship to his own work. Therefore, we will reject methods of imitation which are not on the level of the child, which are dictated means of regimentation. To this end we should reject all of the hectographed or mimeographed sample sheets which we may distribute among our children for the sake of making our teaching easier. You understand, it is much easier to give a child a coloring book to keep him quiet, but whether this means it's also good for the child is another question. And as I said the last time, it is very important, at a time like this in which we live, that we try to make things meaningful to our children; because when they grow up and have nothing meaningful to which they can relate themselves, they will seek other means to satisfy themselves, and these other means are not conducive to their mental health.

What goes on when a child colors in a coloring book? I would like for us to go through the process so that we learn to understand how detrimental this coloring-book approach is to the child. First of all, may I say that not all children are affected by coloring books. If a child's sensitivity is very intense, he can easily shift from an imitative process to a process which is important to him. As a matter of fact, we found that the same percentage of children—sixty-five percent—are affected by coloring books, but thirty-five percent are not at all affected. They can do both creative work and coloring books without any interference. So the argument that my child can do both is no argument because we never know. We also could apply this to other phases of life. We could say, "Well, my child is never affected in his stomach so he can eat everything." You see? Yes, indeed. If we would do a test—I don't know whether it would be worthwhile to do it—if we would have, let us say, a hundred children and we let them drink the water of a pond, maybe half of them will get sick and the other half will not. Their responses to contaminated water, or the water of a pond, will be different. But by no means would we recommend the drinking of water from a pond. So we will not make it a principle, by any means, in the same way that we will not make it a principle to recommend coloring books because some children are not affected by them. The larger number is affected in a detrimental way.

How are they affected? Now, imagine that Johnny has to color a dog in a coloring book—and I become again concrete. What happens to Johnny? Well, first of all, he has no choice. He cannot think of or recall an experience which he has had. Therefore, no activation of his passive knowledge takes place, because he just has to color that which is in the coloring book. He will not adjust to new situations as they arise, because they don't. You see, as he draws, he will not have a selection. "Where will I draw Dad?

How should I—how did he dig the hole?" He doesn't even have the opportunity to identify himself with the experience which he has, because the dog isn't the dog which is his dog and with which he has had any relationship; it's the dog which has been drawn by an adult. So he cannot flexibly shape the situations in which he would like the dog to be. He has no such situations, and he has no such choice. He cannot sharpen his perceptual responses or his refined sensitivities to a dog and add what is important to him. No, everything is ready-made for him; he doesn't even become actively involved in this except for the filling in of the space which is within the outline. He doesn't have an opportunity to organize harmoniously, because there is nothing to organize except to remain within the outlines.

Some teachers may say, "He learns the discipline of remaining within the outlines." Well, even that he doesn't learn. In the experiments which we have made, we have found that more children color beyond the outlines in coloring books but remain within their own outlines which they have created. We've gone over thousands of drawings and have critically looked at them both in coloring books and in free drawings, and we have found that children more frequently remain within the lines they create themselves than within the lines which are created for them in coloring books. So even the discipline is not true, or it is only thought to be true by those who have not engaged in experiments and who think this ought to be a way of discipline. This can readily be seen. A child will remain within the outline of the dog which he has created himself much better, because this dog is meaningful. When someone else creates a dog for him, this dog may not even be the dog he wants so he has no respect for it. Why should he remain within the border lines which are created for him? This may be the reason that so many children sometimes color very aggressively all over the page in a coloring book. We have seen coloring books which were a delight, which resembled scribblings rather than coloring books because the children just scribbled over the outlines, while the same children remained within the outlines when they created their own symbols. You had a question.

Student: I'm very interested in this because my son just completed first grade, and I had the feeling in looking at his workbook that there was a time element involved. Now, what about the time element? They're trying to teach them to get a certain amount done in a certain time. I mean, how do you get around that with this philosophy?

Lowenfeld: We never, never should sacrifice the individual for some acceleration which we would like to do.

You cannot artificially fill the child with arithmetic, you know, unless the child is ready for it. So we cannot get around the question. We will create within the child a feeling for arithmetic even if we tell him, "Draw your own birds." You can use stimulations, as they are here, in a workbook; but there is no reason why there should be stereotypes and why the child

38

cannot draw his own. You can say, for instance; "Do you know what happened this morning? I saw six birds on the telephone wire, and they were sitting there, and you know what I did? I clapped my hands. Three birds flew away because they were frightened." Can you see, can you get the feeling of how you motivate the children with regard to how the birds are frightened and fly away? "Let's draw what happens." Now every child creates his own relationship to the frightened birds: "How many remain in your drawing? Now look at it." You don't need to give children those symbols. You can see that it may take a little bit longer, but, on the other hand, it may not take as long to make things meaningful to children. So, may I say, the time element is only a question of methodology, of how to use it, you know, but it is not a principal concern.

The principal concern is to make teaching meaningful to children. And after it has become meaningful, I'm quite in favor of not remaining, in every instance, and repeating again a meaningful relationship to a number concept. It has to become mechanical at some time. A child has to learn what is seven plus eight. You understand what I mean? You cannot remain always with a concrete type of relationship. Once the child has established a relationship to number concepts, well, it has become meaningful; and then it probably has to become part of the child by repetition. But the creative desire and the respect for individual differences must not be destroyed in these processes.

Student: In this survey that you did with the workbooks, was there any counter survey done with the children who were put in the class where they didn't use workbooks to see what their number concept was?

Lowenfeld: No, we did not check on arithmetic, but we checked on the creative—we wanted to see the effect of workbooks on the creativeness of children. This is another question, you see—if I were concerned with promoting number concepts, I would certainly go into the methods of it, of number concepts, and would then adjust my methods to the way of thinking of children; in other words, a method which does not necessarily have to introduce stereotypes. Do you get what I mean?

Student: Yes, I understand.

Lowenfeld: It would be a wonderful thing if someone would do it and attack it from the other direction.

Student: Dr. Lowenfeld, how does this hold for the teaching of writing—numbers and letters and things like that?

Lowenfeld: Well, quite the same. I am against the method which we often use, to lead the child's hand in writing, you know. This really forces his own motor activity into the preconceived method of the teacher, so I'm more for the free method of writing in which the child uses the slant, which is more adjusted to his own body and his own muscular activity. But the purpose of writing is also the same as the purpose of language, namely, that the child does not write for the writing's sake but writes for the sake of communication. In other words, I would continuously emphasize that writing is only a means to an end. That means, what happens if we don't put a comma here? What happens to the word, to the sentence? Does the sentence change? Do you understand what it means? So I would rather like to see children develop their writing ability as a means to communicate rather than as a means to do calligraphy. Do you see? That means the end would not be calligraphy. I do believe writing must be readable, because we wouldn't be able to understand it, you see? But this is also a means to an end. And if we cannot read it, well, we will turn it back and we will say, "I can't read your writing. You must learn to write clearer so we can write letters to each other. See, I'm going on vacation, and I expect from you a letter; but what good is the letter to me if I can't read it?" Do you see? We should always emphasize, in writing or in reading or in language or in arithmetic, that all these are only means to an end and not ends in themselves. We would be lost without arithmetic when we grow up. You wouldn't even know how to pay for what you want to buy. "What do you like? Do you want a gun? Well, how much is a gun?" Do you see?

And we should make it as meaningful as possible to children on all levels. We fail here to recognize that one area of teaching has meaning and reflects upon another area of teaching, especially in the methods of imitation of which we are speaking. Now, we have seen that those methods which are not serving the individual child and the differences in his growth are then detrimental for education. We shall try to be missionary in regard to that and promote methods which allow the child to express himself individually. This is especially important in the democratic society in which we live. It should be very, very much on your mind that, whenever you promote the regimentation of stereotypes, you actually engage in fascism. See, the method which totalitarian regimes—fascist and communistic regimes—use is the exclusion of the individual and his differences, a regimentation to one kind of thinking. If we engage the same methods in our classrooms, then we are really guilty of disregarding the individual as an individual. Now, may I say that I do not use such means to make you feel that you are guilty of something. I should rather say, "Have respect for the individual." It is unethical not to regard an individual as an individual and to straitjacket him and regiment him into a sameness of expression.

At this time, I often tell a story of an experience which I actually had when I was in a classroom several years ago. It was after Easter, and I saw a frieze of hectograph Easter bunnies in a room. I asked a child, "Which one is yours?" The child looked around and became very irritated—I could feel it—and excited. The child didn't find hers until she looked very carefully around and then she said, "It's this." And I said, "Why is it this?" And the child said, "I remember I had a dirty thumb!" and she had seen the imprint of her thumb.

Now isn't that horrible that a child should identify herself only on the basis of a dirty thumb? Actually, you see, the children were regimented into a sameness of expression. This is fascism. So never engage in such imposing of your own standards and concepts upon children, but always think that they are human beings; and every human being has a right to his own reactions, especially on the level of creativeness. Of course, the teacher wasn't aware of it. No teacher is aware of these implications—of implications that he would ever do anything having a purposely wrong or detrimental aim in his life. No one would ever do it. See, we all are ethically that high that we would not on purpose do something which is detrimental to children. But this is not the question. The question is that we have the responsibility of becoming informed concerning what is detrimental, and the more—the better—we are informed, the less we will be apt to make mistakes.

Now, as we have talked about various kinds of imitation, we have come closer in our understanding to what we mean when we say the child should express himself and should not be dependent upon imposed standards. By that we mean that every child has his own standards which are peculiar to his own thinking, his experiences, his past associations, and so forth. Then, does it mean that we do not expect any child or any two children to react in the same way? Oh, no; not at all—because we know that children, as they go through various developmental stages, have certain things in common. We shall then, in the future, call these stages "developmental stages."

In developmental stages, children at the same stage have certain things in common. For instance, we know that, at a certain time in their lives, all children scribble. That means, they go through a stage which we shall call the "scribbling stage." But it would be neglecting the individual child if we would not look at the scribblings in a differentiated manner. Yes, all children scribble, indeed, at a certain age. But one child scribbles outside of his paper on the desk; another child scribbles very restrictedly in the corner; another child scribbles with very dainty lines; another uses a lot of pressure; another distributes his scribbling well over the paper; another scribbles, oh, let us say, in repeated motions; another scribbles in circular motions. Children scribble differently. But all of them scribble. We will learn both the general developmental characteristics and the individual characteristics of children, so that we learn to establish a more sensitive relationship to each individual child. Now, if a child expresses himself according to his own relationships, we call this type of expression "self-expression." Self-expression is a mode of expression. It means, then, that the child expresses himself according to his own level of thinking, feeling, and perceiving. So

41

self-expression means that the outcome of it is different for each child because it refers always to the child's own self. If a child expresses himself freely, in this way he learns to adjust flexibly in different ways to his thinking and his perceiving and his feeling. If a child expresses himself imitatively, neither his thinking nor his feeling nor his perceiving come into play. Perceiving probably comes into play the most, in a very limited way, because, as he sees something and imitates it, he has to do it according to his perception. Now there is a difference in creative activity and the subject matter with which creative activity deals, that which we generally regard in courses of study as the content of a course. I would like to talk about this difference, because it will bring us a little bit closer, again, to a better understanding of what creativeness means in children.

And this brings me here to the answer of this question. Technique, after all, is only the acquisition of the necessary skills to execute one's own creative desires, which shows again that the individual determines his own standard. In evaluating a product of art, it is the teacher's task to find out whether the child or youth has reached his own standards. The standards of an individual are those which he can conceive of—that means, with which he can identify—which are in the realm of his concepts. Foreign standards are standards which are inconceivable to the child and are, therefore, imposed standards. Indeed, the individual should at all times determine his own standards according to his own reactions. But this does not mean that we are only bystanders. In our motivations, we continuously try to raise this relationship to the environment and to change the standards of individuals. For instance, before being motivated with regard to the story of the birds, the child may not have conceived of a bird as an animal which has so much sensitivity and life, an animal which has wings that he can flap and stretch out, as well as feet and toes that stretch when he lands, and so forth. The child may have had a very simple concept of a bird. He never may have thought that a bird can get hungry, too, and have feelings like a human being, you know. Well, all of a sudden, the concept has changed. But the child determines his own standards through his drawings. You can only motivate the child towards arriving at higher levels of understanding. Now, in evaluating a product of art, it is then the teacher's task to find out whether the child or youth has reached his own standard of feeling, thinking, and perceiving in his drawing. And we shall only be satisfied if we have brought out in the chld all of his potential abilities. Now, this is our aim; we cannot always do it.

There's another statement here which mentions self-expression. The term is often misunderstood. It is wrong to think that self-expression means expression of thoughts and ideas in general terms of content. This is a great mistake, because thoughts and ideas can be expressed imitatively. Yes, indeed. Well, when are they expressed imitatively? Let me give you an example. If a child brings me a drawing and the child says, "I like football playing; I love football playing; I have just played outside with others," and he brings me a drawing of football players, is this self-expression? Is it self-expression? Not necessarily. He could have copied the football players from the *Daily Sentinel Times* or from somewhere else, you know. Unless the football players are experienced by him and are expressed on his own standards—that means, on his own level of thinking, feeling, and perceiving, with his own means—unless this is done, it is not self-expression although it expresses an activity which is closely related to his own football playing. Do you see? It must be done on his own level. This is very important.

Now that brings us to the discussion and understanding that subject matter in art is different than subject matter anywhere else, except probably in English. In history, subject matter is a sequence. See, we know the content from the beginning to the end. We may start here at our home and then go further around to the history of our state, of the country, and to its relationship to foreign countries. In arithmetic, the subject matter may be, well, beginning with the concept of numbers, then addition or subtraction, and so forth. Now in art, the subject matter may remain the same for the child, as well as for the adult. The child draws houses and figures and trees and so forth, and even Rembrandt did the same. He also drew a house and trees and a mountain. That means the subject matter, the content—what is being represented—may remain the same throughout our lives if we engage in drawing or painting or in any creative activity. What changes is our relationship to the subject matter—that changes.

The relationship of a child to his father may be: "My dad has a head and two big legs because I played around the legs. My drawing has a head and two big legs. So my drawing is Daddy." Do you see? Such simple relationships are then the relationships of Johnny, who may be four years or five years old. But Rembrandt also painted his dad. "My Father" is one of his most beautiful portraits, in which he went into the most intricate relationships to his father. And his mother—he painted all the sorrow in the eyes of his mother. He painted the finest reflections of light and shadows and brought out through these reflections some of his sensitive relationships to his mother. He put the body into darkness and brought out the head into light just to show us the veins and the wrinkles and the hands—how hard they had worked. He brought out the most intricate relationships. Yes, indeed. But they also are his relationships to the subject matter, which have changed. Even within the artist, they change as he grows older, although the subject matter may remain the same. For instance, we also know that Rembrandt painted many crucifixions—many. But it's the relationship to his subject matter which changes from one time to the other. So may I say, then, in art it is not the "what" which counts but the "how"—how we relate ourselves to it. Our course, then, will deal with these changing relationships. As we grow, our relationships change, and, therefore, we will try to find out the relationships of Johnny at five years, Johnny at six years, at seven, eight, nine, ten, eleven, twelve; and in this discovery of the changing relationships of the child to his environment and to himself through his creative work, we will discover Johnny.

LECTURE 5

Visual Aids, Art Motivation, Media, and Creativity Research

"A child wants to include a horse in his drawing. If he copies a horse as part of his expression, is the imitation harmful?" Well, this touches upon a vital question, and I would like to be very clear about it. There are situations which we cannot construct as an experience because it is difficult to bring a horse into a classroom, you know. But a child may have had an experience with a horse. We can ask the child, "Have you watched horses?" A horse is such a common thing that we can expect children to have seen horses and to have had experiences with horses. But how about a lion or a tiger, when the experience is no longer as common as an experience with a horse? So I would like to discuss with you those experiences which cannot be produced by associations or by reality, experiences which are rather fictitious in nature and which we cannot readily produce. What shall we do? And this touches the problem, too, when we ask ourselves, "Should we give the child a drawing of a horse, a drawing of a tiger, or what?"

May I say that the nature of children's imaginations is very good. When we speak of something, some kind of image is readily produced in children. But in order to recall an image and use it for drawing, it must be so activated that the details are also available. Therefore, mere verbal recalling or discussion of an image is not enough for children. It is, therefore, important to give children a visual understanding of certain objects which are not obtainable in the classroom or even outside. It is very legitimate to use visual aids for drawing and for art in general. The important thing, however, comes afterwards—we should not remain with the visual aid. So, it is not good to give a child a picture of a horse and say, "Look at it, and copy it," because this picture of a horse, when being copied, will not become an emotional experience for the child nor will it become his mental property. We are interested, of course, in the process which integrates thinking, feeling, and perceiving, because this is one of the major contributions of art teaching. If we drop this contribution and merely remain with the visual experience—as, for instance, "Look at the horse and draw it"—then we cut

45

off the emotions of the child and also what he can recall; that means, the mental property, his relationship. Since we would like to make the experience a total experience in which the whole child is really involved, we cannot leave him merely with the visual aid.

What else should we do? We were talking last year about the very great importance in teaching of dramatizing. Actually, in a way, every teacher should have some ability as an actor or an actress. You don't know how important this is! Only through such an ability will the teacher really get the child involved. There is no doubt about it. I've never yet seen a teacher who stands straight, and the children become excited. It is simply impossible. There is a wall between the adult and the child, anyway. You can only bridge the gap by getting the children excited about what you do. For instance, if you tell the children about the lion in the desert and his life there and how he feels when roaming around, well, it isn't enough if you just show the children a picture. The best thing, of course, would be if you could produce a motion picture about a lion, because this would show the lion in his real-life situation. This is difficult, we all know. But you can produce a picture—every school has a number of pictures. If you don't, take one from a magazine and say: "Now, children, look at this lion. We talked about the lion, you remember, and you didn't know how he looked. Now, I brought you a picture. You see, a lion really is like a very big cat." Now you relate to something which the children know is possible. If not, well, you cannot; and you just have to remain with the picture. You say: "It's really like a big cat. Have you ever seen a cat walking? I've said 'seen' because you scarcely would have heard her. A cat walks very, very softly. Can you hear me? This is how a cat walks. And this is also how a lion walks. Very softly. Softly. You know what a lion eats? Oh, he can get very wild when he is hungry, very wild. You see a lion is like a very big cat, a cat which is that big. Look. Do you see the lion there? A lion when he is hungry eats sheep, even calves. See these lambs there? Baa! See them? Look at them. See, the lion has smelled them. And now he sees them. See how he softly approaches them—Arhrr!—up to the lambs!" You see? Now the picture is no longer a picture. Do you see?

In the child, the picture has become alive; and this is your task—to make the experience a total experience. All the children will be tense when you tell the story. And all of a sudden, the lion has their imaginations. "Now, children, we are going to paint this lion." This photograph is no longer the lion which the children are going to paint. The lion is here and here and in his mind. You see, this is very important on every occasion. It is also important when he draws a horse to give the feeling of a horse—how it is grazing. "Have you ever given him a lump of sugar? How does he feel? Warm and soft. What do you feed a horse?" You know, so that you get within the child the total experience. "Have you ever seen a horse when he eats some hay and some of the dust gets into his nostrils? You know what he does? Like you, he sneezes; but it sounds different, you know? Just do it." Of course, you at least try to get insight or to get the children aware of feelings outside of the classroom. Don't restrain yourselves. You have to lose a little bit of your puritan background in doing those things. But it is very important, you know. And in the classroom, we should just feel one with the children. I've just had some fun—you know, that's why I was late—with the children over there.

There is a very interesting child who is a schizophrenic child, not a very severe case, but he repeats again and again, a hundred times—a thousand times, if you want—a fire engine. He does nothing else but produce a fire engine, very skillfully. Then all of a sudden, he turns around and says, "Now, children, I want to tell a story about the fire engine," you see, and he just talks to them about a fire engine. Then he turns around, erases it, and starts the fire engine over again. And then he turns around and says, "Children, are you ready? I want you to listen now to my story about a fire engine." You see? Now this is one of the severe cases of inability to adjust to a new situation. For him, the fire engine is his escape mechanism—in this case, almost an hallucinatory escape mechanism, as it is in schizophrenic art.

Well, I disturbed him when I came in, and I said: "What's the fire engine doing? I can't see anything." And I shook him on the shoulder a little bit. This disturbance was important. He, all of a sudden, looked at me. "A house is burning," he said.

I said, "I can't see it! Where is it?" And he quickly drew a house and quickly erased it. I said, "Oh, I saw it. I think I saw a house burning, but I don't know." And he drew it again. And I said, "Who is in the house?" "I am," he said. And he quickly replaced his name by another name. You know, as schizophrenic individuals, they cannot speak in terms of I. But I got him to do it.

Such shocks to bring an individual out of his enclosure are very important. That's what we usually do. I did it here, with the lion, in a group motivation. But with a disturbed child whose sensitivity is thwarted, one can only use abrupt means for this interruption. And, you see, for the first time, he even drew a fireman. I said: "I have never seen a fire engine run by itself. Where is the fireman?" He drew it—the fireman up in the engine. He then erased it. But all these were shocks, one after the other, for him. If this is done continuously, such disturbances out of an hallucinatory fixation may bring him out of his situation, because they at least establish a quick contact with the environment, a quick realization.

As I told you yesterday, art education therapy is nothing else but an intense motivation, do you see? We would never be that intense with normal children. But it is only a matter of the degree in which we do that. Of course, when you stimulate a class like I did with the lion to make them aware of their feeling, their perceiving, and their whole individual participation, and a child still draws a fire engine, then you have to use different means. But this we do not expect in a normal classroom situation. So may I say—to finally answer this question after a long way around—yes, any imitation is harmful if it is for the imitation's sake in art or in any other form of creative expression, which includes language. But looking at a picture and getting some forms from there can be helpful if it is done as a means to an end and the whole child gets involved in it. Of course, I didn't describe the lion, you know: "It has a big head and graceful body." I didn't say any of this, because I expected the child to take this from the picture. Do you see? So, the exterior can be presented to the child.

But the feeling and the sensation in the relationship to this exterior has to be motivated by the teacher. We can show children almost anything—say, the big fire of San Francisco. We can show them a picture of San Francisco, if you want, and then we can say, "Now imagine, all of a sudden, people heard some grumbling under the earth, and everything got shaky." You see, they see the picture now shaking and going up and down. "Now one house after the other fell, and some fires started, and then fire engines roared, and this whole thing was a mess." Now, all of a sudden, the picture changes. But it is your task to create these changes. The picture may serve as, let's say, the basic visual concept, but nothing more. And you can do that with almost everything, because art is not the representation of things, you see. Never. It's not the representation of a horse. It's not the representation of a house, nor a fire engine, nor anything. But it is the expression of our subjective relationship to things.

This is what art is and what creative expression is. Since it involves the individual in his relationship, as the individual changes, his relationship changes. The subject matter in art is the changing relationship to ourselves and to the world which surrounds us. So we have to come back to what we said yesterday. "What can be done when the child does face his experience but does not feel that he can draw it? For instance, he can perform the actions and verbalize picking flowers but can't draw the action." This is equally important to the other problem. But, may I say, no child has the desire to draw photographically because it is not in his concept. A child who is very gifted is a child who expresses himself with ease and fluency and readily uses his imagination. We wouldn't call a child gifted who draws a photographic picture. See, this is only a representation and no establishment of a subjective attitude to what surrounds him. Children just don't draw that way. For instance, look at Figure [2]. Now, if you refer to the colored reproduction there, you will see that the child was perfectly happy when painting this, perfectly happy.[4] He didn't even conceive of the fact that he

4. For color reproductions, it will be necessary for the reader to refer to Lowenfeld's text, *Creative and Mental Growth,* 3rd edition.

Fig. 2. "I Am Standing in My Backyard" (6½ years). Color is used purely for enjoyment. First signs of color-object relationships of emotionally significant parts such as eyes, lips, grass, tree, and sky. These are the first signs of the establishment of color schemata. Notice the importance of the ego as compared to the tree. (Courtesy of the Laboratory School, State Teachers College, Indiana, Pa.) [*Note:* For illustration in color, readers are referred to Viktor Lowenfeld, *Creative and Mental Growth*, 3rd ed. (New York: Macmillan, 1957), Plate 3.]

omitted the arms. He was perfectly happy. Why? Because he drew his experience or painted his experience. Now, if a child says, "I can't draw catching a ball or playing tag" or "I can't draw picking flowers," then the child has to go again through the motions and through the feeling of picking flowers so that the experience becomes activated. If a child says, "I can't draw this," it merely means that the experience is not active within him—he cannot recall enough. Just as you would say, "I can't draw a traffic light because I don't know where the red light is—on the bottom or on the top." But as soon as you know it or someone describes it to you, well, even with your meager ability you will be fortified in your understanding, and you at least will make the red on the top and the green on the bottom and the yellow in the center.

The same is true with the child. Therefore, you would have to say: "When did you pick flowers? Let me see how you picked the flowers. Were you standing straight when you were picking the flowers? Oh, there's a beautiful daisy. Would you like to pick this? Now, let's pick it. What color is it? Oh, have you ever had a daisy in your hand? What did you do? You played with it? What did you play? Picking the petals? Oh, I did that, too. Now look at this. Let's pick it. What do you do? Oh, you can't stand straight. Pick it. Oh, you picked it? You bent down? How did you bend down? Did you have your legs close together? Let's find out. Oh, you would fall forward. What did you do? You spread your legs apart so that you could

49

reach it?" In other words, you try to bring every detail into the feeling and consciousness, not the intellectual consciousness but the one which has been felt by the child. And this will produce a more intense relationship to the action. When the child still says, "I can't draw it," then you say, "You don't know how to pick flowers?" Don't refer to the drawing, because you would only call the attention of the child to the product. No, you call the attention of the child to the experience of picking flowers, and you will then fortify this experience again. "You still don't know how to pick flowers? Well, let's go through it again. Did you pick them with a fist? Oh, you couldn't pick a flower with a fist. What did you do? You stretched out your fingers? Now, I would like to see how you stretch out your fingers and how you pick the flowers." You see, a child would have to be very, very closed in, in order not to react even to this stimulation.

When the child starts to do something, it is your task immediately to follow up with still another motivation, such as "Oh, yes, now I see you know how to pick flowers." Do not talk about the drawing. "Your drawing is beautiful"—please, never say that. Don't refer to the final product but to the experience; because the stronger the experience is to the child, the more meaningful will be the final product. The final product takes care of itself. You don't have to do anything about it. The final product is only a result of what goes on in the child. If the child harmoniously relates things to each other, the final product will show it. If the child has a strong feeling for color, the final product will show it. So you don't have to do anything about the final product. But you motivate the child concerning his relationship to what he does, and that will improve him. So, may I say again, it is important when a child says, "I can't draw," to pinch him and say, "What do you want to draw?" When he says, "I can't draw how to pick flowers," well, again, pinch him and say, "How do you pick flowers?" Go into every detail, from his relationship to flowers, his appreciation of flowers, how flowers look, how he wants to have them, why he wants to pick flowers, to the action of picking flowers. We will go through details of motivations as we go through the various developmental stages. And, of course, motivations also change on the various levels, as we shall see.

"It is stated in the text that a discrepancy between chronological age and the appropriate developmental stage, as given in our discussion, can be accepted as a sure sign of mental retardation. Could not this discrepancy be due to other factors, such as emotional disturbances, rather than necessarily being mental retardation?" Yes. Yes, but mental retardation, then, is due to the fact that there is an emotional disturbance. You understand? In other words, we are not yet hitting the cause when we see a child who is eight years old and who still scribbles. There is a great discrepancy between his chronological age—that of eight—and what he produces. His mental readiness to accept his environment is then concerned with motor activity such as scribbling. Here, there is such a discrepancy. We know a scribbling child should be finished with scribbling at age four or five. And if the child of eight is still scribbling, then we would say the child is mentally retarded. Now, we could go further concerning this question. What is the cause of the mental retardation? The cause may be an emotional restriction to accept environment. Indeed, I've had disturbed children with neuroses who could not accept their environments. But as soon as they did, they improved their mental relationships to their environments very quickly. This can happen. And the cause, of course, was an emotional disturbance. But it is not up to us to determine the cause. It is up to us to draw our conclusions from visual conceiving, from what we see. If we see that the eight-year-old child scribbles, we can only say that for an eight-year-old child scribbling is out of range; because we expect a child to scribble when he is two or three or four. But the cause may be an emotional disturbance. This is always closely related.

Now, with regard to materials, the art medium must conform to a child's own desire for expression. What about pencils? So many children love pencils; they prefer them over crayons. Some teachers say that we should never let a child have a pencil for creative expression. Let's not conform to anything. If a child loves a pencil, I don't see anything wrong with the child creatively using a pencil. But if he constantly loves only a pencil, this, too, is a rigidity. Do you see? Then he cannot readily adjust to a new material, and that means also that the child is fixed on one material. He should not merely use pencils, he should not merely use crayons, and he should not merely use paints, because also in the adjustment from one medium to another lies some educationally significant factors.

Student: Isn't it true that most children want to start with a pencil and then color later?

Lowenfeld: It is true, because they are conditioned to the use of a pencil from the parents or from the home environment. They see mother jotting down something with a pencil, and this is the most readily available thing in the home. So children, in the beginning, are most likely conditioned to using a pencil.

Well, it makes no sense to break this down by force, because it's against our belief to do anything by force. We hope that the child loves, or begins to love, crayons and paints. So we spread crayons before him. We will occasionally say, "What color does it have?" or "Is it a sunny day?" or whatever we have that incites the feeling of color and makes him excited in his relationship to color. And then the child will pick up a crayon and gradually will move from this fixation for a pencil to a more flexible use of other materials. We will talk more about this when we go to the discussion of the various developmental stages. All this will be discussed in relationship to actual classroom situations, so this is only a superficial discussion.

"I like your statement, 'Never prefer one child's creative work over that of another. Never give the work of one child as an example to another.' I find many teachers like to point out and brag to others of a certain pupil's outstanding graphic ability for expression. This particular experience of mine might come under the same heading or a similar category. I want to know if I'm wrong or right—when feeling the injustice and dishonesty for the teacher and children involved, I expressed myself right there and then. How would you have answered or handled the following situation? I found that one of my classroom teachers not only had one of her pupils as a bright and shining example, but was even encouraging him to do drawings for others in the class. I discovered it in this way. I came to her room on invitation from the teacher to check the preliminary sketches for a mural. As I was checking, I found several that showed that one person had a hand in making them. I was especially surprised when I found this on Mary's paper also. Mary had such a fine expression of her own. I said, 'Mary, your work looks like Eddie's today, and not like yours.' 'It is Eddie's. Isn't it nice? He did it for me.' I answered, 'But, Mary, I like the way you say things yourself. That is what counts for you. You would not copy all of Eddie's spelling and hand it in as yours. Oh, no, that would be cheating. So accepting Eddie's drawing as yours is not honest.' 'I won't do it again,' says Mary, 'The teacher told us that Eddie could draw for anyone because his looks better.' I was so stunned, I said nothing. What would you have done?"

Well, certainly I think the suggestion for honesty and sincerity is one of the basic principles on which we have to stand. And we always should try, whenever we can, to go as far in truth and sincerity as we can. You know, however, there are some things to which we have to conform. I come to class with a necktie. I don't know why. But these are not things that do harm to my personality. You understand? But there are things which do harm to our personality, namely, when we betray ourselves in matters which are much more significant to us, to our actions and beliefs—for instance, if something is done for us, and we act as if it were done by us. Well, this is a dishonesty such as the one which we have here. Yes, if Eddie does the drawing for Mary, Mary is dishonest if she makes people believe that it is hers. But this is only an extrinsic factor. The intrinsic factor, you know, is that her own drawing, or her own expression, lacks homogeneity and consistency. And, indeed, our whole theory goes to pieces; namely, that the child acts as a whole in his feeling, in his thinking, and in his perceiving as he creates. How can you create your individual relationship with something if someone else does it for you? It's no longer yours, but somebody else's. So it is not only a matter of dishonesty to others, but the child is actually deprived of one of the most important educational experiences—namely, that the child should become involved as a whole in his expression, that he

52

should not become thwarted in his exploring and investigating, that means, in his creative efforts. It's much more than we have heard here.

I would handle this situation like this. If I see that Eddie draws something into Mary's drawing, I would go much deeper and I would say, "But, Mary, did you experience that?" And I would become concrete: "Did you stretch out your hands like this when you caught the ball? You didn't? Eddie stretched it out? But it isn't even his arm! It's only his hand. How can you stretch out your arm with a hand which doesn't belong to it? Oh, Mary, what did you do? You pasted several individuals together. That isn't possible. You stretch out your arm. You catch your ball. Oh, my, and if Eddie puts his hand on it—my, what did you do to this human being?" In other words, go deeper and give the child the feeling of the wholeness of this experience which has to come from him, and do not stress only the extrinsic factor of dishonesty which can only be felt by others. Do you see? That's why I call it extrinsic. So it is very important that we stress the experience to the child and not, again, the final product only.

"I agree with your philosophy and the way of teaching the children arithmetic with the example you gave of six birds sitting on a telephone wire and the clapping of the hands and three flew away. Now, my question is — what do you do in the arithmetic class with the first graders who are still in the scribbling stage? Will the creative motivation still have more meaning for these children with the whole purpose being the learning of arithmetic, or will they also scribble over the whole page in the workbook with no identification with the birds? Are these children at the scribbling stage in the whole educational program? How should the art supervisor go about convincing the elementary teacher that the creative process should and must be used in the whole educational program, not just when the art teacher comes to give an art lesson? How do you do this convincing when you are just supervising and not teaching? What is your opinion of holding creative art workshops for elementary and, possibly, secondary teachers? How do you convince these adults that they can draw and break them away from, 'I can't'?"

It's an involved question, but I'd like to answer it, nevertheless. Well, if you have scribbling children in the first grade, scribbling is an indication that the child is still concerned in his mind, not with mental pictures or imagery—that means, with the establishing of a relationship between what he draws and what he sees or experiences—but rather with expressing body motions, motor activity; therefore, the child isn't even ready for birds. Imaginatively, he can be ready, but not for drawing. I have my grandson, for instance, who imaginatively is ready for many things. He can imagine three birds flying away; but if he draws them, it would be just scribbling. That means he is not yet ready to relate a mental picture to what he wants to represent. His imagery has not been activated to that extent. A scribbling child, therefore, in being forced to fill in birds, would never realize that these birds are birds which he has to fill in. It is essential that we do not force him. There are not too many children at the first-grade level who still are scribbling. If they are, they are not up to the mental level of children in the first grade. But if they are still scribbling, your motivation of clapping the hands and the three birds flying away will be much more fitting without the drawing at all than the filling in of predetermined outlines of concepts which are not in the realm of the child. The child may imagine that the three birds are flying away, and in his mental concept may adjust easier to the number three than in drawing because he is not yet ready to draw it.

What was the other part of the question? Well, how will you convince? We'll talk now about it, because there is a very important issue involved which has not yet been widely spread because it isn't an old issue. May I say that every teacher, in a way, is a missionary if he or she takes the job seriously. And there is no escape from introducing new things or even from being rebuffed and not being accepted. But there is nothing stronger than truth, and if you are convinced of those things which we do as being right, then do it, regardless of how it will be received. I remember very well my first year here at Penn State in 1945, when I taught during a summer session (I began my permanent teaching here in 1946). My students asked me, "But, Mr. Lowenfeld, who will believe us? People don't believe that there is a relationship between the drawings and the mental concepts of children. They think drawing is a skill." You see, we have gone a long way since then, and a wonderful way. It was a very exciting way, and still is. But if we would not have had teachers who believe in what they do, we would not have gone this long way. For today, quite contrary to ten years ago, art in the elementary classroom is a generally accepted means, which it wasn't then. So we have gone a long way.

Now, I shall introduce you to a new concept which also will take quite some time until it settles down in the minds of people—educators, as well as parents—but it is one of the most important concepts which we have brought out, I believe, within the last few years, with regard to art education. We found, by experimenting, that whenever children create their creativeness is not restricted merely to the arts but is used elsewhere. We came about this by referring one creative activity to another sensitivity; and we began this, actually, by trying to find out what kind of criteria are responsible for creativeness. We tried to construct tests which may differentiate creative people from less or non-creative people in the arts. Actually, I have been concerned with this for a long time.

After the last World War, I was asked if we could design such tests for veterans who came out of the service so that they could more readily accept one or another field of occupation. We could use it as a means of guidance. This, for a long time, then, has been with me; and it was in 1950 when one of our doctoral candidates [W. Lambert Brittain] started to take up this matter again. He found that there are certain criteria which are responsible for creativeness. Actually, he began with thirty-four criteria and boiled them down to eight criteria which significantly, in statistical terms, differentiate creative from non-creative, or less creative, people. This is on a continuum, you understand? Every individual is endowed with creative abilities, but in the one they are suppressed, and in the other they come out readily. Those things are usually done or developed in the formative stages of childhood and are usually suppressed, as we now know, during adolescence, during this change from unconscious to conscious activity. Now, may I say that at no time did we intend to construct tests parallel to intelligence tests, because, from the very beginning, I have deeply opposed any efforts to categorize people and put them into another cubbyhole such as a "C-Q," a creative quotient. This would be against my spirit, and I would rather destroy our own findings than have tests constructed which would be used parallel to the intelligence test. But it was important to me to find criteria which may help us in our educational methods, so that we will be better able to bring out creativeness in children. Now, did I say this very clearly?

It is a methodological question, one of helping us to find out how we can best motivate creativeness, which inspired me most strongly to go in this direction. As we were working on our criteria, we came across a study in our literature. At that time the American Psychological Association was holding its convention here on our campus, and the president, J. P. Guilford of the University of Southern California, gave a talk on creative thinking. Later on, we followed up his work. Dr. Guilford was director of a Naval research project to find criteria which are responsible for creativeness, not in the arts but in the sciences. He, too, arrived at eight criteria after long sieving. He started out with thirty-two or so by going over the whole literature of the field, as we did. When we compared his criteria with ours, we were very surprised; because many of his criteria were even named like ours. Dr. Kenneth Beittel of my staff, from whom many of you take courses, then started a study intercorrelating the two tests to find out whether these tests test different things or the same things.

After long and tedious work, we arrived at the conclusion that the two sets of tests can almost be exchanged because they test the same thing. In turn, it means that creativeness in the arts and creativeness in the sciences have the same attributes. By implication it means that—whenever we motivate children in art and try to make them more flexible, fluent, independent in their thinking, creative, and harmoniously organized in their thoughts, their feelings, and their perceptions—whenever we try this in the arts, it may be felt in the sciences and elsewhere. That means that we have arrived at almost a universal concept of creativeness. We know now from experimentation that, whenever creativeness is motivated in one area, it will be seen in the other. But it also implies that, whenever creativeness is thwarted in one area, it may be thwarted in the other. And that greatly adds to our responsibility, as you can readily see, and partly answers this question. So, actually, there is no creativeness now in one specific field, although different people will apply their creativeness differently, of course.

I should graphically give you an understanding of this basic theory which now has been put into practice. It is approximately this: we have here eight criteria—I will discuss them with you later on—which are responsible for creativeness. You have here a painter; you have here a chemist; you have here a mathematician; you have here a sculptor; you have here a musician; you have here, let's say, one who has medical interests—all of these need to possess certain skills, you understand? Now we are not dealing with these certain skills. The painter has a number of skills. I could name some of them. He must be sensitive to color; he must be able to coordinate his motions very sensitively; he must be able to translate, depending on his kind of expressive relationship, into concepts, and so forth; he must have certain attributes. The chemist must have the skill for certain mathematical understandings; he must have the sensitivity to react to biological occurrences; he must have all kinds of abilities. The mathematician must be able to think logically; he must be able to combine things; he has to have many kinds of skills which are different from those of the painter, which are different from those of the sculptor. The sculptor must have a very sensitive tactile reaction. He must be very sensitive to spatial-transfiguration combinations, and so forth. Do you see? The musician must be very sensitive to tones, chords, and their relationships, too. He also has all kinds of skills and aptitudes, and so has the medical person. These are all different. But if a painter doesn't have all of these, including creative attributes, he will only be a craftsman and not a creative painter. If a chemist doesn't have all of these, including creative attributes, he will only be, let us say, a laboratory technician but not a creative chemist. If the mathematician doesn't have all these, including creative attributes, he will not be a creatively thinking mathematician, but one who can readily apply what he has learned—not to new things, however. The same is true with the musician. He will be just a performer and not a creator. This is, then, very important for us—that there are common creative attributes for all of them which are very important. And all of these attributes are promoted in the creative process, as we shall see next time when I go into greater detail concerning them.

Student: Do they have the same degree of these criteria?

Lowenfeld: No, the degree of each of these criteria varies from individual to individual, and that makes for personalities and different kinds of creativeness. But we must have all of them, as we shall see, to some degree.

MOTIVATION, MEDIA, CREATIVITY

Here is really a hypothesis, an assumption, which I hope may ultimately be responsible for the complete changing of our methodology in elementary schools and in kindergartens: we will not stress subject matter as subject matter but rather how it is applied by using the criteria which we use in creative processes.

LECTURE 6

Praise, Criteria of Creativity, and Integration

Praise may be useful even in front of a class. Let us say there are children who were thinking carefully when they played ball; and I can see how they were playing ball—I looked at their drawings. Some children, when catching the ball, were trying to hold the ball with both hands. But I've also seen children who didn't even have their hands up and thought they could catch a ball by having their hands down. Now this would be a start toward class praise: "Let's look at our drawings. Are we really catching the ball?" You fortify your motivation by asking the children to look intently at their drawings and to identify themselves with what they did. Some of the children have done marvelous work because they were thinking of everything. They were thinking that you couldn't catch a ball when you looked down at the ground. They were really looking for the ball and catching it. But there are other children—"Now, let's find out whether you can discover for yourself if you were catching the ball." All the children will look at their drawings; and the best praise is the one which the child finds for himself, because the child knows now that you have seen and you meant him when you said: "There are children who are beautifully catching the ball. I have seen them."

However, if you would like to praise a single child—sometimes a single child needs praise because he lacks confidence; for example, a child who has been working with a stereotype and all of a sudden moves from this stereotype and discovers an individual relationship between the drawing and what he does, like the schizophrenic boy we mentioned yesterday who included a fire with the fire engine and also the fireman. Well, I said, "Wonderful! Wonderful! There is a fireman!" Of course, he erased it immediately because he couldn't stand it to be something in addition to his stereotype. It disturbed him. But I praised him, and I said, "Wonderful! There is a fireman who is in the fire engine." But I did not say, "Wonderful is your drawing." I did not direct attention to the drawing. "Oh, you have made a beautiful drawing"—I didn't say that. In my praise, I again directed the attention back to the experience—what he was able to discover. This prevents the child from becoming over-conscious of the final product. Praise from the teacher is then again the means to an end, namely, a means for the growth of the child rather than praise of the final product. So my praise does not refer to the final product but to how well the child applied himself to the experience, as shown in his final product. We all know that the more the child can involve himself in the experience, the more organized and the more beautiful is the final product. These cannot be separated. We know this, of course.

A student asks: "Is group praise wrong, or should it remain on an individual basis? For example, a teacher motivated nine-year-olds for a scribble design to break the rigid training of previous years and to introduce the fun of using all the colors. The results were so interesting it was just impossible to speak to each child. How could this be handled?"

Just as I said, it is good to praise a whole group, even better than individuals. Let each child discover his own achievement, because in this self-discovery of one's own achievement lies a great educational value. For instance, if you use a scribbling motivation to free children, and you say, "Well, children, I've looked all through your work, and I've found that some of you have done marvelous things by making free motions and applying colors freely as we have discussed previously, but other children are still afraid to use their free lines, are still afraid to apply different colors. Now, let's find out if you, yourself, can see whether you were afraid or whether you did them freely."

Let the child discover it, yes; and then give some criteria which you think are good for free expression and which you think are characteristic of rigid expression. For instance, you may say: "Now, children, look at your drawing. Did you really use the whole area which you had at your disposal? Let's find out. Suppose you go ice skating"—these were nine-year-olds— "suppose you go ice skating. Wouldn't you have fun by going ice skating? Who goes ice skating? Or roller skating?" Well, the children would lift their hands and the teacher would say, "Oh, well, I'm sure if you haven't done it yourself you have watched others do it." Now, you extend the frame of reference; you say, "Suppose this room were your skating rink," and now you would say, "Well, let's skate. What would the children do to try free motions? What do you think, Mary? Would they skate just in the corner up and down there? What would they do?"

Posing questions is always good for inciting answers which lead in the direction of self-expression. They are suggestive questions, of course. There's nothing wrong in doing it. "Would it be free if you just stay in the corner and move back and forth? What? Oh, no it wouldn't be. What would you do, Joe?" "I would run around the whole room if this were the skating rink." "Sure, and would you bump into the wall? No, you would be careful. That means, you would use the skating rink without bumping into the wall, but you would use all the freedom you have within the limitations, wouldn't you? See, these are free motions. So free motions are not motions which are running into the wall, just using freedom without restrictions. No, the restrictions are your walls. Now, let's pretend the sheet of paper is our skating rink. Now, children, look at your motions. Did you bump into the wall? Did you freely run around all over the paper?" Do you see? This might be a criterion. I don't know. I'm just replacing and substituting for you in teaching the lesson which you have suggested.

This would lead to a self-discovery of freedom in using lines and motions and also to a self-discovery of restrictions. The child would all of a sudden feel, "Mmm! I really only moved in one little corner, and I didn't apply my lines freely." Whenever you refer one experience to another experience, you extend the frame of reference. You remember, we talked about this very important factor of extending the frame of reference. And that may lead the child to a self-discovery because, probably, the lines or the motions on the paper, as you have motivated the class, were not meaningful to the child; but skating or running around a skating rink is a meaningful experience. So, they may have now referred the one experience which was meaningless to another experience which was meaningful.

Praise is very important, indeed, but *not indiscriminate praise*. Indiscriminate praise is just as harmful as indiscriminate corrections or help which you give children. So, it is important that our praise deal with motivating art as a means to an end and not as an end in itself. We do not say, "Your drawing is a beautiful drawing, period." That would be an end in itself. For what reason do you praise? So that the child will know, "I have made a beautiful drawing?" Oh, no! The child must gain something from your praise in every moment when you say something.

"How can a supervisor or fellow teacher guide another teacher who stars or gives undue praise to one particular student to the detriment of the others?" Well, it is important that we do as much missionary work in our schools, in our rooms, as is possible, also among teachers. I expect every one of you to spread the gospel when you leave this course—that means, of course, only when you are really convinced. You can only spread something which has taken hold of you and your whole personality. But, if it has, don't keep it to yourself.

One of our tasks as a supervisor is that, if we see an art teacher who has unduly praised only one child, well, we would talk with the art teacher. Of course, we would say: "I recognize that you wanted to bring out the best potential abilities of this single, individual child. I recognize the great value of this." We always stress positive sides of human beings. This is a philosophy, I hope, which we all will, as we grow older, recognize. We do much more good by stressing the positive things and looking away from the negative, you know, because we bring out the good things in people rather than step on those things for which they are not, in most instances, responsible.

So if we tell him, "You have done a good job in bringing out the individual qualities of this one child, but it may be that in this way you may have neglected five others who probably need some boost more than this individual child. It is always better not to harm five others by doing good to one"— you know, in such a way, you could convince him. I'm not sure whether you will.

There are no general prescriptions on how to deal with human beings, because the reactions are often quite unexpected, depending on how flexible the individual is. So it is always good to have individual contact, and we cannot do anything more than express what is our conviction. Even if it will not be effective in this single case, we have done whatever our conscience makes us do. Of course, as I said, we must not expect to be successful at all times; on the contrary, we will learn by mistakes which we make ourselves. I constantly learn. But this is a great thing throughout our life.

I talked yesterday about one of the most important things on which we have now experimented, and that is the establishment of a common denominator, as it were, for creativeness. That is, we know now through experimentation that, whenever we promote creativeness in one field, it may also be applied in another field, provided that the skills which are peculiar to this other field are present, too. You understand? I mean, if someone doesn't have the qualifications of a mathematician, creativeness alone will not make him a creative mathematician. He must have the basic skills. Or, if someone does not have the qualifications or the sensitivities necessary in the arts and also the skills which are necessary in the arts, creativeness alone will not help him. He may be creative in his living, probably, but has not applied this to any specific skill. Indeed, we know that, whenever we promote creativeness in the arts, it may be seen elsewhere. In other words, creativeness has certain general attributes.

Our experiments were conducted with college students, adolescent or post-adolescent individuals. Therefore, we have not yet any experimental proof, other than that of observation, that our findings are also applicable on the level of the child. I have laid down the fundamental theory that creativeness, wherever it may be applied, has the same attributes. Now, this is true. I would not say it if we did not have conclusive evidence for it. But in the book I did not go into the details of enumerating the criteria which are responsible. I leave that for a later writing when we have experimented sufficiently. But for you, I would like to develop these eight criteria so that you may, yourself, experiment and apply them also in your teaching.

As I have said before, these are criteria which we have found in the arts and which were also discovered in the sciences. They were intercorrelated by Dr. Beittel and some of his graduate students, who found that they are basically alike. The first criterion is *sensitivity to problems*. We tested sensitivity to problems by the method of seeing, perceptually seeing, finer differences. You know those multiple-choice tests wherein you have, let us say, five objects which are almost alike, but one is slightly different. How fast can you discover such differences? We tested sensitivity toward visual experiences, but we also tested it on a social level—that means, the ability to sensitively identify with social situations and to see differences there. Seeing unusual things also belongs to the testing of sensitivity to problems. We discussed sensitivity in our basic philosophy in the first class, as you remember, and we all know how important sensitivity is—perceptual sensitivity, as well as our sensitivity which we apply in our ability to identify ourselves with what we do and with the needs of others. You remember when I said, "Johnny cannot draw Daddy unless he identifies himself with the action of Daddy." Do you see? And that goes throughout the arts. No work of art is possible without this sensitive relationship to experiences, perceptual relationships as well as emotional and social relationships. So, sensitivity is one of the basic factors in any creative activity. Sensitivity to problems, however, was also the first criterion which Guilford, in his tests, put down as significantly differentiating between creative scientists and non-creative scientists. You see, there is a close relationship.

The second criterion is *fluency*. Guilford differentiated between various kinds of fluency. We did not. We just called it fluency. But there are various kinds of fluency. One is a fluency which we call ideational fluency, because it deals with the fluency of ideas. The other is called associational fluency. It is a fluency which we apply in our associations with various things. I can give you an example. Associational fluency, for instance, would be if you look at the impact of a wave hitting a rock. What comes to your mind? This would be associational fluency. Do you only look at it and have a blank; or do you feel the energy which the wave applies toward the rock or how old the rock must be—the reflections, the foam, how water can disperse and reflect the sky in its colors? All kinds of things may come to your mind. The more things that come to your mind, the better you are in associational fluency. Ideational fluency is the fluency which you have with ideas; that means, how well you express yourself fluently in using different words, different shapes, different forms, and so forth. In art, this fluency is one of the major abilities that we always use, because whenever we apply a material, a medium, we take into consideration that this medium will react in different ways. For instance, watercolor, as it runs, will merge with another color; and we readily take, fluently take, this reaction which we get and use it in our creative endeavors. So, without applying fluency to creative processes in the arts, we would be rigid and we would not be able to use various art materials for various expressive purposes.

The third criterion is *flexibility;* and here we have spontaneous flexibility and adaptive flexibility. Now, if you teach creatively you should always be spontaneously flexible. For example, if you go into a classroom thinking,

"This time I'm going to teach this certain material," but a child says, "Yesterday I saw the northern lights," and you say, "Sit down, we are going to study about the equator"—now, that wouldn't be flexible, you see. You would not adapt yourself to a given situation. But this flexibility, as you know, is always used in any creative work. If Johnny adapts his mind to a given situation—the backyard scene as we discussed it—well, he continuously adjusts himself to new situations as they arise. And this is the very same thing as if you were to go into a classroom with a preconceived idea and were not able to change according to new stimuli. Your spontaneous flexibility is the flexibility which you have in yourself; the readiness to change, not only to new or given situations, but also within yourself; the readiness to approach new things, for instance; the reactions which you have within yourself in approaching new things—that which we call an experimental attitude in the arts and also in the sciences. You see, some people do not have an experimental attitude at all. They have to have a plan; they even have to know, not only the plan, but also what the end will be. This is the converse to an experimental attitude.

This spontaneous flexibility shows itself in the way you approach things. For instance, some people are socially afraid to apply their spontaneous flexibility. They remain at home rather than meeting new situations. They are afraid to meet these new situations, because they don't know what will happen. Do you see what I mean? They don't want to go out because they don't want to face unforeseen situations, so they remain at home. These are not usually creative people, and this attitude will be seen elsewhere in whatever they do. In art, of course, it shows itself in the readiness to use materials which you have never used before, just for the sake of experimentation. I think one of the most marvelous examples of this is Miss Emerson on our staff—Professor Emerson, for those who have been fortunate in knowing her. Not that I want to single out any one of my staff, because I'm so lucky in having my staff that I could not possibly single out anyone. It's the nicest communion I know. But some people are surprised when I tell them she is going to retire. Yes, she's sixty-five. No one would ever believe it! Every day she experiments with new materials, new methods, trying to find new things. See, this is spontaneous flexibility; that means, the ability to change within one's self and be ready at all times to face new situations. So flexibility is a very important criterion. Now, you look at yourself whenever I say that. How are you? It is best that you listen to what I say now, because then you may discover some of your own weaknesses in your own teaching; and this information concerning creativity may apply to arithmetic and writing and reading and any kind of subject matter, because I believe this is universal and applies not only to art but to science and to whatever you would like to apply it.

The fourth criterion is *synthesis*. I'll explain it—synthesis. You know what we call a synthetic material? Well, we all know it, but I'll explain it to you. A synthetic material is a material which consists of various elements; but when these elements are put together, out comes a new element which is entirely different from all of these single elements. Let us say, in practice you may put together tar and another chemical and another chemical and out comes rubber. We call this synthetic rubber. But the single elements— tar, et cetera—in no way resemble rubber; nor do any of the single chemicals resemble rubber. So, synthesis would mean the integration of various elements into a new element. Do you see? This is synthesis. In art, we also mean that to be the very same thing. We have many brush strokes—out comes a shape. These single brush strokes do not resemble at all the final product. So we synthesize throughout any creative process. We put various things together and arrive at something new. In your elementary classrooms, you may have toothpicks and various kinds of little things; and you put them together and out comes a new form, a shape, a new element which we arrive at by synthesis, by putting various elements together. Now, in every art process we do this constantly. But we do it also in languages. There are various letters, and together they make a new word, do you see? And new words would make a sentence. We have always had synthesis; and the more flexible we are in using our words to make something new, a new meaning, the more creative we are in our ideas and in our language expression, and that applies now to all of us. Inventions are often made in a synthetic way; that means, we have various elements, and all of a sudden when they are put together, well, we arrive often unexpectedly at something new. Great inventions have been made not by planning but rather come about unexpectedly—radium and electricity and many of the great inventions, as you know.

The fifth criterion is *analysis*. Guilford called it analysis, and we called it penetration; but I think analysis is a better term so we adopted his term. Analysis is contrary to synthesis, but it is also an important part of any creative process. You know what it means? When you go to a doctor and say, "Could you analyze my urine?" what does it mean? He has here the total fluid, and now he should make a urine analysis. He has to find out what is in it. He has to break it down into its various components. What is a sentence analysis? You have a whole sentence, and now you want to find out the meaning of each word within the sentence. You break it down into its various parts. Now, may I say again, this is one of the most important parts related to sensitivity. You remember when we said that? We must not remain with the whole. Unless we break it down, we will not become sensitively related to the object, whether it is an object or it is man. Even in our relationships to human beings, we would by no means be satisfied in only looking at human beings as generalities—not from the point of view of races or nationalities or religions or even individuals. Do you understand what I mean? If we just say "Jews" and say—oh, some criterion about Jews—"All Jews are rich," you know, or capitalists; well, how unjust we would be to the individual! Or if we were to say, "All Negroes," and so forth, and give a kind of a criterion, how unjust we would be to the individual! So you see, to remain with the whole prevents us from becoming sensitive to the individual, to the detail. Or if we were to say, "I don't like contemporary art," as we often hear it, this is also the same kind of discriminatory statement— insensitive statement—just as if we were to say, "I don't like Jews," or, "I don't like Catholics," because these all are dogmatic statements. Do you see? This is an injustice both to the generality and to the individual. So if we say, "I don't like contemporary art," this is the same type of discriminatory statement. We may like one piece and may not like another. Because of the effect it may have on us, we shouldn't even say it. To say, "I don't like trees," well, all trees? Going into details is one of the most important fortifications of our sensitive relationships and, as we have seen in both of our studies, is essential to creative thinking and creative processes. Indeed, we always knew it in use; analysis is an aspect of our creative processes. For example, the child says, "A man, a man has what? Head, eyes. My dad has glasses. My dad has a moustache. He has a body and big arms and fingers. Yesterday, he scratched me with his fingernails, so I put the fingernails on him." Do you see? The more he goes into details—and experiences condition the child to greater details, because he would not have included the fingernails if Dad would not have scratched him. Now he becomes aware that he has fingernails. In our teaching, as we shall see, we will constantly motivate those details.

The sixth criterion—we finished five, so this is now the sixth—is called *redefinition*. This is an important criterion in creative processes, and very distinct. It means the redefining of an object by a new use. For example, let us say, we have here a toothpick. What can the toothpick be in a new situation? Let's redefine its meaning. The toothpick can be a spear in a little collage, if you want. A button can be the eye of an elephant, if you want. You know, that means that we redefine the meaning of the object. We do it all the time. We should also do it in teaching language involving the meaning of various words in various situations. We should also redefine the meaning of arithmetic in various situations. In other words, redefinition is one of the important attributes of creative teaching. We usually call it illuminating things from various aspects, seeing things from various points of view. Every good teacher knows how important it is not to present to a class only one situation, but to show how this situation can be redefined in various other situations. Now, in every creative process, we engage in such redefinitions.

The seventh criterion is *consistency of organization*. That means, if we have various parts, how well are they organized in relationship to each other? How meaningfully do they relate to each other? Now, it is this part to which we are most definitely dedicated in art teaching, because the consistency of organization actually is what we usually call aesthetic growth. How coherently does the individual apply his thinking, feeling, and perceiving; and does he express these in a harmonious organization, often also called composition? If it is incoherent, it will not convey the message and it may not be a totally creative product. We feel consistency of harmonious organization is one of the most vital parts of aesthetic growth, as we discussed previously.

The last criterion was called, by both investigators, *originality*. Originality was tested by the uncommonness of responses. You have the stimulus, and you react to it. How uncommon are your reactions? Well, in creative activities, this uncommonness is seen in the inventiveness of individuals, in the exploratory and investigative attitudes of children or adults. So it is very important that we promote it not only in the arts but in every phase of teaching.

Now, you can readily see, after we have discussed these components, that they may well serve to initiate a new methodology in teaching in which we do not only emphasize achievement but in which we also emphasize the creative attributes which go with achievement. Don't misunderstand. I am for achievement, but I'm not for rigid achievement or achievement for its own sake. We should always keep in mind that we are living as free and creative individuals and should take every opportunity to motivate the creativeness in individuals and bring it out wherever we can, whether it is in the arts, in the sciences, in language, or in arithmetic. We should always think foremost of the meaning of the individual.

Now, I would like to talk about another important and often misunderstood factor in teaching art in the elementary classroom, the factor of integration. Often, integration is confused with correlation. By integration, we mean the combining of several elements; but the combining takes place in the individual and not outside. As long as this combining takes place outside, we speak of correlation. I'll give you a practical example. For instance, if we combine several subject matter areas such as history and art, or social studies and art, or social studies and reading, we only correlate two subject matters. We do not integrate them. We must cause integration to happen rather than just correlation. When do we cause integration? When the two combine in the individual's experience. So, integration takes place in the individual, in the child. Now I'll give you two examples with the same subject matters which, in one instance, we can speak of as correlation and, in the other, we can speak of as integration. If a teacher, an elementary teacher, comes to a classroom and says, "Well, children, you know we have talked in history about the settlers and how they landed. Now we will make a drawing of this incident. So, let's draw the settlers—how they landed on the shores of New England"—this is correlation. You correlate two subject matter areas. Integration may accidentally happen if you are a good history teacher—that means, if you make the children so excited about the settling that the children themselves feel like the settlers, then they may use this experience in their creative expression. But this may only accidentally take place.

Integration only takes place if the experience—it may be a historical experience; as a matter of fact, it may be any experience—if the experience takes place within the child. How would you promote this? Only through self-identification. You see, the basis for integration is self-identification. Now, the lesson then would look different. You would say, "Children, have you ever been on a boat? On what kind of a boat were you?" You start with the child, not with the settlers, you see. "On what kind of a boat were you? In a rowboat? Oh, were you in a rowboat in rough water? How did it feel? Oh, it went up and down. Did you feel something in your stomach? When it went up and down, did it tickle you? How did you feel when it went up and down? Oh, and sometimes the rowboat would hit a wave, and it bounced. How did it bounce? Up? You felt it? And you even fell back into your boat! Well, that's fun, isn't it? Well, think, has any one of you been in a big boat? You see, the settlers were in a big boat. It was also bouncing—up and down, you know—and sometimes it wasn't even straight. Does any one of you know what kind of a boat it was? Yes, it was a sailboat. A sailboat. What drives a sailboat? The wind, so the sailors are happy if they have a wind. Oh, yes. But you know what sometimes happens? The boat leans all the way over, and all the people have to go to the other side. So, children, let's try it. If the boat leans this way, where would you go? You would run to the other side so that the boat would again be straight. But sometimes it won't get straight because the wind is very strong. Now, let's think that we all are the children of the settlers. See Daddy there. How is he dressed? Now, let's look at him. Oh, he has a kind of a cape, I see, because it's stormy. He needs to have protection. He comes over. What does he say? He says, 'Children, now remain here. You stand here, we will be soon landing.' You are going soon to the shore, and you will be lowered into another boat that will put you down in rough water. Now, hold on, hold on." You see, the children must feel the wet air. They must feel the strength of the wave. They must even taste the salt on their lips. And the experience must be their experience. They must closely identify with the settlers. And then we could expect from them a creative work, because in it one child may express a line which goes up and down and the line becomes both expression of the feeling as well as of the seeing, and also expression of what he knows. That means thinking, feeling, and perceiving always are integrated into one experience—the experience of being on the boat as the child of a settler. Do you see? So self-identification, to identify one's self with the experience, is basic to any integration.

In correlation, both subjects may suffer; and this probably is one of the criticisms which we could make concerning elementary school art, namely, that the teacher generally is only using art as an interpretation of the subject matter. In this way, the subject matter may suffer and art may suffer, because the subject matter will not be correctly interpreted and art will not be applied at all. Not everything which is done by means of a crayon is a creative experience. Now, this is important for those, especially for those, who are in elementary education. Unless we give the child the real feeling to identify with the situation, we have not done a good job of teaching or of bringing about an art experience. So it is important that, in integration, all of these elements combine within the child. Now, then, we have spoken of the integration of subject matter and of the process of art. I have both in the book in a chapter which reads, "Integration of Art and Society."

There also is something of which we have to be conscious, and I will only briefly touch upon it. I probably mentioned to you one experience of mine which best illuminates what I mean by the integration of art and society so that you will better understand in practical terms what I mean by it. It wasn't long ago that I visited the campus of Chicago University. And as I was driving with my guide through the campus, he stopped at one building and said, "This is the most significant or important building which we have on our campus." As you may know, Chicago University has chosen to build its buildings in a pseudo-Gothic style, that is, in a style which no longer fits our present but which was meant, in the past, to be the style which expressed the ecstasy of religion.

The Gothic cathedrals which were built in the medieval period were meant to express the longing for heaven, to go higher and higher and reach for the unknown. If you are in a real Gothic cathedral, then you almost have the feeling that you are uplifted by the arches, which grow higher and higher the longer we go into the period of Gothic building. Since, structurally, they have to come to an end, they meet in a pointed arch. But in the domes or in the spires of Gothic cathedrals, you can see this expression of going higher and higher without having an end. This was the spirit of the Gothic style. We should also at this time think of architecture as being the shell, the housing, of the spirit which lives in there. If the spirit is great, the glorification in its shell signifies the spirit. In periods in which man was endowed with a great spirit, the architecture that housed the spirit was equally great. In times in which man lacked spirit, man had to go back to past periods to borrow what he did not have. So architecture is not simply something externally visible. Architecture is something which signifies the spirit of man in one way or another. If the spirit of man was the glorification of worldly goods (wealth), like in the Renaissance, then the architecture was a glorification of the wealth of the worldly spirit of man. If the spirit of man was deeply concerned with religion, ecstatically concerned with religion, then the architecture was the most eternal memorial for this ecstasy of spirit, such as we see in medieval buildings—cathedrals, in particular.

So, when I looked at this building, I was not quite aware of what my guide meant until he pointed to a tablet at the right side of the door which read, "In this building, the first atomic fission occurred which changed the outlook of science and the meaning of man." I shuddered for a certain time, because I looked at the building, a Gothic building, and out of the arches grew huge tin pipes heavenward. I thought for a moment, "What a sacrilege!" If Giotto, builder of one of the great Gothic cathedrals in Florence, or part of it at least, would get out of his grave and would see this—there is no ecstasy for religion. What a mess! He would think, "What happened to man? They used my spirit for utterly different purposes."

LECTURE 7

Meaning of Culture, Integration of Art and Society, Competition, Grading, Motivational Procedures, and Discipline

I believe this (the meaning of culture) is a very, very important item of which we should become more conscious as educators, as teachers, and as people who live in this society. I always feel terrible when I come together with people who are educators on a high level, even deans and college presidents, who are completely unaware of the meaning of culture. This is something which shakes me, for they are the ones who should promote those things which are beyond the mere making of a living. I am referring here to the deeper meaning of culture, of those things which surround us— as I mentioned yesterday, for instance, the meaning of architecture. I have scarcely been able to get an understanding by any dean with whom I have talked—deans of colleges of education; moreso of deans of colleges of liberal arts—for the real meaning of architecture as an expression of a time's spirit. You see, as I said yesterday, architecture is the shell which houses a spirit. The greater the spirit, the greater is the glorification of the spirit which is expressed in this shell. It is probably the same experience that you have when you buy an item which is very dear to you or if you already have an item which is very dear to you. Let us say you have a brooch which you received from your mother, and your mother has been dead ever since. You wouldn't wrap this brooch in a newspaper wrapping. You most probably might even want to buy a little box which is nice and soft inside so the brooch will not be hurt. It is the box, then, which glorifies the spirit of the brooch. In the same way that the box glorifies the contents—namely, the brooch—that is, the spirit and your sentiments which you relate to it, so does architecture glorify the spirit which it houses.

This, to me, is one of the most important cultural concepts. I believe it would be wonderful if someone would write a history of cultures and of art on the basis of this concept. He would find that during different periods of art the emphasis is on different kinds of glorifications, as shown in architecture. He would find, for instance, no family buildings or homes of Greek architecture left from the great Greek period of culture. We should not be surprised, if we have read the history of the Greek culture during this period, for the family was entirely subordinated to the religious and social life of the Greek culture. As you may know, mothers even put their little babies on the mountains of the Tiekatoes if the body of the baby did not comply with the measures of beauty as demanded and requested by Greek culture. Is this cruel? Yes, to a certain extent, it is. Just imagine that you are such a mother and your baby is not quite fit, not physically fit—in proportions—so as to stand up to the beauty concept which Greek culture had; and you had to carry your baby into the mountains of the Tiekatoes and leave it there. Your belief must be very strong that the gods and the cult for beauty would not accept your baby within their society. The cult was so strong, the belief was so strong in body culture during this time, that family life—the relationship, even, of a mother to the child—wasn't strong enough to create a glorification of the family spirit. Therefore, no family houses have been left from the great Greek culture, because apparently they didn't stand the times. They didn't stand the weather. They deteriorated rapidly. So we have nothing which reminds us that there were families. But we have beautiful other buildings—for instance, temples—gorgeous temples, in excellent condition some of them, which are witnesses of the glorification of the spirit that lived inside the shell. We know there was a great spirit which demanded the glorification, and it was strong enough to create these wonderful shells which we see in Greek temples. Also, body culture was so strong that even to the present day we have beautiful arenas which bear witness to the great Olympic games. After thousands of years, we still have the glorification of a spirit, as shown in these shells.

It was quite different during the Roman period. During the Roman period, people wanted to live. They had their parties. They had their homes. They wanted comfort. During the Roman period, they were no longer that much interested and fascinated by religious spirits, whatever they may have been. So, from the Roman period we have beautiful homes, incredibly beautiful homes. If we go to Pompeii and look at these buildings, we will be amazed at the comfort which Roman architects produced. The glorification of the spirit of home life during Roman culture was tremendous, so the shell was beautiful. Has any one of you been to Pompeii? Well, then you know of the comforts they had. Incredible! They had little channelways from the kitchen to the dining room in which they put water with a tray on it, and the tray floated from the kitchen to the dining room. Do you see? These are wonderful things that we don't even have today. Yes, and they gathered in the center of their homes where the rain was collected in a little swimming pool. They would gather around the water in the center of the home in the evenings and have beautiful parties. So, we have lovely villas from the period in which the home was glorified. We could go on through all the periods of history and find out what happened.

You know, when Christ was born, the adherence to Christian beliefs was by no means an easy task. It was not like going to church today. People had to do this in hiding. Churches were built underground, and you did not see a glorification, a visible glorification. It was underground. The catacombs took care of it. Once religion became the desire of the people, cathedrals were built; but still these cathedrals needed thick walls—"A mighty fortress is our God." This was the beginning of the Romanesque style, not large windows because people needed darkness inside. They were not yet completely free and not filled with ecstasy but rather with humility. And then, as the humility disappeared and the ecstasy grew, more space was needed and the windows grew. But it became too light, so stained glass windows replaced the windows of the Romanesque period. You could write a history of art on the basis of the spirit which searched for a glorification in the shell. If we then, from this point of view, look at our buildings which we build today, we, too, get a very deep insight into the nature of our culture. It is very important that we as teachers understand it, for we will get rid of many of our prejudices.

Now let us look, from this viewpoint, at our elementary schools of today. May I say that, to me, this is the most encouraging sign of our present period. Wherever you go—whether it is in a little town in the South or in State College; even in State College where the community is rather conservative—our elementary schools are most advanced in design, are contemporary in spirit, using contemporary materials. They are not uniform—oh, no, not by any means. Wherever you go, you will see individual designs of elementary schools, beautiful designs. Whether you are in Atlanta, Georgia, or whether you are in Chicago or whether you are in any other community in which an elementary school is built, we never borrow a pattern from the past. Do you realize that? We never do it. No school board would ever have in its mind to say, "We are building a colonial elementary school." This is entirely impossible. Do you realize that? We never borrow the spirit of the past for an elementary school. The spirit of the elementary school is strong enough to seek a glorification in its shell. This is the most encouraging thing. I prefer it to having started on the college level, on a level of higher learning, because it's always better to start at the roots.

This contemporary spirit as shown in architecture is not seen in institutions of higher learning. On the contrary, we have here great contradictions. Princeton built a nuclear physics building in the Gothic style. What a nonsense! And, imagine, they are not even aware of it. This is the sad thing, because any psychological treatment—whether it's the analytic treatment or any other type of therapeutic treatment—consists of making us aware of things. As long as things are in the subconscious, we cannot even deal with

72

them. So imagine what it means when people build nuclear physics buildings in the Gothic style. Even for the great advancement of our scientific spirit in schools of higher learning, we don't find a glorification of it. We go back and borrow from the past. Do you see the implications of it? I hope you feel it. Now, gradually, there is some awakening taking place. In some universities, we begin gradually to get away from it. But even here on this campus, five years ago, before the student union building was built, no one would have dared to build in a style other than pseudo-Georgian, because we would have been afraid to do something which does not fit the pattern. You see, this fitting to a pattern is an inflexible attitude and shows the inability to adjust to changing needs.

This was quite different during great periods of art in which culture and spirit were in unity. I'll give you an example of this; I stated it in the text. Imagine that we are living during the medieval period, sometime around the thirteenth century, and witnessed the building of the great cathedral in Florence or of Saint Stephen's Cathedral in my home town of Vienna, Austria. All of these cathedrals were built in several styles, all in one building. Saint Stephen's Cathedral, one of the most marvelous Gothic cathedrals, was started during the Romanesque period, with thick walls and small windows; but the building went on over a period of several hundred years. And, as the period changed, the style changed. So we have in Saint Stephen's, which was begun in the eleventh century, a very early Romanesque building, with thick walls and those small windows. Then we have the later Romanesque style, with the larger round windows but still without the stained glass, just the very primitive, thick, turned glass. As it grew, of course, the early Gothic came. A feeling of ecstasy started, and this grew and grew and grew and grew until we reached the spire which is completely dissolved as it reaches higher and higher and has not a single flat space on the walls. And when it was finished, the Gothic was ended and Baroque had started. So all of the interior, including the altars—with the exception of the chancel—are in Baroque. And there was no one who came in and worshipped who was disturbed by the divergence in styles—four styles, or even five—in one building, one great building. The same is true for almost any of the cathedrals.

When the cathedral in Florence was built, it was started in the early Gothic period. And then Giotto, who constructed this very inspiring spire, died. Well, all the people in the town went together and said, "What should we do?" And they appointed one of the most progressive and contemporary architects of his time, Brunelleschi, to continue the cathedral in Florence. Brunelleschi, for his time, was at least as contemporary as Frank Lloyd Wright is today. He became a devoted Christian, full of the spirit of religion, and continued in the spirit of religion—but according to his own concept, not Giotto's concept. In his concept, Brunelleschi envisioned that a cathedral should have a cupola, a dome, which encloses the hall in which people worship—a heavenlike structure. So Brunelleschi constructed the first dome of its kind—which signified the beginning of the Renaissance, as those who have studied art history know. A dome was not as easy to construct then as it is today. He had to overcome many obstacles because there was no steel or concrete, only wood. And he did it! And when you go to Florence and look up, you have a feeling of heaven. This was the beginning of the Renaissance. According to Vasari, a contemporary historian of that time, the people streamed in and watched with great excitement as the building grew. The whole square was filled with people when the cathedral was opened. There was no voice which complained that the dome had not been finished as it was started. People, in their spirits, were so flexible that they accepted the change. Do you see the difference?

Today, when we build a chapel in an institution of higher learning—and I'm sorry to refer to the chapel on our campus—we do not deliver in the building our beliefs in the religion of our time. On the contrary, we go back into colonial periods or Georgian periods and borrow something, probably because of a lack of enthusiasm for our individual religious beliefs that we have today. If Dr. Milton Eisenhower—and I had a personal talk with him; it's no secret—if Dr. Milton Eisenhower would have been aware of the cultural meaning of architecture as a glorification of the spirit which it houses, he would have seen that he has erected a memorial which stands for our lack of belief rather than for our belief. May I say, indeed, he did it with the most sincere and best intentions. Yes, indeed, we all do things with our best intentions. But this is no excuse for doing things wrong. We have not signified, in such a chapel, that which we signify in our elementary school buildings, where we are showing our belief in the meaning of elementary education and our regard for our children.

There are signs, as I have told you, of a departure in which we see that our belief now becomes strengthened and is in unity with our time. But these tendencies are still weak. The more we become aware of this implication, the more will we contribute to our upright citizens who believe in the time in which they live. We are apt to become schizophrenic, in a way, if we withdraw after teaching progressive methods, and nothing but progressive methods, and then go home and retire in a colonial environment. This is the problem. May I say that it is no one's individual problem, but it is the problem of our time. This is what we should be conscious of. You see, if you have bought a colonial home, or a home which is not in agreement with the structural means and the spirit of our time, there's nothing wrong if you are conscious of the implications. And this "if" is important. But if you go to Sears and Roebuck to select a colonial-type furniture which isn't colonial— as you all know, it has been produced on an assembly line—it really is a sacrilege to colonial furniture, which is really beautiful if you look at real colonial furniture, if you go to Williamsburg and see what has been done. But, you see, we never go out in a horse and buggy. No one of us would do that. We try to select the finest car; the most streamlined model is not good enough. We go and buy dishwashers and washing machines and all of these comforts. We wouldn't have a colonial bathroom. Yes, but as soon as we step from those commodities into the living room, we unconsciously step over centuries. This is a problem with which we should be greatly concerned, because the living room also should be a glorification of the spirit which moves there. And this glorification should not be borrowed from the past; because if we are strong enough, we believe in it in the present.

These are some of the implications, of which I would like to make you conscious, concerning the integration of art and society. Indeed, you see how society is so confused that we have here, on the one hand, assembly-line products which are all alike because we have strong tendencies which hammer upon us for conformity. On the other hand, we are puzzled when we stand in front of most of the contemporary art works for we cannot identify ourselves with them. Only after long and hard work can we get into the spirit. What does this mean? May I say this, and I hope you will think about it—even if you do not understand contemporary art, the single works of contemporary art, just have in your mind that the artists who produced these works could easily have produced communicative works of art such as landscapes, flowerpieces, and things which can be easily understood by the masses. But, voluntarily, they went into exile, an exile which means individuality. This is their exile. Today, every single artist has almost to invent art as if it would have been here for the first time. Why? Oh, you see, today someone paints like someone else. Then one says, "Oh, he imitates van Gogh or he paints like Picasso or he paints like—see, this is like . . . ," and so forth. What happened? During the Renaissance, people did that on purpose. They belonged to the Venetian School; they belonged to the Florentine School; and one painter even painted on the paintings of another painter.

Has it changed? Yes, indeed, it has. Now think about it. Future historians—let us say, in the year 3000—may look back and say, "This was the beginning of a great industrial era, the machine era, in which mass products were turned out. Now let's look at art." They may even say, "You see, art saved the individual from succumbing to this mass production. Art emphasized individual differences, overemphasized them so much that the masses lost contact with art because they couldn't understand it. But the artist said, 'I am an individual; I am an individual; I am an individual,' and all of them glorified their own individuality by being different, one from another." In this glorification of the individual as we see it today in art, we see a great mission—a mission to counteract conformity, to counteract mass production, which looms large in our society. If no one would do it, we might succumb to the social achievements of our time. This is probably one of the great meanings of contemporary art. So don't turn your back, but take your hat off to these individuals who are people who sacrificed their communicability and went voluntarily into an exile. They have a mission, although many of them may not even be conscious of this mission. These are some of the implications which we have to see as educators, and I hope I have opened some of your eyes so that we can look more deeply into the meaning of things which surround us.

After this discussion of the integration of art and society, I come to another implication which we should deal with and which more intimately relates to our classrooms, and that is the meaning of competition—including the meaning of free enterprise, which is a very basic issue in our society. Now, as we all know, children are different from adults; and most of our difficulties in education result from using our adult attitudes on children. Children, as you know, play differently from the way adults do. A child may take a pencil in his hands and zoom through the air and say, "Ahrhrhr," and the pencil may become an airplane. If we adults were to do this, we would be considered insane. Such a difference is seen between the adult's controlled imagination and action and the child's unconscious imagination and action. A child may pick up anything, a piece of wood, and it may become a train when he pushes it and says, "Chss, Chss, Chss, Chss, Chss." In the next moment, it may be a machine gun with accompanying noises, "Pscho, Pscho," you know. For us adults, a piece of wood is a piece of wood and not a machine gun, nor is it a train. So our imaginations are controlled, while the child's imagination is uncontrolled; and he readily translates almost anything into his own form of action. We should keep this always in mind. Things which we readily accept in an adult society are not accepted on a child's level, for a child does not rationalize as we do. We rationalize and say a pencil is a pencil; a child does not. A pencil may be a gun, and a piece of wood may be almost anything.

Now, I say this because I do not believe that forms such as free enterprise or competition, which are accepted in a society, are readily applied in our classrooms, for there is a great difference between our goals and the goals of children. On the contrary, I would say that, as long as we believe that education in itself has a great value, we should not introduce into our classrooms values outside of (extrinsic to) the values which we create. I would feel terribly bad if you had to be paid in order to listen to me. You understand? I feel that what I say and what I believe in are important enough for their own sakes. In other words, we should not pay money here in order to get students to come to class. This would degrade me. It would mean that education, or what I say, has no value and that I need some stimulus in addition to what I say, such as a dollar or something else, in order to have people come. But this is generally accepted in a free enterprise system. This is the nature of our advertising and the selling of products. The coupons, you know—this is the system. You need additional coupons in order to buy. It's not the quality of the product, but it's the additional stimulus which makes you do it. Now, imagine if we transfer this into the classrooms, and we say, "Now, children, the one who makes the best drawing will get a dollar." You see, you do exactly the same thing. We would then no longer believe that the child finds satisfaction in making a drawing, but rather that the dollar is a greater incentive. That means we deprive ourselves of our own spirit. So, in the classroom, I shall distinguish between two kinds of competition.

The one I call *forced* competition. Forced competition, I understand, is competition with extrinsic values, values which do not lie within the educational procedures. The child must find so much satisfaction in his art work that he is eager to express himself and loves it for the doing's sake. As soon as we introduce extrinsic values, such as prizes—dollars or whatever else the prizes consist of—we weaken our point. We deprive education of the spirit and introduce material values. Education is not a material value. It's a satisfaction which we gain from extending our own self—our knowledge, our sensitivities, and whatever accompanies this. From this deep satisfaction, we gain our rewards. No one ever has to pay you to fall in love. Our reward is the deep and vital satisfaction which we have in this highest communication with another. We would deprive love of its meaning if we were to say, "Those who fall in love get a dollar." You see? And the same is true for religion: "Those who go to church get a dollar." Imagine! We would deprive religion of its meaning and deprive it of its spirit. If we do not go to church because we would like to be in unity with the universe or with God, the dollar will not help us. And the same is true for education. Any extrinsic reward deprives education of its most effective means, and that is the satisfaction which you gain from education as a means to extend yourself through learning.

There is a form of competition which we accept readily and love. I call this *natural* competition. The most natural competition is the competition with one's own self. I would like to do better tomorrow than I have done today—that means, I like to compete with myself. And this never stops. We call it growth. Growth is the most natural form of competition. But there are other natural forms of competition which go on by themselves in a classroom. Mary wants to do better than John—this is a natural form of competition. It's not because John receives an extrinsic reward, but rather that Mary would just like to be as good as someone else. This is the finest spirit in a classroom and belongs, indeed, to natural competition.

Unfortunately, we have adopted one means in our teaching which comes very close to extrinsic values and, therefore, to forced competition—especially if it is misused. This is grading. If we use in a classroom situation the expression, "Mary, you won't get the grade, or you won't make the mark," then we are "done for" as teachers. We don't believe in our mission of extending Mary's field of interest, her knowledge, and her sensitivities. We, rather, use an extrinsic means as a threat and say: "Mary, look at that! If you don't learn, you will not get the grade." The grade is then something extrinsic. Yet, as you know, we need some record of our students and our children. But as long as we consider this record (grade) as a basic means, we are done for as teachers and do not recognize our mission. If we look at it as a necessary evil, that's much better. Then we keep in mind, "Well, Mary just didn't do well," and record it.

In creative activity, a grade is always a nonsense. Imagine that Johnny, who has been inhibited his whole life—he is seven and he has always been restricted—draws stereotypes. And one day I catch his spirit, and now he departs from his stereotype a little bit. He has started something which probably isn't even recognizable unless we are sensitive to it. Now, Johnny needs some praise because he has found himself for the first time. But compared to Joe, he's still bad. If I were to give him a poor grade because he doesn't compare with Joe, well, I would be giving him an additional blow on his head to the one he has already from his inhibitions. What should we then do? In creative activity, if we can, we should only grade with descriptive grades. But if we have to stick to letter or numerical grades, then I would suggest that you grade each individual child on the basis of his own progress, not by comparing one child with another because that always creates injustice. I would tell this to my group. I would say: "Children, you know we all are individuals and every child expresses himself differently. You see, you all live in different houses. You all live in different environments. Your mother is different than Mary's mother. We all are different. In order to do justice to your differences, I shall look at your works as you produce them. And I shall keep in mind how you progress, so I will not compare Mary with Joe because they are different. I will only compare what Mary did yesterday with what she does today and with what she will do tomorrow." This eliminates some of the injustice which grading brings about. It does not eliminate all of it.

May I repeat again, I believe that grading is an extrinsic value. In all our subjects, we should therefore not—and never—emphasize grading as a means to get children to work. We are licked if we do it as teachers. As a matter of fact, by doing so, we stamp ourselves as being too weak to be able to compete with those things which have the connotation, "I am better than the children." The grades become something fearful, something for which children have been conditioned by the parents and the past and their environment. We should not contribute to this condition. On the contrary, we should try to do everything we can to make the grade something insignificant, merely a record and nothing more. I know that this is a very controversial issue, and I hope I will have some points of view on my desk tomorrow which we may discuss. But I feel very strongly about this, very strongly. I hope I have given you the best comparison by comparing education with religion, as a spiritual value for which we cannot be paid by extrinsic means.

As we talked about grading, I would now like to talk about other classroom procedures which are important to me—motivational procedures. As you may have learned from our discussions concerning basic philosophy, for us it is very, very important that the child gains in his attitude towards his environment, that he improves in his seeing, that he improves in his feeling relationships, and that he improves in his knowledge. Any motivation which doesn't do that is not a good motivation. We will discuss concretely motivations for children in the various developmental stages. We will hear how we should motivate children who are still scribbling. We will hear how we should motivate children who are still in the first, second or third, fourth or fifth grades, and so forth. But, at this time, I would like to discuss general procedures which, to me, appear important so that a good motivation will not fall short.

I have seen teachers who really inspire a class by giving them a strong motivation, and all the children are with the teacher—think with the teacher, feel with her—and are ready. And then the teacher says, "And now, children, we are going to distribute the materials." Then there is much noise—you know what it means to distribute materials—and the whole motivation is gone. The sequence in which we distribute materials or give the child an understanding of what materials he is going to use is very important. And the motivation should always be kept properly intact. We should never disturb the child from the moment of motivation to the actual beginning of the creative process. The creative process, therefore, should always follow immediately after the motivation. The distribution of materials should always be done first.

When you distribute materials, please let your children do the work. Don't do it for them. It's an entirely wrong attitude to think that the children will be more quiet if you do it, going around and distributing the materials. You know, sometimes the children feel that they get a present from the teacher if the teacher distributes the materials, and some children look at the teacher and say, "Thank you," when they get the crayons, and so forth. The teacher also gets the feeling that she is distributing presents. This is a wrong attitude toward materials. Materials are things with which the child expresses himself. Of course, we should be thankful for everything, but not to the teacher. We should be thankful to God that we use our language to express ourselves, that we can communicate. This is marvelous, wonderful. But we don't owe it to a single person. This is something of a spiritual value in which we believe. It is not the crayon in which we believe, but the thing which we can do with the crayon. Do you see? So, yes, a certain humbleness is essential, but it isn't brought about by making the child say, "Thank you." It's brought about by the teacher's attitude.

Here we speak about a very important point—less important probably for those who have been teaching for years, but more important for those who have not been teaching (and we have some among us)—and that is the meaning of discipline. As we distribute or have the children distribute materials, we should be aware that this is part of the classroom atmosphere. And please don't misunderstand me when I say, "Any spirit can only develop in an environment which is conducive to the spirit." No chaos is ever conducive to the spirit of promoting harmonious organization as we do it in aesthetic experiences. Therefore, it is of vital significance that a class is started in order. How should you produce order? Never overshout a class; because the louder you speak or shout, the louder will be your children. Never start a class in a hustle-bustle. Be collected even if you have to stand in front of the door for a few seconds and calm down and then go into the class relaxed. Any of your nervousness will immediately be felt by the children for, thank God, they are still sensitive in their natural reactions.

LECTURE 8

Subjective Evaluation, Objective Evaluation, and Evaluation via the Various Components of Growth

You all know that there are limitations to what we can do, so if we come into a school situation in which there is chaos, we cannot help but simply do what we can do; and we may fail. If an individual is in a situation of chaos in which there is a weak principal who cannot remove the chaos, who has not even the desire to do it, and who blames the teacher for not being able to establish a better, harmonious organization in relationship to the children within the classroom, well, then, the teacher is often doomed to failure. We are not magicians; and, as I said before, we cannot change a situation which has been established for a long time by simply coming in. We can try, and we should try. But if there is a principal who does not support the teacher and who is a politician more than an educator, then we are left alone with our educational ideals. I want to say that I have gone through such situations, indeed, with my students. It would be desirable if such a situation would become known to the school board and other authorities. There are means, of course, democratic means, by which such situations can be improved. If there is chaos and there are several of the teachers who feel that this is undesirable, I don't see anything wrong or disloyal if they get together and discuss the situation. This is perfectly all right because you are not disloyal. You can look at it from two sides. Think of how the children could improve in their learning. So if you don't do anything, you would be disloyal to the children. Do you see? And this is more important to me than to be disloyal to a principal who places politics above education. Therefore, it is important that teachers use their own minds and see correctly. And for this reason, a course such as this is designed so that we get an attitude toward what is desirable and what is not desirable. But, may I say again, there are situations which are difficult to change.

There is a note here: "Do you believe that there is a lot of bad art produced on the basis that it is different and revolutionary or individualistic? Do I have a right not to accept an adult artist like Pollack, who paints by splashing? And must I accept the child splashing in paint?" Now, here is another way of controlling paint. It is not from the brush to the canvas, but it is like throwing a ball, you see? You can control it, as you control the ball in golf so it will land in the hole. In other words, the artist has now tried to control another form of technique as one of the many searches for individual differences. But Jackson Pollack tries hard in his organization. Those who have seen original Jackson Pollacks and who have been before them and have seen the canvases can no longer say this is mere splashing.

Now, may I say, when we apply it to child art, it is somewhat different; although here some may say "the child artist." If we were to say that, I would be against it because the child is not an artist. Indeed, the child distinguishes himself from the artist in one very important aspect, namely, that the artist always thinks of the final product as the main outcome of his creative endeavors while for children the process is the more important part, the doing of the thing. Now and then, even a child can experiment and can do something, depending on his level of development; but it is different. We must not compare the child with, let's say, Jackson Pollack in his desires. "Must I stand by and watch the adult artist paint by splashing and say, 'Johnny, the artist is expressing himself'?" Now, may I say, Jackson Pollack never refers to child art and would be quite opposed if he were to see children trying to do the same thing that he tries to do. So, here is an ambiguous statement which is not true at all. May I divide the question, then? "Must I stand by and watch the adult artist paint by splashing?" Yes, why should you not? You don't need to buy the painting if you don't like it. But to say something detrimental about the artist is none of your business, because most probably you have not gone into the spirit and understanding of the endeavors of the artist. And as long as you cannot show him that he is betraying himself on purpose and betraying others on purpose, let him splash the paint. He will not hurt you. So, indeed, learn to be more tolerant. This will make you a better teacher.

Now the other question is different: "Shall I accept Johnny splashing the paint?" Surely not, especially not, if he just tries nothing. If he occasionally would like to find out what happens, well, it can be fun, but it is rather difficult in a classroom because it may be diverting other children from their own work. So you have an entirely different situation, a situation for which you are responsible in your own sincerity and your own attitude. I would say that I would not let a child splash paint, let us say, 99 times out of a 100. Do you understand what I mean? But once, probably when I have a feeling that the child is trying to find something here, I would. I would depart from the rule that I would not usually want them to do it. But this is something entirely different than the first question. I'm very grateful to the writer of these lines, because it gave me this opportunity to underline what we said yesterday and to make some statements with regard to ethics and philosophy as teachers and as human beings which I feel are so important in a time which is intolerant and which does not regard the needs of others as prime values—in a time in which society's set of values is geared more towards material goods.

Now, I would like to discuss with you the last part of our basic philosophy, and that is "evaluation." When we evaluate, we have to think, first of all, why do we evaluate? May I say here that the best evaluation which we can do is an evaluation for the sake of learning to know children better and thus penetrate their thinking, their feeling, and their perceiving. Learning to identify ourselves better with their needs is one of the prime aspects for evaluation. But, as you know, there are two kinds of evaluation. One kind of evaluation just serves the purpose which I have mentioned, namely, to find out in which way the child reacts, and thus we learn to know how we can better motivate the child. But there is also an evaluation which we would call an evaluation by external criteria—that means, an evaluation which is meant to place the child on a continuum from good to bad according to his products. Let us discuss both types of evaluation. Let me call the one evaluation, which is meant to help the child subjectively, subjective evaluation. And let me call the other evaluation, which tries objectively to put the child on a continuum from poor art products to good art products, objective evaluation. Usually, we will not use the second kind of evaluation at all, because we'll always do injustice to the individual child by placing him on a continuum from poor to good and by forgetting the child and his relationship to his work. It is then important that we always emphasize the evaluation which gives us more insight into children.

As I said previously, one of the great educational contributions which art makes to our educational system is that art deals with all segments of growth. In our evaluation, therefore, we will be concerned with learning to understand the criteria which are indicative of the various components of growth. We should be able, after this course, to look at a drawing and say to ourselves, "This child needs greater flexibility because apparently he is emotionally restricted." We should be able to say to ourselves that this child apparently cannot think orderly, but thinks chaotically. He still has no feeling for establishing some harmonious relationships in his mind and, therefore, cannot express it. We would then think to ourselves, "This child needs more motivation in aesthetic growth." We also should be able to say: "This child is a poor observer. He does not include those details which are a result of observation. Therefore, I should motivate or stimulate the child more in his ability to observe and to become visually sensitive to his environment." So, we should be able to say that; but in order to be able to say that to ourselves, we must learn to understand which criteria are indicative of which growth components.

While I feel badly about discussing separately the various components of growth which are surely united in the creative process and are seen as a whole in the final product, we will have to do it throughout the course because we cannot talk about several things simultaneously. Therefore, we have to get an understanding of what criteria are indicative of intellectual growth, emotional growth, perceptual growth, aesthetic growth, social growth, and so forth. But, in the end, we will relate them all to one another because it is the nature of personality that those things are very much integrated.

If I were to demonstrate to you what we mean by it in a more, let us say, artificial sense—but probably better to our understanding—then I would say that what we are going to do now is this. We have here a test tube which we call personality. Now, look at it; it's here. So far, there is nothing in it. But there are all kinds of individuals. Their mixture of the different growth components is very individual. There are none alike, none probably in the whole world—none. The differences in amounts of the various components account for the differences in individualities. Let us say, there is Johnny. Johnny is a good thinker, and he rationalizes always. He observes very well. He's sharp in his observation, but emotionally he is not touched by things. He is good in organizing things, but he depends mainly on that which he is told. He is not an independent thinker, nor is he very inventive or exploratory in his attitude.

Now, let's find out how Johnny would make out here in this test tube. We would, for Johnny, put quite a lot of intellectual growth into it, because he's a good and sharp thinker. We would put probably a very little amount of emotional growth into it, because he never relates himself emotionally to his environment. But, look, he's a sharp observer, and he uses his sensory experiences very well. So I'll put quite a large amount of perceptual growth into it. I didn't speak of his relationship to his environment. He doesn't make friends. He doesn't cooperate because he thinks only of himself, so we'll put little social growth into it. We said he's a good organizer and harmoniously organizes those things which he sees and thinks about. We'll put a lot of aesthetic growth into it. But he is not independent in his thinking, so we'll put little creative growth into it. Now, you have it all here; but this is not the personality of Johnny unless we take the test tube and shake it very hard so that none of these components remain isolated, and then we would have the personality of Johnny.

You can now readily see that there are no two individuals alike; because the amounts which we would have to put into the test tube, that are responsible for the various components of growth, are all different. So now when we discuss the various components of growth and how they are seen in the creative work of children, it is in general, not in specifics; because specifically we will deal with them according to their developmental levels. Specific characteristics will be seen in the different growth components for a scribbling child, for a six-year-old, or for an eight- or ten-year-old. We will now deal merely with general criteria, so that we will get an understanding of the evaluation which deals with growth components. Then, let us once and forever say this, "We only do it in order to become more sensitive to the child and never in order to cubbyhole children on a continuum or to say, 'This child is more intellectual and less emotional, and so forth.' " I underline this and repeat it. Please do not go back into your schools and try to classify and diagnose children, because we shouldn't do it. We should, however, become more sensitive. We always become more sensitive when we break down a generalization into details, as we have learned. And when we break down growth into its single components, indeed, we become more sensitive to growth and to the meaning of it. I hope I have been clear in that.

Let's begin, then, with intellectual growth and the criteria which are indicative of intellectual growth [see the General Evaluation Chart]. As I told you previously, we all have two kinds of knowledge: an active knowledge and a passive knowledge. I hope you remember that we call active knowledge the knowledge which we have and use, such as a large vocabulary that is at our disposal at any time. We call passive knowledge the knowledge which we have, but which isn't handy. It doesn't come to our mind. We cannot use it. There are many words which we would recognize when we see them but which are not ready for use. In children's drawings, only the active knowledge is seen, the knowledge which children recall actively while drawing; that means, the knowledge which is emotionally significant to them during the act of drawing. This changes, and education or motivations are mainly responsible for such changes.

In the same manner in which you change your active vocabulary when you go through a good English course, children should change their richness of concepts when they go through art lessons. In drawings, then, the details which children put down will be mainly indicative of their active knowledge. Since active knowledge is closely related to the child's intellect, the active knowledge or the details which we see in children's drawings are indicative of intellectual growth—now do not misunderstand—not the way in which the details are drawn. They may be drawn poorly—you know, what we call poorly—or they may be drawn very effectively. No values are attached to the details, but the presence of details is mainly indicative of intellectual growth.

You know that this has actually been used by a number of researchers to establish some intelligence tests? The Goodenough Intelligence Scale is based on this assumption: that children who are intelligent have a larger active knowledge, and, therefore, the amount of details is indicative of intelligence in children. We always forget at this point that we also have within ourselves as a person or personality an intelligence which is potentially available to us but which we cannot use because it is restricted by

Objective Criteria	Little	Some	Much
Is the child's creative work adequate for his stage of development in representing the:			
1. figure			
2. space			
3. color			
Technique adequate for expression.			
Technique is part and parcel of child's work.			
What degree of effort does final product represent?			
Meaningfulness of single parts of work as detail.			
Meaningfulness of single parts of work as part of environment.			
To what extent did child follow a mode of expression?			
To what extent does any change upset the meaning of the work?			

Degree of Self-identification	Yes	No
1. Constant stereotyped repetitions		
2. Now and then stereotyped repetitions		
3. Mere objective reports		
4. Some inclusion of self by adding special characteristics to objective report		
5. Indirect or direct inclusion of the self		

	Attributes of Growth	Little	Some	Much
Emotional Growth	Free from stereotyping. Lack of generalization of objects (no trees are alike, etc.). Constant deviations from generalizations. Inclusion of experiences of the self. Use of free lines and brush strokes.			
Intellectual Growth	Inclusion of many subject matter details. Differentiation in color. Other indications of active knowledge.			
Physical Growth	Visual and motor coordination (how well he guides lines). Conscious projection of body movements (representation of them). Unconscious projection of body (body image). Skillful use of techniques.			
Perceptual Growth	Visual experiences: light shadows perspective space color differentiation Non-visual experiences: tactile texture auditive Kinesthetic experiences (body movements).			
Social Growth	Faces his own experiences in his work. Identification with the needs of others. Inclusion and characterization of social environments (home, school, factory, office). Participation in group work. Appreciation of other cultures. Enjoyment of cooperation, directly (through work) or indirectly (through the topic).			
Aesthetic Growth	Integration of thinking, feeling, and perceiving. Sensitiveness toward harmonious color. " " " texture. " " " lines. " " " shapes. Preference for decorative design patterns.			
Creative Growth	Independence without copying. Originality without imitating style of others. Creativeness and inventiveness in regard to content. Can immediately be distinguished from others in mode of expression. Is entirely different from others.			

86

other factors; and this, unfortunately, is not and cannot be tested well with our present intelligence tests. Our intelligence may be very restricted by our emotional inability to express it. Do you see? So, we have a greater potential intelligence than the one which actually functions. We have, then, a functional intelligence and a potential intelligence. Functional intelligence is the intelligence which we can use, like our active knowledge. It functions. But many of us have a greater intelligence which slumbers and is not being used because it has not been brought out. Maybe our upbringing has restricted us in the use of our intelligence. This is important, because also in art—in our children's drawings—we will only see that intelligence which functions. A child may be very intelligent, yet in his drawings we will see that the child is emotionally restricted and his intelligence, therefore, may not be functioning.

I told you about this little schizophrenic boy we have who is making rapid progress. He has now almost completely departed, in these few days, from his stereotyped fire engine. This is something that is very gratifying to me. Dr. Mattil told me yesterday it was just like turning a switch. Now he no longer turns around and says, "Listen, children, there is a fire engine," and starts his story. He already is concerned with farming and all kinds of things, and his flexibility is rapidly expanding. Sometimes we have such gratifying experiences if we push the right button. He is a very intelligent child, but his intelligence could not be used because he was restricted emotionally. In our classrooms, we have many such individuals. We will talk about them. Indeed, the comment is often made that a child draws beautifully but his intelligence is very restricted—"He's dumb." You know, we hear such words from teachers. Well, you may find the answer now. It means that the child most probably has no outlet in intelligence and, therefore, concentrates all his energies on harmonious organization and perception and other areas. But if he is able to organize harmoniously, this is also an intelligence; only it is a different kind of intelligence, one with which we do not deal in our common intelligence tests.

We have made experiments—Dr. Burkhart is mainly responsible for this—in which a confirmation was brought to some research which had been done elsewhere, namely, that intelligence, as tested by our intelligence tests, is not related to creativeness. Isn't that sad? In other words, when we test intelligence by our common tests, we may not find out whether this individual is creative or not. That does not mean creative just in the arts, it means creative. We may have here a very, very valuable individual who may be highly creative but may not test as high in intelligence. But the individual may be more valuable as a citizen in his ability to invent and explore than the individual who has an intelligence quotient of 160 and is regarded as a genius but is not creative and doesn't know what to do with all his knowledge. That value is mainly, according to our tests, the ability to achieve. I do not know of any tests which do justice to those creative components we have mentioned. This is one of the faults of our system, as you can readily see. These discrepancies may be true, but what we have to do is to motivate children so that they will become more balanced in their knowledge, in their perception, and in their feelings.

The knowledge which a child may have—that means, as shown by the details which he represents in his drawings—may not be of much use to him unless he can use it freely for different purposes and to adjust to new situations readily. Emotional growth will be responsible for determining whether he can use his intellect readily and can bring out the potential abilities which he has in his intelligence. Emotional growth, then, is the growth which is responsible for the individual's adjustments to new situations, for his flexibility. In children's drawings, the most reliable factor indicative of emotional growth is the lack or absence of stereotypes; that means, how frequently does a child change his concepts in his drawings? How much does he repeat the same concept for the same object, and how much does he depart from it? Does he always use the same kind of house or does he change from one house to another house when he draws houses? Does he always use the same concept for a tree when he draws a tree, or does he use different concepts for trees? Does he vary his concepts? Does he use the same subject matter, or does he depart and use all kinds of subject matter? The flexibility with which children approach subject matter and representation, then, is indicative of emotional growth.

You will look differently now at children's drawings. You will look at Ann's drawing and see that whenever she draws a tree, she draws the same tree; whenever she draws a figure, she draws the same figure; whenever she draws a house, she draws the same house. You will look at another drawing from three weeks back—oh, still the same house. Well, Ann is not very flexible. She apparently does not adjust easily to new images, to new situations in her thinking; and, therefore, Ann needs some motivation for greater flexibility. We will discuss the motivational factors when we go through the different levels in the development of children, because they are as different in the first, second, and third grades as you can imagine. But it is important for us that we know and recognize the needs of Ann. We are now clear. The lowest level of emotional growth is indicated by stereotypes. If children consistently and continuously draw the same thing, with no deviations, this is a very important factor. The more of this we see in children's drawings, the more rigid are the children.

Student: What if they continually change in every way?

Lowenfeld: What if they continually change in every way? Then they are most flexible, and emotionally they are always ready to take in new suggestions, new experiences, and to change accordingly.

This is only one factor that is indicative of emotional growth, but at this time we'll leave it at that, because today I want to give you merely a feeling of what is indicative in children's drawings of the various components of growth. Indeed, if a child is emotionally flexible and highly intelligent, he still can be asocial; that means, not concerned about others nor identifying with others nor cooperating with others. Now, may I say here again, with all the emphasis which I can give to it, that, please, it is not necessary for all children to be social. We have built a rather conformist attitude with regard to that, and we stamp a child who does not, oh, play football or who reads and stays at home rather than making things with others—we stamp him as an outcast without ever giving thought to the fact that probably most of the great contributors to mankind have been such outcasts. In this drive for conformity, we may forget the Beethovens of our time, for Beethoven, too, was no mixer. So, when we say that one is low in social growth—that means, in his ability to mix with others, cooperate, or even identify with the needs of others—we will keep in mind that this is not necessarily bad. Indeed, it is desirable that individuals generally are not shy, think of the needs of others, readily cooperate, and give what they have to mankind. But some may not be able to do that, and we have to look at them with magnifying glasses. Condemning is no means for education, you understand. And, if we condemn an individual because he's not a mixer, well, we haven't done anything for him. Let's rather think it over. Does this individual child, in his desire to remain an isolate, have something special which he contributes; that means, does he really concentrate in his thoughts and in his feelings on something which should be cultivated? You see, here is where we fail to look at the individual child, rather we treat them all as a mass.

We know, of course, that social growth begins with the identification of one's own needs, and then it gradually shifts to identifying with the needs of others, thus ending with a cooperative attitude. In children's drawings we can readily see that. I'll give you four criteria, on a continuum, in children's drawings which document this ability, or inability, to identify with the needs of others. The lowest, as I have said, is the repetition of the same thing. With this, the child documents that he cannot even identify with his own needs, because his own needs are shifting from one area to another and he cannot. He, therefore, escapes his own self by using a mechanism such as a repetition of the same object—"My child always draws airplanes," do you see? This is a mechanism. Or "My child always draws a fire engine," such as our little boy who is the schizophrenic child. This is the inability not only to identify with one's own experience but also to identify with the needs of others.

The second stage is what I call generalizations. When the child does depart from stereotype repetitions and draws different things, they always are alike—all houses are alike, all trees are alike, all figures are alike. The same things are always alike. He escapes into generalizations, because he does not yet identify with different houses or with different individuals. For him, every individual is an individual but all are alike. He has no ability yet to differentiate. This is a higher step of identification or of social growth than the first one, because it indicates that the child already extends the self at least to other things, environmental things, as they occur; but he has not yet mustered the ability to differentiate.

The third of the steps is seen in the child's ability to characterize, that means, to recognize that houses are different. He has found out, even by external factors, that people have different needs. He has found out that this child has pants and this one has skirts. Even that girls and boys are different is already a discovery. As soon as the child sees that figures are not all alike but that they are different, he characterizes them—sometimes by little characterizations. Depending on his social growth, he will characterize them more or less.

There is a fourth criterion—one which is most indicative of social growth and which is very objective, inasmuch as it has been tested by several researchers—and that is the ability of the child to establish spatial relationships in his drawings. By spatial relationships, we understand the child's ability to express meaningfully the relationship of one object or figure to another object or figure. Do you understand? I'll give you a practical example. For instance, a child who draws himself picking an apple from a tree, but who draws himself standing here and draws the apple tree there with apparently no relationship between himself and the apple tree, is found to be an asocial child. But a child who draws himself picking the apple and establishes a spatial correlation between himself and the apple is the child who is socially more cooperative, because he readily achieves the relationship between himself and others. Children who disperse figures in the drawing without relating them to each other—one standing here stiffly, another standing there stiffly, another standing there stiffly—do not feel the relationship between the figures and, therefore, establish less spatial correlation and have less feeling for each other. So spatial correlations or relationships are also indicative of social growth.

Now you know a lot already when you look at children's drawings. You can see whether a child is flexible, whether a child is aware of many details and, therefore, is highly intelligent, whether a child is identifying with the needs of others by ever-changing characterizations of objects, and whether a child is able to establish spatial relationships. I said that evaluating these factors is one means we can use to detect social growth. The other means is not as easy to detect, but I'll give it to you, nevertheless. It is the child's ability to include in his drawings factors which are indicative of social activities. I'll give you an example of this. If you look at a drawing, such as a backyard drawing, and it contains only the most essential things—let us say, a fence and nothing else; nothing that indicates man's desire to change the backyard, such as an ax, a saw, a shovel, and other things which show man's activities—this child is less socially inclined than one who fills his drawings with those details which are suggestive of man's activities. Do I make myself clear in that, although it is less objective as a criterion? This factor overlaps with emotional growth, because in society if someone is shy and does not want to make contacts, he rather stays at home. Therefore, he would be less able to identify a variety of social activities in his drawings. This is an emotional as well as a social factor.

Perceptual growth is usually indicated in children's drawings by their ability to observe and see things and include things which are perceived with our senses, such as textures—tactile activities. A child who includes details may only be intelligent; but if the details also carry special patterns—such as the veins in leaves each being drawn differently from the others—then he must have observed this. To draw leaves indicates a knowledge of leaves on a tree, but to differentiate each leaf suggests that visual observation has taken place. Later on, perceptual growth is mainly indicated by the individual's ability to see changing differences: in light, that means he includes light and shadow; in distance, that means distant things are drawn in diminishing sizes; and in color, that means color which is close appears different (more intense) than color which is in the distance, which involves including the effects of atmosphere. These are indicative of perceptual growth. If a child includes texture in a lawn by little strokes wherein we feel the grass instead of simply leaving it plain, this indicates that the feeling of the child was for texture. Whenever the child includes texture, such as little cobblestones, and whenever we can feel texture, the child was experiencing perceptual growth.

Aesthetic growth is indicated by the child's ability to organize harmoniously his subject matter in the drawing area, that is, to distribute harmoniously on the area of the paper what he has to say. For instance, a child who draws everything small and in one corner has not experienced the meaningful relationship of his figures to the area of space which he has at his disposal. We see aesthetic growth indicated by the child's ability to harmoniously organize his thinking and feeling and perceiving in relationship to the drawing area which he has at his disposal. You understand, then, aesthetically highly developed children will always use those spaces or areas which they have at their disposal and will distribute their subject matter—their thinking, their feeling, and their perceiving—over this drawing area.

Creative growth is the last component of growth—except for physical growth. Creative growth is responsible for the child's independence in his own creations—whether he independently selects his subject matter, whether he independently creates his own concepts, or whether he, rather, relies on others. Children who love to copy are not creative, because they are dependent—or their creativeness is suppressed. They may be potentially creative, but it has been suppressed by coloring books, as we have mentioned, and by other means. But as long as they have the desire to explore and investigate and create independently, not relying upon others, they are creative.

I have not mentioned physical growth before, because it probably is the least important component in art. But we have the means for evaluating it. Control of motor coordination is mainly indicative of physical growth. Do children remain within an outline, or do they go beyond it? How they sensitively control their own body is indicative of physical growth.

Now, as I have told you before, we will not have a feeling for the child's personality unless we shake this test tube and mix them all and find the relationships among emotional, intellectual, physical, perceptual, aesthetic, social, and creative growth. We have the most marvelous means in art education for doing that; it is already done for us in the creative product. If we look at the creative product of the child, we see all these components already integrated for us. We don't even have to shake it, because the child has done this for us; and if we then see how the various components relate to one another, we get a feeling for the child's personality. Now, as I said before, developing an understanding of the various developmental stages will be one of the main functions of our class. How to bring out the potential abilities in children through art is one of the major responsibilities of art education, which we will learn about throughout the rest of this course. This concludes the lessons on our basic philosophy.

LECTURE 9

Exhibits; Creative Experience for the Teacher; and Introduction to Scribbling Stage: Impulses, Kinesthetic Experiences, Focus, and Control

These exhibits we call educational exhibits. Educational exhibits always have a purpose, and the purpose is not merely to hang pictures. In a classroom exhibit where you put up the drawings and paintings of the children in your class, the purpose sometimes may be merely to expose those experiences which you value. Through the selections which you make in your classroom exhibits, you will give educational direction. So it is not good in a classroom exhibit to indiscriminately exhibit drawings or paintings of all children. This is a misunderstanding of education. If we were to exhibit drawings that are copied and drawings that are imitative such as Mickey Mouse drawings and those things that have the influence of some commercial product in them, we would only indicate that we agree with them. Therefore, we would not exhibit drawings indiscriminately. And, indeed, we would not exhibit the best artistic drawings, because that, again, would direct the attention of the children to the final product and to the fact that the final product is judged only by aesthetic measures. It would, indeed, be undemocratic to exhibit only the best drawings of a few selected students who can achieve the aesthetic organization which fits your adult taste. No, we shall exhibit the most expressive drawings of each child.

Who determines that? Well, you and the child together. Don't ever be afraid to ask a child, "Tell me something about your drawing." And don't be afraid to criticize the child. Let us say, Mary comes and tells something about her drawing which isn't in her drawing. For example, she has drawn a house and nothing else, and she says: "This is our house; we are playing in the yard behind the house; we have planted a vegetable garden, and Mother is working in it. She loves to garden." She tells the whole story now of how her mother loves gardening. You look at the drawing, and you say, "But, Mary, I can't see anything about what you have just told me." So I would not exhibit this drawing, because Mary only said things while in her drawing she did not express them. I would criticize it. I would say: "Now, Mary, you have told me a good story, and I know now what you do at your house, and in your house, and behind your house, and what Mother does in her garden. But next time when you draw your house you think about it; and then I would like to see everything. Now, let's find out when you show me the next drawing and when you tell me about your next drawing whether you draw everything you were thinking about." Do you see? This is a motivation for the next time. I wouldn't accept the present drawing for the exhibit, because it is empty. Don't accept stereotypes; but if a child deviates, after having been restricted for a long time, and all of a sudden discovers some kind of freedom by changing his stereotypes, then, of course, this would be the drawing which is the most expressive drawing for this child and should be exhibited. So "most expressive" is, indeed, a relative value judgment, because it always refers to the individual child. The answer is not to exhibit indiscriminately, not to exhibit the best drawings only, but to exhibit the most expressive drawings of the child.

Here is a question which eliminates itself, because I shall do that later. It says: "Would you care to bring in some children's work and demonstrate the method of evaluation? We would derive much from this, I feel." Yes, I shall continuously do it from now on and use the drawings which you have in the book for better communication. From now on, we shall evaluate drawings, indeed, by means of practical examples; but I did not do it up until now for a specific purpose. Do you know the purpose? Up to this time, I didn't speak of any particular developmental stage, or age, did I? No. We laid down a general philosophy, and, therefore, I did not want to commit myself to a specific age level or developmental stage. Had I chosen a drawing of an eight-year-old child, we would have had to go into specific evaluation of eight-year-old children, of this particular stage of development, and for this reason I did not do it. So, I shall be glad to do it in the future.

Now, I still would like to say one other word about another point which I did not touch upon in our discussion of the basic philosophy, and this is whether it is necessary for the teacher to engage in creative work herself. You see, very often we hear from teachers who say, "I can't do a thing in art," and imply with that that they cannot teach art. "I'm not an artist myself. How can I teach children art?" This is what we hear continuously. We even hear more of that from administrators. Almost as a rule, when I'm introduced, they say: "Well, I'm sorry I don't understand anything about art." This usually is the first thing that you hear. My answer usually is that I'm sorry that administrators so freely admit that they don't understand one of the most important occupations of children—one which may become the catalyst in an educational system which not only emphasizes subject matter but the child, for art emphasizes all components of growth, not only the intellect. You see, instead of being ashamed that they don't understand anything about art, they freely admit it and think this is washing their hands of their responsibility by saying, "I don't understand anything." I then usually ask the administrator, "Would you also say, 'I don't understand anything about English or even arithmetic, which is a greater specialty because it does not embrace all of these components of growth'?" They would not admit that.

So, may I say in the very beginning, I believe that we all should know how the child develops creatively in order to motivate him. This is especially important on the lower levels, but, indeed, it is also important to have experienced creative processes. As I told you previously, if one never has been in love, you can explain to him what it means to be in love, but it will leave the individual cold. He cannot empathize; he doesn't feel anything of what love may be—how it may shape a whole individual and how love may take hold of him so much so that for the time being it may be his whole life. You can explain this to people, but only those will vibrate inside who have been in love. It will be meaningless to those who don't know what love means.

The same is true with the creative process. If you have never had the feeling, on whatever level it may be, of what it means to create something out of nothing, then you don't know what the creative process means. But if you have once had the feeling of creating, then something will tick inside you. When you see that the child creates something out of nothing and that the child organizes, you will look at the colors differently. You will look at the subject matter differently and how the child deals with it. You will no longer compare it with nature. On the contrary, you will feel that the concept the child created is like a flower which God created, and He didn't have an example for doing it. He did it all out of Himself. And, therefore, we have this great variety of flowers. Every work of a child will be a new flower if it is his own creation. But if it is not his own creation, if you insist that it should be like something else, you remove the very backbone of creative activity and make the child imitative. That is true, as we shall see, for proportions, as well as for the invention of subject matter and thought. But, you can only feel that if you, yourself, have once created such relationships. Therefore, I would advise every teacher to engage, at one time or another, in some creative processes. However, emphasis on creative activities on the part of the teacher is different.

I would say that there is no person who has never created. You may be creative in your kitchen; and I hope you are, because then the kitchen may be fun. It may be also drudgery if you do the same thing all day. Even figuring out how you can use your kitchen space most efficiently may be creative. But we all do things in our lives which necessitate our own individual solution at a particular moment which cannot be reproduced. Therefore, we all, at some time or another, are creative. But we are not always creative in using a specific medium and perhaps not an art medium. So it might be good for all of us to try out ourselves in using some art media. In the beginning with the small child, when our own creative processes may only be interfering, this is of lesser importance. I say lesser because one can become a wonderful kindergarten teacher or elementary school teacher in the lower grades, in particular, without having engaged very much in creative processes in the visual arts.

However, no one will ever be a good teacher who has not engaged in creative thinking, because creative thinking embraces the ability to empathize, to put one's self into the situation of somebody else. Without this, no teaching is possible, especially not on the lower levels. It is more difficult to put yourself into the place of a little child than to put yourself into the place of an adolescent or a grown-up, because you can always think that the grown-up has the same concepts that you have with regard to imagery, with regard to thinking, and so forth. The child is entirely different from you in his reactions, thinking, and perceiving. So, may I say, the ability to creatively teach by putting yourself into the situation is more difficult with children than with grown-ups. But the necessity of doing creative work in the visual arts—that means, in using the media which we use in the arts—becomes more important the higher you are in the developmental levels. You may feel rather lost if you were to teach sixth- or seventh-grade art without having had any experiences yourself, but you may not feel lost if you can put yourself into the place of children if you teach art in the kindergarten; however, you may miss something—some enjoyment of your own in the appreciation of what children can do. This is very important for keeping you alive as a teacher.

So, may I say again, it is very important that we, ourselves, at one time or another have engaged in creative processes on all levels. It's good for you anyway—for all of you, whether you are art teachers or not—because it's a wonderful feeling on whatever level it may take place. It becomes essential when you teach art in the upper grades, because there the ability to promote skills—that means, to identify with materials—becomes very important. As I told you, identification with materials means that we should be able to predict their behaviors or their reactions—how watercolor will behave when two colors merge, for example—and that we should know about a great variety of materials so that we give the child enough motivation to use this flexibility in creative processes.

Now, let me shift to our actual subject matter. We start with our thinking right at the beginning. When a child is born, he comes to this world endowed with certain impulses. I use the definition for impulse that it is a reaction to a stimulus but that this reaction is not taught. We have certain impulses which we can identify at birth. One of these impulses is what?

Student: Reaction to light.

Lowenfeld: The reaction to light? No, this is not an impulse. Reactions to light are not impulses. Children will not react to light. Their pupils will not contract or expand if they come closer to light. On the contrary, this is something which develops.

Student: Suckling?

Lowenfeld: Suckling. Yes, it's one of the most amazing impulses. If you bring the baby close to a breast, it will start suckling. No one has ever taught the baby how to suckle. But suckling is one of the impulses—the reaction to a stimulus which is not taught. There are others.

Student: Grasping and crying.

Lowenfeld: Also grasping. Yes, if you give the child your finger—not right at birth but later on, you know—this reflex develops later, but he doesn't need to be taught. Crying, breathing—these, too—but there are not many which the child has when he is born. Animals often have more impulses after birth; for instance, the chicken. A baby chick, when it leaves the eggshell, has more impulses to work with than a baby does.

Student: Would I be out of turn if I were to mention the experience of losing my ability to swallow at one time? I had to be taught how to eat all over again, and I was amazed when I found out that my grasping and sucking motions were gone.

Lowenfeld: Well, that's all right; but this may be an exception. There are exceptions always. Some children are born without the ability to suckle. There are other such exceptions, as you may know; but, in general, suckling is one of the inborn impulses. There are also other impulses which develop without being taught. Can you tell me some of these impulses which develop without being taught?

Student: Creeping.

Lowenfeld: Creeping, yes. Even if you leave a child alone, he will not lie only on his back; but he will turn around and sometimes start to crawl, to creep, and will react this way. Yes, there are several impulses which develop. Another one, which we don't know yet whether it is taught or whether it develops, is smiling. You know how parents wait for the first smile as a great experience. But it is not known whether this is an impulse which develops without being taught or is learned by example. Indeed, we think it is an impulse which develops without being taught, because children all over the whole world smile. Since the opposite—crying—is definitely an impulse which hasn't been taught, we take for granted that this, too, is one.

Student: Don't you think that smiling would be one that develops instead of being learned because in blind children, in blind babies, they don't see anyone smiling and yet they smile?

Lowenfeld: And yet they smile. Correct, correct. Yes.

Student: Is there an impulse to imitate what you see?

Lowenfeld: There is an impulse to imitate, but we will call it something different. This is an impulse which, for a long time, has not even been considered an impulse. Only recently, probably five years ago, psychologists agreed that this is an impulse. You see, an impulse usually is considered a reaction without which we cannot exist. Without breathing, you cannot exist. Without crying, you cannot exist—or, you will emotionally deteriorate in a way if you do not have the outlet of crying.

We call this other impulse the impulse to explore and investigate. Imitation is another way of exploring and investigating. And this impulse to explore and investigate we may also call the creative impulse, because it doesn't remain with the exploration and investigation. It means also to use what one has explored and investigated for new adventures; and this, indeed, is an important impulse without which man cannot exist. Can you give me an example of the truth of this statement? What would happen if you were not to explore and investigate how hot a flame is? You would burn. Do you see? Or that, when you step into deep water, you would drown. So your ability to explore and investigate and react accordingly is one of the impulses on which we greatly rely in creative activities. You can see that this, the creative impulse or investigative impulse, is one of the very, very important things in our lives because without it we would be lost. And there is a direct line from the exploratory and investigative impulses which deal with the existence of man to those which go beyond the stage of existence, such as art.

You know, babies in the beginning explore and investigate, namely, through what? By taking things into the mouth or grasping things; that means, through the ego, through the self, not through intermediaries but through the self, through the body self. The body plays a very important role—the most important role—in the very beginning. Within the body, a very specific experience—that which we call body movement, or body motion—occurs, which is probably in the very beginning almost the sole means by which the child expresses himself. Even when the baby is still in the womb, he kicks or moves or turns—this being the reaction to some stimuli. What kind of stimuli? We are not yet sure whether they express mere physical reactions or already express reactions which go beyond chemical and physical stimuli. We don't know. But, at any rate, we know that after the child is born he begins to move or rather continues his movement of kicking—of course, uncoordinated kicking, as we would say.

All movements which relate to the body we shall call kinesthetic experiences. We differentiate between two kinds of kinesthetic experiences: the one we call active kinesthetic experiences; and the other, passive. What are active kinesthetic experiences? What would you call those experiences? Kicking. The things which you do consciously or unconsciously; because kicking is, indeed, in the beginning not done consciously. As you know, it is uncontrolled, and the child kicks even in sleep. The baby moves constantly when he lies on his back. This is an active kinesthetic experience. Of course, we actively experience our body movements whenever we engage in sports—running or playing football or whatever we do. Swimming is an active experience of our own body movements. What do we call passive kinesthetic experiences?

Student: One's that we recall.

Lowenfeld: No, not one when it is recalled. You can recall active and you can recall passive kinesthetic experiences. The recall of kinesthetic experience we could even call kinesthetic imagery, you know.

Student: Vicarious experience?

Lowenfeld: No, vicarious kinesthetic experiences belong to kinesthetic imagery. I'm thinking of how I was running across the field and how I was breathing heavily in order to reach the post. You see, I am recalling an active kinesthetic experience.

Student: I'm not meaning vicarious in the same way. I thought vicarious experience was that kind of experience which . . . like you said, we don't all have to experience being drowned, you see. I mean vicariously from the experience that is gone or from the experience that someone else has had.

Lowenfeld: No, no, it's the very same thing. For instance, if we watch the racing of people in a movie—see, we have here the movie screen, and we see people are racing with all the power to get to the end—we are not actively engaging in the racing, but it's in our imagery. Depending upon how much we are able to empathize, we can be exhausted after this; because we actively engaged in a kinesthetic imagery. No, passive kinesthetic experiences are of a different nature.

Student: When someone else initiates the action—you must feel that the result is either of the mother rocking the baby or. . . .

Lowenfeld: That's correct. If we are moved, not if we move ourselves. You know, one of the most common passive kinesthetic experiences is rocking.

Student: In a boat?

Lowenfeld: In a boat, yes; when the boat rocks you up and down, don't you feel it? Yes, it's a passive kinesthetic experience; you can't do anything about it. You are moved. In an elevator and in traveling, in general, even if you sit in a car—then, you are passively engaging in kinesthetic experiences by being moved.

Student: Both could be going on at the same time.

Lowenfeld: Both can be going on at the same time—yes, indeed. For instance, if you were to sit in a car and turn the wheel, you engage in an active kinesthetic experience by moving the wheel in a curve but also you are passively engaged because you are moved by the car. They can and do overlap.

Student: What is a heartbeat? Is it a natural kinesthetic experience?

Lowenfeld: A heartbeat? A heartbeat is not a kinesthetic experience at all because you don't feel it; but it may become a kinesthetic experience after running, when you really feel the movement within your body—such as muscular contractions. This may also be part of kinesthetic experiences. Yet we usually don't include contractions of muscles, as such—or muscular innovations, the digestive apparatus, or a heartbeat—under the nature of kinesthetic experiences.

Let's say that active kinesthetic experiences are the movements which we actively do with our body, and passive kinesthetic experiences are those movements which we passively experience, that is, when the body is moved without engaging actively in it. This becomes very important to us, because we know that the baby is very much affected by kinesthetic experiences, both active and passive. Kinesthetic experiences of a passive nature, such as rocking a baby or holding it in one's arms and rocking it somewhat, has a very calming effect upon babies, as you all know. Why? Because it has a strong influence on babies and the influence is often stronger than that which disturbs the baby.

Never forget that the crying of a baby does not always indicate the same as if you were to cry. We cry mainly for emotional reasons or because of pain. We don't cry when we feel uncomfortable. For instance, we would not cry when it gets too hot in here, because we have our verbal expression. We would say, "Open the window or the door." Or, we might even say, "Isn't this a hot day?" And that makes us feel better. The baby can't do that. A baby, when it is too hot, cries. A baby, when it feels uncomfortable—not pain—cries. Of course, it cries also when it feels pain. So the differentiation of expression within a baby is rather limited, because the only vocabulary which he has at his disposal is crying. Do you get this?

Student: Would pain be considered a kinesthetic experience?

Lowenfeld: No, absolutely not. It's a body experience. So is pinching. If I pinch you, it's not a kinesthetic experience. For the one who pinches, it may be slightly because he moves his fingers; but for the one who is being pinched, it's simply a body experience. Not all body experiences are kinesthetic experiences, you see? If I have a stomachache, it's not a kinesthetic experience. It's a body experience. A kinesthetic experience is only when the body moves actively or passively.

Kinesthetic experiences for the baby are very important because, outside of crying, for some time they are the only expression. Do you see? We often don't realize that. When a child kicks or moves, this is part of his own self, the same way that crying is. If a child feels uncomfortable and cries because he is uncomfortable and you pick up the child and rock him, then the feeling of the passive kinesthetic experience of being rocked is stronger than the uncomfortable feeling which he may have had even when it was caused by some gas. So the child stops crying and falls asleep. Passive kinesthetic experiences, as well as active kinesthetic experiences, are very important for children, very important; and we must realize that, because we will then look at scribbling somewhat differently. You see, I gave you this whole introduction only to make you feel the importance which it has when the child, for the first time, actively engages in kinesthetic experiences and controls them—and that doesn't happen very soon.

When the child is one year old, the child still does not scribble; but a one-year-old child engages in quite a number of kinesthetic experiences. He sits. He walks—and walking, indeed, is an active kinesthetic experience. But one day (when the child is approximately two years old) if you give him a crayon, he may pick up the crayon—maybe by the wrong end or the right end, upside-down or right-side-up—and he will engage in experiences, sometimes apparently looking at the crayon and other times looking elsewhere, but out of this he gains great satisfaction. This is an active engagement on the part of the child in kinesthetic experiences. You will see that kinesthetic experiences, being the very first ones which allow the child to express himself outside of crying, are quite significant, indeed.

All children in the whole world begin with scribbling. Whether they are Chinese, Eskimos, Americans, or Europeans, they begin with scribbling. Whether they are Catholics or Jews, they begin with scribbling. So we can say that scribbling is a developmental characteristic because it is part and parcel of growth. All children, then, at a certain time, engage in scribbling—that means, belong to the developmental stage of scribbling. The normal child—the average child, let's rather say—begins with scribbling when he is two years old. But let me emphasize here that a half year up or a half year down may not make any difference. So we regard average as being a child who begins with scribbling between one-and-a-half and two-and-a-half years. Within this range, the average child should develop an urge to express himself in motions. The first scribbling is uncontrolled; and we shall see that we call it uncontrolled scribbling or disordered scribbling. It merely expresses the child's enjoyment in active motions. It is done, usually, without the control of the eye.

At this time, I would like to call your attention to a very important fact. If we would like to reexperience or empathize with the scribbling child and feel how he feels when he scribbles, we must not think it is the same as if we adults scribble. It's quite different. First of all, the size of motions is always relative to the size of the body. If a child engages in a motion, let us say, which is twelve inches long or high, it is not the same as if we engage in a motion which is twelve inches high. For us, it would be a yard. So it is relative. It should always be regarded relative to the body size. The same is true with all other things.

We consider the size of the baby relative to the motions which he makes and vice versa. If a baby, let us say, is two feet and I am six feet, I would

Fig. 3. Disordered scribbling of a 2½-year-old child showing no control of motions.

have to translate it into three times the motion if I were to apply it to myself. Do you get what I mean? And the same is true with all other sizes. A square in your town, for instance, which you may have in your memory as a tremendously big square when you saw it as a child, may be very small when you come back as an adult because size relationships have changed. I don't know whether you have experienced that. The same is true for hills or mountains. A hill which may have looked to you very high when you were a child may all of a sudden be a small hill when you come back as an adult. These things change relative to your own body size, and we must always remember that. So, when the child scribbles, this may be a big motion for him, while for you it may only appear as a small motion.

Another factor—when you look at scribbling, you see the scribbling sharply focused. When the child looks at his scribbling, his eyes do not focus on the scribbling. Adjustment of the eye muscles does not take place until later. The child looks at his scribbling in the same way you would look into an empty space, and your eyes don't adjust. Can you do that? Just look into a blank; and then, as you look into the blank, look also at your paper. You can't read what you have written, because it also is fuzzy. This is how the

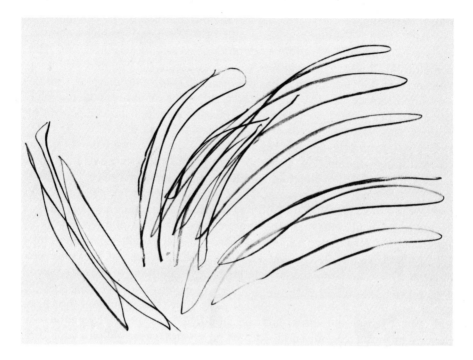

Fig. 4. Longitudinal scribbling of a 3-year-old child showing repeated motions and thus established control of motor activity.

child sees the world; he actually, physiologically, sees the world differently from the way you see it. Therefore, he hasn't any urge to control his lines, because they all are simply blurred expressions of his body or kinesthetic activity.

We shall see that the child of two years or two-and-a-half years, on an average, discovers that there is a relationship between the line on the paper and the motion of his arm. This is a big discovery. It's like this. If you look in a blurred manner at your lines and all of a sudden you can focus, you discover a line. You catch it, and you say, "There is a line," and you make it over and over again. See, there is a drive in us that, when we once achieve control, we love to conquer it. We love to move out of the accidental stage into a stage which we can control. Even in the child, this desire is already very strong. So, when the child discovers that he can control the lines, "Look, I can draw a line; I can"—of course, this is done unconsciously—the child wants to repeat the motion over and over again. And this scribbling we call longitudinal scribbling, because it is usually done in a longitudinal fashion.

Now, let's look at some of the illustrations. Next time, I shall bring you a lot of scribblings so that you will see the different kinds of scribbling. You see that Figure [3] shows an uncontrolled or disordered scribbling. In this, you see no repetition of motions; all motions go in different directions. But, in Figure [4], this scribbling differs very greatly from the previous scribbling. You see that the child already has the desire to control his motions, and this is an important desire. It brings to the child, for the first time, the feeling of active mastery of motor coordination. He discovers that he can control his motions and, out of this discovery, he develops his desire to do it. It's probably here that leadership begins, because the child wants to control an external thing—the motion. If he does not get satisfaction out of it, he may become frustrated. So the child should be given an opportunity to scribble until he can control his motions. With this control, he learns to focus his eyes upon a line. Usually, the child who scribbles longitudinally has already started to focus his eyes upon the lines. This controlled scribbling is not only important for scribbling but, indeed, has an effect upon the whole child.

Mothers, especially, should know that and should not frustrate their children by asking from them something they cannot do. If you ask a child who is two years old to eat properly, he will be frustrated. He may put the spoon into the cereal and try to eat, but he may land it here on the cheek and then, by trial and error, find the mouth. Do you see? But a child who engages in motor coordination—that is, in controlled scribbling—should be able to put the spoon into the cereal and land it at the mouth. You see, we have here a gauge of the child's ability for motor coordination. As soon as the child coordinates his motions, which is immediately seen in his scribbling—that means, as soon as the child starts his longitudinal scribbling—he is ready to coordinate his motions with his visual activity. Seeing and movement, then, are one. Up to this time, we would have frustrated the child by asking the child for proper motor coordination because he cannot conceive of it. Anything of which we cannot conceive frustrates us, because we do not know what we are asked to do.

LECTURE 10

Integration of Art and Society; Scribbling Stage: Evaluation of Intellectual and Emotional Growth

During the colonial period, the jobs of people like us were restricted in a more individual fashion. People were concerned with what they did individually in a much more limited sense than we are today. We have greatly expanded, not only in our standard of living, but also in the life which we live. Distances no longer exist as they did at that time. Just think, if someone wanted to travel from Williamsburg, Virginia, to Richmond, it was an event at that time because it took a long time by horse and buggy. Today, we can reach it in an hour by car and in a few minutes by plane. Our perspective of life has completely changed.

Now we would like to get rid of those superfluous things which are unnecessary for our lives, such as ornaments on furniture which only are dust catchers but which people enjoyed in colonial times, when they also enjoyed wigs. They also enjoyed those crinolines, and they enjoyed many other things. They had time to sit down and gossip. They did not need to restrict the period of relaxation to a certain time—like when we go home from the office. Our lives have completely changed, compared to the lives of people in the culture which was prevalent during the colonial period. Now, to keep the colonial period preserved in one area of living, such as in the living room, while we live entirely differently—we don't wear wigs and go driving in horse-drawn buggies—would be, of course, insincere and inconsistent.

But may I say, if we choose colonial furniture because we appreciate this period and do it for special purposes of appreciation, there's nothing to say against it; because one may have a certain sentimental attitude toward it—toward genuine furniture of any style—and this belongs to the art appreciation of past cultures. Any sentimental feelings of a genuine nature should be untouched, because they are of great value. If you have a chair for which you have a great sentimental feeling because it is the chair of your grandfather or your father, don't touch these feelings. To me they are, in a way, holy; because these are sensitivities, you remember. We spoke of them as something more important in our lives than anything else.

I'm speaking here of people who go and buy outmoded furniture, furniture of past styles, simply because they don't know what exists presently or because they have built up a kind of—oh, let us say—discriminatory attitude towards the contemporary furniture of a functional nature which serves our time, as contrasted to other styles of furniture. They go to Sears and Roebuck and select, not colonial furniture, but only a pseudo-colonial-styled furniture—which is a bad and poor imitation of what was done during the colonial period—out of, let's say, ignorance for what their responsibility is as a citizen living in this era. And may I include in that, anyone, including the President of the United States, who goes and builds or imitates colonial-type buildings. We serve our present period; we should embrace the people who live today and not those who lived in the past, with their wigs and crinolines for which we have little understanding.

But, it is not the fault of any single individual, including the President of the United States, whom I only use as a symbol. It is the fault of our time, the confusion in which we live—the very same issue which I mentioned when I said I looked at the Gothic building in Chicago out of which huge tin pipes grew. This is the confusion. The very same tin pipes which serve nuclear energy grow out of the very same shape which served religion in past times. This is a sacrilege, and we should be sensitive toward it. If we are not sensitive toward it, then it is a fault of our time and we should do something as educators toward improving these divergent attitudes.

Of course, being a part of our time includes our ability to see the beauty of functional furniture and discover it and relate ourselves and our work to it in our life. Don't misunderstand; if you buy furniture—if you buy even a dishwasher or anything of this nature—you should not blindly say, "This is contemporary; therefore I like it." That would also be discriminatory in nature. You should always keep your sensitivity at hand and say, "I like this better than this." But, you should become sensitive toward the single item. There are good contemporary designs; there are also poor contemporary designs, of course. We may not always choose the good one because we may not have the background for doing so. But my duty as a teacher, especially when we think of the integration of art and society, is to call your attention to this discrepancy which exists.

Again, I can only point out this fact, how Giotto, one of the great Gothic builders and painters, would feel if he were to step out of his grave and were to look at these tin pipes growing out of the rose window. The rose window is the upper part of the Gothic window arch which was really thought to be the glorification of religious ecstasy, and now you have these tin pipes there. Can you feel it? It's the same as if someone laughs at you when you cry bitterly about an experience which has meant very much to you inside. Therefore, look at this very personally so that you can identify with the situation.

If we were to have a more harmonious relationship between our-selves and our environment, we would have less trouble in this world, too; because, as we know, environment is one of the most important educators or influences. As the environment and our relationships with ourselves are messed up, we may become messed up. These are the implications which are not seen and, again, I don't make any one person responsible for that because they all do it with the best of intentions, including the President of the United States. I'm referring, obviously, to his home in Gettysburg which he built in colonial style. Why? We shouldn't be ashamed of living in the present time, even if we are near the battlegrounds of Gettysburg; but it's not his fault. He did it with the very best intentions in his mind. I hope I made myself understandable. But it is one of the confusions of the present period in which we live. We as teachers should open our eyes to it.

Yesterday, we went a little bit further in our understanding of what scribbling means. Now do you know what we will do? We will become more sensitive towards scribbling. We may have established a discriminatory atti-tude towards scribbling; because in the beginning everything that was a scribble meant to us scribbling, and we could not differentiate between different kinds of scribblings. You remember I said in the very beginning, the more we can differentiate our generalizations into greater details, the more discriminatory we are and the more sensitive we become. Now you will see what we do with scribbling. At the present time, you can differenti-ate between disordered scribbling and longitudinal scribbling. But you also know that, when you go into a kindergarten and look at a child who scribbles in a disorderly fashion, this child is merely enjoying his motor activity and he actively engages in it.

As soon as you see that the child scribbles like this—that means, longi-tudinally—you can be sure that this child now has already conquered some-thing, namely, a relationship between his motion and his vision. His eyes control his scribbling, and now he repeats the scribbling. The implication of this is clear, as I said before; namely, the child now actually can do things which require motor coordination and that means also eating or any chore which requires motor coordination.

A typical disordered scribbling is this. Do you see? This is a scribbling of a child who is two years and two months, as you have it here. And we have also scribbles which are controlled, as you shall see—different kinds of scribbles which are controlled, about which we shall speak today. There are scribbles like this, you see; this is a controlled scribble—it's longitudinal. Longitudinal scribbling is usually done by children with the lower arm, not engaging the whole arm, but with the lower arm. He discovers this first and it has, as we heard, some very important meanings; namely, that the child relates his scribbling to the motions which he is doing and, therefore, has

Fig. 5. Circular scribbling of a 3-year-old child showing simply the urge for variation.

discovered that there is a relationship between his body motion and what he looks at, what he sees.

After some time, when the child is probably between two-and-one-half and three, the child may try and discover other versions. You see, always when we are conquering something and become perfectionists in one phase, we like to go on to new adventures. And as we go on to new adventures, we discover that variations are possible. In this discovery, the child now finds that he can make circular motions like this; look at Figure [5]. These are clearly different from longitudinal motions and represent a higher stage in the development of children. We call it circular motion.

Very often, circular and longitudinal motions are done at the same time by some children. Usually, circular scribbling follows longitudinal scribbling—normally between two-and-one-half and three years. As I said before, a half year up or down does not make any difference. So, if a child still scribbles longitudinally when he is three-and-one-half, don't worry. The child is all right and average. Or, if a child scribbles longitudinally or circularly when the child is two, don't think he is a genius. The child is just a little bit advanced, but he is still average. So, circular scribbling means merely a greater enjoyment of the variations of motions. Yes?

Student: Would you compare circular scribbling with the first stages of unorganized scribbling? I'd like to hear you go over that again.

Lowenfeld: No, I don't compare it. The unorganized scribbling—look again at Figure [3]. Can you see the difference? Your judgment should always relate to that. In unorganized scribbling, we have no repetitions; or if there are some repetitions, they are only accidental—you know what I mean, repetitions of motions. While in a circular or longitudinal scribbling, you have the feeling of repetition, of a repeated motion. Do you see it? There is quite a distinct difference. You will have no difficulty when you go into a kindergarten in differentiating between them, especially if you watch the children, too. If children do this repetition, they even go with the body in a rhythm so you can see it.

We have a motion picture here which, if I have time, I would like to show you at the end, because it goes quickly through all the stages—or most of the stages. We have children who start disorderly and then all of a sudden discover that they can repeat the motion. There are two children who sit close to each other, and the one hasn't yet discovered it but sees how the other child is doing this. Then all of a sudden, all are repeating their motions and discovering the rhythm. It is contagious, and it's all right. This is not forced competition. This is natural competition because it grows out of the spirit of the whole group. No one has told them to do it, but they just do it.

Now, however, comes a very big step, and I would like that you conceive of it as such. If someone were to ask me to name the most important stages in human development outside of birth and death, I would say it is the stage which we are now to discuss. It is one, and probably adolescence is the other, because the two constitute the most important changes in human development. We know of adolescence, the changes from childhood to adulthood, as one important stage. But we have not yet conceived of the stage which we shall discuss now as such an important stage. In fact, even child psychologists do not yet recognize it. It is the stage when the child one day starts to name his scribbling and says spontaneously while he is scribbling, "This is a choo-choo train." Or he may say, like the drawing in the book, "Mother is going shopping" [Figure 6]. Yet we neither see a choo-choo train, nor do we see Mother going shopping, because the child is still concerned with motions.

What is so important in this stage? The importance of this stage can only be really appreciated if you know that here is a change in thinking—from making motions to thinking in terms of images, mental pictures. When the child was merely scribbling circularly or longitudinally, the child didn't think of anything but just enjoyed his motions. No mental picture occurred to the child during the act of making the motions or movements. But all of a

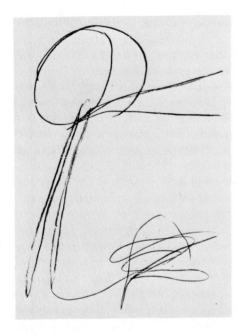

Fig. 6. "Mother Goes Shopping" (4-year-old). Indicates naming of scribbling. Notice the different kinds of motions.

sudden the child thinks of something. He thinks of a choo-choo train. He has a mental picture. So the significance is that his thinking for the first time refers to the outside, while a motion is still part of the body self, of the ego, with which the child has been concerned up to this time. From now on, the child will refer to something outside of himself by referring to the choo-choo train or to Dad or to Mother going shopping, or whatever he names his drawing. So, may I say, the significance is, then, that the child's thinking has changed from a thinking in terms of kinesthetic experiences to a thinking in terms of mental pictures.

Student: Will this naming happen before he's scribbling, while he's scribbling, or after he's scribbling?

Lowenfeld: While he is scribbling—while he is scribbling. He scribbles and says, "This is a choo-choo train."

When you go by a child in a kindergarten, the child may look up and say, "It's a choo-choo train," or he may say something to his scribbling. Don't force the child. Don't say, "What's that?" because the child may be embarrassed and invent something if he is insecure. The secure child will say nothing, you know, simply go on with his scribbling. But the insecure child wants to please you and may invent something on this occasion. So wait for the spontaneous response of the child who is scribbling—when he spontaneously names his scribbling. But this has great implications.

Student: At what age level does this generally occur?

Lowenfeld: This generally occurs when the child is three-and-a-half or four years. You see, we have half years of differences or distances between the various forms of scribbling. On the average, we would say the child starts scribbling at two, disordered scribbling, which he practices until he is two-and-a-half. When two-and-a-half, he should discover longitudinal scribbling; that means there is a relationship between his motor activity and what he sees, his visual world. We call it visual-motor coordination, you know—motor activity is the activity which he does with his hands when he moves, and coordination means that he now coordinates his motor activity with his vision. This lasts usually from two-and-a-half to three; circular scribbling from three to three-and-a-half; and the naming of scribbling from three-and-a-half to four. Yes, on the average, a half year up or down does not make any difference.

Student: Say a child has not had the opportunity to scribble at all. He's four years old, and he picks up a pencil. Will he start with unorganized scribbling?

Lowenfeld: No, usually he is in the developmental stage in which he ought to be; because if he hasn't had an opportunity to scribble with a crayon, he may have scribbled in the sand, or he may have given expression to his scribbling somehow without you knowing it. So, he should be up to his mental age in his development—should have caught up—except if he's not alert enough. You see, this is not a drawing achievement—that one starts to think in terms of mental pictures. This is clearly an achievement in growth. As we said in the beginning, we only use drawing as a means to an end and not as an end in itself. We would not say the child has advanced in his drawing when he names the scribbling. The child has grown so that he now thinks in terms of a mental picture. But this has great implications.

Student: If a child is scribbling and a friend makes little marks, is that the same? I mean, you know, if you just take a pen and make motions? Is that the same thing?

Lowenfeld: It's the same thing.

Student: It's not important to him, then?

Lowenfeld: No, it's the same thing. You see, if a child makes marks without having a crayon—but with a clothespin, let us say—well, it doesn't satisfy him, and he may not arrive as soon at the satisfaction of seeing what he has done. It will hold him back, probably, but he will feel that he has gone through the same motions.

Now, I have not yet seen a psychology book on child art or child development which gives us an answer as to how far back our memory goes, except that we find there arbitrary answers. How far back can adults remember in their memory? They usually say, "We do not remember anything before the third year of life." That's what they usually say. But may I add that we have a much better statement. We can now say that children who

111

think in terms of kinesthetic experiences cannot produce a memory image on which we usually can rely in our memory. See, when I ask you, "What did you do last year at this time? Where were you?"—well, you have here a kind of filing system, you know, by which you recall. This filing system consists to a great extent of memory images. You don't think in abstract terms. You have a reference file; and this reference file usually calls upon pictures; for instance, "I was at my father's house." In that, you think now of sensory experiences to which you relate your father's house. You may think also of the visual image. Unless we have such a reference file, our thinking is greatly weakened. Our ability to recall kinesthetic thinking is very weak, because the differentiation in kinesthetic thinking—thinking in different kinds of motions—is not great. You can think of a drop of an airplane, for instance, as a distinct memory—you know, when you feel the bump—and you may recall it. That would be a kinesthetic memory image. You understand? But the child doesn't have such distinct memory images with regard to kinesthesis, because his whole thinking at this time is restricted to terms of kinesthesis.

So, a new kind of thinking starts—a thinking in terms of mental pictures—and that opens up a whole field of new activities, especially with regard to memory. It is from this time on that children refer to events which have taken place and which they can recall in terms of mental pictures. So we can now say—in much better conscience than an arbitrary date—that, as soon as man begins to think in terms of mental pictures, his memory images start to function, and that usually is at three-and-a-half years. So, we usually can think back in our memory as far as three-and-a-half. Now, this is something of a new discovery which we still don't see quoted or mentioned. We have something of an advance here in art education, namely, that we have tangible evidence of what children do and we use this evidence for our research.

Now we know quite a lot about a child when we go into a kindergarten. We can look around and say, "Oh, this child is already enjoying his motor activity because he is doing circular scribbling." Or we say, "Oh, this child already refers to his mental pictures because he is naming his scribbling." But up to this time, we have not considered the individual child. We have only considered stages in development, and we have categorized children into groups: "This group of children belongs to disordered scribbling, and this group of children. . . ." But we have not yet been able to find differences in children's scribblings, and it is this that we would like to do now. You see, we go deeper and deeper into the understanding of details. Why? Only for the purpose of becoming more sensitive to the individual child.

There should be no misunderstanding about our purposes. I emphasize this, because you may hear criticism that we are trying to put children into cubbyholes and so forth. Oh, no, we are not trying to categorize or label children or to use our knowledge for any other purpose than to go deeper into the details so that we become more sensitive toward the individual child. As long as we say, "This child is in the scribbling stage," we have generalized only; and we put all children under one hat, as it were, without seeing the individual child. Not even now do we see the individual child; we only have a better knowledge than what we have had. Scribbling has become more important to us. We don't yet know anything about classroom procedures and what we should do in order to motivate children in scribbling; we will arrive at this later. We don't even know what material we should give them. We will hear about that later. But don't be impatient. We are doing something very exciting in finding out what happens to the individual child now.

As we discussed in the beginning, all components of growth are within the scribbling child, too. The scribbling child grows intellectually; the scribbling child grows emotionally, and physically, and perceptually, and socially, and aesthetically, and creatively. We would like to find out now what criteria are indicative of the various components of growth in the scribbling stage. The criteria, which I mentioned in the beginning of this course, are based upon research. This particular study is a study of 400 children which I myself did. However, not all the criteria are based upon research which I did. I'll make quotations whenever they are needed. Questions in the charts are based upon criteria. They were also tried out in terms of the criteria— that means, questions which were invalid and questions which were unreliable are not included. So we have here only questions which significantly relate to the scribbling of children and their expression in terms of growth components.

In general, intellectual growth is seen by the discrepancy between the developmental stage and the chronological age. For example, we said that longitudinal scribbling should be done between two-and-a-half, the average, and three years. We said half a year up or down doesn't make any difference. But if we go into the first grade, we see Mary who is six years old and still scribbles longitudinally. There is a greater discrepancy than a half a year up or down. There is a discrepancy here of probably three years down. Then we would say, "Mary must be mentally retarded," not because she does not know drawing—oh, no, indeed not—but because a six-year-old child should think at least in terms of mental pictures. She should even be anxious to establish a relationship between her mental image and what she draws. This is a mental characteristic. Do I make myself clear? I would not like to hear from any one of you: "This child is not gifted in drawing." Do you see? There is a difference. If Mary does not draw in terms of her mental pictures but still scribbles longitudinally, it is not because she is not gifted in drawing, because drawing is only an expression of her growth—that means, she has not yet matured to the point that she has discovered that there is a relationship between what she thinks in terms of a mental picture, or image, and what she draws. So we would say she is retarded.

May I warn you at this time: don't say that she is retarded merely for the purpose of making a diagnosis. You are saying it in order to become more sensitive to Mary. Since Mary isn't responsible for that, you don't want to degrade her because she hasn't been able to catch up with the other children (on the average). So it is important that we do it in order to become more sensitive to Mary's needs. What we should do, we will discuss later.

Student: What do you do with your first grader who is in the disordered stage of scribbling and is also naming the scribble? How do you account for that?

Lowenfeld: Oh, then you didn't recognize it. Look, a child who is naming his scribbling may mix up motions of all kinds. In other words, the child may say, "There's a choo-choo train, and there is Mother going shopping." You may think this is disordered, but it isn't. It's a combination of various kinds of scribbling which takes place during—oh, it is not true?

Student: That isn't what it was. It was definitely disordered scribbling.

Lowenfeld: It was definitely disordered scribbling, and the child named it. Then the naming isn't true, you understand. The child has been asked, "What are you doing?" And the child now thinks that he has to please adults and so he names his scribbling all the time. You see? This may be true, too. In other words, this is one of the controls which we have. We will, in this way, often differentiate true naming from false naming. If a child cannot yet control his scribbling, motor control, then the child isn't ready for naming. But if he names in spite of it, the naming is something which the child has accepted and does not produce spontaneously.

Student: That's the answer then, because this happened when I was student teaching. The elementary teacher asked the little boy—I mean, he was perfectly happy just scribbling—and she asked him, "What is it?" He got a shocked look on his face, and then he told her what it was.

Lowenfeld: Yes, see; this is your control, your gauge, you see.

And now may I say this, please, to all of you. After this course, I'm sure you will be much richer in your understanding of children's art, but I do not expect you to be already at home in dealing with it. This, for some of you, may be a new revelation. The more practice you have, the more sensitive will you become to such situations. When I go into a kindergarten, I immediately sense it if there is a discrepancy between the naming and what the child does. You may not. But you will be more sensitive than you were previously; and what the child does will be more meaningful to you, although your reference file may not yet be ready to be used. You understand what I mean? Especially with regard to the growth criteria? Do you think I ever look at the growth criteria when I look at a child's drawing? This occurs to me almost intuitively now, just as it occurs to you intuitively what word you should use for an expression if you are at home in your language. But if you are not at home in your language, you would have to find out, "What word should I use for 'comprehension'?" you know, or for any word which is not quite on the tip of your tongue. This is true also for the subject with which we are dealing here. But the more you get practice in looking at children's drawings and the deeper you go into your understanding of these growth components and the meaning of them, the more readily will this be available to you. When you can forget it altogether and you intuitively look again at the drawing, those things will come to you almost spontaneously.

May I, then, continue. Intellectual growth is usually seen by the discrepancy between chronological age and the developmental stage. For instance, if I show you this drawing, this scribbling, and ask you, "Is this child intellectually on the level of average or advanced?" what would you say?

Student: How old is he?

Lowenfeld: His age we don't know. You should say: "I don't know. Tell me his age." Then I would turn around the drawing, and I would say: "His age is two years and six months." You see, then you would say: "Fine. This is just where he ought to be." You would say, then, that this is probably average.

Now, you refer the developmental stage to the chronological age or vice versa. But you should still not make such a judgment unless you have at least three drawings obtained from this child. You should make it a rule not to look at only one drawing of a child, because the child may be upset at the time, and being upset always creates different reactions. You will have to obtain three scribblings from this child, and then look at the three scribblings. If they agree with each other, then you should look at the chronological age of the child and compare it with the data which you have indicating where the child should be, and then you will say, "This is fine."

May I ask you at this time to open your book and look at the charts which we have provided. See, we have here a Summary Chart for the Scribbling Stage and an Evaluation Chart for the Scribbling Stage. You have an asterisk there which says, "This evaluation chart can only be used if samples of scribbling are done in crayon." This is important because we shall see that scribbling cannot be as easily detected in another medium. I have examples here of scribblings which were done, not in crayon, but in paint. In paint, you often cannot see what has happened, because the paint has blurred and you can't see whether it is disordered or whether the child has controlled his brush strokes. So we use crayon if we want to find out more and become more sensitive about the child. The first question here says, "Are there uncontrolled lines only?" We evaluated one drawing with regard to intellectual growth. Are there uncontrolled lines only? What would you say?

Stage	Characteristics	Human Figure	Space	Color	Design	Stimulation Topics	Technique
Scribbling (1) Dis-ordered.	Kinesthetic experience. No control of motions.	None.	None.	No conscious approach. Use of color for mere enjoyment without any intentions.	None.	Through encouragement. Do not interrupt or discourage or divert child from scribbling.	Large black crayon. Smooth paper. Poster paint. Finger paint only for maladjusted children.
(2) Longitudinal.	Repeated motions, establishment of co-ordination between visual and motor activity. Control of motions.	None.	None, or only kinesthetically.	Same as above.	None.	Same as above.	Same as above.
(3) Circular.	Self-assurance of control through deviations of type of motions.	None.	Kinesthetically.	Same as above.	None.	Same as above.	Same as above.
(4) Naming of scribbling	Change from kinesthetic to imaginative thinking. Mixing of motions with frequent interruption.	Only imaginatively by the act of naming.	Purely imaginatively.	Color used to distinguish different meanings of scribbling.	None.	In the direction of the child's thinking by continuing the child's story.	Colored crayons (four colors). Poster paint. Plasticine throughout scribbling stage.

EVALUATION CHART *
Scribbling Stage

	Mental Age		No	Yes
Intellectual Growth	2–3	Are there uncontrolled lines only? Does he only pound or knead clay?		
	2½–3½	Are all motions controlled, repeated motions: longitudinal or circular? Does he form coils with clay? Does he enjoy breaking the clay?		
	3–4	Does the child name his scribbling? Does he name his pieces of clay?		

		None	Some	Much
Emotional Growth	Does the child enjoy his scribbling? Is the scribbling free from stereotyped repetitions? such as: Is the scribbling free from interrupted lines? Are the child's motions determined and forceful? Does the intensity and direction of the motions change?			
Social Growth	Does the child concentrate on his motions? Is it difficult to divert the child?			
Perceptual Growth	Does the child show the desire for large motions? (Kinesthetic freedom.) Does the child enjoy tactual sensations when working with clay? Does the child control his motions visually? When he names his scribbling, does he use different colors to differentiate different meanings?			
Physical Growth	Are the motions vigorous? Are the lines bold? Does the child use his whole arm?			
Aesthetic Growth	Does the child distribute his motions over the whole paper? Does the child show a feeling for balance in his distribution of dense and loose scribbling?			
Creative Growth	Is the child independent in his scribbling? When scribbling with other children does the child remain uninfluenced? Is he generally opposed to imitating? When naming his scribbling does he develop stories independently?			

* This evaluation chart can only be used if samples of scribbling are done in crayon.

Student: Yes.

Lowenfeld: Yes. You check "yes." As soon as you check "yes," you look at the mental age, and you see that his mental age is between two and three. Do you see? This is how the chart is used. But, if I would say, for instance, "Are there uncontrolled lines only?" and you would say, "No," then we would go on to the next question. Well, we have not talked about questions with regard to clay, so we'll go to the next: "Are all motions controlled, repeated motions: longitudinal or circular?" Yes—so we would now check "Yes." So this child's mental level is between two-and-a-half and three-and-a-half. Do you see? Or if we were to say, "No," then we would have to go to the next question: "Does the child name his scribbling?" Yes; then the child would be between three and four in his mental age, on the average. This is just for us.

But, you see, this will be of no value if we just repeat a performance which we can do by testing; although testing on this level, as those in child development know, is very limited because we just don't have many tests for children of this chronological age. So it is a good help, but it wouldn't mean anything if we only looked at his intellect. You see, we should now conceive of an individual as a whole. We should be ashamed of ourselves if we were only to look at his intellect, because we know that his intellect may not even come out if the child is emotionally restricted. So we look at the other components of growth, and there we come closer and closer to finding out about the individual differences in children.

Children who are emotionally free in scribbling show it by a great diversity in the use of and pressure on materials—let's say, changing the intensity of lines, such as we see here. See, there's a soft line. Then the child enjoys his scribbling. He goes off and makes dark lines, and so forth. The child frequently changes the intensity of the lines. Children who always draw with the same pressure do not show as much enjoyment in their scribbling as children who sometimes put on great pressure and another time less. They also are not as flexible in their adjustment, but rather remain with the same pressure all the time once they have started. So, a sign of emotional growth is different intensity.

A still better sign of emotional growth is when the child scribbles freely, continuously, without interruption of his motions. Children who frequently interrupt their motions in their scribbling have less confidence than children who continuously scribble. For instance, this is a very healthy scribbling. But the scribbling which you have reproduced, for instance, in Figure [4], is not as healthy because the child scribbles a little bit, then pauses, probably looks around, then scribbles another bit, then again pauses for no reason. If he were enjoying it, he would go on and would get some excitement out of his continuous scribbling. The more the scribbling is interrupted, the less stable the child may be emotionally—unless we see an extreme of this, that

117

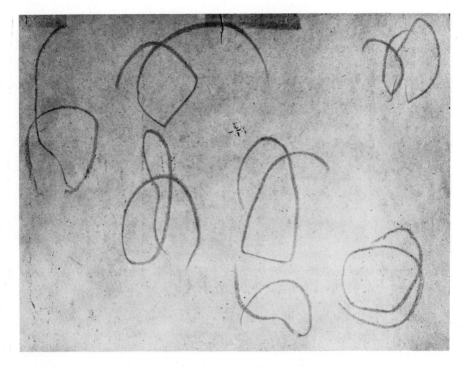

Fig. 7. Stereotyped motions, repeating the same rigid movement.

is, when the child does not freely scribble at all but engages in stereotypes, in the repetition of a same motion. For instance, you see here an interrupted scribbling. Can you see it? Well, the child scribbles a little bit here; then something happens to him—he doesn't want to go on. He starts again, something happens, starts again—and then he scribbles more. Do you see? This is not as healthy as when the child really enjoys himself and goes on and on. We also see children who feel not as free in their scribbling.

Now, I'll show you various scribblings. See that, where the child interrupts very frequently? And now I would like to show you a scribbling which we call stereotyped scribbling, where the child is not free and does not engage in free motions but sticks to the same motions again and again, like here [Figure 7]. Can you see what happens? The child then produces the same kind of motions again and again—not exactly the same, but basically. This motion which you see here consists of a loop. This child has lost freedom in engaging in free motions. Now the reason for that may differ from one child to another. In one child, this may merely be a period through which he goes because he wants to imitate writing. Let us say, the parents write letters and encourage that, "Are you writing me a letter,

Johnny?" You see, now Johnny wants to write a letter and does a thing like this.

Student: Yes, I remember doing that.

Lowenfeld: Now this may be only for one stage; but even for this stage it is unhealthy, because scribbling should not be misused for letter writing of an adult nature and we should not encourage it, as so many parents do. "Write me a letter." What a silly idea! A child of three should write a letter! The parents know it. This is a confusion of adult imposition and childish behavior. And many parents, you know, just say: "Oh, just let me alone. Write a letter." Something of this sort, you know. They don't just say, "Let me alone," but "Write a letter." And some are even satisfied if the child fills one page after the other with the same kind of interrupted scribbling. We should be sensitive to this, because scribbling fulfills an important purpose in the development of children and should not be misused by adults for their own purposes or to be pleased.

Student: This type of thing—is this true for all children or just for this age group, two to four?

Lowenfeld: Well, if the child is in the scribbling stage, he will express his stereotype reaction in this manner. If he is in another stage, he would express it in a different manner. But stereotypes, as we have heard in our general evaluation, always indicate emotional restriction or emotional maladjustment, depending on how frequently and persistently they occur. Now, if we have this one drawing and we have two other drawings by the same child and only the one shows the stereotypes, the repetitions, and the others do not, what would you say? The child may have been upset on this day. Do you see? I would discard it. I would not think of it at all, because this is just an incident in the child's life. But if I have three drawings done on different days and they all show the same kind of stereotyped, stiff repetition, then I would be alarmed inside and would say, "This child has established a certain inflexibility, and if I'm not doing anything about it, the child may remain backward in his emotional growth." Do you see? These are the implications. That means that I have to be sensitive toward it.

Now we will discuss what we should do about motivation. We will go through all the details concerning what we should do about it, so that we shall learn what we should do with such children. But, you remember, in one of my lectures in the beginning, I mentioned to you that we should always start on the level of the child. This is a principle, an educational principle. Also here, we should start on the level of the child, and, you remember, I already gave you some advice on how to motivate the child away from this stereotyped scribbling. You remember that?

You should refer to another motion which is meaningful to the child; for instance, skating. I would say: "Look, if you were skating in this room, would you only skate this way and stop? Then go here and skate this way and stop?" You see? You could say, "Let me see how you would skate." And the child, in his skating, may not be restricted; because skating is a more direct transference of motion into action. Of course, the restricted child may not even want to start running or be in motion. Well, then you would not speak of skating. You would say: "Do you play tag? Let's play tag. You catch me." You see, if the child says, "Mmm," and stands there—as such a restricted child may—you would say: "Come on. Catch me. Come on. Come on." And you would, of course, try to encourage the child. "Can you catch me?" And then you would start running, and probably he would start running over a large area. Then, you would say, "Oh, well, now let's try to show how we run and catch on the paper." You would relate one motion to another motion and the child may, through this motivation—for a short time, at least—depart from his stereotype.

LECTURE 11

Scribbling Stage: Evaluation of Social, Perceptual, Physical, and Aesthetic Growth

When the child starts to imitate writing rather than engaging in free motions, we should know that this is not a healthy activity even if we think that the child is advanced. A child might even try to write a letter, which usually does not take place, of course, at two or two-and-a-half or so. But at three or three-and-a-half, the child may begin to write an L or an E or an N, you know, which are usually the first letters because they consist of straight lines; and the eager parent may be thrilled, "My child is already writing letters."

Now, this is an engagement which is not a healthy engagement if we look at it as a part of the total development of a child, unless the child really has the desire to write letters for himself and at the same time continues to engage in free scribbling—controlled, longitudinal, or circular scribbling, or the naming of scribbling. But if the letter writing is done at the cost of other things, such as free engagement in scribbling or the naming of scribbling or whatever, then we should know that it is introduced at a wrong time or it is forced upon the child and is, therefore, harmful to the child. What we should do about these children we shall not discuss now. We will discuss it later, because I hope we will get to the point where we will discuss motivations; and it would only be a repetition.

So, may I again say, anything which is done at the cost of some other phase of growth is harmful, because we hope that we can stimulate the child to grow as a whole and not in slices of subject matter areas or even growth areas such as intellect and so forth. It would, in the same way, be harmful if a child would merely engage in scribbling and never would arrive at writing, do you see? It would be a prolonged scribbling, then, and the child would not arrive at the realization of communicating with the outside world, which is also wrong—that means, not advantageous to the total development of the child.

Now, let me continue from where we stopped yesterday. Briefly, I would like to repeat, as we said at that time, that we now conceive of creative activity, even scribbling, in a more differentiated way. Even today, if we were to go into a kindergarten, we would already be more sensitive to the child's activities, wouldn't we? It is for this purpose of becoming more sensitive to the child and his activities that we go into greater details and learn to know the various growth phases and the criteria which are indicative of them. Yesterday, we discussed the criteria that are important for determining the child's intellectual and emotional growth in scribbling. We discovered that we could find out via his scribbling whether a child is advanced in his intellect or whether he is retarded or whether he is just average. I shouldn't say "just," because average is the right thing to be for a child. May I say, a half year up or down will not make any difference, as we have previously indicated. But it is the discrepancy between the chronological age of the child and what we expect him to do in his developmental stage in scribbling which will give us insight into his intellectual growth.

We have said that there are various things, or criteria, indicative of emotional growth. One is the intensity which the child uses in his scribbling. If a child's scribbling is very even, with no varying intensity at all, we can see from that that the child's emotions do not change and that we are dealing with a child who is not excited about what he is doing but rather does it as routine work. Therefore, the intensity of the line remains the same. We expect children to enjoy their scribbling and, therefore, to become excited about their activity. This excitedness will be seen in the change of intensity in the lines.

We also said that children who are greatly engrossed in their scribbling will move continuously; they will not interrupt their scribbling activity but will rather go ahead with continuous lines. Now, children who are frequently interrupting their lines in scribbling are not concentrating on their scribbling, but are easily diverted and most probably look around. Always we should remember that our observation of children should be a part of our evaluation. If we see that a child frequently interrupts his scribbling, looks around, and sees what others are doing, this is always a sign that the child does not really enjoy his scribbling, that he has no confidence in his motor activity, that he needs to look around; and, therefore, we would say that interrupted scribbling is not conducive to emotional growth. As a matter of fact, it may already show that the child may not be well-adjusted—not to his scribbling, please, but to his motor activity. Motor activity is an activity which does not only show in scribbling, but it also shows itself in speech because motor activity is a part of speech. It shows itself in moving about. It shows itself in almost any activity because, whenever we move or whenever we act, our body motions are put into action.

Kinesthetic experiences as expressed in scribbling are an expression of a very important activity of the child. Therefore, if a child interrupts his scribbling, we should not say the child isn't good in his scribbling, please.

See, it is a part of the expression of the kinesthetic experience of the child. We know that kinesthetic sensations of the child are of tremendous importance at this stage, because they are one of the major forms of expression of children. Now, since we know this is true, we will say that interrupted scribbling is a sign of the child's lack of confidence in his motor activity—I emphasize this because I did not say in his scribbling. Do you see? We refer time and again from the child's personality back to the creative process and vice versa.

We also said that a most detrimental development for children in scribbling is stereotyped repetition; that is, when the child no longer can engage in any free motion but is stifled and remains with the repetition of a little motion which is restricted in itself to a certain sign or symbol. I said a stereotyped repetition is one which is repeated in the same way, time and again. Also remember, we said yesterday that we should never get our feeling for the child only from one drawing or from one scribble, but that we should always have at least three scribblings in front of us before we establish a relationship to the child through his scribbling; because a child may often be upset one day and may react differently from other days. If it only occurs once, well, we put aside the one drawing and look at the others because we take for granted that the child had difficulty on this one day.

Now, let's look again and look at the evaluation charts for the scribbling stage. I'll pull out a scribbling which we may continue to evaluate in terms of the characteristics that we see in it. If I show you this drawing, or this scribbling, and if I tell you that this child is three years and six months, according to what is on the rear of the scribbling, would any one of you want to comment on this? Don't be afraid. Just say what you think.

Student: He's normal.

Lowenfeld: What would you say about the child's needs?

Student: Looks as if it were interrupted, but he already has longitudinal strokes in it.

Lowenfeld: Right, it appears that the child is in the longitudinal stage of scribbling.

Student: It's vigorous?

Lowenfeld: Is this good for a child who is three years and six months?

Student: Yes.

Lowenfeld: It's all right. It's slightly below average, now, isn't it? What did we say is the average? Two-and-a-half, isn't it?

Student: Two-and-a-half to three.

Lowenfeld: Two-and-a-half to three, we said, And this is three and six months. We said a half year up or down will not hurt; so we would still say it's average, although we would have in the back of our minds that it's a little bit below average—you know? He's perfectly O.K.; but he's three years and six months, so he is on the lower edge. Do you see? Three years and six months is on the lower edge of perfectly O.K., not on the upper edge of perfectly O.K.

I said that a half a year up or down is always all right. I stated that longitudinal scribbling usually begins at two-and-a-half years and lasts a half a year. At three years, the child should engage in circular scribbling. So, when I said two-and-a-half and it lasts a half a year, then the average age is two-and-a-half to three. But I said also, "Half a year up or down would not make any difference." So, half a year down would be two years or up would be three-and-a-half, so anything between two and three-and-a-half would still be average. But we always, even if it is average, should keep in mind the lower and the upper edge of average. If it is the lower edge of average, we should be a little bit sensitive. We should be sensitized that there may be some special considerations as to why the child is low; and if there are none, then we just forget it. But if we look at this scribbling, we will see that there may be some reasons as to why the child hasn't progressed a little bit faster.

What are the reasons? Well, what about the intensity of the lines? They're very heavy as you can see. They're not changing much. They're all very heavy, except here we have a little change. Do you see it? So we may draw from that a slight conclusion for ourselves—that apparently this child is very intense at the time he does his scribbling because he puts lots of pressure on it; but he doesn't change much. On the contrary, we see that he interrupts his lines frequently. Now, our observation of the child would help us in finding out what the child does when he interrupts. Is it a kind of nervousness which doesn't make the child go ahead? Does he look around? What does he do while he interrupts? That would help us in developing our sensitivities toward the child, because then we probably would know why the child is not more advanced intellectually. Maybe he's a child who cannot concentrate. This might be a reason. And because he cannot concentrate at continuous motions, he interrupts them. This is as far as we went yesterday.

Student: We don't know actually if the child has made circular lines in another drawing. Or, also, he might have named that drawing. We don't know.

Lowenfeld: That's correct. It's most likely, though, if we had three drawings, not one, that the child would have done nothing else but longitudinal scribbling in the three drawings. We need to look at three drawings done not on the same day but on different days. Whether the child names his drawing or not, we cannot definitely say unless we are present.

But, as we shall see today, the naming of scribbling looks different from mere longitudinal lines. As soon as the child names his scribbling, we see clusters of lines—circular or longitudinal—then longer lines which extend to something. For instance, this is naming of scribbling. You see a difference? Here the child meant this to be, I believe, a tree; and this is the playground, and he is running around. You would think that this is just a mixture of longitudinal and circular scribbling. It is not. It is the naming of scribbling, but we don't know it unless we are present. So, the naming of scribbling is restricted to classroom activity and to our presence.

Indeed, we always will get more out of drawings if we also know the child and are present during the creative process. You remember, in the very beginning, we pointed out that for us the creative process is of more importance than the final product. Also, the creative process will be of greater importance to us in establishing greater sensitivity to the child than merely looking at the final product. But, since we are not in the children's art classes and cannot possibly have this class and the children's art class at the same time, we must just look at the final product as a substitute.

Student: If the child just scribbled the upper section there and then left the rest of the paper blank, would we consider this the same thing?

Lowenfeld: No, we would not. Our judgment would change. If the child simply has this one section, our judgment will somewhat change; because we feel that the child has done his scribbling and has stopped it but has not radically interrupted his scribbling, since no interruption can be seen in this part. But, indeed, we would look at the other drawings, because it could be a rather short kind of a scribbling span; and we need to look at two other drawings of the child, two other scribblings. If all his scribblings are in short spans, we would keep in our mind that this child does not scribble for a long period. He may stop and, therefore, may not be able to concentrate over a long period on scribbling. But he is not erratic—starting and stopping and starting and stopping and starting and stopping. This is different. Is this clear in our mind? Yes?

Student: Would it occur that a child who would do a drawing like this is perfectly normal in his general behavior and gives you no symptoms of any other kind? Could you still draw conclusions from this?

Lowenfeld: You would still draw conclusions from that, but you would be more watchful for the general behavior of that child. You understand?

Student: Well, I mean, suppose you don't see anything in his general behavior that you might conclude from this. Is that possible?

Lowenfeld: Well, we should be careful if the general behavior and the drawing do not go hand in hand. We should still be very sensitive to the child, having in the back of our minds that this, you know, is part of the general behavior of the child—the scribbling is part of his general behavior. But if it isn't shown in the other part of his general behavior, outside of scribbling, well, we know from psychology that what we see in an individual's behavior—not only in children's behaviors but also in adults' behaviors—is not always the true behavior of individuals. On the contrary, this may be a "very well-brought-up child," one who behaves very well, and, therefore, we don't see anything of this. Well, he may have been thwarted through, let's say, too restrictive behavior—do you see what I mean?—in the same way as individual adults are often thwarted because they cannot freely engage in what would be good for them in a free exchange of ideas, or in a free social exchange, and so forth, because in the past they have been restricted to a rather formal education, and you wouldn't see anything of the difficulty.

I don't know who has read this—the review in the *New York Times,* which appeared a few weeks ago, about a very, very interesting book, *Why Men Don't Cry.* Have you read it? It's a very interesting treatise on the subject that men in our society are discouraged from expressing their emotions more so than women. For instance, if Johnny starts crying about something, we call him a sissy and discourage the free expression of emotions. Yet this person, a psychologist and anthropologist, says that this may be one of the very important criteria responsible for our heart illnesses, which are seen more in men than in women because men restrain themselves much more in expressing their emotional experiences. He says it's good for people to cry or to give expression to their emotions. And he says, furthermore—from experiments and investigations which he and others conducted on a large scale—that, in countries in which there is such a social custom as there is in the United States or in England or in other countries where men are considered sissies when they express themselves emotionally, we have more heart ailments in men and less in women than we have in countries where men cry and it is also an accepted social custom. For instance, in France the ratio of heart ailments between men and women is almost equal, he says, and he attributes that mainly to the expression of emotions in men.

So, what we see in persons, in individuals, is not always their true behavior. If a child, in his behavior (other than in his creative processes), does not show any indication of what we see in the child's drawing—well, maybe the child's drawing is *the* one general behavior in which he freely engages in this type of expression, while in his other behaviors he restrains himself according to, or depending on, his upbringing.

Now this is as far as we went yesterday, and today we will find out what criteria are indicative of the various other growth components. Still, I'd like to insert here that you should never forget when I said that the most important part of a personality, or characteristic of a personality, is that all these components of growth are so thoroughly mixed that we cannot differentiate the one from the other. Remember when I mixed the contents in the test tube? I shook it so hard that none of these parts still remained isolated. We shall see that they all are here simultaneously. And we will only discuss them separately because we have no way of discussing them simultaneously. This is simply a way out, as you know.

In social growth, we heard that it is very important, first of all, to identify with the work which we are doing; because only when we can identify ourselves with our own work will we be able later to engage also in projecting this identification to the needs of others. This, indeed, is social growth, because without it no cooperation takes place. Therefore, we begin with the self. Children who do not concentrate on their own scribbling lack the very basis for social growth, because it hasn't become important to them. Their own work is unimportant. If they do not identify themselves with what they are and do at this stage, later they will have difficulty in extending the self because the self is not established. So, it is the most important criterion. We ask ourselves, "Does the child concentrate on his motions?" [Refer to the Evaluation Chart for the Scribbling Stage.]

We cannot answer this question unless we observe the child. We cannot answer it simply by looking at the scribbling. But when the child scribbles, we can see whether the child looks around, doesn't want to engage in scribbling, sits there and laughs, or does other things. Then, we would say "None," and we would make our check mark under the "None." But if we see that the child concentrates now and then at scribbling—he scribbles, is quite concentrated, then looks around, does nothing for a time, then goes on again—then we would make the check mark under "Some." And if the child constantly scribbles and watches his scribbling and cannot be diverted easily, we would put our check mark under "Much." The child concentrates much on his scribbling. If we would like to differentiate even more, we can put a check mark somewhere in between the three columns.

Directly related to this question, of course, is whether the child is easily diverted from his scribbling. If the child is easily diverted, we can also see it when we observe the child. For instance, if a car goes by and creates a certain noise, does the child look around? If someone walks in the doorway, you will see many children just go on with their scribbling; it doesn't make any difference to them. Others will look up. Is the child diverted by the scribbling of others? That means, does he look around and then get his inspiration or his encouragement from someone else? Such diversions from scribbling also account for a lack of concentration. Therefore, we ask, "Is it difficult to divert the child?" Well, we would say, "Not at all difficult; the child can easily be diverted," and we would then put a check under "None." Is it difficult? Not at all. If it's quite difficult to divert the child—something must really go on in order to divert the child—we would put it under "Some." If the child cannot be diverted, if it's very, very difficult—you could even shoot outside and Mary would go on with her scribbling—then you would put it under "Much."

You see that we have only two questions here under social growth. What accounts for that? You can see that we have many questions under emotional growth. You can also see that we have quite a number of questions under perceptual growth but only a very few questions under social growth.

Student: He's not yet a social person.

Lowenfeld: Correct. A child of two or two-and-a-half or three or three-and-a-half years just is not yet a social person. Social growth just doesn't play an important role in young children. If you were to go and watch the children of this age level—or, rather, this developmental stage—in their play in a nursery school, you would see that their social inclination is rather weak at this period. One child may play in this direction, and another child goes right straight ahead and goes in that direction. The active desire to cooperate is not yet developed. We may get children together by encouraging them; but actively, on their part, there is not yet a desire to cooperate or to engage in social activities. Therefore, we have very few criteria which indicate social growth. The number of questions which you have here may even be indicative of the importance that a growth segment has within a period of development. If we consider perceptual growth, we will probably have more to say; although it isn't yet developed, either.

Before we engage in discussing perceptual growth, I would like to insert a consideration which we have omitted previously, and that is scribbling with other materials—not pencil or paint or crayon, but scribbling with three-dimensional materials such as clay. We shouldn't call it scribbling, actually, but it is a parallel development. Since it is most important for perceptual growth, it is quite proper that I discuss it now.

Children should have an opportunity to use all kinds of materials. It is also very important for them to have three-dimensional materials which you can hold and grasp, because these offer entirely new avenues for the child. Do you see? To hold something in one's hands is a more direct experience than to have a kind of remote control over a crayon and produce lines on the paper. So, if children engage directly in clay modeling, or in clay work, they have a more direct experience. This experience is important to them because it involves other functions, other kinds of motor activities, than scribbling. In the beginning, we will see that, if we give children clay or plasticene—which is oil clay, as you know—they will begin by pounding and kneading it. In the beginning, they may not do anything else but put their hands on it and pound the clay and, later on, knead or squeeze the clay. This is the stage parallel to disordered scribbling. The pounding is uncontrolled; the squeezing is uncontrolled. They are not doing anything in particular with the clay which demands a certain control.

After the child has gone through this kneading and pounding—between two and two-and-a-half years, usually—at two-and-a-half the child usually starts to form coils and noodles, to break pieces of clay into little parts, or even to roll the clay. This breaking into parts assumes already a certain control. The more the child equally breaks parts or makes his noodles and coils, the greater is the control. We have no differentiation here, as we have between longitudinal and circular scribbling; we have merely the indication that the child breaks the pieces of clay and forms coils or balls as one stage in the development which we call the stage comparable to controlled scribbling.

At one point, however, the child may pick up a piece of clay, a lump or one of the coils, and lead it around and say "Psch, Psch—this is a train." You see, it is here when clay assumes a special role. He cannot do this with the lines on the paper. So the naming in clay work may often be of help to children who do not name their scribbling at this time. For instance, if you feel that the child is retarded in his naming, in the realization of a mental picture, it may greatly help the child if you give him clay and let him play with clay. The child may arrive earlier at the naming in clay than he does in scribbling. Why is this true? The motivation is here. To pick up a piece of clay and to move it in a way which is natural to the child gets his imagination stimulated. Do you understand? We don't have that as readily available in scribbling. The child can't move a line; he cannot actually move the object as he does with the lump of clay. He may pick up the clay and say, "Ahahng," and this may be an airplane. In other words, he has the opportunity to hold the real symbol and engage in a mental picture, in imaginative thinking. It is here that the tactile and kinesthetic experiences motivate the child in his thinking, in his concrete thinking; because the holding is something concrete, and the moving is something concrete, and the two together may easily stimulate or motivate the child's thinking in terms of images. Because holding—touching—is a perceptual experience and because moving is a perceptual experience, I'll discuss this while we are discussing perceptual growth.

Perceptual growth is seen, first of all, in the child's kinesthetic freedom; that is, whether he freely engages in motor activities in his scribbling or in his clay work or in both. But we can see that better in his scribbling. Therefore, the first question reads: "Does the child show the desire for large motions, that is, kinesthetic freedom?" What would you say here? Who would say, "None"? Raise your hands. Who would say, "Some"? Raise your hands. Who would say, "Much"? Raise your hands. Do you see, we are almost in 100 percent agreement. We would say, "Some." He engages somewhat in large motions. They are not very large motions which go over the whole paper. This would be "Much." They are not "None" because they are somewhat large motions. So we would say the child engages somewhat in large motions.

Student: Wouldn't this depend an awful lot on physical growth?

Lowenfeld: It does. There is overlapping, as we shall see, of various growth components, including emotional growth. There are always overlappings; but the questions, as we formulate them, mainly count for the type of growth which we are discussing. It is interesting that we all agree here concerning this child, and it is not surprising, of course.

Now, the second question deals immediately with tactile experiences, and that's why I discussed the clay work. "Does the child enjoy tactile sensations when working with clay?" This needs a definition of what we call enjoyment, but all who have worked with children in a nursery school know it without my description. They know when the child approaches the clay with two fingers and is somewhat hesitant to hold the clay. There are children, of course—especially if you were to teach blind children—who always start with a kind of hesitancy when touching something of a consistency which they are not used to. Other children like to roll and touch the clay with just the flat hand, you know, and sometimes hold the clay; and still other children love to engage in holding the clay and really digging into it. There are differences. Experience will help us to differentiate between this hesitancy of touching it when the child does not want to engage in tactile sensations at all, and when the child sometimes just embraces the clay, and when the child loves to dig into the clay and gets a beautiful sensation out of it. Now, these are the three different phases; and, according to these different phases, we would say, "Not at all," "Somewhat," or "Much." All this makes us more sensitive to the child; because we learn now to observe the child in detail and this, as we said in the very beginning, calls for greater sensitivity.

The third question can only be answered when we are present with the child and can observe him. It asks whether the child visually controls his motions—not at all, somewhat, or much. Well, we can only answer it by watching children. Some children just scribble and look around; they don't control their motions visually at all. Other children look at their scribbling and then sometimes look out the window; and still other children even go with their face, up and down—we see even the eyes go up and down—and control their motions very much with their vision. So, according to the control, we would put our check mark on either "None," "Some," or "Much."

The fourth question deals with the naming of scribbling, and we would not bother at all with this question unless the child names his scribbling. So we would leave it blank and would not make any check mark if the child has not arrived at naming of scribbling. No check mark, as we shall see later, does not interfere at all with our total picture of the child. It reads, "When he names his scribbling, does he use different colors to differentiate different meanings?" The differentiation of color is one of the aspects of perceptual growth. Some children introduce colors when they name their scribbling merely to differentiate between different things. This child did not, although he had different colors at his disposal. He could have made the scribbling of a tree brown or green or blue and the running around yellow, because they are two different things. If the child does it, then, he is perceptually more advanced than if he does not do it. If he always does it, then we would put the check mark under "Much." If he now and then uses different colors, we would put it under "Some." If he never uses different colors, we would put the check mark under "None."

Now, this brings to an end our understanding of how perceptual growth is seen in scribbling. You see now, that we don't neglect any kind of growth during the creative process, and it no longer remains a generality. This is what we call the total child, and we now know what we mean by total child—we reach every phase of the child wherever it is.

Of course, we are also interested in the child's physical growth. I have stated previously that the sole responsibility for physical growth should remain with those who are responsible for physical growth—the parents and the physician—because there are so many activities, especially food habits, which are very important for the physical growth of the child. These other activities, such as physical activities in gymnastics and the child's body activities, would give us a better picture than his scribbling. But we will, of course, look also at scribbling from the point of view of physical growth.

We know from experimentation that children, according to their physical stamina, use the pressure of the crayon either lightly or strongly. This becomes a habit with children. A child who is weak and often ill has not much superfluous energy. He will make it a part of his physical make-up, his physical characteristics, to use a crayon lightly. But if he is emotionally well developed, even in his light use of a crayon, we will see different pressures. Do you understand? Only if he were physically not strong and emotionally not quite stable, would he use fine lines all the way through and not differentiate them. Yes?

Student: Should we encourage a child who has weak lines to try to make them heavier?

Lowenfeld: It would not be wrong, but we should not over-exert a child. We should always take the child's physique, his physical make-up, into consideration in our motivations. For instance, it would not help the child who is, let's say, weak if we were to ask him, through some motivation, whether he always goes on his tiptoes and very lightly or whether he can run strongly and use all his muscles. Although it may be good for him, it would not be good to force him into some kind of motion. But we all know that cause and effect are very closely interrelated and that a child who may engage in running strongly, or in putting pressure on the crayon, may also become used to it, or more used to it, and improve his muscular stamina. Do I make myself clear? So, this is interrelated. But if we look at children's scribbling, we will see that children who use vigorous motions are the stronger children in their physical growth. Therefore, the first question is: "Are the motions vigorous?" This is a value judgment. We can say that they are "Not at all" vigorous, "Somewhat" vigorous, or "Much" vigorous. What would you say of this drawing here?

Student: "Much."

Lowenfeld: You see, we all would agree this is "Much," especially if we make some kind of comparison with other children, do you see? Then we would all agree—at least, on a three-point scale, we would agree on the same point.

The next question is: "Are the lines bold?" This is, of course, in direct relationship with and simply fortifies the first question. "Does the child use his whole arm?" Well, if we observe him, we can say, "None," or "Now and then—Some," or "Always." "Always" would be "Much." These are the physical characteristics, you know; and we see that we have not many questions in this particular area.

We have also means of evaluating a child's aesthetic development, even as early as scribbling. This is a revelation for many of us, also for those in art education, because we thought that aesthetic growth begins only when we can appreciate things. Oh, no, it begins on the unconscious level. Aesthetic growth reveals itself in scribbling by the child's unconscious desire to use what he has at his disposal and to bring into a harmonious relationship the material which he has—crayons and the sheet of paper—with his motions. This is his way of expressing harmonious relationships. Harmonious relationships are, of course, aesthetic growth. You remember, we said aesthetic growth consists of the growth which takes place from a chaos to a better and more harmonious organization. It is on a continuum, as we said, and in scribbling we will immediately see it. In scribbling it shows by how the child distributes his lines—whether he remains in a corner and uses only a very small section of the paper or whether he goes over the whole sheet of paper.

Look at these scribblings. This is a scribbling of a child, and this is a scribbling of a child. Do you see? I could show you many more. This is a scribbling of a child, and we can find out now the aesthetic relationship. How is aesthetic growth shown in this? Does he use the whole sheet of paper in relationship to his motions? No, he remains on one side. Why? We don't know; he just does. We would say, in art education, it's because he hasn't discovered the other side of the sheet of paper—and no implications, please—not because he's frustrated and so forth. We would simply say because he hasn't discovered the other side of the sheet—the other part of the paper. So this is part of his aesthetic growth; that means, he has not thought of the relationship of his marks on the paper to the area which he has at his disposal. We shall later see that we can, of course, motivate for developing this awareness.

LECTURE 12

Scribbling Stage: Evaluation of Creative Growth; Procedures; Techniques; and Art Materials

We have three scribblings by this child. We look at them and we see that one scribbling covers only half of the paper. The two other scribblings cover the full paper. It may have been, then, under very accidental circumstances that this child would not have covered the whole paper. We try to protect ourselves from such haphazard circumstances by evaluating three scribblings, but it still is better if you are with the child. There is no doubt.

"In evaluating the response of small children to clay, how can one determine whether the response is natural or conditioned by previous experience or parental attitudes towards this medium?" I'll answer this question first. We cannot determine the cause of it, but it is part of the child's behavior. You remember, we said in the very beginning that we differentiate between potential abilities and functional abilities. We said that, in children's drawings, we can only see the child's functional abilities. So if a child has become restricted by parental conditioning, we would see only the present condition of the child. Of course, we may find out, if we are sensitive to the fact that children react differently under different circumstances (let us say, in a school situation and at home with parents). This is what is being called a double reaction, and a Frenchman [Luquet] calls it "duplicity of styles."[5]

If we see that the child has such double reactions, then we should know that there must be some restricting circumstances at work. They may be parental, or they may be in a teacher-created situation. Sometimes the child works freer in the classroom than at home, because parents want to see finished pictures and the teacher has a broader understanding of the child and encourages the child to create more freely. So, the child now creates two different kinds of reactions. I'm sorry that there is no one here who is working in clinical psychology. All who work in clinical psychology are aware of this difference. Do you know the difference between a child in a play-therapy situation and outside? Do you know what a play-therapy situa-

5. George H. Luquet, *Les Dessin d'un Enfant* (Paris: Alcan, 1913).

133

tion is? For those who do not know, I will explain. You see, some children are very aggressive, but only show this aggressiveness now and then because they have been restricted in their normal life. They show it in certain reactions only. Let us say, as long as the parent or the guardian is there, the child behaves very properly; and as soon as he leaves, the child beats the sister or pinches her and does all kinds of aggressive things. But, as soon as the parent comes back, the child is afraid.

Such tendencies can be worked out in a play-therapy situation, where children are put into a situation of complete freedom and they are told they can do whatever they want to do. They are given material like clay; and if they want to throw it around, they can do so and let out their aggressiveness and freely express themselves. Or they get dolls which are constructed in such a way that they can tear off the head or the legs or the arms, and they do it. Of course, the therapist may put in a question and say, "Who is this?" And the child may say, "This is Mother" or "This is Sister," depending upon who the person is on whom he would like to take out this aggressiveness, you know.

Now, it may not be that simple, but this is the principle of it. When the child goes out of this play-therapy situation—this clinical situation—the child will not throw the clay around, will not feel as free as in this play-therapy situation. Through play, the child gets rid of his aggressiveness. There, too, is a duplicity of styles, a duplicity of behaviors. This, we find, is not rare. But finding it out in a single drawing or even in three drawings is difficult. Often, the duplicity is so buried that we can only see what functions and not that which is underneath. But we are not supposed to be here to find out what is underneath. This is the function of the psychologist and not of the teacher. Here is where I object to our interfering, because we don't have the proper understanding and knowledge and background to go into some kind of a diagnostic or therapeutic activity that goes beyond teaching. Do I make myself clear on that?

So, we take the child as he functions; and in his drawings we will, of course, then see that maybe the child is restricted. That we can see. If the child, for instance, repeats certain symbols and scribbles interruptedly or with hooks only, then we can only say the child is restricted. We cannot say why the child is restricted. This we leave up to the psychologist. We shall, indeed, engage in motivations which may lead the child out of his restrictions. But these motivations are motivations which are within the realm of teaching and do not go beyond it into interpretations which lead, let us say, to a statement that the child has this complex or this neurosis, and so forth. Do you see? This would go beyond our ability.

Student: In other words, to us every child is normal?

Lowenfeld: Well, to begin with, yes; we presume that we have children in the classroom situation who are normal—unless we are convinced, through their drawings or through other behaviors, that there should be something done. But, instead of doing it ourselves, we will most often refer the child to the school psychologist or to the parent whenever we find something which alarms us and which is confirmed over a period of time.

So, to answer the first question—"In evaluating the response of small children to clay, how can one determine whether the response is natural or conditioned by previous experience or parental attitudes toward this medium?"—we cannot. Only in circumstances where we see such a duplicity of styles can we do it. If we see that a child reacts one time this way and another time another way, then we see that there is something weird because the child reacts to different situations differently. We would then ask ourselves, "What is the natural reaction?" For instance, as I told you, the one schizophrenic child whom we have in the children's art classes reacts also differently. On the blackboard he reacts by drawing perspective drawings—in the beginning, the fire engine. On the paper he paints perfectly in planes (the plane of the sky coming down to meet the plane of the earth), like other children. So my assumption or my guess is that probably when he uses paint, which is a new material for him, he approaches his imagery anew, freshly. But when he uses chalk—this is like the crayon or pencil which he is used to using at home—then he goes back into the old conditioned kind of perspective drawing, which he has probably taken over as a stereotype, and continues it.

If you see such a duplicity, then you have to ask yourself: "Now which is closer to the child and his development? Where is he freer? Where does he have more variations?" He doesn't have any variations in his perspective, except that he draws the same fire engine again and again in different sizes. That's his perspective reaction. But when he draws on a plane, he has as many different kinds of symbols as normal children have. From this duplicity of reactions, I can see that most probably the painting is his true reaction, and the chalk, crayon, or pencil work is his stifled reaction because he cannot do anything within this reaction. Now we encourage painting rather than drawing on the blackboard. Do you understand? In such situations, we can recognize it. Often we cannot.

"If a child does not enjoy tactile sensations when working with clay, how can it be determined whether some lack in perceptual growth is responsible rather than the feeling, perhaps, that 'Mother won't like my dirty hands or my dirty dress,' or 'This is strange, and therefore I don't like it,' which according to the book would be a lack of intellectual, exploratory growth, rather than perceptual?"

Now, may I say this. We can only take off from where the child is. You see, his inhibitions which are or were created by Mother—that "You have dirty hands," and so forth—are responsible for his lack of perceptual growth. It's the same thing if you have a child who is highly intelligent but, because of his emotional restrictions, he cannot use his intelligence; therefore, it will not be shown. Potentially, he may be highly intelligent. Potentially, this child may be highly perceptual in his growth, but it doesn't function. We can only see what functions. At all times, we may be wrong in judging the potential abilities of the child; but we certainly will try to develop the potential abilities and bring them out when we see that the child is afraid to engage in perceptual experiences in his clay work but freely engages in perceptual experiences in his motor coordination; for example, in scribbling. Here, we see again such a duplicity. And, if we see such a duplicity—a freedom on the one hand and a restriction on the other hand—well, then we have to try to motivate the child so that he will be free also in the use of clay. How we shall do that we will discuss today; that belongs to motivation. So, we will see such duplicity in styles whenever a potential ability contradicts the functional, or vice versa. Do we have any questions on that?

Indeed, sometimes we may have the wrong idea in regard to a child's potential abilities; but we will always have the right idea in regard to what functions, because that which functions is visible. So, if a child doesn't want to touch clay, well, he is certainly inhibited in his tactual experiences and doesn't want to engage in tactile experiences. Therefore, his perceptual growth is low in regard to this. Why is it low? Well, it is most likely because he is inhibited by his parents or by other circumstances; but this is no longer within the framework of what we usually do. You will see in the book how evaluation never deals in one area—let us say, with one question—and, if this question is negative, then we have only our own judgment. We always have at least two questions of divergent nature, and sometimes, of course, many more. You see, the only areas where we have but two questions are social growth and aesthetic growth; and usually they don't refer to any particular medium, but are general: "How much does the child concentrate?" You see? This is a general attribute. We will never base our judgment, for instance, of perceptual growth only on the tactile engagement of children; there are several other questions.

I was given here various scribblings—three. Now, these were not done on different days. They were all done on the same day, probably in sequence, one after the other. Therefore, they would not serve as the basis for establishing greater sensitivity to the child, since we want to do it on the basis of three drawings. These are actually one drawing because they were done at the same time. Yet, even here, we see certain differences. Now, look. Here you have a scribbling which is rather interrupted and which is also not covering the whole paper, only one part of it. The same child has made this other drawing which is non-interrupted—a scribbling that is very empty but of different intensities and which goes on continuously. Can you see it? And the same is true here in the third drawing.

Even if a child has made three scribblings and we see that two are more or less alike in their nature, we should discard the one that is unlike the others. Why? Because we think that it must have been done under certain different circumstances. But we would be more happy if we had three scribblings from the same child done on different days, probably even within a week. This would be more valuable to us in establishing a greater understanding of this child. But if I look at these two scribblings, they are so much alike that we can say that this child—if he doesn't name his scribbling—engages already in controlled scribbling and in disordered scribbling. Therefore, the child may be one of those children who develop circular and longitudinal scribbling at the same time as simply controlled scribbling. He is in the stage in between. As you can see, there are both scribblings here. Now, you must not think that growth takes place from one day to another, that a child on one day does disordered scribbling and the next day he goes into the next stage and does longitudinal scribbling. There are always, in growth, stages of transition in which the child has not yet reached the next stage because he still is attached to the previous one. Here he engages in some trial-and-error activities, such as controlling his lines. So, you may find both stages in one drawing. What would you say then? You would simply say that the child is between disordered scribbling and longitudinal scribbling. His mental growth would then be, probably, two-and-a-half, and a half a year up or down would not make any difference. How old is this child?

Student: Two years and ten months.

Lowenfeld: Two years and ten months is exactly what we said. Then, we would consider that average.

So, this is a very fine scribbling and a free scribbling. Of course, we would like to see more. The child, if he has many such spells of interrupted scribbling, well, we should encourage him probably more in his freedom. But if it only happens occasionally, we will simply ignore it. This definitely is an interrupted scribbling, as you can see, and one in which the child has not become aware of the total space or area which he has at his disposal; while here, in this drawing, he is marvelous. He not once goes beyond, goes even into the corner here, and goes back, and goes around over the whole page. So this is a very fine scribbling in pencil. Now, did I answer this question for you?

We simply consider that there are such stages of transition in which both developmental stages can be seen. Most often you will see that, when a child is in such a transitional stage, he will scribble in the advanced way when he's fresh and, when he gets tired, he will revert to the other stage, to the previous stage. This we see throughout the development of children— that when they get tired, they usually retrogress to a former stage if they are in a stage of transition. This should not in any way surprise us.

We still have not finished our discussion on the evaluation of scribbling, so we would like to refer again to the Evaluation Chart, Scribbling Stage, and look at the other characteristics. We had just discussed aesthetic growth and we had arrived at this conclusion: that aesthetic growth can be seen in such small children by the distribution of their scribbling over the area which they have at their disposal. All aesthetic growth consists of bringing into harmonious relationship our actions, our thoughts and imagery, our perceptions, our feelings, and our thinking. Whenever these are brought into some harmonious relationship, we engage in aesthetic growth. Since the thinking of the child during scribbling is mainly kinesthetic, we would say that if kinesthetic experiences are brought into harmonious relationship with the area of the paper which the child has at his disposal, then the child engages in aesthetic growth.

The last of the criteria we call creative growth, and we said previously that such growth is seen in children's independence, in their exploratory attitude, in their inventive attitude. So the first question deals exactly with attitude in children's scribblings: "Is the child independent in his scribbling?" We can only see it by observing the child. We cannot make a statement here. If a child is independent in his scribbling, you can see whether the child concentrates on his scribbling and doesn't look around. You can see whether the child needs someone else to stimulate him—for motivation. If he is independent in his scribbling, we would say—depending on how independent he is—"None," "Some," or "Much." "When scribbling with other children, does the child remain uninfluenced?" Well, this also can only be observed. So you see how important it is that we are present when children work and that we simply cannot answer certain questions unless we observe the child. You see, the next question is: "Is he generally opposed to imitating?" Does he create all by himself? Now, many children always say to their parents: "Do it for me. Can you do it? Do it again." We have to differentiate between children who investigate and experiment in this "doing it again." This is a stage in children's development when they love to see and to hear repetition. "A sheep goes, 'Mahha'."

"Do it again."

"Mahha."

"Again."

"Mahha."

You know that this is a kind of enjoyment which a child has, and it is not a lack of creative growth. But, if a child in his scribbling depends on others and needs to be fostered: "How would you do it?" or "Show me how you would do it," or "Can you draw something for me?"—all such questions are accounting for a lack of creativeness. "Why?" is another question. But the present status is a lack of creativeness. The "why" may be that the child has been inhibited by coloring books. Indeed, if a child is given coloring books early and has been shown how to fill them in, well, the child will always need coloring books and will rely upon them and will ask for them. This has destroyed some independence and has interfered with his investigatory attitudes, and now the child asks for them. Some of his potentially creative abilities, then, have been repressed. They no longer function; therefore, we don't see them. And since we are only judging what functions, we would then say: "This child is less creative."

"When naming his scribbling, does he develop stories independently?" Now, when naming the scribbling, we will watch. Does the child spontaneously say, "This is Mother going shopping; she is going to the A&P store," and he makes a motion in the meantime. "There she's picking up some groceries." And the child flows out with stories independently. This will be a more creative child than the one who says, "This is Mother," and no longer continues with the trend of thought and even depends on your questioning. So we will see from these questions whether the creativeness of the child functions. We will not see whether the child potentially is creative, because the child may be more creative than what functions.

Now we come to the real need for our evaluation. We will never see anything of the potential abilities as long as we remain with a single growth criteria. Now comes the shaking, and that's really the meat. There we will see and discover potential abilities; namely, we will now relate creative growth to emotional growth, and emotional growth to intellectual growth, and intellectual growth to perceptual growth, and so forth. And as soon as we see that there are great discrepancies, we may then say: "Well, this child could not function creatively because he has been inhibited emotionally." There we may discover such differences and may sense that there is more in the child than we can see in the single growth segments.

We can, for instance, discover that the child's intellectual advancement has not been able to function because the child engages in stereotypes and, therefore, he's backward in his development. Let us say you have a six-year-old child, and the six-year-old child doesn't function intellectually. You see that the child engages in stereotypes. Of course, you would say that, functionally, his intellect has not developed. But it may be due to the fact that the child has not established the freedom for learning so that he can use his intellect. We can see that, because the child frequently interrupts his scribbling or the child engages in stereotypes. Then we should be doubly cautious. Anything we think, we should keep to ourselves; because it is here where it becomes most important to us as teachers. We will then be more sensitive to the child and see that this child needs more encouragement in his emotional growth. The child will then unfold intellectually, also. As we have experienced it time and again in our children's art classes, the children come in restricted and then unfold and leave entirely different—moreso during the school year when we have them over longer periods than during the summer session. But this, indeed, happens. So, only when we bring into some relationship all of these components of growth will we discover some discrepancies. Out of these discrepancies, we then can sense some of the differences in children's growth.

It is here where intuition comes into play. You see, everyone who has worked in psychology and tries to interpret some of the projective techniques, such as the Rorschach tests, will know that all knowledge of a criterion—an analysis of Rorschach—will not help you unless you can bring into play all of these characteristics. That takes place by intuition to a great extent; that means, you sense those relationships rather than construct them. It is here where good teachers are differentiated from poor teachers. You see, teaching cannot be learned if you don't have it in here. In teaching, your intuitive abilities to enthuse a child and to make him feel with you and love you are not things which can be taught. They must be in you with all the friendliness and love which you have had in your past experiences. These qualities always will remain with you whether you would like to embrace the world or whether you would like to kick it. These are basic attitudes, and here is one of these examples where intuitive qualities are important.

So if you look at the total scribbling of the child, all of a sudden the picture puzzle will close in on yourself; and you will get a new attitude toward the child, although you will not be able to close in as well unless you have become sensitive to the details. It is for this purpose that we are taking part in this course. But we will have to digest it inside ourselves, and we have to use it whenever we are ready. Now, we have brought to an end the evaluation of scribbling; but unless we are able to use all our knowledge which we have accumulated in the classroom, it will not be of much help.

Therefore, it now becomes essential that we should talk about the important things which go on in a class, such as motivation (how should we motivate children during scribbling?) and the use of materials (what kind of materials should we use for children in scribbling?). Let me first talk about materials because it is a simpler matter, although in the book it is reversed in the discussion. I had it reversed and remained with it; but I think now that it might even be better to discuss materials first and then motivation, because after we know the materials which we would like to use we can better talk about how to motivate children with these materials.

Before we talk about materials, let me state a very important principle. We should always distinguish between procedures and techniques. A procedure in art consists merely of the handling of those parts of a material which are impersonal. Procedures can be taught and should be explained in a classroom situation. Technique, however, is how the procedure is used; and this is highly personal and must be left up to the child. I'll give you practical examples of the two. For instance, if we were to have the material watercolor, we would have a container with water and we would have a button which consists of paint. You should then say to the child: "Look, you first have to wet your brush. And then depending on how much you rub on the button, you will get the color darker or lighter. If you rub much on the button, you'll get your color so that you can't see through it." We call this opaque, depending on the level of the child and his understanding of language, of course. "You will also see that, when you use your brush very wet, the two colors may merge together. They will run. But if you use your color dry with not much water, you can see the single brush strokes." This all is still procedure. "Now you try it out for yourself. When you paint a sky, what will happen? Or when you paint anything, what will happen?" From now on, the child must have all his freedom in using the procedure in his own way. This will mean that the child develops his own technique or his own individual interpretation of the procedure.

If I explain it to the art education majors on a higher level—it's easier to explain it on a higher level—it would then be—for example, in the procedure of etching—that you would say: "In etching, you take first a copper plate, or a zinc plate; there are different ways we can etch, but the procedure is this way. You first cover the zinc plate with asphalt. Asphalt does not let the acid penetrate into the zinc plate. Then you take your etching needle, and you scratch out those lines which you later will cover with acid. The acid will only penetrate into the zinc plate on those parts where the asphalt has been removed. Now, the broader the line, the thicker the etching—the wider the etching. The longer you let it in the acid, the deeper will be the etching. The acid will eat into the plate and the deeper the line, the darker it will be; because when you print, there will be much printing ink that accumulates in this deep groove, much more than in a shallow groove. This is all procedure. Now you do your etching." We should not interfere with the individual way of the person in using strong or bold lines or in shading or in remaining with lines only. This is his individual way of expression, his technique for which he and only he is responsible.

I've explained this so clearly and so intensely, because I believe that we often interfere with the child's technique—his individual way of using a procedure. If we keep the two apart, the impersonal attributes of the material and the individual way of using it, then we have clarified an important issue. Is there any question about it in your mind? The more we come down to simple materials, the less we have to say about procedure. For instance, the procedure with a crayon—one of the procedures may be that you call the child's attention to the fact that using the crayon with pressure and with no pressure result in different line qualities. The child may also arrive at that realization by trial and error. But, then, leave it up to the child whether he wants to use different pressures. In using crayon, I wouldn't give any explanation on procedures, because the procedure is so simple that it is almost self-evident. As you go a little further in the complexity of materials, you have to explain some of the procedures; but leave the child the freedom of applying these procedures in his own way.

Student: What about demonstrations? For example, would this only be done verbally?

Lowenfeld: No, you can demonstrate procedures as much as you want, as long as you do not develop in these procedures your own technique—that means, your individual interpretation—and thus use your procedure wrongly. When you say, "Now, children, you know you can use the chalk many ways: you can draw a very fine line and you can draw an intense line. It can be so fine that from a distance you can't even see it"—this is still procedure. When you say, "If you want to, you can also use the crayon broadside"—this is also procedure. But if you say, "Now, children, you know you can use the crayon to make a fine line and you can also use the crayon to make a strong line as I do. And you can use your crayon also to make a broad line as in my drawing"—well, you explain here your own technique with the procedure and, therefore, impose upon the children your own concept. Do you see what I mean? Now, we must not mix the two. A procedure is only the explanation of a material and not any interpretation of it. In the same way—when you make an etching or explain the procedure for an etching, you can have a plate on which you simply explain and demonstrate the different grooves and then etch this plate and print it. It doesn't say anything but is just a scratching plate, one on which you have tried out the different kinds of lines and etchings. This is still procedure. But if you make an etching of your own and show it to your students and say, "See how differently you can etch?" then your students will look at your etching and will say, "Yes, I'm going to do the same thing." You see, they will then use your own individual interpretation for their own individual expression. Therefore, you have imposed upon them. Is this clear?

Student: Do I understand that it's all right to let children practice procedures on a piece of paper?

Lowenfeld: No, I did not say that. We don't teach procedure for the procedure's sake—there's no sense in that. You're simply developing craftsmanship, or something of that sort, without giving it any relationship to feeling, thinking, and perceiving. We never separate the one from the other except when we explain it as teachers. I did not say the children should separate them. I said we teachers should.

Student: But shouldn't we help children to try out different types of procedures?

Lowenfeld: No, children try them out with their own techniques. They try them out while they express themselves. Why should they be separated? Then procedures become exercises—boring—with no quality or expressive tendencies. If you separate the one from the other in children, you arrive at the dullest kind of teaching. We separate grammar from expression; and that's bad, because a child never develops an urge to master a procedure (grammar) merely for the procedure's (grammar's) sake. Unfortunately, in teaching music we still do that. It's an unfortunate thing, because most of the children will begin to lose their real enjoyment of playing. Some of the good music teachers already use that which we know in art education, but many of them don't. They teach first the scales—and this is procedure—instead of learning the scales by expressing one's self and seeing how a scale can do different things within a song or within various forms of musical expression. But here we are backward—you know, those who still separate grammar from expression. Yes?

Student: What happens when we show them pictures, such as showing them watercolors that have been painted by one person in one technique?

Lowenfeld: Well, with children I would not mix up appreciation of pictures and procedural explanations, because the child has not developed an understanding of the final product. He is not interested in the technical devices which an artist uses. So I would never, in an appreciation of art class on the elementary level, go into technical explanations whatsoever. I would only remain with a content analysis, if we may call it that. That means, the first thing I would ask the child is: "Do you like it? What do you like in this picture? Why do you like it?" And the child would then react to it. I would try to make the child more and more feel or empathize or identify with the situation which is expressed in this painting, but I would never go into a technical explanation.

Student: What problems are there in having a child listen to a piece of music without words and make up his own story and own drawing?

Lowenfeld: That's fine. If a child listens to music and interprets it in his own way, I don't see anything wrong; because any stimulus, whether it involves sounds or visions or dreams or imagination or stories, can be used for the individual interpretation of the child. Music is often a very good stimulus for getting the child's imagination to become free and flexible.

We have now distinguished (differentiated) between procedure and technique. Another important part in a discussion of the use of materials is that we should know that a material is only good for the child which serves the child's needs. That cuts out a number of materials, in the very beginning, which are detrimental for the child. I'll explain this when we discuss the materials that are good for scribbling. But, may I say that I'm opposing, clearly opposing, the point of view which many art educators have when they say: "Give the child all the materials, and the child will select what he wants. Give him paint, give him plenty of materials. This is the most important thing." I hear art educators say that who have considerable reputations. I'm clearly opposed to it, not only by experience but by experiments. It is not good if a child is frustrated by materials which do not serve the child's needs. In the same way, you do not give the child all kinds of foods and say, "Well, you select what is good for you and that's all," and leave it up to the child. You don't do that, because you know that the child does not discriminate between what is good for him and what is not good for him. We also do not confront the child with all kinds of art materials. The child will simply gasp and be confused, because the child·will shift from the one to the other. The one may be frustrating; the other may be stimulating. We are really superfluous as teachers in our guidance if we promote this attitude.

I'll give you now an example of how this works in scribbling. We know that the major need of the child during scribbling is motor coordination—first, motor activity; then, motor coordination. This is tremendously important. Arnold Gesell, the child psychologist—with whom many of you may be acquainted—in his latest volume promotes kinesthetic experiences as the most fundamental experiences in child development. It took him many years to arrive at this conclusion: he says all environmental contact is made through kinesthesis—language is developed through kinesthesis; social growth is developed through kinesthesis. So, motor activity—that means, the activity of our body—is of utmost importance. If we know that, then we know that it is very important during the scribbling stage to foster motor activity, or motor coordination, and then to shift from thinking in terms of kinesthesis to thinking in terms of mental pictures. So, a material which does not promote motor activity is not a good material for this age or for this developmental stage.

Now, let's find out what would happen if I were to give watercolors to a child of two or two-and-a-half or three. What would happen? The child would take the watercolors, and he would start scribbling. Soon the brush would be dry, and he would start to engrave with the metal part on through the sheet. The sheet would tear; the child would be frustrated. He would not see any motion. Or, if the brush were wet, the child would make lines and the lines would merge and would render a sheet with paint strokes which could not be distinguished as such in their motions. The child may end up with a solid area; and the child would no longer have the enjoyment of controlling his lines, because he would end up with this. This scribbling has not been motivated and is just one of the scribblings which has naturally been done. I'll tell you about it later.

So, the major material during scribbling will be one with which the child can control his motions and get the satisfaction of continued or repeated motions; because if he doesn't get the satisfaction, he will become frustrated. Just like you—if you don't get satisfaction out of some activity, you will become frustrated because you don't see any results. You don't feel any accomplishment; you just don't feel that anything happened. So the best material for children will be crayons—indeed, thick crayons—probably the type of crayons which the child can hold this way, with all his fingers around it; a marking crayon which the child can use, with pressure on it, to go over the whole page and the marking crayon will not break.

If you don't have marking crayons, I strongly advise you not to give children new boxes of crayons but to always break the crayons before you give them out. The reason for this: many children are brought up with the attitude that they should keep things new, and they will. Then you have a kind of competitive situation in a classroom in which one child points out, "I still have my whole box." Another child uses the crayon very efficiently, but all of a sudden the crayon breaks and the child is frustrated. I've seen children start to cry when a crayon breaks. Yes, and they sit there with the two halves and then they put them back, and the crayon is no longer new. Even if the points are disappearing, children who are used to keeping things in good shape get frustrated. So the best thing to do to prevent this is to break the crayons. Children can use them more effectively, anyway. You double your materials, you know. Put them on trays and put them in front of the children. The children will select the kind of crayon stumps which they like to use. Best, of course, is to buy those crayons that are now on the market which have no paper wrapper at all.

"Is it essential—is it necessary—that we provide the child with many colored crayons?" No, it isn't necessary at all for scribbling. The child most definitely remains with one color in continuous scribbling. The experiments which we made when we gave children different-colored crayons showed that most of the children remain with one color. They just pick yellow or red or blue and remain with this color throughout their scribbling. Only those children change colors who lack confidence. They like to pick up one and then the other; through this they interrupt their scribbling, which is most welcome to them because they lack confidence. So, in the beginning, I would say that a black crayon would be the best thing for scribbling. Don't feel badly if you must give them black crayons.

"What kind of paper should you use?" Well, smooth paper is better than rough paper. Newsprint, unprinted newsprint and also printed newsprint, serves the purpose excellently. You can use old newspapers with crayons, because the child neglects the print underneath and simply scribbles over it. For this, old newspaper is fine. Don't be choosy in materials according to adult standards. The child won't see the print. For him, the paper is simply gray; and the child goes over it.

"What about size?" Adjust sizes to the child, please, and don't be persistent that children should use a particular size. Don't make the size too large. May I say that the sizes 12 by 18 inches or 18 by 24 inches are probably the largest you should use for scribbling children, but 12 by 18 inches may be much better. In my experiment, I used 12 by 18 inches. Sometimes when children only covered part of the paper, I gave them smaller paper to find out whether they still would draw into a corner and whether the smaller paper would fit better to their own size. This is a very nice and simple experiment which you can do with your own child if you have one at home or with children in kindergarten. If you see that a child reacts by drawing in one corner, like here, and does not use the rest of the paper continuously, then you simply give him a smaller sheet of paper.

LECTURE 13

Methodological Approaches for Johnny and Mary;
Scribbling: Value of Motion for the Very Young Child;
Fingerpainting; Other Art Media; and Motivation

This is the situation:[6] "Johnny is eight years old. His mother likes to show him how to draw more accurately. When he draws an animal or a person doing something, his mother will say, 'Oh, that doesn't look like a rabbit's face. Make it shorter, like this.' She then draws one for him. Or she will say, 'The cowboy's arms are too long. They're out of proportion.' Gradually Johnny has shown less and less interest in drawing until now he prefers just to spend his time coloring the pictures in the third-grade reader.

"Below are four alternate teaching methods to use in aiding Johnny to regain his ability to express himself. Place a 1 opposite the method you would most recommend. Place a 2 opposite the choice of the second best, 3 opposite the third best, and 4 opposite the least effective one." Now A is: "Encourage him to talk about what he likes to do; have him act out what he does; concentrate on how he feels inside while doing it; then have him draw again. B: Encourage him to continue drawing, but supply him with many illustrations of animals and people in a variety of positions so that he can better understand physical proportions." Then "C: Suggest that he work in another medium, such as clay, and avoid asking him to draw anymore; however, encourage him to talk about his own experience and express his own feelings about that experience through clay." Then "D: Have him visit the local zoo and make sketches of rabbits. In class, have children pose for him in various positions so that he can better comprehend how the human figure actually appears in action."

Now, let's first discuss Johnny and his reaction and the reaction of Mother. Johnny is eight years old. We haven't talked about an eight-year-old child. So far, as you know, we have just talked about the child in general and the scribbling child, who is from two to four. So we are not prepared to say anything about Johnny, who is eight years old, except what we have

---

6. Dr. Lowenfeld had given the class a test which included situational questions. Here, he is discussing and evaluating several of these questions as a post-test learning experience.

learned as a general basic philosophy. Now we hear that his mother likes to show him how to draw more accurately. Well, that's no good. Why? Well, "accurately" is an adult concept, while Johnny has his own concept. Therefore, to impose a concept which is called "accurate" would not be good for Johnny. He would lose confidence in his own way of expression. "When he draws an animal or a person doing something, his mother will say, 'Oh, that doesn't look like a rabbit's face.' " Well, as we may hear it from Mother, "Make it shorter," because the way she sees the rabbit is different from the way Johnny conceives of the rabbit.

You see, seeing and conceiving are somewhat different: conceiving is a mental activity, while seeing is a perceptual activity. Do you understand? Now, Johnny may simply conceive of a rabbit. A rabbit has a head, and he has two eyes, and he has a snout. According to that, he may make it a triangle or a square or an oval or a circle. But Mother insists that it should be shorter and not that long. Then she draws one for him. Is this good? No? Why? Well, it encourages imitation for imitation's sake, as we heard—forced imitation, you know.

Student: It frustrates him because he can't possibly draw like that?

Lowenfeld: He could not possibly draw like Mother does because he's eight years and Mother may be twenty-six or thirty, more or less. Now, she draws one for him, and she says: "The cowboy's arms are too long. They are out of proportion." Well, what looks out of proportion for Mother may be just right in proportion for Johnny, because Johnny doesn't think in terms of visual proportions but in terms of how he feels. So the jumping rabbit may have very big legs because he's jumping and uses his legs; and Johnny, while identifying himself with the rabbit very closely, adds long legs to the rabbit. "Gradually Johnny has shown less and less interest in drawing until now he prefers just to spend his time coloring the pictures in the third-grade reader." This is a situation which may be actually encountered.

Now, first we heard, "Encourage him to talk about what he likes to do; have him act out what he does; concentrate on how he feels inside while doing it; then have him draw again"—this is, of course, the first choice we always should take. We should not assume that the child is already lost or has lost confidence and cannot go on. We should first try to motivate him as we would like children to be motivated; namely, we should encourage his thinking, his knowledge about a rabbit, and his feeling—how the rabbit jumps. Have him even act out how the rabbit jumps. That involves him and gives him still greater opportunity for self-identification and, thus, to integrate his knowledge, his feeling, and his perceiving into his drawings. So that was Number 1.

But if this doesn't work, we would still not give him an illustration, nor would we immediately go to a zoo and show him animals so that he could sketch from nature; because Johnny is eight years old. We should rather try to shift to another medium. Maybe he hasn't been affected in his mind in working in another medium. Mother only has shown him and has imposed upon his drawings; so he still may be more flexible in another medium. So, we give him another medium. That means Number 2 was then C: "Suggest that he work in another medium, such as clay, and avoid asking him to draw any more . . . ," since in drawing he may have established a stereotype or a kind of frustration because he has been frustrated in drawing by his mother. "However, encourage him to talk about his own experience"—we can do that at any rate—and then it says, "And express his own feelings about that experience through clay."

Number 3 . . . if using another medium does not work, probably we should go to a zoo and show him rabbits or similar animals which encourage clear perception. But it would be a method which would not be advisable at this time, because he may not be able to draw from nature. If the child already suffers from a feeling of inferiority or has been frustrated in his drawing attempts, he might want to try drawing the right proportion, as it is in nature, because Mother has told him to draw it so. But it would be a less advisable situation. With normal children who have not been frustrated, it's all right to go out, and very good even, and confront them with nature. In our children's art classes, we go out and look at the lambs and the sheep; and the children get a closer feeling and then go home and draw with the picture in mind. You see, that is possible.

However, it is entirely impossible to say, "Encourage him to continue drawing, but supply him with many illustrations of animals and people . . . ," you see, because that encourages copying. So, B would be Number 4.

The next question was: "Mary, eight years old, sometimes exaggerates the size of her figures in her drawings. Occasionally she draws a person much larger than the house into which the person is going. Sometimes she draws the trees and houses much larger than we normally see them in relationship to human figures. Rank the following four statements, in order, from the most reasonable to the least reasonable method of handling her." First, "A: Recommend her case to a psychiatrist for consultation and investigation; B: Watch her more closely than those who do not exaggerate relative sizes of figures and environment; C: Pay less attention to her than to her classmates who do not engage in exaggerations; and D: Consider her a normal child."

Well, first let's look at Mary. Mary is eight years old. We haven't discussed her age level, as you know, but only the basic philosophy. "She sometimes exaggerates the size of her figures in her drawings." Well, we know that all children sometimes exaggerate the figures in drawings, especially if a figure is more important that an environmental factor; so this is normal. "Sometimes she draws the trees and houses much larger than we normally see them. . . ." Of course. When the trees and houses appear to her as very large compared to her in size, then she will exaggerate them.

149

And sometimes she exaggerates the human figure in comparison to the house—much larger than we normally see it.

In rating the statements, we would never recommend her to a psychiatrist, because we know that she is normal. We would, therefore, consider her a normal child. This is Number 1 and was letter D. We would even pay less attention to her than to those children who always draw accurately in proportion. Why?

Student: They have been influenced by adult concepts.

Lowenfeld: You see, if a child always draws accurately in proportion, then we should keep in mind that this child has no specific emotional relationship to any specific item; and that is not good.

Children should exaggerate certain parts to which they are more closely emotionally bound. This child suppresses her emotional feelings toward a certain item and everything appears to be alike in size. There is a certain stereotype regarding size if a child always—a child of eight years—draws things accurately. "Watch her more closely than those who do not exaggerate relative sizes of figures and environment"—we would not do this. And "Recommend her case to a psychiatrist . . . ," we would do even less.

So the correct sequence of the statements is: "Consider her a normal child"; "Pay less attention to her than to her classmates who do not exaggerate"; then "Watch her more closely than those who do not exaggerate"; and "Recommend her case to a psychiatrist." It was very good reasoning for those who did it correctly. It was not an easy sequence for those who engaged in it for the first time in their thinking; therefore, I'm very proud that a large number of you answered it correctly. Now, let us continue with our discussion.

We had finished our evaluations and had started to talk about the difference between procedures and techniques in relation to scribbling. We said that every child has to find his own way of applying materials. We also said that no materials are good for a child on any level if they do not serve the child's needs. We have found that the child's needs during scribbling are mainly motor activity to establish motor coordination and to enjoy his motions. We now know that to gain confidence in one's own body motions is almost the key to freedom in your later life. Once you become restricted in one motor activity or body motion, you may become restricted in others. This may be shown in many cases.

At Bellevue Hospital, for instance, they have established some relationship between restrictions in scribbling and stammering—stuttering. We have not been able to establish that in our own investigation on stammering and stuttering, which was done by Dr. Wright Putney as one of our doctoral dissertations, an excellent dissertation. However, he was not dealing with subjects who were small enough to be in the scribbling stage, so it was not included in his dissertation.

In the Bellevue Hospital study, some relationship between stereotypes in scribbling and stammering was established. This shouldn't be surprising to us. Why? Both involve motor coordination. Proper speech habits are established at the very same time when children start scribbling. Do you see? Between two and two-and-one-half years, most children establish their speech habits. But it is also the time when the child starts to coordinate his motions with his vision. Now, that is most interesting and only confirms our philosophy that one trait in human development does not remain isolated. So what the child does in the motions with his hands may be seen also in his motions elsewhere, such as with his tongue, with his whole mouth, and in the relationship between breathing, speaking habits, and so forth. We should know now that, if we don't give the child a material which encourages motor coordination, we may fail to reach the child in a very, very important activity. I can't stress that enough.

I hope I have some kindergarten teachers here. I'm certain I have some future or present mothers with me. Mrs. March related to me yesterday—or day before yesterday at our evening gathering—that it would be wonderful for future mothers to have this course. I agree, yes. For instance, it would be wonderful if high school students on the senior level would get something of our basic philosophy, because it is there where we would get the best break. They are the future mothers. Where should we start, if not there? But we have not come that far in our break, that means, in reaching individuals. This very class which I have here indicates that we reach individuals on various levels of understanding who even voluntarily come here and try to gain knowledge of what art means to our children and to our future society. Administrators are becoming increasingly aware of the meaning of art for children and thus pay more attention to it.

Even people in industry are becoming more aware of how we can make people more creative in their thinking. This starts always at the root. Yet, we have not arrived at the general concept that we must not begin at the top. It is much more difficult to make people more creative on the level of adulthood or even adolescence than on the level of childhood. We always realize things at the top level first, because we discover them there. That we have to compete in industry with all kinds of industries, as you know, is a top-level industrial problem at the present time. So all kinds of books appear and requests appear with regard to making people more creative in industry. But they don't think yet in terms that they will become more creative if we start on the childhood level. Do you see? It's still the cure of the rash—which has been caused by an upset stomach—with the use of ointments on the surface. The upset stomach reaches far back into childhood; and if we want to cure it, we have to begin in childhood. This is very important. So we should know that materials are very important at all times.

Today, I would like to discuss other materials which may be of advantage. One of the materials which was very much in fashion sometime ago is fingerpainting. I hope you all know what fingerpainting is. I'm quite sure—being in an elementary classroom as art, elementary, or special education teachers—that you have come across fingerpainting. Who does not know what fingerpainting is? Will you raise your hands? Don't be modest. You are not modest, you are silly, if you don't raise your hand if you don't know, because we are frank with one another. There's nothing wrong with not knowing about fingerpainting. So, who does not know about fingerpainting? Well, then I presume that you all know what fingerpainting is.

Now, you see, we have done special research with regard to fingerpainting, because we also wanted to find out what children do when they do fingerpainting and how they react. We placed some of our graduate students from a previous class, quite a few years ago, in nursery schools. We found that children, when they do fingerpainting, actually don't do it for the motor activity but do it for other purposes—unless they are catered to in this kind of activity. That means, the teacher says, "Now, children, we are using the fingerpaints with free motions," and the children will then imitate merely what the teacher says; but still they revert to other things, such as clapping their hands and enjoying the consistency of the fingerpaints.

Through questionnaires and through firsthand observation, we have established that those children who try to clap their hands (and this was the majority) retrogress into another stage, the stage which Sigmund Freud calls the anal-erotic stage—anus, anal, anal-erotic. You know what erotic means? Erotic means love. Eros is the god of love, and erotic means related to love. The anus, you know, is the opening from which our excrements leave. When children play with their excrement, they fall in love with it; because they want to keep it. You see, it's something of their own, psychoanalytically seen. Almost all children naturally go through a stage which Freud calls the anal-erotic stage, the stage in which children love to play with their own dirt. At two or two-and-a-half years, the average child has usually grown out of this stage. But we have found that playing with dirt-like consistencies, such as fingerpaints, may lead them back again to the enjoyment of playing with dirt.

Now, may I say that there is nothing wrong with playing with dirt, and don't ever discourage your child during this stage when he wants to play with a consistency which is dirt-like—but not with his own excrements, because we should encourage children to grow up and become socially acceptable. There are certain things which we must not encourage; but unless we give the child a substitute where the child can satisfy his needs, such as sand, wet sand, and let him play and let the sand go through his fingers so that he will get the satisfaction of playing with sand, we have actually no right to discourage a child. Do you see? So we give the child pails of wet sand in kindergarten and let the child exercise and get his feelings satisfied.

When we give the child a material which is used for purposes other than the satisfaction of the need for consistency, then we would like the child to use it accordingly. We have found that the direct use of their fingers with fingerpaints actually retrogresses them into a former stage of development. We think of the child as one growing from the stage of direct use of their fingers to a stage where there is an indirect use, such as holding the crayon and using the crayon. There is no longer the direct contact with the fingers, except in clay work where it is intended to be. We find that with the normal child—and I emphasize the normal child, the average child—there should be no use of fingerpaints in kindergarten at a time when the child really cannot take advantage of this beautiful material or medium. We will see that, later on, the child can take beautiful advantage and can do all kinds of things with fingerpaints in the elementary classroom, when the distance to the anal-erotic stage is already far enough so that he will not retrogress. Do you understand? You retrogress easier when the distance is small to the stage which you have just left. Then you revert. But if the distance is large enough, well, there are too many experiences in between, and your desires have changed.

Student: About what age would the child again be able to do finger-painting?

Lowenfeld: In elementary school where, let us say, one stage after scribbling has passed. Perhaps at ages eight, nine, and up; but not between two and four, because here the average child is too close to this stage.

Now, this is for the special education people, in particular, but for all of us to know. If a child, for instance, scribbles in a stereotyped fashion or interruptedly—that means, if we feel that the child has not gained his motor enjoyment and, therefore, interrupts his scribbling frequently or scribbles in stereotypes—then we need an additional motivation for the child to engage in free motions. This additional motivation may be the consistency that the child loves to play with—dirt or fingerpaints, as a matter of fact, and, therefore, he would rather like to do that than play with crayons. We may then prefer this little retrogression to free him in his motor activity. Therefore, it has been proved that motor activity with mentally retarded or emotionally maladjusted children may properly be stimulated by fingerpainting.

We said that a smooth paper is better than a rough paper. For finger-painting, a special paper is necessary because fingerpainting must not be done on any absorbent surface. It must be done on a glued, smooth paper. There is a fingerpainting paper on the market; or, if you don't want to use that because it is too expensive, use kraft paper. Kraft paper, which is glued properly and is non-absorbent, can be used. You can also use waxed paper if you put into your fingerpaints some glycerine; otherwise, they will curdle and will not stay on the waxed paper. But best, of course, is a glued paper or the very best fingerpaint paper, which is also a very smooth-surfaced paper. Yes?

Student: How about glazed shelf paper?

Lowenfeld: Very good, excellent, yes.

Now, what about giving the child different-colored crayons? Well, I told you at the very beginning, one dark-colored crayon—a black crayon, a blue crayon, a red crayon—is best; but not a yellow crayon, because with a yellow crayon the child cannot as easily control his motions as with a darker crayon. When the child moves into the naming stage, the child should have at his disposal different colors; because he may want to signify with different-colored crayons that there are different actions or that there are different objects.

When I said crayon is the best means, I did not mean that we should exclude other media; because other media may be used for different purposes than for the purpose of motor control. And, certainly, the scribbling child has different needs than those of merely controlling his motions or engaging in motor activity. Sometimes we should give the child poster paint. Some of the emotional needs can sometimes be better satisfied than the needs of motor activity by means of poster paint and a brush. So, there is nothing wrong in giving the child some poster paint now and then.

What are the occasions? I'd just like to give you one example which we had recently in our children's art classes. One child has a sister, and there was a great rivalry when the new baby sister was born. Well, it's always a problem. The child would like to do away with the sister; but, of course, the child is being taught by mother that she should kiss the newborn, the new sister, and should be friendly to her with the best intentions. We all would like to eliminate this feeling of jealousy; but deep inside, there will be some jealousy because no child is a superhuman being. So there must be some way to give the child opportunities for living through this jealousy without suppressing it.

Now, we had the following here in our classes—the following episode of the child who got a new baby sister. The child was scribbling very properly before but retrogressed when the baby was born. The child was already naming her scribbling; but, when the baby was born, the child retrogressed into disordered scribbling. Such retrogressions are common. But children grow out of them soon if they are handled well. We gave the child paint because we felt that at this time a change in medium would be good, and maybe some of the inward feelings could be expressed better by paint than by crayon. What happened was this. The child started to scribble first with the paint; slopped the paint on the paper; and then, all of a sudden, the child started to name again, saying, "This is my baby sister." And then she took the whole painting and painted it over so that you couldn't see baby sister at all and enjoyed it tremendously—that means, she wiped her out, and no one could see baby sister again. Such aggressive tendencies can easily be painted out if the child is given an opportunity to do so. It cannot be as easily done in crayon, because you will always see baby sister through the lines—you cannot eliminate her—nor can you as easily slop something on top as you can with paint. So, if there are such tendencies—and we never know—they are always on a continuum from being just present to being strongly present in the child. We never know if a child needs an additional means of emotional outlet. So we give the child, all children, some paint now and then so the child may engage in such activities.

Our main medium during scribbling is crayon, and we don't even need many colors, just one, but we also use clay or plasticene. In my book I said plasticene is preferable, but I mean only preferable for those who cannot store their clay. Storing clay is always connected with keeping it in a damp place so that it will not become hard, and, therefore, it is more difficult to use in a kindergarten. You can use clay, just as well if it is not too wet, especially now that we have plastic bags. Clay keeps very nicely and stays moist in plastic bags; but in plastic bags, it may develop some odor which children don't like. You'll have to take this into consideration. It's always good to keep children in a pleasant environment, which includes also a consideration for the odor of the clay. We have, then, other media such as poster paint which occasionally should be used. Working in materials will not be discussed in detail in this course, because you have another basic course in which working in crafts and materials is discussed.

I would like to point out at this time that, indeed, giving children an acquaintance with various kinds of textures cannot be started soon enough, if it is merely for appreciation—to touch velvet, to touch feathers, and to enjoy themselves. I'm not in favor of forcing children to make collages as early as that and of putting them together, because children have no appreciation whatsoever for harmonious organization at a time when they scarcely can handle those materials. It's difficult for a child to handle feathers, and the establishment of some form of organization with collage materials is almost impossible.

Now, how should we motivate children in scribbling? An important principle should be applied at all times—the principle that we should always start on the level of the individual and should extend the frame of reference of the individual beyond his thinking, feeling, and perceiving. So, when a child scribbles, his frame of reference is motion. His frame of reference is not scribbling, please, because we refer always from the drawing activity back to the child; and for the child, scribbling is motion. Therefore, his frame of reference is motion.

Now, is there any doubt about this? Please ask, because this is a very, very important principle which we will use all the way through our course. If we would like to extend the frame of reference of the child, it does not mean we want to extend his scribbling. The frame of reference is motor activity—his enjoyment in motion—that means, the child's basic experience. The basic experience of the child is movement. If the child, for instance, does not move freely, we use other forms of movement to extend his frame of reference, whether the movement is dancing, running, playing tag, skating, swinging, or doing something—whatever the movement is. Whatever refers to motion, now refers to the frame of reference of the child. So how can we then free a child who, let us say, moves in a restricted fashion, who interrupts his scribbling frequently? Our motivation should then be to extend the frame of reference of motion to a motion which is not frequently interrupted. Could you name one? Running, skating, swinging—do you see? These would be motions to which we now could refer.

I've just tried it out with Robin. Some of you met him at the picnic. You know, it's always wonderful to see how methods work, even if you know they will work. You can refer, even with a two- or two-and-a-half-year-old child, to motions outside. Robin is now two-and-a-half; he's my grandchild. Now he's running around on the paper. He calls me Pompa, which is Grandpa; and he says: "Pompa, I'm running, I'm running." And he runs with his crayon around on the paper in beautiful free motions. Do you see?

You can also establish a restriction for freedom; that means, a frame of reference to the boundaries of the paper. Let us say, the child always scribbles beyond the paper and onto the paper which is underneath. First, let me say this. If you have a sheet of paper on which the child scribbles and if the sheet of paper is on a desk or cardboard, the cardboard or the desk or whatever is underneath should be of a different color than the paper on which the child scribbles. Why? So he sees the difference, you see? Many kindergarten teachers say that we can scribble on newspapers and place newspapers underneath. This is not good, because we would like the child at some point or another to establish a harmonious relationship between his motions and the area of the paper which he has at his disposal. Why do we want to do that? I wish one of the elementary school teachers would give me an answer. Why do we want to do that?

Student: Only because we would like to give the child a feeling for boundary.

Lowenfeld: Is there another reason for it?

Student: For aesthetic growth.

Lowenfeld: To force aesthetic growth? What does that mean? Look, I will give you an example which you will understand. You have a weekly allowance, which you call your budget, with which you can obtain food? You shouldn't go beyond it, no? That means you should stay within the limit of your pocketbook. That means you bring your food into a harmonious relationship with what you can spend. True? You relate one thing, food, to another thing, your pocketbook. You have to remain within this boundary. That's also part of aesthetic growth. Economy in relating one thing to another is, of course, a part of aesthetic growth. But it also means something else for you. You want to get the best for the amount of money which you have. You don't want to keep only within the boundaries, but you also shop around and find out how you can use it most adequately. So you bring economy, in a deeper sense, into relationship with what you have and with the best that you can get. This is very important. This is exactly what we stimulate for here, not just with regard to your pocketbook but for every situation—namely, to bring one thing into relationship with another. The given thing is your budget, and the flexible thing is the kind and amount of food which you can buy. The given thing is the boundary of the paper; the flexible things are the motions and how you handle them. Do you see these relationships?

There are many relationships in life to which you can apply that. A deeper philosophical relationship, of course, is how you can get into a harmonious relationship with yourself—your limitations and your possibilities. Only a few can do it; but once you do it, then you feel at peace with yourself. You are not always looking over the fence at what others have, but you try to get along peacefully and happily and thank God for what you have. And I'm not speaking theoretically. I thanked God when I was alive in a cellar in Austria when the Nazis were hunting for me, because others were no longer alive. So I'm not speaking theoretically. I am speaking from all levels up. Now I thank God for what I have, probably even undeserved, because, as you know, my restrictions are myself. You see, from getting along with your budget to getting along with yourself are the implications in keeping within the boundaries in scribbling. I hope I imbued this very deeply in you so that we are not thinking merely of external reasons.

Now, when you keep your child within the boundaries, that means that the child learns to recognize early in the stage of scribbling his possibilities and his limitations. The possibilities are to use the whole paper, and the limitations are his boundaries—that the paper is only a certain size. How can we encourage this? By extending the frame of reference. "Robin, now look, think how you would play and run around somewhere which is surrounded by water. Oh, you could not run into the water, you know. What would happen, Robin? You mustn't run into the water. Why? Can you swim? Because you can't run in water. Can you run on water? Oh, no! Oh, no! So let's be careful. Now look, all around your paper is water. Now we make a game. Let's find out." And now the child plays the game. You know, he goes into the farthest corner and looks at me and laughs. In this way, we establish a higher responsibility for the self in regard to movement. Do you see? And that can't start early enough. That means, we bring into harmonious relationship the marks on the paper to the boundaries, not for the sake of boundaries but for the sake of bringing one thing into harmonious relationship with another, as you know; and this goes all the way up into spiritual, deeply spiritual, experiences. Now you can also say: "Well, if this were surrounded by a fence, could you run into the fence? You would hurt yourself if you ran into the fence, so you must remain within the fence. Look, your paper has a fence around it. Now let's see how we can run on the paper, but not into the fence." Do you see? We extend the frame of reference. These are the motivations for scribbling; but there is no need for such motivations for the average child, because the average child will use the whole paper. He will freely scribble and will not need any additional motivation. Only the child who has become restricted in his movements will need additional motivation.

I have not finished the last motivation, which involves the naming of scribbling. I will briefly cover it so we can begin tomorrow with the next stage. The naming of scribbling, however, needs to be motivated also with the average child, because it is important to give the child confidence as soon as he discovers this very, very important stage of the change from thinking in terms of kinesthetic experience to mental pictures. We must extend the frame of reference of the child concerning the newly won confidence of thinking in terms of mental pictures. So, if the child says, "This is a choo-choo train," we simply go on and ask him questions about the choo-choo train. "Does it go fast? Who sits in the choo-choo train?" Even if we don't see any reference in his scribbling to our questions, we should encourage the child's thinking in terms of mental pictures and not in terms of his scribbling. His thinking in terms of mental pictures, however, is encouraged if we simply continue that particular frame of mind of the child. "Mother is going shopping. What is she shopping for? Where does she go?" and so forth. We go on with the child's thinking so as to encourage him and give him confidence in this type of thinking. Now, I hope you know what scribbling means, and I hope you understand it.

LECTURE 14

The Pre-Schematic Stage: Group Motivation, Discovering a Relationship between Drawing and Experience, Percepts and Concepts, Accidents in Art Work, and Analysis of Drawings

You can tell children in great detail what happens in winter when birds don't find any food, when they are flying around and flapping their wings. And then you ask, "Who has ever watched birds?" Now all of the children can participate and give their individual reactions with regard to their own sensitivity to their environment and to themselves. "Who has ever felt like a bird when it is hungry and flying?" And the same approach that you use with birds, you can also use with other things, such as playing tag, or experiences on a picnic, or whatever experiences refer to topics in which all children in grades one, two, three, and four have participated.

You give them a mass motivation which is like being present at the same experience, at the same situation.[7] Grade one, grade two, grade three, grade four can all watch a football game or can go to a fair, a country fair, or can go to a circus. And grade one, grade two, grade three, grade four will all come home with different kinds of impressions. You actually focus your attention on the individual after the motivation. But, first, you have motivated all four grades, probably at the same time, by an intense feeling of participation in the situation; that means, you tried hard to make them identify themselves with the environment and the action which took place. Such a motivation, by necessity—because of the action or the environment—may not be particularly focused at any one grade. Usually, we would give a different kind of motivation to a first grade, or a second or third or fourth grade, as you shall hear today. But it will not do harm to any of these grades if we give a common motivation with which they all can identify, such as: "Did you watch the circus move into town? How did they put up their tents? Did you see the elephant pulling on the ropes? What else did they

7. The discussion concerning group motivation of several grade levels simultaneously is in response to a question from a student in the class.

159

do?" And Mary, who is in the first grade, can just as well answer as John, who is in the fourth grade. They will give you their reactions. But, then, after you have distributed materials to all of them—probably the first graders may have crayons, while the second graders may have poster paint; and the third graders may have poster paint, too; and the fourth graders may already have watercolor or thinner poster paint—and after the motivation, you say, "Now, let's all express our experience." Then you go around and give different kinds of suggestions to the first grader than you give to the fourth grader. It is here, in your reactions and in your after-motivation, if we may call it that, that individual differences at the various grade levels will be seen.

Now we shall hear how we fortify this motivation. I don't want to confuse you, because we haven't even talked about the first graders. It is my understanding that a common motivation does not do harm; on the contrary, it will be helpful to each child. But then, when the children have started with their own individual work, your reaction to the individual child will be geared to his or her developmental stage. I didn't answer this question last time, although I should have.

And now, in our discussion we'll switch to the next stage. I hope you all now know how to motivate children in kindergarten who are in the scribbling stage. You will look at scribbling more sensitively, because you have become aware of the detailed differences. See, sensitivity is always a breaking down of generalizations into detailed reactions; and, actually, it is this that we have tried to do. We have found out that there are detailed reactions with regard to general developmental stages, such as disordered, longitudinal, and circular scribbling, and the naming of scribbling. But we have also found that within these stages we have individual differences, namely, children who freely do their disordered scribbling, children who daintily do their disordered scribbling, children who interruptedly do their disordered scribbling, children who boldly do their disordered scribbling, children who remain in one corner and do their disordered scribbling, and also children who cannot continuously do their disordered scribbling because they are restricted to stereotypes. What we have just said about disordered scribbling is also true for longitudinal and circular and naming. We will have a more sensitive understanding of the individual child if we are sensitive in our reactions to the different mixtures, because none of these may even appear isolated as such. We may have a scribbling which is in between disordered and longitudinal. We may see some longitudinal lines superimposed on disordered scribbling. This is where Robin, my grandchild, is now. There are stages of transition, do you see? You will also see that some children always interrupt their scribbling and can never continually scribble; other children only now and then interrupt their scribbling. So, we have all kinds of transitions and characteristics within these stages. To become sensitive to these differences is the task of a teacher who empathizes, who puts himself into the place of the children.

When we talk about the next stage, we should not presume that on one day the child names his scribbling and the next day moves into the next developmental area. This is not human growth, indeed not, because human growth takes place gradually; so here we will have some form of transition. However, I would like to give you a feeling of how this transition takes place in the child. Let us say, we have Johnny, who scribbles and names his scribbling. At one time or another, he will discover that, while naming, there may be motions that are representative of something which comes close to his mental picture, such as a circular motion expressing a head and a longitudinal motion expressing a body. Then we arrive at a transitional stage of naming in which we already see some kind of relationship between what he names and what he draws. Such a transitional stage of representation can be seen in Figure [6]. I shall always refer in my discussions to the illustrations in the book so that you have something to hold onto. When we come to the discussion of the evaluation of children's drawings, I again shall make use of our collection of drawings which we have here that refer to the stage we are discussing.

In Figure [6], you see a child who still scribbles and names his scribbling—in this case, "Mother goes shopping." But when you are sensitive, you have already some kind of indication that the child apparently used a circular motion here for a head and a longitudinal motion or two for legs. If we strain our imagination, we can even see two arms. Only after he says, "Mother goes shopping," has he reverted to scribbling again. Can you see that? This is a transitional stage. We still call it naming of scribbling because there is no clear representational attempt; but there will come a time when the child makes a great discovery. Now, I don't know whether you can put yourself into the child's place. Let's try it. Let's all concentrate as much as we can and think that we are thinking of Mother; we are scribbling and we say, "Mother goes shopping," just as if we were to doodle; and, all of a sudden, we discover in our doodling: "Oh, this could be Mother. This is Mother, because Mother has a head and two legs! Mother has a head and two legs! Look, Daddy, this is Mother."

This is a discovery, a great discovery, because the child has, for the very first time in his whole life, discovered that he can actually establish a relationship between his mental picture and his drawing, whatever the relationship may be. So don't ever criticize a relationship, because the very great discovery is that he can establish a relationship between his drawing and his mental picture. Imagine what would happen if we were never able to do that! Our mental pictures would always remain abstract and never become concrete. We would never be able to say, "My mother has—," and then go on and enumerate what mother has. Of course, in the very beginning, this relationship is one which is very simple: "My mother has a head and two legs. My drawing has a head and two legs. This is my mother!" Such a relationship is very simple. As the child grows, these relationships become more complex; this is actually a miracle which takes place.

My grandchild, Robin—I will refer to him because I have him now close at home—is still scribbling, but he discovers in a picture book the most minute things. This is a multiple-choice type of discovery. It's as if I say, "A man has: wings, arms, a snout, a tail." You would say that he has arms. You wouldn't say he has wings; you wouldn't say he has a snout, do you see? You would just select one. This is a multiple-choice type of discovery. So, when a child is confronted with a picture of a bird, he will say, "This is a bird and this is not a man." Because he's confronted with it, this is a multiple-choice type of decision. Yet, when Robin draws something for himself, he never refers to such a mental picture. He always scribbles and is perfectly happy and satisfied and even calls it a picture. "I'm running around in this picture," he says. You know, since we have motivated the running motions, that he is not naming his scribbling when this is done; it's only when he does it spontaneously. He's perfectly satisfied, on his active level, with kinesthetic thinking; but on his passive level, in a multiple-choice situation, he can pick out the minutest details and say, "Look at the puppy," as he did yesterday in a picture book. Here is human development in its most intricate manifestation.

But one time there will come a great moment for Robin. He will discover that there is a relationship between his mental picture and his drawing. His relationship will be based not on what he sees, no, indeed not—Mother having only a head and two legs is not what he sees—but on what actively motivated him during the process of drawing. The relationship, then, depends not on seeing but on what he knows during the process of drawing—not on what he knows, period, because the child knows more about Mother than that Mother only has a head and two legs. This is significant because we now know that the child in his drawing only draws his active knowledge—the knowledge which he readily has available during the process of drawing. Yes, indeed, he knows much more than he draws, or as he draws, but he doesn't use it. So, in the beginning, the relationship which he establishes is the most important part—the discovery that he can draw a mental picture. Now, it may be that his mental picture right in the beginning consists of more than a head and two legs. All of a sudden this inspiration may come to him, this discovery. He sees a circle and two legs, and then he adds the eyes because Mother is looking for him. Then his thinking would be: "Look, there is a head and two eyes and two legs. Mommy has two eyes and a head and two legs. My drawing is Mommy."

He has discovered that there is a relationship between his drawing and outside experiences. This relationship is built upon a translation of what he actively knows and what he sees. We call this translation a concept. A concept is based upon the individual's knowledge of something. The knowledge which actively motivates him, we call a child's concept in his drawings. To conceive of something means to know of something and to relate it to one's own experience. This we call a concept. What else do we know that is in contrast to a concept? Contrasting to a concept is a percept. There is great confusion everywhere, let me tell you, whenever you see writings on concept and percept. Concept comes from conceiving and is a mental activity. Percept comes from perceiving, which is a sensory activity. When it is done with the eyes, then it's visual perceiving. When it's done with the hands, then it is tactile perceiving—perceiving through the sense of touch. When it is done through motions, then it's kinesthetic perceiving. You can perceive space; you see that you are surrounded by space. When you can touch the space, then it's your tactile space percept. You have heard of space perception? You can perceive space visually, like perspective—the things which are in the distance apparently diminish in size. This is not so for the blind; the blind individual has no perspective feeling. For him, the tree, whether it is far away or close, is the same size; it doesn't change. He has no visual percept of space, but he has a concept of space— that is, a mental understanding of space. Do you understand?

Let's differentiate the two expressions right at the beginning, and then we will have no confusion and we'll understand. Do you have any questions with regard to the two? I'd like to get this well into your minds. The one deals with thinking, with your mental understanding and mental picture; the other, with your sensory experience, what you actually see. So, when the child draws a head like this and the legs like this, this is no percept; this is a concept, because the child has never seen a man like that. Do you see? He only conceives of a man like that. This is his concept. His concept is then this: "A man has a head, two legs, and two feet. My drawing has a head, two legs, and two feet. Therefore, my drawing is a man." You wanted to say something?

Student: The first time he puts that down on paper, could it be accidental; and then he applies his concept of that when it first happens?

Lowenfeld: When it first happens, it sometimes may be accidental, but there's a philosophic belief we have which says that you cannot ever learn from an accident unless you are ready to learn from it. Do you see? If the child would have such an accident during the disordered scribbling stage and would all of a sudden make a head which might stimulate him to see Mommy in this head, he would never be able to see it because he isn't ready for it. But, during the naming of scribbling, he is ready for it because he thinks already in terms of mental pictures and his readiness stimulates him to take advantage of an accident. So, an accident is only a happy accident if we can take advantage of it.

And that may also apply to the use of materials; for instance, when we use watercolor. Watercolor may make the most beautiful accidental things. But, at the time, when the child draws a head and then an eye, and all of a sudden the paint runs down because he had it vertically on an easel, this would—for the child—be destroying his concept. It's not a happy accident, because he cannot use it to advantage. Or, if he were to make the sky up here and the sky then started running down because the paint was too wet, this would be a sad accident because the child cannot take advantage of it.

This is an aspect of one's philosophy toward life. When we can take advantage of accidental things, we are ready. The more flexible we are, the more ready we are to take advantage of those accidents which may occur in life. You see, when you go home, you may go across the lawn. You have in your mind, "I have to go there," and nothing in the world may divert your attention. You have your mind set. To the left and to the right may be the most beautiful things which offer themselves to you and say, "Look at me; look at me," but you don't take advantage of these aspects even if they are wonderful. If your mind is set and not flexible enough, you don't take advantage; you are not ready to accept these accidental aspects. The same is true for the child. The child who scribbles in a disordered fashion does not take advantage. Within the scribbling, there might be a round circle into which he can put his mental picture of Mommy or Dad or something. Do I make myself clear?

That gives us also the understanding of why, for instance, a paint which runs and destroys the child's concept would only be detrimental to the child; because he cannot take advantage of it. So, watercolor—which easily runs— if used at the time when the child needs to formulate his concepts, would be a very poor medium. You see how the two are closely integrated? You cannot separate the one from the other—the material which you use from the child's needs. The child now wants to form his concepts. Once he has discovered them, he wants to repeat them; he even wants to enrich them. If you give him a material which is detrimental to this enrichment, which constantly runs and destroys his concepts, his knowledge about things, then you are doing something which is discouraging to the child.

Student: Do most children draw these head and leg sorts of things?

Lowenfeld: Most children begin with head and leg representations. They are normal for a four-and-a-half or five-year-old child. This concept, or this transitional stage, actually is between four and five years.

The stage which we are now to discuss is between five and seven, or you may also say four and seven. As I told you, a half year up or down will not make any difference. Once the child has discovered that there is a relationship, he will constantly try to improve this relationship if he is alert and not fixed in his mind. He will change his concepts from one day to another or even in one drawing. This flexibility in the changing of concepts is very important for children at this developmental stage.

164

Now, I have to go a little bit further, and I hope I won't confuse you. A concept—that is, a knowledge of a mental picture—does not need to be translated into a drawing. But when it is translated into a drawing such as this, we call it a schema. So we can say the drawing concepts of children are schemata. These are the drawing concepts. We soon will arrive at a stage when children, all children, have established such a schema and signify that they have established such a schema by repeating the schema. Like all children say, "Again, again," when you play with them—when they want to gain an experience more definitely, they engage in repetition. Repetition is an important learning factor; but this does not take place before children are probably seven years of age.

The stage which precedes this schema stage, or schematic stage, we call the pre-schematic stage. Whenever the child discovers his first concepts in his drawings but is not yet sure of them, we call this the pre-schematic stage. It usually lasts, as I said, between four and seven years of age. During this pre-schematic stage, the child frequently changes his concepts, his drawing concepts. Therefore, this is one of the most outstanding characteristics of the pre-schematic stage—namely, if we look at the child's drawing and see that he draws a man today this way and tomorrow draws it quite differently, then we know that he is in the pre-schematic stage.

There is a danger, however, of which we should be very alert as teachers. The danger is that the child, when he discovers something, will repeat it again and again and thus will prevent himself from discovering new things. This is the sign of a retarded child. Retarded children have a tendency to remain with the same concepts much more than average children do. For instance, mongoloid children—sometimes they are even twenty years old—just draw head-feet representations and nothing else but head-feet representations, because their mental level is probably that of a five- or six-year-old child. They have been fixed in their mentality at this stage and can no longer flexibly apply their knowledge to new concepts, to changing concepts.

Now, in Figure [8], you see a drawing of a more advanced concept; at least, one which is clearly expressed and formulated. In the very beginning, you will see that children only vaguely express their drawing concepts; but later on, they express them with greater vigor because they have collected more confidence and, therefore, express these concepts more clearly. This child, in Figure [8], said, "I am on the street." So you see he was concerned with himself—"I am on the street." This child, in particular, was in an accident; and you see what comes out: "There is an ambulance. There am I. And there are airplanes"—on the lower right corner. You see that he had not brought himself into some other relationship to airplanes and to the ambulance than that of a conceptual relationship; namely, he said: "I am on the street. There is an ambulance. There are airplanes." That means that this is as far as his thinking allowed him to go. There is no spatial relation-

Fig. 8. "I Am on the Street" (5½ years). No spatial correlations are perceived. Proportions are drawn according to significance. Head-feet representation. (Pre-Schematic Stage)

ship between himself and the street and the ambulance and the airplanes. He did not say: "I am on the street. The airplanes are above in the sky; and the ambulance is also on the street." He did not say that, because he had not yet established this higher form of conceptual relationship. But he said: "I am looking. I am looking; therefore, I have eyes."

He omitted the mouth and the nose because they were not actively in his mind. Of course, if you were to ask him, "What's that?" and you pointed at his nose, he would readily say, "Nose." "What's that?" "Mouth." "What's that?" "Cheek." "What's that?" "Neck." Oh, yes, a four-and-a-half-year-old child or a five-and-a-half-year-old child would readily know that. Every five-and-a-half-year-old child would even know such details as fingernails if I were to point them out to him: "What's that?" He would say, "Fingernails," but only as a matter of choosing as in a multiple-choice situation. Do you see? He sees the fingernails. They have been activated in his mind, and so he recognizes them. But when he draws them, he will be satisfied with the expression of his conceptual relationship only. So this child thought: "I'm in the accident. I'm looking. The eyes are

Fig. 9. "I Am Running for My Ball" (5-year-old boy).

in my head. I have legs. I have feet. I have two arms and two hands." That's all that he said. "There is an ambulance. The ambulance has four wheels and a red cross. There are planes." And that is all the child said. This, by the way, is a child who had gone through the London blitz, so you will understand why he included the planes and why he included the red cross. Our ambulances usually don't have a red cross on them. This child was right in the midst there. It came out even on this low level of expression. You see? He confronted himself again in this situation.

Now, if we turn to Figures [9, 10, and 11], I would like for you to look at these three drawings at the same time. You will see what I meant when I said that children frequently change their concepts. These three drawings were done in a period of three months. In the first drawing, he said—his name was Micky but he printed Vicki—"I am running for my ball." There is an entirely different concept which he expressed here than that which he expressed in the later drawing, "Mother is looking for me," or which he expressed in the next drawing, "I and my dog." There he was entirely different in his concepts. Now, let's find out what made him different in his concepts and we'll probably get a deeper insight into the nature of this pre-schematic stage. First of all, we see that the child included in the first drawing, "I am running for my ball," those things which apparently were important to him. Yes, the active knowledge always consists of those parts which are on the mind of the child while he is drawing; therefore, they are actively on his mind. What was actively on his mind? "I have a head; I have ears"—most markedly ears, as you can see. Why? Probably he was quite impressed by listening to the bouncing of the ball, but we don't know that. But since he has drawn a ball, the ears most probably are in some relationship to it.

There may be another relationship, as we later will hear when we go through the growth components and see what is responsible for the growth of children. At that time, we will see that children who are affected in their physical growth in certain parts of their bodies usually exaggerate that part of the body continuously—not once, but continuously. Let us say, if the child is frequently plagued by earaches, then he has a greater sensitivity and a higher active knowledge about his ears. They are constantly part of his body reference, of his body feelings. And, therefore, he becomes over-alert.

Fig. 10. "Mother Is Looking for Me" (drawing by the same 5-year-old boy). Note frequent change of symbols.

Even in his subconsciousness, they are always with him as an active part; and he continuously exaggerates them in his drawings. If a child continuously exaggerates a nose in his drawings, he may have sinus trouble. Blind children continuously exaggerate the eyes; and deaf children, usually their ears. Children who are crippled emphasize the legs, because they are over-conscious of their legs.

Be cautious, however, in such statements. You see what I do when I see such a statement in a class—when I see a child continuously exaggerate the ears, then I become sensitively aware of this exaggeration. I go by and I pull the ear of Johnny. And if he says, "Ouch, ouch," then I know. I know that either this was just a casual "ouch," or it was a more meaningful expression, and it hurt him. So I will do it again and say, "Johnny, does this hurt you?" "Wahhh," and he may start crying, even at the time, because he has now become conscious of his pain. In this way, you may discover some defects. But, when you see your first exaggeration, don't say, "This child must have earaches," or something like that. This would be silly. We said that we are not discovering things for diagnostic purposes. We are discovering these

Fig. 11. "I and My Dog" (drawing by the same 5-year-old boy). Notice change of representative symbols, proportions of value, use of geometric lines.

169

things to become more sensitive to the child's needs. Unless we know of them, we will not become sensitive.

Student: You said sometimes they omitted parts, too.

Lowenfeld: Yes. If children omit some part, it may also account for some feeling concerning the part. But there is no significant, statistically significant, relationship between omissions of body parts and body defects as there is between exaggerations and body defects. Did I say this clearly? We have no significant relationship between omissions and body defects, but we have a significant relationship between exaggerations and body defects. So, Micky may have had constant earaches, or frequent earaches, because he drew the ears always in an exaggerated manner.

Now, let's look at whether he really did. Let's look at Figure [10]. Here the ears are not present at all. But in Figure [11], he has them again exaggerated, do you see? So there we should be more sensitive to Micky, because he has exaggerated the ears frequently. Let me continue. He drew the legs very dark in the drawing, "I am running after my ball"—yes, indeed, because he used the legs for running. "I am running"—therefore, the legs were important. There is a slight slant to the body; you know a kind of a diagonal slant. This often is an indication of the child's desire for motion. He cannot express it differently, so he expressed it by giving himself a slant so that he will push forward. He felt the weight of running in one direction. He has the eyes quite differentiated. He has, as you can see, a circle for eyeballs and probably another dot for the iris, although he didn't account for it; but it is a differentiated expression for eyes. He has a nose, and he has a mouth. Now this is all he knew of himself. Then he drew the ball. So probably he indicated: "I am running. Look! I am running." These are a definite expression for the eyes. "I'm listening to the bouncing of the ball"—these are the ears, and there is the ball. "I want to get it. I want to get it. I want to get it, and it's going." You see? Now, he suppressed his arms because he couldn't get it. Do you see? So he omitted the arms. This would be a feeling interpretation of the drawing of the child so that we can put ourselves into the place of the child. The feeling of being afraid—that we can't use our arms—often results in omissions. We can't use our arms so the child runs and runs, and the ball is going there and there and is going down the hill and so on. The child may have omitted the arms for this reason. But there is a reason, because a child who is five years old knows that he has arms and would have included them at this time if they were to play a vital role.

In Figure [10], we see that he called it, "Mother is looking for me." Now, I will tell you the whole story because I was there. He said: "I am in the yard. Mother is in the flower garden. Mother is looking for me. She is calling for me, 'Micky,' but I am hiding behind the house. Mother has told me not to step into the pond. We have a little pond in our back yard." Now

170

let's look at how he did it. He drew a house in the center. The house—what is his concept of a house? For him, the concept is only: "A house has walls and a roof, a steeple. It has windows and a door. The door has a peephole." Oh! See the peephole is the only detail which he applied there. This is something Micky was conscious of. Probably Mother was looking out through the peephole for him, and it impressed him so he included the peephole. Otherwise, he wouldn't have used it. "I'm behind the house." You can see how he was behind the house. Mother was in the flower garden, "She's calling me." You see the three big flowers? That symbolizes the flower garden. This is the concept formation of a flower garden. It's not the visual percept but the concept which he had of a flower garden. A flower garden has flowers. The flowers do not need to look like flowers; they are just his concept. And there is grass in the flower garden, too, and there is Mother.

Now, look carefully. He gave Mother four eyes. I asked him: "Now what is Mother doing?" He said: "She's looking for me. She's looking there and there." He wanted to indicate that mother was looking to the left and to the right and has given her two pairs of eyes, you see? This is often signifi- cant. And this is the same thing that I told you, do you remember? I told you a story where we had a similar incident, when the birds were flapping their wings. I said that some of the birds were drawn with four wings. Do you see? It is the same movement which is expressed with another pair of wings; here, the looking around is expressed with another pair of eyes. Also "I am looking around," so he has given himself two pairs of eyes. You see now that he has two legs and a body, so he has changed his concept again if we compare it with the previous drawing, Figure [9]. At the top of him, you see a square that is blue, blue paint in it. He said: "This is the pond. Mother has told us to be careful and not to step into the pond." So this was on his mind. I shall repeat again his experience: "I am hiding behind the house. I am ready to leave at any time." He didn't give as definite a concept of his legs as he did in the other drawing. "I'm hiding behind the house. For that I don't need the arms. I am looking around. Mother is calling me." So he had in his mind only the head of Mother, not the body. "She is looking around and calls, 'Micky'," so Mother has her mouth wide open. "She's in the flower garden. There is also grass. The house is in between us. The house has a steeple. It has windows and a door which has a hole to look through." Here we have the experience of this child.

You understand, we only use the data which we see for our interpreta- tion and nothing else. We do not use symbols which allow us inferences. For example, because the child has only drawn the head of Mother, he wants her to be decapitated. Such things we would not say. We would not say it's invalid, but it is not according to our background that we can say it. It doesn't fit into an art education concept. We only interpret what we see.

Since he has not drawn the body and legs of Mother, we say these are not important to him. They are not actively in his mind, and that's how far we go. Is this clear? This is very important; and I will tell you why.

I do not want to underestimate what we can do in art education. We should get a very sensitive understanding of the child within the framework of our basic philosophy, and we should not go beyond it. For those who are majoring in art education, it will not be new to you that there are tendencies in the field to minimize our interpretive ability, and thus deprive us of a marvelous means which we have at our disposal, because some are afraid that we will engage in something which we usually should leave to psychiatrists or psychologists who have the background for it. But instead of truly confining our ways, outlining them, noting how far we should go, they deny the right to us at all. You see, there is a great difference in that. We should use all of our knowledge and abilities and, if we don't use them, we fall short in art education. We cannot just say, "Look only at the aesthetic experience of the child and be satisfied with that." We would lose much of our sensitivity toward the child, and we would not take advantage at all of the wealth which we have at our disposal.

We should also be conscious that art, throughout the history of man, has dealt with concepts which are only visually perceivable, and it is within this framework that we will work. During the medieval period, too, we knew that, when the Lord was expressed very large and the Apostles small, it did not mean that the Lord was larger than the Apostles. It meant that he was more significant and the Apostles were not as significant. So this value relationship—that it was more actively on the artist's mind—we have continuously used as our art tradition in the interpretation of art works, of creative products. To drop them in child art would be ridiculous for fear that we will do injustice to aesthetic experiences. It is this that I meant in my talk at our conference, when I clearly pointed at those who are now holding the banner for aesthetic experiences only and are afraid, really, to use their sensitivities concerning child art.

If we compare this drawing to the next one, Figure [11], we will see what changes the child has gone through—terrific changes in a relatively short time. Now he said: "I am looking for my dog. I am going into the backyard. The grass is high. I am there all alone." So he surrounded himself by sky. This dark outline around the page is blue and signifies the sky. "I'm all alone. I look to the left, I look to the right, I look above; and there is nothing but sky." So he must have felt alone, you see. This sensitivity I would like you to feel, so that you become alert to such a line. It means: "I am alone. I am looking for my dog. I am alone in the backyard. My dog— there is my dog! It's in the grass!" And now he stretched out his fingers and said: "I want to grab it. There is my dog. I lost it." This was his experience. Do you see how the grass is lower where he has stepped it down and where it's higher surrounding him? So the grass played an important role. He has become sensitive to the high grass around himself, to listening for his dog— "There is my dog," and then he grabs him. There were no arms in the previous drawings. Now you see the real significance of his mental image, the image which was important to him. He knew that he had arms before, also that he had fingers, but now he used them as part of his concept.

So, we see that there is a great flexibility in the relationship of the pre-schematic child to his experience. We should use this flexibility as much as we can in our motivations.

LECTURE 15

The Pre-Schematic Stage: Percepts and Concepts Reviewed, Characteristics of Drawings, and Evaluation of Intellectual Growth

It says here, "Please give an example of a percept as compared to a concept." An example of a child's concept is a head, two legs, two feet. Now, I'll give you definitions for a concept and a percept, and a method by which you can easily differentiate the one from the other. Whenever we speak of a concept, we think of the child's own mental translation into some kind of idea or symbol whatever he may have perceived in the past. Since this symbol in art represents something, we shall call the concept in art a representative symbol. It can be differentiated from a percept, which is perceived, by separating a part from the whole. If I separate the parts of a concept from the whole—or, in a schema, the parts from the whole—then the single parts lose their meaning. That's the best kind of experiment you can make. For instance, if you separate the head from the body in this drawing, what is the head when you don't see the whole drawing?

Student: A circle.

Lowenfeld: It's a circle. It's a zero. It may be anything. What is this other part? Maybe a letter, I don't know. You see, no one would say it's a leg even if I draw it here and add an arm. Well, I shouldn't have said that. But if I would have asked you, "What is this that I now draw?" I don't think there would have been a single student in this class who would have said, "I don't know." Am I right? You all immediately recognize that this is the arm of this man. But if I would *not* have drawn it attached to the body and would have asked, "What do you think this part is by itself?" no one of you would have recognized it even if I had separated it into further parts and said, "What is this and what is this?" You would not have recognized it. In a concept or in a schema, the single parts lose their meaning when isolated from the whole or when separated from the whole.

Now, in a percept, this is not the case. In art if I perceive something and do not translate it into a symbol but leave it as a perception, as that which I perceive, then we approach, more or less, realistic drawings. The part will

174

no longer lose its meaning when isolated from the whole. So, of course, you would not have a schema, but a drawing which approaches realistic drawing. If you were then to separate the hand, it would remain a hand—a recognizable hand. If you were then to separate the arm, it would remain an arm; or the feet, and they would remain recognizable feet. If you were to separate the hair, you would still feel that this is hair due to its texture and its quality. So, in a percept, whenever you separate the single parts from the whole, they retain their meaning. Do you understand? I will have to draw a realistic drawing on the blackboard in order to show you. You see? Now, if a child draws like this with sketchy lines, even if it is more or less primitive, you can see that there is a tendency to characterize the single parts. If I separate this part, then it will be recognizable. You no longer can say, "I don't know what it is." Even if it isn't like a hand, it reminds you of a hand. Therefore, percept plays an important part. Do I make myself clear?

We move, then, from a concept towards a percept; and there are all kinds of stages in between, of course. You see, her dress looks this way; and we would not clearly say that it is a dress when we isolate it, but we will still recognize it. It reminds us of a dress. Do you see what is meant? A better formation or percept would be if we were to get something of the texture in it or how the dress falls. We would then get a little bit more of a feeling for the dress. We will talk about that when we arrive at the realistic stage. It's significant. There's a difference between, let us say, whether a child includes those details which change in the dress through movement or whether he simply draws a straight hemline. There's a difference; but both already belong to percept—that means, they are moving towards it. When the hemline is straight, it may be a transition towards a clearer percept. But if I were to define the two, then I would say the one (concept) loses its meaning when separated into its single parts while the other (percept) retains its meaning.

I have still another question here: "What is being done to further art education at the principals' conference now being held?" That's a good question. Very little. Very little. I have a meeting tomorrow noon with a small fraction of the principals and superintendents at the State College Hotel. I don't know how many there will be. I think art education should be a significant part of the conference which we have here and which I greatly criticize. In spite of art education being an important part of the College of Education—because we are a separate department equal to the Departments of Educational Psychology or Industrial Arts—when it comes to a principals' or superintendents' conference, no attempt is made by the Department of Education, which includes administration, to integrate or at least give an understanding about art education at such an important meeting.

There are other states who are more alert than we are. I believe that it is high time we also awaken. Now, may I say that, during the past year—to answer not this question but another question—I've been fortunate in addressing the education associations of ten states, which is a quite large number. These were not art education associations; they were education associations. In some instances, I gave the main address, as in Atlanta. Even Georgia is now more alert than we are. We should have art education right in the spotlight here, you see. I don't know—we have just not awakened here to this concept in administration, but I'm not distressed about it. Things sometimes move slower in some states which are more traditionally bound than in others; therefore, I feel our superintendents and principals will probably have less understanding than those in other states, but gradually they will grasp the importance of creativeness and the meaning of art in our schools.

So, to answer your question directly, I have a meeting tomorrow noon, a luncheon meeting, at which time I will meet superintendents and principals as part of this conference to explain to them the meaning of art in our public schools. Again, I don't know how many there will be. Have I answered all questions? Are there any other questions?

Student: The illustration done by Charles [Figure 8]. I think the title is, "I am Walking on the Street"—where there's an ambulance. . . . There he uses the symbol of a loop for hands and feet. Is that the usual concept?

Lowenfeld: No, there is no usual concept. Children are very inventive in their concepts.

We will talk today about it but, since you asked, children may use such a concept for hands. Children may use a loop for hands. Children may use a loop and fingers for hands. Children may use something like this for hands. There are all kinds of symbol formations. And the same is true of symbols for other body parts, such as for feet; although this loop is more commonly accepted as the symbol for feet than it is for hands. We find all kinds of inventions by children. A concept depends, probably first, on kinds of relationships and the child's inventions. The symbol is a pure invention. Just imagine that the child is the Creator, with a capital C, and he says, "And there are hands." Well, for him, this is so, and there is a hand. He invented it for himself, as his concept, just as we as a species have grown up with the kind of hands which we have; but it doesn't mean that the hand of an inhabitant of another planet wouldn't be different from ours. This is a hand, by common agreement, of the earth inhabitants. But the child doesn't care for this percept. He conceives of a hand as being of his own invention; therefore, he introduces a hand like this, a hand like this, or even a hand that is just a line. For him, it may also be a symbol for both arm and hand. Some children don't include a hand at all.

And that brings us right to our discussion for today, because we will now find out what we should expect from children in terms of symbol formation or in terms of their active knowledge with regard to hands, with regard to their bodies, with regard to environment, with regard to color, and so forth. From now on, although they never appear separated in children's drawings, we shall always discuss separately what we expect from children in terms of drawing a figure, what we expect from them in terms of drawing their environment, and what we expect from them in terms of color and probably design.

As the pre-schematic child advances, he will include more details, depending upon his active knowledge. We shall see that the more intelligent child will include more details because he's more alert and has discovered more of himself and his environment, and the less intelligent child will discover less. Intelligence usually is seen in the amount of details which children include in their concepts of which they have become actively aware. That, of course, depends on their alertness, not on how it is drawn, because the "how" would be another characteristic. It may be more a part of aesthetic considerations, as we shall see in our evaluation. The what—the kind of details which children include, especially during the pre-schematic stage— is responsible for the child's functional intelligence. He may be high in his potential intelligence but he may be restricted by emotions and other things, so what we see in the child's drawings is actually the alertness which functions. The number of details is indicative of that.

We expect, of course, certain things to appear, that means, in terms of an average. The average child during the pre-schematic stage—that is, between four and seven—will begin with the head-feet representations and will end up with the head, the neck, the body, the arms, and separate symbols for hands, legs, feet, the features—eyes, nose, and mouth—and either the ears or the hair, usually not both. Instead of the body, the child may also introduce a symbol which reminds us of clothes, such as a triangular shape which reminds us of a skirt. This can be introduced in lieu of the body. This is what we should expect at the pre-schematic stage. If a child is below that, if he still draws head-feet representations when he is seven years, he is backward—not in his drawings but in his alertness. Do you understand? We never refer to the drawings when we say something about the child, because our goal is always the child and not the drawings. I hope I have made that clear, but I would like to emphasize this again and again so that we always refer back to the child. When the child has not discovered more of himself and the environment, the child has not been alert enough to discover them. We would then not say that the drawing isn't good enough, because the drawing is always good enough since it merely represents the child's present level. But we would say that the child's alertness has not been that which we expect of the average pre-schematic child.

Student: Is the active knowledge the quality in evaluation? Are there any differences if the child discovers it himself or if he has been sensitized to it, as has been mentioned?

Lowenfeld: Yes, indeed.

Student: Suppose the child starts to draw at this age and looks at his picture and says, "I didn't put the nose in, but I have the feet," and so on. In other words, he has some idea of what he wants to have.

Lowenfeld: If a child makes a drawing like you have here, and I motivate this child through an experience—we always motivate through experience—I don't have to say "You didn't draw the nose," or "You didn't draw the eyes." That's a correction, an imposition, which doesn't relate to any experience. What would be a motivational experience? Such an experience would be what? To come to class and to make him sensitive to a nose? Yes, you would say: "Lefph, I have a stopped-up nose today. I can scarcely breathe through my nose. Children, have you ever had such a stuffed up feeling? See, I can't speak through my nose." And every child will think of a stopped-up nose. Then we would say, "Well, let's draw ourselves—how we feel today." There may not be a single child who would fail to introduce the nose as part of his increased active knowledge. Next time, he may omit it again; but through repeated sensitization he will include it finally in the same way as we include a new word in our vocabulary. When you learn a foreign language, you will hear a word for the first time. You will remember it, but you won't include it in your conversation. If you hear it ten times again, then all of a sudden you will find that you'll catch yourself using it. It has become a part of your active vocabulary. You see, this is the same process.

Student: Do you think that it's possible for a child of that age to constantly leave off part of the body and then say, "I didn't put it on because I didn't want it on, or I just—."

Lowenfeld: It is not usual, because a child isn't conscious of his activity. There may be some children—exceptions—who may say, "I don't want to draw this," you know. "I don't want to draw it. I don't want it. I don't want it." Yes, you may find children of this sort—as an exception, but not as a rule.

Student: I'm still confused about what would be the definition of drawing, then? How do you refer to children in the elementary grades as having a talent for drawing and some not having a talent for drawing?

Lowenfeld: I don't. I only refer to children who can express themselves easier and more freely and others who are restricted. Some have, let us say, more ability to harmoniously organize their drawings and bring them into relationship to the area, use the material in relationship to what it can do, and, thus, are higher in aesthetic growth. Is that clear?

Student: What if you found a child in first grade drawing a more representative drawing?

Lowenfeld: I'd be very happy if it is really a part of the child, and I would say the child in his developmental level is advanced. He conceives of himself already as a moving part. He conceives of the details much in advance of his own level. I would say he's on the level of a nine-year-old child or an eleven-year-old child. But I refer to the child rather than to the drawing so that I become more sensitive and understanding of the child. Let's not divide children into those who are talented or not talented on the basis of products, but let's rather remain sensitive to the child and his needs. Of course, if we see that the child draws such drawings—which is very unlikely, but it may be so in very exceptional cases—then we would say the child most probably is advanced in his growth and, therefore, should be rather with children of an advanced stage than remain with this group, because he will stand out and will not be touched by our motivations as much as he would be if he were in a fourth grade or a fifth grade. You see? I believe we should not be rigid about this.

Student: Is it possible for a child to show a development such as this, an advanced development in his art expression, and still not have the achievements that would go along with a higher developmental stage?

Lowenfeld: Did you hear? "Is it possible for a child to have or to develop such kind of a percept in his drawings, an advanced stage of development, but yet not show any achievement in his other work?" Yes, it is possible. It is possible.

It's also possible the other way around—that he shows achievement but this achievement is not seen in his drawing. In both instances, we should be alert and should know that, if the child develops in his drawing percept or concept to an advanced stage, the child's ability is advanced and he is probably restricted in his other intellectual pursuits. Because of this restriction, he has found an outlet in his drawings where he can show his free development. This is only on the functional level. Potentially, I should say, "No." The child in his alertness and in his motor control has advanced, but verbally he has probably been restricted and cannot express it. Therefore, we should work with him on his verbal level. Vice versa—if we see that the child is verbally expressing himself very richly and is intellectually advanced but he draws stereotypes and his drawings are on a low level, we should then know that the child's intellectual growth in one area has not kept up with that in another area. Therefore, his perceptual growth and his emotional growth, probably also his aesthetic growth, have suffered in his development; and we should emphasize then the other forms of growth development. That's why we consider creative expression to be so important. It gives us a feeling of a balanced development.

We have to remember again and again that being highly developed in one area of achievement is still an old concept to which we do not like to subscribe. We still tend to think of the classroom as the room in which learning takes place and not growth. Learning deals mainly with developing the intellect by the accumulation of knowledge. When we make such statements, we are still in our mind a little bit old-fashioned, because we still think of the compartmentalization of the child. We think achievement is the highest form that we can gain in life, especially if we think of intellectual achievement or knowledge. Yet we all know that we can have the richest knowledge and can be the most unhappy people and not know what to do with all the knowledge which we possess if we don't have the freedom to use it, if we feel restricted, if we feel that a nervous breakdown at all times may come over us. All this is something which should become a part of our concept, too. Now we think of the total growth of the child—"the child as a whole," you know, as we have been hearing it during the last two years. But what we do in our educational system to promote it is another question. So this, indeed, will give us a good feeling of where the child stands in his total development. If we find such discrepancies, of course, we should be very alert and sensitive to them.

Student: Well, then, when you use the word "retarded," are you referring to capacity?

Lowenfeld: The total capacity in his growth. If a child is retarded, I feel that he is retarded emotionally; he is retarded in his reactions, in his ability to think and feel and perceive.

Student: Then, when you say restricted, you mean he has a capacity for this but it's—.

Lowenfeld: He may have a capacity.

There are two forces which determine man and his actions: the one is, without any doubt, heredity; and the other is, without any doubt, environment. As we cannot touch heredity in education—God, thanks—we touch environment. You know why I say, "God, thanks"? Well, we are glad that we have these individual differences. If we ever touch heredity, we will come out all the same in assembly lines. So we touch environment. Environment is education in the broadest sense. It is what influences man. So we concentrate, of course, on these influences.

You may have a retarded child who has in his genes the inability to grow at the pace of the average because he is hereditarily, let's say, held back. But you may also have a retarded child who has the potentialities for intellectual development, for becoming an intelligent child, and for a total development like every other child; but for some reason, he has been held back. It may be an emotional condition, a restriction. It may be a child neurosis that may have been responsible for pulling him back and which does not let the child develop so as to take in what he finds in his environment. There may be many conditions.

But when I say retarded, then the total drawing will express it. I mean if a child of seven years still draws like this, as you see it on the blackboard—head and feet representations—we would then say the child is retarded, of course, only functionally. We would not make any other statement at this time. And we would also have to look at three drawings; if he draws head and feet representations in each drawing, then we would say he is retarded. Retarded in what? Retarded in his active knowledge, certainly, because he should know more about his body. Then we would see that a knowledge of himself and his environment would also introduce a greater flexibility of expression.

You see, this is interwoven in the same way as when you learn a language, and you can only say, "Yes" or "No." With "Yes" and "No," you have no opportunity to express yourself emotionally, except if you use your body and say "Yes" or "No," and then you show something of your emotions, too. But outside of this, you wouldn't be able to say anything about yourself at all. An enriched vocabulary will also give you a greater opportunity to express yourself verbally. The same is true also in drawing or painting. This child cannot say in his drawing, "I am hungry," because he doesn't even express the mouth and he doesn't have any feeling for this. Nor will he be able to say: "I like this or that. I like to play in my yard." How would he do it? He would have to add an enriched vocabulary of forms in order to express it. Therefore, the enriched vocabulary of forms is closely related to emotional expression. We see it here as a total form of expression of the child.

Let's go on, because I would like to finish today this part so I can go into motivation and the practical part tomorrow. We pointed out what the child should know about himself and his active knowledge with regard to space, that means, his environment. We know that the child begins with dispersing things as he or she does in language. Have you ever gotten a little note from a six-year-old child, between six and seven? She will say: "I am on the beach. There is sand. There are waves. There is also a shell. Kisses, Mary." Do you see? The child will not bring things into proper relationship to one another. She will not say, "I was walking on the beach, and I found, on the beach, shells." This comes later. We are now in the "There is" stage when the child simply names the things as they come to his or her mind. The same is true in drawing. He'll simply draw: "There am I. There is the ambulance. There are airplanes. There is the sky"—without bringing them into any spatial relationship. This is part of the child's thinking.

In the beginning, we then say the child has no feeling for space relations. His objects in space are dispersed. But later, as the child develops, he should arrive at some kind of spatial order. This order is determined by the "I" and "my"—that means, by his own emotions and how he relates himself to what belongs to him, his belongingness. For example, in "I and my dog" [Figure 11], he has some kind of spatial relationship because he brings himself into relationship to the yard and to his dog because he has established an "I" and "my" relationship of belongingness. This belongingness very often determines the spatial relationships in drawings of children during the pre-schematic stage. Did I express this clearly? The child begins with a merely dispersed relationship—"There is this; there is that"—and he disperses the objects, including himself, over the area of his drawing sheet. As he approaches the end of the pre-schematic stage, some order comes into it; and this order is determined by his feeling of belonging, by his emotions.

What is the child's color perception during this stage? In the very beginning, the child doesn't relate himself to color at all. We have very fine examples in the book if you would like to look at Figures [12] and [13]. You have here reproductions of two paintings which indicate completely that there is no color-object relationship in pre-schematic drawings.

Student: You said color perception?

Lowenfeld: Color perception. Yes, I said that the child perceives color—let us say, perceives that the lawn is green. If you ask him, "What color is the lawn?" he will say, "Green." If you say "What color is the car?"

Fig. 12. "Mommy and Daddy" (4 years old). Color is enjoyed for its own sake. There is no desire to establish color-object relationships during this stage of development. This child has just left the scribbling stage. Notice the circular motions used as "heads." The green "moustache" apparently established a significant relationship to "Daddy." [*Note:* For color, see Lowenfeld, op.cit., Plate 1.]

Fig. 13. "I Am in a Lightning Storm" (6 years old). The child has no desire for "correct" color relationships. The use of a few colors may often satisfy his urge for expression. To direct the child at "proper" color relationships would be an interference with his expression. Let the child discover his own relationships; this discovery is a vital experience for the child. (Teacher: Jean Holland, Duke of York School, Toronto) [*Note:* For color, see Lowenfeld, op.cit., Plate 2.]

he will say, "Orange," or whatever the color of the car is. At five years, children usually have a clear color perception, but they have not yet developed their color concept. There you have a very clear difference between the two: color perception is developed but color concept is not yet developed because, as you can see, one head is blue, the lips are green, the body is blue. If you turn to Figure [13], you see that the child paints himself a bluish-green and the rain purple. His color concept in his drawing in no way relates to his ability to perceive, although he perceives clearly. Even Robin knows colors. He has a few cars, and he says the red and the yellow and the green and clearly points to them. He has already a color perception but no color concept when he draws because he doesn't even relate color to naming. Percept and concept are apart, not related.

If you look at the drawing in Figure [2], you see that the child gives himself or herself a green outline, green legs, red lips, and a blue sky. Things partly relate already to a color concept but not as a whole. We can then say that during the pre-schematic stage the child simply enjoys his color just as it comes. I tried to give this color enjoyment its real name and called it "the decorative stage" of color. Those who know French know what "de coeur" means. "De coeur," anyone know it? "De coeur" means from the heart. "Coeur" means the heart, and "de" means from—from the heart.

They enjoy. Decorative, then, means color merely out of enjoyment. They enjoy green; they take green.

I'd like to give you a description of a little experiment which we did a few years ago. Dr. Corcoran, who did his doctoral dissertation on the relationship of color in children's drawings, tried in a nursery school to put all kinds of paint on the shelves for the children to use. When the children came to the nursery school, they used first the color in which the brush was placed. See, they accepted a path of least resistance. If the brush was first in green, they started out with green. The next day he put the brush, just for experimental purposes, in red; they all started out with red. You see, there was no specific need for a certain color. We also have experimented with regard to emotional relationships and color, and we have not come to any clear conclusion that any particular color expresses a certain emotion of the child. On the contrary, we have found that associations play a much more important role.

Student: Did he ever put a brush into all of the colors?

Lowenfeld: Yes, we did that, too—by accident, apparently—and usually the color was chosen which could easily be reached, the first and closest color, and not one in between. We did all kinds of experiments. They were done in conjunction with our Psychology Department. Dr. Lefly and Dr. Corcoran collaborated very closely in this experiment.

Student: Was this experiment published?

Lowenfeld: I think it was part of his pilot study, but I am not sure if he included it in his dissertation. But his dissertation is quite extensive and would contain some statement on that, too, I'm quite sure.

In his dissertation, he deals with color preference also. He made a very lovely experiment, if you are interested in this. I shouldn't even start telling you about it because I will become involved since I so much enjoyed the instrument which he used for this purpose. He wanted to find out about the color preference of children. But since children don't prefer color for the color's sake, he wanted to attach the color to things which children know, such as a dancer with different dresses. One had a green dress; one had a purple dress; one had a red dress; one had a yellow dress; one had a brown dress; and so forth. He made an instrument—that means, a sheet on which the different-colored dancers were printed. Then he asked the children, "Which of these dancers do you like best?" Thus, he would immediately find out the preference for color, the liking of colors. Then he said, "Which of these dancers do you think dances always sad dances? Which of these dancers is most happy?" He wanted to find out if children relate certain colors to certain emotions—happiness, for instance. Then he said, "Which of these dancers looks closest to you?" He wanted to find out if some colors appear more advanced.

He also did that with other things besides dancers. For instance, there were clowns. There were seven or so circus clowns: "Which of these clowns feels saddest?" There were different houses painted in different colors. The houses were considered in the same way. He said: "Now, in one of these houses, people have a good time at a gay party. They are very happy. Which of the houses do you think is the house in which the people are very happy?" Then he said: "In one of the houses, a person died. All the people are crying and are very unhappy about it. Which is the house?" He wanted to find out if, in all these instances, colors were related to feelings; and you only could do it this way. He found absolutely no relationship. So it was a significant study with a negative outcome, but in some few instances positive findings.

In general, similar likes and dislikes were not expressed by children; but, as we found out, color choices are mainly based on past associations. For instance, if a child had a grandma who mainly wore a purple dress and gave the child candy, the grandma will remain nicely in the child's memory, and purple may be a lovely color. So past associations may have some significance. There are absolutely no emotions attached to color, as such, but only for color in relationship to objects because of past associations; and we found no clear indications with regard to that. This is in contradiction to some of the studies which we have in the field in which colors are attributed to certain emotions. When we look at these drawings, some children may draw purple and yellow and brown. They do not need to be sad children, please, because these colors impress you sadly, or look dark, and so forth. There are children who use bright colors, and they do not need to be especially bright children since we know that the average child prefers bright colors.

From this stage when there is no color-object reference—that means, from the mere decorative stage in the beginning of the pre-schematic stage—the child gradually moves into the stage in which he relates colors to objects. He does that whenever he has some emotional relationship that relates the color to the object.

Now, I would like briefly to look at the Evaluation Chart, Pre-Schematic Stage. There we will only see that what we have discussed is confirmed for the differentiation of individual children. I'll discuss actual drawings with you tomorrow when we talk about motivation; but, now, let me go through the evaluation chart so that you may use it. As your home-work, I would like you to do the following: Look at the painting where the child is in the storm [Figure 13], and try to evaluate this drawing according to the evaluation chart. Put a check mark where you feel it belongs. First we say, "Does the child's representation of a man show more than head and feet?" If it does show more, then we would move on. "Does the child draw more than head, body, arms, legs, features?" If this is "Yes," we would stop here and say the child's mental age is between five-and-a-half and seven.

Characteristics	Human Figure	Space	Color	Design	Stimulation Topics	Technique
(1) Discovery of *relationship* between drawing, thinking, and reality. (2) Search for concept. (3) Change of form symbols because of constant search for them.	Circular motion for head. Longitudinal for legs and arms. Head-feet representations develop to more complex form concept. Symbols depending on active knowledge during the act of drawing.	No orderly space relations except emotionally. "There is a table; there is a door; there is a window; a chair." "This is *my* doll" (emotional relationship).	No relationship to reality. Color according to emotional appeal.	No conscious approach.	Activating of passive knowledge related mainly to self (body parts).	Crayons, clay, powder paints, (thick) large bristle brushes, large sheets of paper (absorbent). Also, unprinted newspaper.

EVALUATION CHART
Pre-schematic Stage

	Mental Age		No	Yes		
Intellectual Growth	4–5½	Does the child's representation of a "man" show more than head and feet?				
	5½–7	Does the child draw more than head, body, arms, legs, features? Are eyes, nose, mouth indicated? Are the features represented with different representative symbols?				

		None	Some	Much
	As compared with previous drawings is there an increase of details? (Active knowledge) Is the child's drawing representational? Does the drawing show details?			
Emotional Growth	Does the child frequently change his concepts for "man," "tree," or details like "eye," "nose," etc.? Is the child free from stereotyped repetitions? Are parts which are important to the child somewhat exaggerated? Is there a lack of continued and too much exaggeration? Is the drawing definite in lines and color, showing the child's confidence in his work? Does the child relate things which are important to him?			
Social Growth	Is the child's work related to a definite experience? Is there any order determined by emotional relationships? Does the child show spatial correlations: sky above, ground below? Does the child show awareness of a particular environment (home, school, etc.)?			
Perceptual Growth	Does the child use lines other than geometric? (Lines when separated from the whole do not lose meaning.) Does the child indicate movements or sounds? Does the child relate color to objects? Does the child start in his modeling from the whole lump of clay?			
Physical Growth	Is there a lack of continuous omission of the same body part? Is there a lack of continuous exaggeration of the same body part? Are the child's lines determined and vigorous? Does the child include body actions?			
Aesthetic Growth	Is the meaningful space well distributed against the meaningless space? Does the organization of the subject matter seem equally important to its content? Do colors appear to be distributed decoratively? Does the child show a desire for decoration?			
Creative Growth	Does the child use his independent concepts? If the child works in a group, does he remain uninfluenced? When the child is alone does he spontaneously create in any medium? When the child is alone does he refrain from imitating for imitation's sake?			

"Are eyes, nose, mouth indicated?" If we say "Yes," then it is more on the side of seven. "Are the features represented with different representative symbols?" Now this I have not explained, but it means that a child, for instance, draws eyes, nose, and mouth using the same representative symbol. If I were to isolate the symbol, you would not be able to differentiate the one from the other. They all are dots. But if the child, for instance, deviates on the nose, then the nose is a different representative symbol than the eyes and mouth. Now, differences in representative symbols for the features represent a higher active knowledge and, therefore, a higher intelligence. This has been borne out and has been the basis for an intelligence test. As you may know, the Goodenough "Draw a Man Test" is based on the differences in details, actually the active knowledge of the child. If we were to say "Yes" for this last question, then the child's mental level would be more toward seven or would actually be seven.

There are other questions which refer to intellectual growth: "As compared with previous drawings, is there an increase of details?" If the child increases the number of details in his drawings, it is a sign of greater intelligence than if the child remains with the same details. You will see that emotional growth is closely related to intellectual growth on this level, because once a child has become inflexible he has no way of taking in more knowledge. "Is the child's drawing representational?" If it is not representational, we would not evaluate it because evaluation of abstract drawings or so-called "designs" is almost impossible. "Does the drawing show details?" By details we mean, let's say, the mouth has teeth, the nose has nostrils, the head has ears, the hand has fingers. These are details.

LECTURE 16

The Pre-Schematic Stage: Aspects of Motivation, Evaluation of Intellectual, Emotional, Social, and Perceptual Growth

---

Student: Do you use motivation and stimulation synonymously?

Lowenfeld: Synonymously, yes. Yesterday when I talked about language, I said that after a good language lesson you should have a better vocabulary, a more active use of your vocabulary. You remember I said that after my lectures, at the end of this summer session, you will have a larger vocabulary with regard to children's drawings. You will speak about many things which were only passively in your mind and now have been activated. So this course probably will do something even to your language. But I hope you won't get the accent. It would be an imposition.

But, you see, in art it is similar to when you motivate children, or stimulate children, with regard to a certain experience. After this motivation, the child will respond and may add something like the stopped-up nose, you know. Motivate the child to add the nose even if you have to say: "Now, children, when you blow your nose, don't blow your nose, phff, all at once. That's not good. Hold one nostril, phff, and blow, and then hold the other nostril, phff, and blow." After this motivation, the child will probably include the nostrils—will make two dots or something. But next time, the child may again have forgotten this activation. It will not be present with the child. So don't be disappointed if a motivation only lasts for one class hour. But if you continously motivate a child, day after day, to bccome more sensitive to himself and his environment, then one day this motivation will become a part of his permanent activated knowledge of forms. Do you understand what I mean by knowledge of forms? That means, knowledge of having nostrils or of having ears or of having whatever. At one point after continued motivation, like keeping certain words in your active vocabulary, the child, too, will keep the form. So don't be disappointed if this does not take place right in the beginning.

Now I will go to the other questions. "What is your opinion of using pressed crayons in the pre-schematic and even the schematic stage?" Very good. My opinion is that they are a very fine material, pressed crayons; they are very fine. They are just like wax crayons except that the fabrication is slightly different. Also, chalk is a good material. We will talk more about materials later.

"I have occasionally observed the following in my classes: A child in the pre-schematic stage, while drawing an experience such as 'I am playing in my backyard,' will talk about the picture in terms of 'he'—he's running, he wants his ball, his ball is gone, et cetera. When I ask 'Who is this?' the child will say, 'Oh, it's I,' and then continue to explain his drawing in terms of 'he.' What, if anything, does this tell about the child? Would one have to mark the degree of self-identification on the evaluation chart as poor?" No, one would not; because this "he" is often an indication of the child's objectivism. You know, the understanding of the "I" is one of the most difficult things for children. It creates a better feeling for the child in talking about himself if he often says "he." "He didn't do this," he can more easily say, "and he was naughty," than to say, "and I was naughty." Or, "He was falling and hurt his knee," than "I was falling and hurt my knee." You see, this is often the case. As a matter of fact, in children who are retarded or children who are emotionally maladjusted, this distance, this creative distance, is almost a rule. I've worked in institutions for mentally and emotionally maladjusted children where you can't even talk to the child as "you." The child would withdraw. So, when motivating a child of this type, I use the third person.

There was a child whom I described in *Creative and Mental Growth* as a sample case of neurosis. The child had a traumatic shock—that means, a shock which disturbed her mental balance—that occurred early in childhood. The child was eleven and could not adjust flexibly to any given situation. On the contrary, when you asked the child, "Virginia, could you blow your nose?" for Virginia this meant a serious adjustment. It meant "Blowing my nose? Blowing my nose? Where is my handkerchief? I don't know where my handkerchief is. How should I get it out? I can't bring it to my nose! Oh, why should I blow my nose?" This was her reaction, you see, and she became stiff. But when I was sitting close to her and said: "Eeffnph, my nose is stopped-up today. My nose was running all day long. Virginia's nose is running, too. She could blow her nose. She has her hankie in her pocket. Virginia, could you blow your nose?" See, I have conditioned her by talking first, step by step, in a third person until I approached her. This is a means which is used in therapy with maladjusted individuals. So the "he" or "she" is the same kind of approach which the child used—she blows her nose—in getting a greater distance. That is done subconsciously, not consciously. So there is nothing alarming or wrong with a child who says, "She did this and this or this and this." It's easier to talk in this more objective language, and it does not mean that the child is less involved.

There is another question here: "If the child habitually looks at his previously completed drawing and decides that this or that should be changed or added, does that mean that he feels his experience has not been adequately expressed? Suppose he looks at something and says, 'I forgot to put my hat in,' or 'I have to add arms,' or whatever it may be. Is it possible to stimulate a child in such a way that his first expression will satisfy him? Is there a particular stimulation appropriate in the above case?" Yes. If a child does not concentrate on the experience, such things will happen. If a child really is involved in his drawings, such things will not happen. So this is a sign of a lack of self-identification, a lack of involvement, and therefore would be part of both social and emotional growth.

Children who concentrate on their drawings will never say, "I forgot this," or "I forgot that," because they are right into it and the experience is over when they have finished. When children continuously do things of this sort (forget things or change things), not only once but again and again, for them the best material would be clay with which they can make changes during the process. It would be frustrating to have them paint and then make changes, because sometimes it may occur to them that they wanted hands not down but up. They drew the hands mechanically, as it were, as their schema or concept, and all of a sudden remembered afterwards you can't throw a ball by having the hands down. "I should have had the hands up." Do you see? Now there is nothing to do but make a new drawing and use this new body awareness as a starting point for your motivation and say: "Now, Mary, I want you to think right from the beginning. Now close your eyes and concentrate on how you throw a ball. While you are drawing, go through every step of how you throw the ball. Then you will never forget where your hands are, or anything else." If this is effective, then keep on. But if the child is still dissatisfied in the end, this may reflect a mental habit, one in which the child says—like many children say—"I don't want to do that. I don't want to do that."

If you have little children around your house, you know that children establish such negative habits even when they want to do something. They say, "I don't want to do it." Then use clay, because this may break the habit. "All right, change it," you would say, and the child would lift the arm of a clay figure. "All right, put a hat on it," and the child would put on a hat. He would see that this habit is without success, as it were, in drawing attention to himself. You know, one becomes satisfied, and anything which satisfies us wears itself out, even love—that's the artist's love. Now, I hope I answered this question.

"When a child of seven-and-a-half years, or four-and-a-half to six years, begins working with clay, is it more natural to start with the whole piece rather than build up his work in pieces?" No, it is more natural to start with pieces. Most children start with pieces, and only a small percentage pull out the details from the whole lump of clay. We will talk about this today. So do not change a child's mode of expression. If a child starts with pieces, this is a way of thinking. He says, "A man consists of a head, a body, arms, legs." These are pieces, concepts. And sometimes, early in childhood, the child doesn't even have the desire to assemble them. He leaves them.

Student: I don't find the children a problem. I find the teachers a problem.

Lowenfeld: Oh, yes. With the teachers, this is a big problem. I shouldn't mention the institution which produced a film and scrapped it afterwards, because I was on the doctoral committee as a consultant. It's a very reputable institution known all over the United States, at which a doctoral candidate produced a film on modeling motivations and modeling procedures. In the film, there was a teacher who said, "Now, in order that you can fire clay, don't put the pieces together—look, pull the clay out," not knowing that actually putting things together is an entirely different mental process than pulling them out. We will talk about this today. It's very fascinating, actually.

"As the child enriches his symbols, are there places where it is difficult to classify? For example, that 'eye' in Figure [13] is still a symbol for an eye; but if removed from the drawing, it would still look like an eye or eye symbol rather than a meaningless abstract form." Yes, obviously there are difficulties because, in our association, we already relate symbols to actual forms. For instance, if I were to ask you, "What is this?" some of you would say, "This is an eye." Some of you would no doubt arrive at this as an eye, quite with ease. No? But it's still a concept. Why? Because we connect our percept to the child's concept and then establish an association. It becomes quite difficult for us to see whether it is really an eye or is still a geometric symbol. So, yes, it becomes sometimes difficult. If I make this circle, you will all recognize it as what? A head, do you see? But it also is a concept because there is no feeling. This immediately tells you that there is a difference. There is no feeling that this is an arm. This is simply a straight line. If I separate this from this, then you have this. Would you say this is an arm? No. But in connection with the head and body you would. So we have to be careful in our evaluation. In most instances, it isn't difficult. In some instances, it may become difficult. Especially it will become difficult when we deal with children who are nine years old, when we have a stage of transition from a concept to a percept. Well, these are, I believe, all of the questions.

Now, let's go ahead with our evaluation. Turn to the Evaluation Chart, Pre-Schematic Stage. Shall we evaluate the same drawing which we started to evaluate yesterday—Figure [13]? Now we ask, where would the child be in intellectual growth? "Are eyes, mouth, nose indicated?" Yes. "Are the features represented with different representative symbols?" Yes. So we say the child is at what mental age? Seven? It's seven. But the child's chronological age is six. Well, we said half a year up or down would not matter, but this is a year; so the child is somewhat advanced.

Student: What about the first question in that same group, though? "Does the child draw more than head, body, arms, legs, features?"

Lowenfeld: Does the child draw more than a head, body, legs, and features?

Student: Not for the figure, he doesn't. He doesn't put clothes on.

Lowenfeld: Yes, he did, partly. I mean you get the feeling, at least, of having clothes on. And if you look closely, you will also get the feeling that he has used a separate symbol for hands, although it is very difficult to determine.

Student: He almost seems to be holding something.

Lowenfeld: Yes, he wants to protect himself from the rain, you see? This is something which goes beyond, let's say, the usual. "Are eyes, nose, mouth indicated?" Yes. "Are the features represented with different representative symbols?" Yes. So he probably is on the lower end, between six and seven.

Now we will see how we make out in the other parts of the evaluation. "As compared with previous drawings, is there an increase of details?" We don't know. Actually, for learning purposes, it would be better if we were to use for the evaluation a situation where we have three drawings, as in Figures [9, 10, and 11]. Here we would say, "Yes, there is an increase." Shall we remain with the colored plate [Figure 13]?

Student: Yes.

Lowenfeld: All right. Then we can't answer this last question concerning an increase of details. "Is the child's drawing representational?" Yes. "Does the drawing show details?" Yes.

Student: "Some."

Lowenfeld: "Some," right; not "Much." Why? What points towards "Some"? Rain, features, especially eyelashes, are unusual for children of this chronological age. Therefore, we would say "Some." In other instances, the child did not show much detail; for instance, no buttons and no fingers are clearly expressed. Details are not present so we would say "Some." Yes.

Student: In answering some of these questions, I find difficulty in that some should be answered by "Yes" or "No" rather than "Some" and "Much." Now, you've answered some of these, such as, "Is the child's drawing representational?" by a "Yes" or "No." Does that mean "Some" or "Much"?

Lowenfeld: No; we can find in some drawings that the child does not draw representationally, but only now and then. Then we would say "Some." One drawing is representational, the other is not representational.

You see, we look at several drawings. We never evaluate one drawing alone—and that refers to spontaneous drawing, not teacher-dictated drawing. If in one drawing the child says, "I'm painting a design," and dabs and colors and so forth, and two other drawings are representational, we would not say "Much" representation. We would say "Some." If two of the three drawings are not representational, we would say between "None" and "Some." If the child always dabbles, you know, and makes only dots and so forth continuously, we would say "None." So evaluation is made over a period of time. It is possible to evaluate a child's drawings when the child has a tendency to be representational and also to satisfy himself by design forms, which is rare. But if he always uses design forms, we can't evaluate the child's drawings at all, as I said previously.

Student: I hate to slow things up, but could you explain what you mean by representational here? I was confusing it, I think, with the geometric forms which, when isolated, would still seem like geometric forms.

Lowenfeld: No, representational refers to the child's intentions.

Student: Oh—thank you.

Lowenfeld: Representational refers to when the child says, "This is a man; this is a house," even if the house or man doesn't look like nature or like what we see. It is according to the child's intention.

Student: About the details—I think the child is concerned more with the rain than with herself. And the eyes looking up, that is a definite detail; but look at the variation in the rain. Down near the bottom, the drops become smaller; and she even makes splashes in the puddles.

Lowenfeld: Mmmm. Yes, there are some details, but not many.

Student: She's concerned not with buttons and things, but with the storm only.

Lowenfeld: Yes, right. That's why I said it's difficult to evaluate a child from only one drawing. I would have to see three drawings or three paintings in order to really answer this question. We can better evaluate if we look at three drawings. Now, it may be that the child here concentrates on the rain and, therefore, draws the storm really in detail, much in detail. And at another time, the child draws a flower garden much in detail. Then we would say "Much." From this one drawing, however, I would say "Some," because I have no indication as to how the child reacts to other details in other drawings. As a matter of fact, I have a feeling that he doesn't deal in details with himself nor does he deal in details with environmental factors outside of the storm. But this was a good suggestion, and I'm grateful for it.

With regard to emotional growth, the most important thing during the pre-schematic stage is the constant change, the search for new concepts. If a child doesn't search, if he remains stiff, he has a tendency towards stereotypes. So the first question, "Does the child frequently change his concepts for man, tree, or details like eye, nose, etc.?" can only be answered if we

Fig. 14. "Playing Tag on the School Ground" (6½ years old). Notice the exaggerated arm of the catching boy and the omitted arms of the captive. Also notice the geometric lines; school ground is expressed by base line only.

were to have several drawings. We cannot say anything from one painting. You see, it's for this reason that I have, especially for the pre-schematic stage, three drawings reproduced in the book, three by one child. In the other drawings, we would say "Very much."

"Is the child free from stereotyped repetitions?" We don't know from this one drawing, but we can quite surely say "Yes," because the child has put so much in this drawing in terms of expression that we would not feel that the child would repeat the same symbols for the same things. So we would say the child is free from stereotyped repetitions.

"Are parts which are important to the child somewhat exaggerated?" Yes, the arms are very much a part of the child and are exaggerated because they are important. So is the head. The head is as large as, probably, the whole body, not in terms of adult inferences but in terms of the child; his subjective feeling is not an exaggeration for the child. He is looking up, and he is so much concerned with this looking up that his head is just the most important part of his body feeling.

"Is there a lack of continued and too much exaggeration?" Now, if the child continues exaggeration, too much exaggeration, we said that there is a tendency toward a physical defect. It wouldn't apparently go under emotional growth. But there is also another factor. I would like that we identify at this point with the child very, very sincerely and intensely. See, there are children when they draw who become so involved with one part that they lose contact with the rest. For instance, I had one such drawing reproduced in the book for another phase, when I tried to explain the change from children's drawings to adolescent drawings—Figure [14]. You see, it's the child "playing tag." This child is so much concerned with catching the other child that, while he was catching, he forgot the body and everything else and simply continued the arm more and more and more until he reached him. So the feeling is this: this boy is catching the other boy, and the other boy is running away; he is running away, but this boy wants to catch him. He can't catch him; now he catches him. Do you see? He loses contact with the original body; thus, he isolates himself emotionally from the rest. This is also a negative sign of emotional growth: when children lose themselves in one part and forget their relationship to the rest. You see, it's kind of the same feeling which you may have when you are upset. You almost forget the rest of your life and concentrate so much on this item which looms so large in your mind that the rest of the world doesn't mean anything. But in a state of upsetness, this is understandable. However, if this is continued, then it becomes a part of one's personality—this isolation of the self from the rest.

This answers the question which I was given and which I said I would explain when we came to it. Now is this understood? Can you put yourself into the place of such children? See, they lose contact with the rest of what they have drawn and now go on and go on. Some children go on indefinitely until their desire is fulfilled, regardless as to what has happened in the past or even right now, you know, and go on and go on. You can see this in children. This is, indeed, a lack of emotional growth.

Student: Is that stiffness in the figures themselves, so that the only motion is in the extended hands, one of the indications?

Lowenfeld: That's one of the indications, yes. But the stiffness may also be due to the fact that the child doesn't have any means yet to express motion other than making long legs for running and shorter legs for not running as fast.

Student: In this picture [Figure 14] in the book, I miss the arms on the little fellow who's running away.

Lowenfeld: On this one, probably because he's running away and he isn't catching, so—.

Student: The running is important to the child.

Lowenfeld: Yes. Now, let's go on since we have answered this one question which was asked. So, it is a part not only of physical growth, but also of emotional growth.

"Is the drawing definite in lines and color, showing the child's confidence in his work?" We would say "Much."

"Does the child relate things which are important to him?" "Much." The rain, you know, the storm—this is all related to him. So we have more check signs on the "Much" side than on the "Some" side.

I forgot to say when we were evaluating the scribbling of children that, if you were to connect these check signs with a line, you would get a very interesting profile of the child, do you see? You would get a profile, if you turn the chart around and say that the "Much" indicates where the child is strong, the lows ("None") in the curve would indicate where the child is weak.

Social growth: "Is the child's work related to a definite experience?" You remember, we said this is the basis for social growth—to identify one's self with one's own experience because only from the self can you extend to others. Yes, we would say he identifies. What would you say: "None," "Some," or "Much"?

Student: "Much."

Lowenfeld: "Much." You see, we all agree.

"Is there any order determined by emotional relationships?"

Student: What do you mean?

Lowenfeld: Sky above is an order; top is an order; bottom is an order. Rain coming from above is an order. Clouds over earth is an order. Rain falling upon the child; the child wants to protect himself. This all is an order. You see? There is a very definite order determined by emotional relationships, so we can say "Much."

"Does the child show spatial correlations: sky above, ground below?" Yes, "Much."

"Does the child show awareness of a particular environment (home, school, etc.)?" Now what do you think?

Student: "None."

Lowenfeld: The only particular environment is the storm, and we would have to see at least two other drawings in order to determine this. I venture to say that the child has a strong feeling for this environment, because he was quite conscious of the importance of covering himself from the rain in a storm.

Now, I would like to say a few words about the importance of this so that we understand why this refers to social growth. You see, social growth starts with a certain responsibility, responsibility for myself and later for my little brother, and later for the home, and still later for the community and for society in general. These are steps of social growth. When I said in the very beginning that our system of methods and teaching in our schools still lags far behind and still adheres to the same forms as we did, probably, a hundred years ago, this is what I meant. We are not even conscious of these steps in social growth unless we learn them accidentally. It's not a part of any curriculum, nor do we know how to foster it or motivate it.

Here you see that this form, or developmental aspect, of social growth shows itself in the children's drawings. This is wonderful. Here the child shows that he has a responsibility for himself on a stormy day to cover himself, to recognize the storm, "not just myself, but the storm and its effect upon me." We need two more drawings in order to find out whether this is continuously a part of the child's responsibility, social responsibility, to find out what happens to himself in various situations; because from then on he will get a feeling not only of what happens to me, but what happens to others. "What happens to Dad? What happens to my pet? What happens to my immediate environment?" From this, then, to—later on, during the gang age, we will discuss "What happens to my peers? How do I relate to them? How do I grow with them? Do I neglect environment completely with the peer group, or do I put them into a certain environment?" You see, these social relationships continuously show themselves. But during the pre-schematic stage, it is the "I" and the "my" which are most important; so if the child relates himself to this "I" and "my," then we can be sure that the foundation is laid for the extension of the "I" and "my" to the "I" and "you" or to the "we." This is important.

Now, perceptual growth. "Does the child use lines other than geometric?" Well, "Some." Where?

Student: The eyes.

Lowenfeld: No. The eyes are not other than geometric. You see, the eye is still a geometric symbol here, a simplification; but more important is the rain. The rain is simply and clearly a result of an emotional impact and is also a geometric line. Most of the drawing is geometric in nature. When isolated from the whole, the parts lose their identity. You see, when we say the eye—I can understand that someone said the eye is not geometric because, if I draw this on the blackboard, we would say this is an eye. This is the symbol which the child uses, but we think it's an eye only because we, with our past experiences, connect it with an eye. But where are the lids?

Student: There is an eyebrow.

Lowenfeld: The eyebrow is there, too, yes; but where are the lids and where is the shape of the eye? There is no indication of the eye as it relates to nature. It's still a simplification of geometric lines. Only by our past association does it become an eye, you know. Let's continue. We see that the child has some kind of percept which he refers also to his concepts. "Does the child indicate movements or sounds?"

Student: Yes.

Lowenfeld: What would you say?

Student: "Much."

Lowenfeld: I wouldn't know whether I should say "Some" or whether I should say "Much." Sometimes we will have to make a dot in between the lines and choose the five-point scale rather than the three-point scale. It is between "Some" and "Much," because movement is shown in several aspects—in the hands, you know, moving them up, and covering himself. There is a body movement which is quite unusual. And in the rain as it comes down is a definite movement. So there is movement, yes.

Student: Is that a blot up there on the right? The jagged line down along the right side—could that be the lightning?

Lowenfeld: I think that's the sun. Yes, we will talk about this now so we'll get an understanding of it.

Children develop concepts gradually of everything, such as a head—a head has eyes, a nose, and a mouth. Therefore, a head has these features. A sky—a sky has a sun. Therefore, the concept of sky is sky plus sun. A body has buttons, because I always button my shirt; so the button becomes a part of the body concept. In many children's concepts, we automatically see the buttons attached to the body. You know, in many children's concepts, they draw the arms and part of the arms are already the fingers. In many children's drawings, the sky would not be complete if the sun were not included whether the sun is shining or not. It is a part of the child's concept. So we see in many children's drawings that the sun is always included whether it's raining, whether it's storming, or whether it's beautiful. Yes?

Student: Do you think that the simplifications of the drawings like the sun that are put in a workbook—it's always the kind of sun that a child draws. Do you think that the child forms any of his concepts from these workbook concepts?

Lowenfeld: Oh, he does; but especially this concept of the sun is rather a workbook concept that is taken from the child's concept. In other words, the sun is an important concept of every child, usually. And that goes throughout the world, not only the Western Hemisphere; it's in China, in Japan, in Indonesia. Everywhere in the world for the concept of the sky, the sun is a part of it. When it is night, the child simply paints over it and makes a star of it—not every child, but most children.

Student: Is it significant that he has no ears in this drawing?

Lowenfeld: It may be significant. I don't know. If the child continuously omits the ears—even when you stimulate the child's listening for something, and the child still does not react—it may be. That may account for—yes?

Student: That he evidently heard no sound in the storm.

Lowenfeld: Right, right. It wasn't important to him. He did hear it, but it was not important. It was a more important feeling that he had to protect himself. Not the hearing, but the protecting of the body was more important.

Student: Wouldn't he change color in the storm?

Lowenfeld: Not necessarily. The child here stuck to two colors as you can see. Color is not always related to objects during this stage in particular, so it doesn't matter whether the child makes himself green and makes the sun purple. Do you see? We must get away from our adult concepts. We shouldn't even stimulate for a color-object relationship unless the child discovers it himself. However, as soon as we see that the child discovers such a relationship, then we come in and motivate for it. This is a general principle, you understand, which we use in education. We should not motivate for anything unless we feel that the child is ready for it.

Student: I wasn't thinking of color; but if a child were to make his sun blue, then I would say he's considering another object. Since the color is the same as the rain, I was thinking that maybe it was just more rain.

Lowenfeld: He may relate it to the rest, but I doubt that. The child at this stage apparently has not yet related color to object, and therefore doesn't do it anywhere. Why should he do it with the sun? Do you see? It's not logical. If he would have related, let's say, a certain color to the eyes, another color to the lips, and another color to the ground, I would say, yes, he may have related it unconsciously or purposefully to the rain. But there is no other indication in the whole painting which points towards that. We always think of consistency, do you see? If we see that there is one relationship, then we can count on another. But if we see there are no relationships, why should he relate color to the sun? Only because we have a feeling for it as adults?

Student: Back to the sun—why is it that children usually put the sun up in the corner, in one corner or the other?

Lowenfeld: I have no explanation for using the corner, except—.

Student: They do.

Lowenfeld: Yes, they do. The concept that the sky is on top simply is this: there is the sky, there is air, and there is the ground. So the child draws the sky on top. The sun is a part of the sky; he doesn't put it in the middle but most likely in the corner because the sky isn't broken up that way, you know. It's a desire not to break up the sky but simply to have the sun as part of it. But this is not a very good explanation.

Student: Could it be because we see the sun more readily in the early morning and the evening since it is so bright?

Lowenfeld: I doubt it. I doubt that this is true because it would mean that the child obeys a perceptual experience.

Student: Well, we very rarely look right at the sun. That's one thing.

Lowenfeld: Yes, that's right. It may be, but I have no other explanation. I believe that the child just doesn't want to break up the skyline anymore than he has to. He draws the sky first and then attaches the sun.

Well, let's go on. "Does the child relate color to objects?" No.

"Does the child start in his modeling from the whole lump of clay?" Let me go through a more extensive explanation, because I feel that this is an important concept. The concept as to how children start in their clay modeling is important because, through their clay work, better than through any other work, we gain for the first time an important insight into one phase of the child's personality, one phase which is completely in the realm of an art education interpretation because it stems from visual data, that which we see. From experimentation we have found that some children start their product with pieces and assemble these pieces and arrive finally, after assembling these pieces, at the total form, at the whole. Other children start with the whole lump of clay and pull out the details, and, finally, by pulling out or indenting details—not adding but indenting details such as the eyes or pulling out the nose and making a hole for the mouth—arrive at their final product in a different way.

Let's look at these two kinds of processes. It's fascinating. You know, I would love to talk to you about this part alone for at least an hour, because it's one of the most interesting things which occurs. If you are used to thinking first in terms of details, you jot them down—you write them down—and then out of these details you arrive at a whole concept. This is a different kind of personality than one who thinks in terms of the whole and breaks it down into details. Actually, I think that, if we observe, we see first the whole tree and then we discover the details in the whole. We see that the tree has a trunk. It has branches. It has twigs. It has leaves. Let's go closer and see what kind of leaves. Visual observation means first seeing the whole and then the details. Generally in life, we call these two processes synthesis and analysis.

In synthesis, we have first the details; and after putting them down and combining them, we arrive at a whole. I will give you an example. In the making of synthetic rubber, we have all kinds of details: tar, coal—I don't know what we have in the way of chemicals, but there are many. Then we distill them and boil them and out comes rubber. We put details together and the product, then, is synthetic rubber. The synthetic product is a result of a combination of many details which form a new whole—rubber. We speak of analysis when we start with the whole, like the whole sentence. Then we break down the whole sentence into the meaningful details. What is the meaning of each word in the sentence? Where is the subject; where is the—you know. This is sentence analysis. Or if you go to a physician and say, "I would like to have a urine analysis," you bring him the whole urine and he finds out the details which are in the urine. This process we call analysis.

In modeling, then, we call the process in which we start with the details the synthetic process of modeling. A child starts with the head, the body, the legs, the arms—makes separate coils for each—and then puts the pieces together into a synthesis called man, a figure. Other children start with the whole. They have the whole lump of clay and pull out the details—that means, they arrive at the details by analysis, saying, "Oh, the body has arms and legs, and we pull them out." Do you see? So these are two different processes which refer to two different kinds of thinking. To change one process into the other would mean thwarting an individual, because we would force him to think in another fashion than the way he is used to thinking.

Now, let us briefly talk about personalities. I have said one characteristic of children who are perceptual, who depend much on observation, will be that the children model analytically. Dr. Zawacki, one of our doctors, made a study on synthetical and analytical approaches to modeling. He confirmed my studies which indicated that children who assemble things synthetically are more inclined mechanically and think conceptually. And children who pull out the clay are more the children who observe, at least in their tendencies. Dependent on how well they observe, they will then pull out many details or few details. But these are two important characteristics concerning their perceptual growth. Especially if a child models analytically, we would say, "Does the child start in his modeling from the whole lump of clay?" If we say "Much–Always," then we would say the child is perceptually inclined and, therefore, is high in his perceptual growth.

LECTURE 17

The Pre-Schematic Stage: Evaluation of Physical, Aesthetic, and Creative Growth; and Motivation

Student: At both of these levels you ask "Does the child model analytically?" Why is analytical asked rather than synthetical?

Lowenfeld: Well, I'll let you answer that. According to our discussion, the answer should be in your mind. Why?

Student: That's a higher level.

Lowenfeld: No, it's not. Well, analytic modeling is a higher level of what? Perception—because the one points toward perception and the other [synthetic modeling] points toward a mental concept. Do you see? Since this question is under perceptual growth on the chart, the child who models analytically would rate high while the child who models synthetically would not ̇rate as high in perceptual growth. You see, we said yesterday that observation is actually analytical seeing.

Observation is actually seeing in details, that means seeing first the whole and then the details. We analyze from the whole to the parts. Any observation is that. What do you do when you paint? You look first at the whole, and then you break it down into the kind of details to which you are inclined, either details in subject matter or details in lights and shadows. But whatever you do, you start with the whole—probably paint over the whole tree, and then go on and divide it into lights and darks, and so forth. This is a breaking down of the whole into details. Observation always consists of this breaking things down from the whole into details. It's a part of ourselves. When I give you a brooch—look at this brooch, a beautiful piece of jewelry. What do you do? You see it first—the whole—and then you put on your glasses and look at the details in order to observe more closely what you have before you. Now, I think we answered the question.

There is another question: "I understand that geometric lines are those which, when separated from the whole, lose their meaning. Why would the rain in the drawing in Figure [13] not be considered geometric when the eyes are considered so?" I *would* consider the rain as geometric. I would not consider it as realistic; I would not consider it in any other way but geomet-

202

ric. If you think that I have considered it differently, then that would be a misunderstanding. I said yesterday, as you remember, that the rain indicates movement and geometric lines can also indicate movement. This does not mean that we don't consider the rain lines to be geometric lines. Indeed, each stroke, as such, is a geometric line, and when it is isolated, it will be a line and no one will recognize it as rain. You see, the realistic representation of rain is when you have all kinds of shadings included. Even if I tried to indicate it on the blackboard, you will already get a different feeling for the rain. We will have much more understanding of what the non-geometric lines actually mean, the perceptual lines, when we come to the discussion of the child who deals with perceptual lines. We have not come to that fully. We have many more characteristics which will be a help to us in separating a concept from a percept. We only have covered concept so far. Yes, indeed, I would consider them as geometric. If I didn't answer your question, don't nod, please; but get up and say, "You didn't answer my question." And I will be most happy, you know, because this always is a challenge.

"What is creativity? I feel that it is necessary to have imagination for creativity, but it is possible to imagine without being creative. Is this a correct assumption, or does imagination presume creativity?" Imagination does not presume creativity, absolutely not! There is even one form of imagination which is completely mechanical. It is quite common in children. It is called eidetic imagery. Those who are in psychology will be acquainted with this term. You don't need to know it, but when I'm asked such a question I like to give a full answer. Eidetic imagery is the imagery which is so forceful that it is almost like reality. It's like a photographic image, so vivid that we almost think that it is reality. Psychologist Gaensch, a German psychologist, and later Gordon Allport at Harvard University, were intensely concerned with the term, eidetic imagery. To give a picture of what eidetic imagery means, I'll illustrate it for you. Eidetic imagery is always awakened whenever your imagery becomes very much stimulated, so much stimulated that you almost see reality in front of you. Some people keep this imagery, especially children, and no longer differentiate between reality and imagery.

But this imagery has nothing to do with creativity, because it is almost a mechanical or photographic picture which you have in your mind. I believe that the cave drawings in Southern France and elsewhere in Paleolithic caves are mainly due to eidetic imagery and not due to the ability to observe or create, as they have been considered previously. The ability for having such skills and the ability for being so creative would be in complete contradiction to the primitivity of mind of those Paleolithic cave inhabitants. They were the very first from whom we have some kind of cultural achievements. It would be entirely impossible—according to their brain structure and the size and the weight of their brain, which we know of through the skulls we have at our disposal—that they engaged in such complicated things which are beyond the species of an ape. Also, the ape does not create, in spite of the fingerpaintings which you may have seen. We have not yet discovered whether any other species but man creates. And man a hundred thousand years ago—six hundred thousand years ago, as Paleolithic time is—did not have the capacity to create.

Now, we were pondering about them. What made them draw such adequate paintings? I'll give you a picture of them, and the eidetic imagery helps us out. You see, hunting a bison was not an easy business, because what did man have at his disposal? Just a rock, probably a rock which is more pointed than another rock which he found. But, you know, a bison is a pretty heavy and forceful animal. If you hit a bison with a rock, it may not do anything to him unless you hit him just right. So the Paleolithic cave inhabitants, who were hunters, only depended on what they could do with their hunting skills of throwing a rock at an animal and killing it, probably hiding for days in order to get even close to a bison. Then they threw the rock, and often in this throwing they were disappointed. They went away hungry, almost starving, because they could not kill the bison.

In such stages of starvation or of being hungry, your imagination becomes much more vivid. The more you are run down, the more vivid becomes your imagination, and it does do some tricky things with you. You know that even from your own imagination, your own experiences. So you must imagine there is a primitive inhabitant of a cave. He looks at the bison. He is obsessed by it because he has an empty stomach. He's going to kill it, but it isn't killed! Now he has to go back into his cave. But the bison follows him, follows him everywhere he goes. There it is. There it is. But it isn't there. Do you see? This is an eidetic image.

He comes back from his hunting, and now he sees the bison. And now, in order to get rid of it—he had so much instinct; you see, that's the beginning of creative instincts—he took earth, mixed it with oil or fat or grease, and traced his eidetic image onto the wall of the cave. It is almost as if I were behind you and would project with a projector a bison on the wall and you would now trace it—only there was no projector; the projector wasn't there. That is what we call eidetic imagery. Did I make this understandable? Imagery is not connected with creativity unless it is translated. Unless it is translated and integrated with your feelings, with your mind, and with your ability to organize harmoniously, it will not become a creative experience. So we have to distinguish between creativity and imagination. Of course, these are two different things.

And now I have not a direct question, but a request. Sometime ago in the *National Geographic Magazine* appeared an article[8] which some of you

8. Newman Bumstead, "Children's Art Around the World," *National Geographic Magazine,* Vol. 111, No. 3 (March 1957), pp. 365–387.

may have read, "Children's Art Around the World," an article with beautiful illustrations in color made by children from around the world. While I greatly appreciate the efforts to collect paintings of children from around the world, the description of them is entirely inadequate. For example, in one instance [Figure 15], it says, "Five-year-old Barbara Foley of New York had just started at the United Nations International School when she painted this class portrait"—actually, it is a series of stereotypes. "She exaggerated the significant detail—the faces—as young children often do. Writes Barbara, who is now 12: 'I am the girl pictured without legs [here on the top]. I suppose I didn't feel the need to do more than show my face. The girl with the red face was Eve from China. She cried a lot, so her eyes always looked scarlet. The girl at lower left was Alice from Africa. She wasn't used to the winter climate in America, so she wore three caps to keep her ears warm. The others are Linda, a Czechoslovakian girl (top right), and Susan, an American. Susan was a happy girl, as you can see by her smile.' "

Now, you see, these are forced interpretations which are really a self-betrayal. They are against all that we know about creative activity. For instance, as you can see, all have the same smile. That's her concept of a mouth. Don't think that it is a smile when children draw that way. It is part

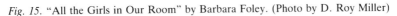

Fig. 15. "All the Girls in Our Room" by Barbara Foley. (Photo by D. Roy Miller)

of the concept of a mouth. Actually, why should this girl smile and not the others if they all have the same concept? So you can see that it is merely that the child added something later on when she was confronted with the drawing. It's also, I think, an exaggeration to think of one's own self without legs and that this was done on purpose. Such things are done subconsciously. Indeed, these are stereotypes, as you can see. All the girls are alike, even have the same kind of hairdo. Everywhere is the same symbol or concept applied. The arms are the same; the legs are the same. Only the one has no legs, so there is a little deviation from a stereotype seen in the various drawings. If you would ask me, I would say that this is not the Chinese girl. This is probably, she, herself, who considered herself more important and, therefore, gave herself a red color. But I also am interpreting this without the child and do not know whether this interpretation is correct. At any rate, I would never relate the crying to the red eyes. A five-year-old child does not discover such relationships and then draw the whole face like that. So I believe that the interpretations of this drawing, as well as of the other drawings, are out of focus and are not done with the sensitive understanding of children's works. But the attempt to collect drawings from all countries is a very noble one and, indeed, contributes to the understanding of international relationships. Thank you very much.

I believe we have answered all questions, and we can now continue with our discussion. We have discussed evaluation with regard to social growth and perceptual growth. Now, we would like to discuss physical, aesthetic, and creative growth, and then shake our tube very well so that all of these growth components will integrate in the creative product. Then we shall go on with motivation.

Under physical growth on the Evaluation Chart, Pre-Schematic Stage, the first question is: "Is there a lack of continuous omission of the same body part?" And then it says immediately, "Is there a lack of continuous exaggeration of the same body part?" Since I wrote these questions, I would like to say that we have established a significant relationship between exaggeration of a particular body part and a physical defect of the part. But another study has been done which tried to verify omission of a body part also as significant with regard to the effect which physical defects have on children, and we could not establish a verification on that. Children omit, then, not only because of some body defect, but they also omit because things were unimportant, things were unrelated to them, and so forth. We have not as clearly an indication as in the exaggeration of a body part, although there is some indication that children who have body defects also may omit those parts.

For instance, in this painting [Figure 13], we have no ears. This could mean that the child was not conscious of his hearing, but it could also mean that the child probably would like to suppress his ears on account of some ill experiences which he has had with his ears. But we would only be able to make any kind of a justifiable statement if we were to have at least three drawings at our disposal. And even if three drawings are all the same with regard to the symbol, we would still not be able to make a justifiable statement unless we verify this with other behavioral attributes or characteristics. So don't make any pronounced statements. Yes, please?

Student: What if there is a lack of continuous—I mean, there shouldn't be continuous omission.

Lowenfeld: That's right. Very often you see that the questions are negatively stated. It would be only logical to state a question positively. Why do you think that is done? Because, as a rule, I kept the "Much" always as the higher achievement. If there is much lack, it is good. Do you see? We kept questions uniform for our profile; if the curve bulges out on the right, then it's good. If it is on "None," it's not good. Therefore, I had often to state negative questions: "Is there much lack of omissions?" If there is much lack, it's good. If there is continuous omission, or continuous exaggeration, it's bad. That is why we have sometimes stated negative questions.

"Are the child's lines determined and vigorous?—None, some, much?"

Student: Yes, "Much."

"Does the child include body actions?" Yes, we have here a picture of the physical growth of the child which should be verified, indeed, by the child's own reactions.

Now, let's turn to aesthetic growth. "Is the meaningful space well distributed against meaningless space?" Now, I would like to clarify a little bit that which we call meaningful and meaningless space. Would anyone like to comment on this? Meaningful space is the space which the child determines through his drawing activity, which the child circumscribes with lines, and which the child may fill in actually with paint. This is the meaningful space. For instance, if a child makes a base line here and fills in the space below the line with grass, then the grass is the meaningful space and above is the meaningless space. If the child makes a tree and does not even fill in the tree, the tree is the meaningful space because it is meant to be something. Meaningless space has not yet been defined by the child, actively defined. When the child draws a skyline, then this is also meaningful space because it belongs to the sky. The relationship of the meaningless space, which is undefined, to the meaningful space, which is defined, is responsible for harmonious organization. If a child draws things very small—for instance, there is one small figure—unless the child got the feeling of being very small and expresses this with some specific expression, such as the feeling of being lost and alone, in general, we would then say there is not a good relationship between the meaningful and meaningless space.

Student: What if he just draws the base line and doesn't color the grass in? Is the part below it meaningless?

Lowenfeld: It's meaningful.

Student: It's still meaningful because it's circumscribed.

Lowenfeld: Yes, indeed, because from here on everything is base. You see? Yes?

Student: It probably happens very rarely, and maybe not at all, but suppose Johnny starts and paints all the spaces. Everything is painted.

Lowenfeld: Well, when you have everything to be meaningful space—. This may happen, indeed, but then it is the distribution between one meaningful area and the other meaningful areas which counts. Suppose the child covers everything in the painting—let us say, the child makes this all blue sky and covers it, and here the tree, and covers this, and everything is covered. Well, then it is the relationship between this meaningful space (blue sky area) and that meaningful space (the tree), because the sky has now become meaningful, which accounts for a harmonious organization.

"Does the organization of the subject matter seem equally important to its content?" Well, it is very important that we find out if the organization of the subject matter is equally important to what it means. For instance, if the child makes a small figure and if this really means "I feel small in this vast world," then the content and the subject matter have been related very well. But if he draws the figures very small and he feels big, then the content is not related to the subject matter. This, too, is a bad sign of harmonious organization; because in a harmonious organization, feeling, thinking, and perceiving should be closely integrated. So this is a sign of aesthetic growth. Ask yourself this question, "Did the child really express what he wanted to express?" If he did not express it well, then there is no harmonious relationship between his content and his subject matter. If the subject matter is small figures but the child's intention is strength, and strong figures in no way are expressed in what he drew, then there is no relationship between the two. If there is no relationship, then some phase of harmonious organization is lacking.

"Does the child show a desire for decoration?" Now, if this desire is present, then he is very high in his desire for harmonious organization, because decoration is something additional and shows something like an overflow of a desire to express things which are beautiful and harmonious in their organization. Yes?

Student: In regard to decoration, why is it that when children use cut paper their concept seems to be advanced in comparison to when they just draw or paint? Take, for example, a tree. Usually, a child in this stage does make his lollipop trees; but if he's doing cut paper, he'll put in the trunk with branches on it.

Lowenfeld: Because cutting paper more readily leads to a synthetic process. You see, he is almost forced to start by thinking, "Now, how should I cut the paper? First the trunk . . . , " and so forth. This may be the reason for it.

But there are other discrepancies we have not yet been able to explain, which are still unexplainable phenomena. One of these is the tremendous difference which we discover in children between building with cubes and scribbling. Have you seen the complex patterns which small children build with cubes or with wooden things? I just watched Robin at home. We gave him cut up little pieces of wood from the scrap box. How he tried to build and combine them is in complete contradiction to his scribbling. Do you see that there is some force at work when children have something in their hands which probably relates more to a multiple-choice recognition than to their active participation in creative processes? But still, this has not been investigated and may relate to your question, too. That's why I brought it in.

Now, let's look at the section for creative growth. "Does the child use his independent concepts?" Again, independence in concepts, as you understand, is very important for creative growth. Or, does he rely upon Mickey Mouse pictures, or coloring books, and so forth? If he does, then his creativeness has already been thwarted. It may potentially be there, don't misunderstand, but it may have been thwarted. We only can see the functional creativeness which is working in children's drawings.

"If the child works in a group, does he remain uninfluenced?" As you remember, we had similar questions during scribbling. They are similar except that we would now say about his concepts what we previously said about his scribbling.

"When the child is alone, does he spontaneously create in any medium?" Or, do you have to say, "Johnny, now you may draw something for me?" Do you see? If you know a child, you can readily say whether he never spontaneously draws, whether he sometimes spontaneously draws, or whether he always draws spontaneously. This distinction we can clearly make on a very reliable scale which we have tried out. You see, we tried out these questions by exposing individuals to certain situations and asking them, after observing a child, "Do you feel that the child always spontaneously draws, only sometimes spontaneously draws, or never spontaneously draws?" We found out that there was 100 percent agreement among people. So we can, through observation, come to a valid judgment.

"When the child is alone, does he refrain from imitating for imitation's sake?" Now, this is another proof. When he is alone, he may not be under the influence of other extrinsic factors: therefore, he may then give real expression as to where he stands—of course, also being influenced by previous experiences. When he is alone, does he refrain from imitation or does he always ask for a coloring book or something to draw from? "Please draw this for me," is also an indication of a desire to imitate and a lack of confidence in one's own creativeness.

Student: Isn't imitation a factor concerning intellectual growth?
Lowenfeld: No, imitation for the imitation's sake is not.

You see, imitation for the sake of imitation is like a parrot. If you can imitate very well, you don't need to be very intelligent. You have only, let us say, the gift of imitation, which is not related actually to intelligence. As a good example, I could give you Einstein. Did any one of you ever hear Einstein speak? Einstein was here in this country for many, many years; but if you were to have compared my accent with his, you would have been surprised. You could scarcely understand Einstein, so bad was his English pronunciation. He spoke with a very strong accent. Now, if imitation would be, as you say, a part of the intelligence of individuals, Einstein wouldn't have been very intelligent, then. No, imitation is not a part of intelligence. And Toscanini! Have you ever heard Toscanini speak? Well, even with his musical ears—this has nothing to do with it; it's another faculty. You may have people who can imitate very well, but their intelligence does not need to be highly developed.

Now, let's shake all these components of growth and look again at the painting which we have before us [Figure 13]. Now, we will get a total impression of the individual, who is probably, with his six years of age, an intelligent child. I'll presume that we have now three drawings before us, not one, and that he is emotionally very sensitive because we saw his curve was going up very much on the high side. With regard to observation, he refers mainly to his subjective interpretation although his kinesthesis may be highly developed. His feeling for motion is the most developed feeling in the area of perceptual growth, as you remember. We are not quite sure whether this child would be as highly cooperative as he is intelligent. We have no proof from this drawing whether he has become aware of his environment, but we know that he identifies with his own experience very closely and that he has the basis for social growth. So we shall lead him through motivation into the social growth which is desirable. As we shall see in the next stage of development, this should come out. So we shall wait.

We know that the child is extremely harmonious in the relationships in this drawing. He distributed amazingly and beautifully the meaningless and meaningful space. There is almost no space left in this drawing in which the parts which were meaningful are not distributed beautifully. So his outstanding characteristics are his intelligence, his emotional sensitivity, and his ability to organize harmoniously. We have here a very wonderful and desirable child if this is true for other drawings, too. Indeed, we can even, from this one drawing, say that he is a creative child because we do not see any desire to depend on others' thinking, although we do not know whether the child creates spontaneously or whether he needs a motivation. We would better understand this child if we were to be present with him and especially if we were to have more than one drawing. So we get a wonderful feeling for this child without even knowing him. But think how much better our feeling for the child would be if we were to know the child. And, of course, we should always use our sensitivities for knowing children and not for diagnosing drawings distant from the child.

Now, let me come to the most important part, the practical part, of all our knowledge. What should we do with all this knowledge in the classroom? You remember very well, I hope, that we said a motivation which does not reach the child is not a good motivation. That means only motivations are good which fulfill the child's needs. "What are the child's needs?" is then the question which will determine our motivations. First of all, we know the child needs to discover a relationship between his mental picture and the outside. So he, for the very first time, relates first to himself in his work and then to the environment in his work. This need should be fulfilled through motivation. Another need, which we know from our discussion of the pre-schematic child, is that the child is searching for his concepts and in this search he should become satisfied. What are these concepts, and what are they dealing with? This question will lead us to the third important need. We know that children of this age are always concerned with the "I" and "my." We have to fulfill these three basic needs of the child in order to do justice to the child during the pre-schematic stage.

Student: Would you please repeat that third need?

Lowenfeld: I said that we know from observation and experimentation that these concepts are mainly focused around the "I" and "my": "I and my dog," or "I am brushing my teeth," do you see? The "I" and "my" play a most important role during the pre-schematic stage, because all the discoveries are made within the "I" and "my" relationship. The child is still self-centered and regards himself as the focus of his experiences. He has not yet extended himself towards the outside, towards the environment. Therefore, these three basic needs must be satisfied by our motivations. You see, once you know the needs, the motivation is simple and is almost just a mechanics.

Since this is the first stage in which children are representational in their drawings, I would like to discuss more clearly how we should motivate children so that they will be affected by our motivations. First, the most important thing is that we use some of the children's basic experiences, experiences with which they can sensitively identify themselves. Now that doesn't mean that we should only take experiences which are from their real world. They can be fictitious, indeed, but then we have to present them to our children so dramatically that they become a part of their experience. For this, we have to select a topic. The topic should be focused around the "I" and "my," like "I am brushing my teeth" or "I am loving my pet." Such topics you have in your book, a series of such topics: "I and my mother," "I and my house," "I am brushing my teeth," "I am drinking my milk," "I am blowing my nose." As you can see, all of these topics are focused on some kind of activation of passive knowledge. How should we activate the passive knowledge of the child? For each motivation, there is that part which should be activated. For example, for the stimulation "I am brushing my teeth," I would like to activate the feeling for teeth. For "I am drinking my milk," I would like to activate the feeling for mouth. For "I and my mother," I would like to activate the size relationship between I (myself) and my mother. We should always do this by means of experiences and not comparisons.

How should a motivation be organized? Every good motivation should consist of a statement which introduces the atmosphere. Let me say clearly, so that we cannot fail—on this level, without becoming stiff and rigid or inflexible in that which we do, the introduction should consist of a "when and where": "When do you get up in the morning? Where do you get up in the morning?" Here we introduce the situation. When we have introduced the situation for "when and where," then we should state the "what." And after the "what," we should give a long explanation on the "how"—how it should be done. I'll give you a practical example. The "how," then, is the point of culmination; and every motivation should have a point of culmination so that the child is not left somewhere in a vacuum of not knowing what it is with which he is dealing. His experience should really be clear in his feeling. For that, the teacher must know his point of culmination. A motivation becomes entirely confused if we talk around and around and around and leave the child entirely on his own. This would be the very same thing that it would be in arithmetic or in reading if you leave the child entirely alone and do not give him any guidance with which he can strengthen his experience so that he can get the feeling of "Now, I know where I am."

The child, as well as the teacher, needs confidence. You need confidence in knowing how to motivate the child, and the child needs confidence in knowing what he got out of it, especially in feeling. An example of a topic which I have in the book is, "I am brushing my teeth." We need to keep in our minds that we have seen in the classroom that the children don't draw teeth. Teeth are not activated in their minds. See, we could use all kinds of motivations. We could give the class, "I am chewing my candy"—this would be another motivation with teeth—or "I am biting the carrot." Do you see?

It means to introduce the motivation in such a way that the children will feel it when they bite off the carrot, or when they chew the candy, or when they brush their teeth. It depends greatly on your intuitive qualities, the way you present this topic, so that you, yourself, are in it and identify yourself with the situation. As long as you, yourself, remain outside, you cannot expect the children to be in it. And this is where we greatly fail. I would advise every teacher to go through a good course in dramatics in order to be able to teach effectively. This is more important than you think it is, because only then will we give the children the feeling that learning for us is just as important as it is for them. You cannot expect children to gain in their knowledge and in their confidence and in their feeling and in their emotional growth and in their sensitivity toward perception if you stay here and have a high wall around you which is a barrier between you and the children. No, you have to be into the motivation just as the children should be into it.

So if you motivate, "I am brushing my teeth," you should go into every detail. You should say, "When do you get up in the morning? Children, when do you get up? What? At seven? How long does it take you to dress? When do you get up? Why so early?" We get a feeling for the life of the children. "Because I have to catch the bus." "When does your bus leave?" You see, we start with entirely different things than our point of culmination. We introduce an atmosphere of interest, of self-identification, in the very beginning. "Where do you sleep? Where is your bedroom? On the second floor? All by yourself?" Now we get to know something about the "when and where," and then we would gradually lead into the experience and say: "What do you do in the morning? What? Eat your breakfast? Right at the beginning? Oh, no, Mary, you forgot many things. First, I think, you rub your eyes, don't you? And then you don't even know where you are. You look around. Oh, it's a rainy day—Don't you? Or you go to breakfast in your pajamas. Do you? What do you do?"

Now you create a feeling of how the child feels. Then you say: "Well, you go to breakfast without brushing your teeth? Now, I'll tell you this is very bad, because there are all kinds of—what did you have yesterday for supper? Don't you feel it? Oh, you should get rid of all those things which you still have in your mouth and should be fresh for breakfast so that you can enjoy it better. Oh, now brushing our teeth—I'll tell you how we are going to brush our teeth. Johnny, do you know? How do you brush your teeth? How do you hold your toothbrush? With just two fingers you hold the toothbrush? Do you brush your teeth up? You know what happened to me? Did it happen to you, too? I got the brush caught there and it hurt. I was bleeding. I was crying. See, when you get in there with your toothbrush, it hurts! So be careful when you brush your teeth. Don't get it in there. But it is even better if you brush your teeth this way, vertically, you know, like this. Do you know why? You can't hurt yourself? Well, that's one reason, but there is another reason. You see, if you brush this way, you won't get those things out of your teeth which are not tasting good. So get them out. Without toothpaste? You like toothpaste? Hm? You eat it? It's not good. It's for brushing your teeth. But don't be afraid if you swallow some of it; it doesn't matter. So let's brush our teeth. Now let's think about it. Let's brush our teeth. And now what? Do we go to breakfast with all the toothpaste in there? Oh, no, we wouldn't do that."

You see, we remain now for quite a while at the point of culmination. And then we would say in our final conclusion of the motivation—every motivation should have a summary or conclusion: "Now, children, we are going to paint how we get up in the morning, go to the bathroom, and brush our teeth." You see? It is important that we have here a little summary.

Then we should not say, "And now let's distribute our materials." The whole motivation would be gone and noise would—you know. We should all have the materials distributed before, as we pointed out in the classroom procedures. Do you remember? Now the children are ready. Everyone feels his teeth. Some even have pain in there, but everyone is conscious of his teeth. There will not be a single child who will not include them. Do you believe it? You may make experiments. Yes, indeed, it depends on your motivation. If you were not good, you will see it in the drawings of your class. Yes, please?

Student: How long do you think the average motivation should take?

Lowenfeld: It usually takes longer than the drawing. It's good to remain with a good motivation, because the motivation is the sensitizing aspect, you see. It depends, of course, on the topic; but as you have seen now, probably it took me five minutes or ten minutes. I don't know. I didn't look at my watch.

Student: When the motivation is so intense, and the kids are really interested, and they're really expressing themselves, and the period comes to an end, what do you do?

Lowenfeld: The teacher did not harmoniously organize this motivation with regard to the time; therefore, it's low in aesthetic growth.

Student: You walk into a classroom and you see that happen so often. Here the kids are, busily working away, and the teacher says: "All right. It's time to clean up. We have arithmetic."

Lowenfeld: But it is very important that you get into a harmonious relationship, that you should hustle with your time, with the means which you have at your disposal—the facilities and so forth.

It is very, very important that you should not stop a motivation and say, "Now, children, next time we will draw how we brush our teeth." That would be very bad as you can visualize. But in this way, whenever the opportunity arises in the elementary school—sometimes every day, other times not every day—you must keep flexible. Whenever you include a new sensitive relationship, you make the child more sensitive to himself and to his environment; and this is very, very important. Yes?

Student: That would be a good time to point up your identification and good relationship with the classroom teacher.

Lowenfeld: Yes, indeed. As an art teacher, your relationship with the classroom teacher should always be one in which the classroom teacher feels that you are part of the classroom. You should give yourself to the lesson. You should not dash in, give a motivation, leave everything in disorder, and go, so that the classroom teacher has to clean up the mess, you know.

LECTURE 18

The Schematic Stage: Self-Assurance via Repetition of Symbols, Order in Space, Space-Time Concepts and Symbols, Pure and Subjective Schemata, and Three Deviations from the Schema

This is a very important stage—one which is not a stage of great intellectual achievements, but when for the first time we shall see the child's social growth come into the foreground—because this may be the basis for the child's development of active participation in the formation of society or, let's say, in the ability to cooperate. We shall see that this stage assumes great significance, but one which has not yet been actually recognized as such. We often think that active cooperation develops much earlier in the life of children. This, as we have seen, is not true. Passive cooperation develops much earlier. But passive cooperation is somewhat different from active cooperation, the cooperation in which the child discovers a feeling of being a part of a larger whole, a part of the environment, a part of belonging to this environment, and an active desire to contribute to this environment. It's a very interesting factor which leads us to this understanding in art, and we shall talk about it during this stage.

Intellectually, there actually is kind of a standstill, you know. Nature provides us in our growth with such intermissions—something like, let us say, a rest-pause. This is one case where we clearly can point to such a pause. The child has been very flexible and has been searching for concepts during the pre-schematic stage; that is, the healthy child, the alert child, the child who can freely grow. But there are other children who have arrived relatively soon at this intellectual pause, at this rest stop. These are the children who are less alert and less active in their thinking, sometimes even retarded. So we arrive here at a very peculiar stage. Usually we say, "When a child moves from one stage of development to another, this is progress." Not so here. We rather would like to extend the pre-schematic stage as long as we can to keep the child flexible in his concepts so that he will finally arrive at this pause, at this stop, with rich concepts and not with poor concepts.

Let me try, at least, to give you a feeling of how the child arrives at such concepts. Have you ever played with a child of five, six, or seven years, or even earlier? It is repetition which makes the child assured that he has grasped your story or the issue involved.

Repetition, then, is a very important learning factor, as you all are aware. "Do it again. Do it again. Do it again," are words with which we all are familiar, especially those who have brought up children of their own. This "do it again" is something which, in the beginning, is a kind of passive learning factor, something like a game. Robin does it already, and he is two-and-a-half. If he likes something, a noise which I make, he says, "Do it again. Do it again. Do it again." I can make it a hundred times, you know, and he just has fun in listening to it again and again. But usually he does not actively do things again for himself, at this age, in order to learn. By the way, he does do some things by himself without being told to do so. For instance, he tries to pull a lever to find out whether the light comes on. He tries to do this again and again in order to assure himself that he succeeded in doing it. But this is, again, a multiple-choice arrangement. He didn't produce the lever—it's there, and the light comes on when he snaps it over in the other direction. Actively, he does it whenever he forms his own concepts.

Now that may be soon—whenever the child has arrived at such a rest stop. This approximately is the way: a child draws or discovers that there is a relationship between his drawing and Mother. The relationship may be this: "My drawing has a head, a body, and two legs; and on the head, there is hair. My mother has a head and a body and two legs, and there is hair, and, therefore, my drawing is Mother." Now, he loves that he has achieved this concept; and by repetition, he may assure himself that he can draw Mother—"I can draw Mother." Or he may generalize and say, "I can draw a figure," and then draws it over again and again. This feeling of self-assurance becomes more important than the search for a new concept. This is especially true for children who lack confidence and need this self-assurance rather than the investigation into further concepts.

So we see that children who have not the desire to increase their knowledge and search for new concepts and add things according to their new active knowledge—such children remain with a poor schema early. And this may be the schema with which they are satisfied. Maybe there are just two eyes. They manipulate now with this schema and remain with it whenever they need a drawing of a man: "All men are alike. This is a man. My dad has a head and two eyes and a nose and a mouth and a body and legs and arms; therefore, this is Dad. My mother has a head and a body and two legs and two arms and two eyes and a nose and a mouth; therefore, this is Mother." Do you see?

The relationship becomes one of little differentiation and soon stops in its enrichment. Therefore, our desire as teachers should be to keep the child flexible as long as we can by motivating him more strongly if we see that he has a tendency to arrive early at a schema. This arrival at a schema signifies that the child has arrived early at the schematic stage, the stage which usually, on an average, lasts from seven to nine years of age. But such an early arrival is no advancement for the child. On the contrary, it stops him from further investigating the richness of concepts. So it is the only stage, probably, in human development where the next stage does not represent immediate progress. This is very peculiar. Yet, at some point or another, all children arrive at this stage which we call the schematic stage; but some children arrive rather late, because they continuously and flexibly search and search for new symbols, concepts. Those who arrive late at this stage have a very rich concept, because they have enriched it over a longer period of time.

In the human figure, the child should include a differentiation of features—the symbol for eyes should be different from the symbol for nose; the symbol for nose should be different from the symbol for mouth. The child should include hair in his concept. The child should include the neck in his concept. The child should include a body in his concept. The child should include arms and separate symbols for hands, fingers, legs, and feet. Again, we may substitute clothes for the body. These go to make up the average symbol for a human figure which the child uses and which the child should have accomplished by the time he is seven. Any greater differentiation of the features is then beyond it, and anything less is below it. So this is, let us say, the minimum average symbol formation which we expect from children at this stage.

In his environment, however, is the greatest change; because here, for the first time, he discovers an objective order—an objective order in the environment. This objective order is signified by the child's understanding that he now knows that he is on the ground, the tree is on the ground, the house is on the ground, Daddy is on the ground. We all share the same ground, and this ground is usually signified by a base line. So this is the first symbol which shows this sharing experience—this experience of, as I called it, a mass consciousness—that I'm not alone, "I'm on the same ground as Daddy is, where Joe is, and Mary is, and the dog is, and the tree is, and the house is; we all are on the same ground." This is the first active knowledge of a sharing experience. Indeed, experiments which correlate social growth with the growth as seen in the creative drawings of children have shown that there is a very significant correlation between the objective spatial relationship which children represent in drawings and their ability to cooperate actively.

There are other significant relationships between this sharing experience and spatial relationships which may be interesting for those who are teaching in the elementary classroom. Dr. Russell made an investigation with regard to reading achievement and spatial relationships.[9] Among other things, she found that children who are good readers have good spatial correlations in their drawings. Children who are poor readers still do not express spatial relationships in their drawings. We have now a study under way at the University of Southern California by one of our doctoral candidates with regard to reading readiness. As far as present indications show, there is a very close relationship between the discovery of base lines and reading readiness. This means that children who cannot relate letters to one another and see a common word picture—which is also a spatial relationship—may be less inclined to read than those who do see their spatial relationships and discover them actively. There are all kinds of implications here, but most important for our understanding is the desire for active cooperation and, therefore, the most fundamental step toward social growth. We could even say that citizenship has its basic starting point during this stage of development, because it is here that the child discovers his active membership in a larger group.

In children's drawings, this is expressed by a base line. The first experience of a base line may have nothing to do with this discovery—it may be purely coincidental. A base line, in the very beginning, is not a visual expression, as you know. We can't see a base line underneath our feet, nor can we see trees standing on a line or houses standing on a line. Often, the understanding and investigation of primitive art leads toward a better understanding of the art of children. In this case it does, because we see that in primitive art, primitive people often use the line simply as an expression for movement. When an Indian tribesman wanted to say, "I moved from this point to this point, and I was crossing a river, and, now I'm on the other side of the river," he made a drawing which approximates this drawing of a base line by a child—that means "I went from here to here along this line."

Indeed, when you remember your childhood games, there are many of these games which are based on moving along a line, drawing a line, and so forth—moving along, not stepping over it. You know these games. They all have their basic experience in moving along a line. So, actually, the origin of the base line is a kinesthetic origin; namely, body movement or body motion. The body moves along the line, and the child has the feeling as he moves that he leaves behind him a line along which he has moved. So the origin of the base line is, like that in primitive art, one of kinesthetic origin. We even see this in our comic strips in which movement is also usually expressed by line. If you have a ball flying, you see the ball flying along a line. This means that it moved along this line, and it may even leave some additional lines of movement. You have seen these signs for movement.

9. Irene Russell, "A Study of Relationship Between Reading Achievement and Creative Expression," *Research Bulletin* (The Eastern Arts Association), Vol. 1, No. 1 (1950).

Moving along a line, therefore, shows the very meaning of a line which is movement. Then, the origin of the line is kinesthetic. As the child moved along a line, he developed the thought, the concept—a thought concept. It's not a percept, because you cannot see a base line, you understand; it's a concept. He had developed his concept by noting, "As I moved along the line, I passed a tree, I passed a house, and I passed Daddy," and so forth. And then he placed everything on this line. This line became the base line. The base line, then, signifies the objective relationship of various objects which are put on the same ground. Yes?

Student: Is this true if children use the bottom of the paper as the base line?

Lowenfeld: Correct. Some children don't bother to draw a line but use the bottom of the paper as a base line. This may be the very first beginning—to use the bottom of the paper as the base line and to place everything on this line. It's a mental line, then, not an actual line.

The base line functions in many different ways. As we discuss the base line, we shall have to discuss another concept which also develops during this stage of development. This is the concept of space and time. Space and time concepts are what we call all concepts in which several time phases are represented in one space. I would like for us to open our books to Figure [16]. In Figure [16] we have the simple schema of a child. Is the schema below average? Is it average according to what we have said, or is it above average? Now, what is the consensus? Who thinks it is average? Put up your hands. Who thinks it is below average? Put up your hands. Well, you need the age—let's say seven years. Average? Below average? Above average? There apparently is some feeling it may be below average. Why do you say it is below average?

Student: Not very rich in concepts.

Lowenfeld: Details? What should it have? Well, first of all, we know that the active knowledge of a child of seven years usually is: "I have a head. I have eyes, eyebrows; the nose is standing out; therefore, it is on the side"—apparently in this case—"and a mouth." Now, this schema would not be much below average. You have differentiated symbols for the features. He included the ear. He did not include the hair, but the ear replaces the hair. He has a neck, a body, legs, feet, arms, hands—but not hands with fingers. So here we have a schema of a figure that is slightly below average, slightly. But what is more below? He does not include what? That he stands on the ground. The base line is not included in this concept. Do you see? You should have the feeling, "I am standing on the ground." However, when he draws an experience as we see in Figure [17], he does include the base line. The experience here is: "I have lost my pencil in the dark. I'm searching for the pencil and groping for it. I found the pencil. I put it into my pocket and enjoy having the pencil." In this drawing, you see that the

Fig. 16. Schematic representation of "A Man." In schematic representation, no conscious experiences are represented.

child has deviated from his schema. He expressed his subjective experience, namely, that of looking or searching for a pencil.

We shall, then, in the future distinguish between the pure schema and the subjective schema. The pure schema is the schema the child draws whenever no conscious experience is expressed—that is, when you say, "Mary, draw a man," or "Johnny, draw a man or draw a figure." In this Figure [16], no conscious experience is expressed. We call it, then, the pure schema. The pure schema shows the active knowledge which the child has of a figure—or if you say, "Draw a tree," of a tree; or if you say, "Draw a house," of a house. But whenever you motivate the child with regard to a certain experience or whenever the child is self-motivated with regard to a certain experience—such as, "I'm drawing Daddy," "I'm drawing a big man, the policeman," or "I'm drawing myself searching for my pencil"— then this experience motivates the child to deviate from his schema. We call this the subjective schema. The subjective schema is the schematic drawing of a child in which an experience is expressed. Actually, when we compare the subjective schema with the pure schema, we can see the child's experi-

Fig. 17. "Searching for the Lost Pencil." The schema has been modified according to the experience. Emphasis is on meaningful parts; unimportant parts are neglected. Several sequences are expressed in one drawing. Use of geometric lines. (Schematic Stage)

ence because the deviations from the pure schema are indicative of the child's experience.

Now, look at these two drawings [Figures 16 and 17]. In Figure [16], you have a pure schema, that is, when the child was asked to "Draw a man." Those who know the Goodenough Test—the Goodenough Test is based on the pure schema: "Draw a man as well as you can"—recognize that no motivation is involved. So Dr. Goodenough expected the children to draw their active knowledge. The test is wrong in that Dr. Goodenough only asked for one drawing, while we would ask for three drawings in order to assure ourselves that we are right in assuming that this is the pure schema.

You see, what may happen if a child takes the test of Dr. Goodenough—the "Draw a Man Test," the intelligence test to which I refer—is this: The child may have walked to school. On his way to school, he had to cross the street. This is nothing unusual. There was the policeman waiting for all of the children to assemble, and the policeman takes this child by his hand. Little Johnny looks up at the policeman, feels his big hand holding his small hand, feels it very definitely; and as Johnny walks across the street, he has in his mind; "My, he has a big hand; the policeman has a big hand." After he walks across the street, he arrives at school with the concept of a policeman in mind. Now he takes the intelligence test. The teacher says, "Now, children, draw a man as well as you can." Johnny, of course, draws a man as well as he can. He remembers everything about the policeman. He remembers his big hand; he remembers his fingers, how he was holding his little hand; and he remembers the big legs and feet.

So, he relates his schema to an experience of which the teacher is not aware. In drawing a man, he now relates his man not to the pure schema but to a subjective schema, that of drawing the policeman. No one will be aware of it unless we compare this drawing of a man with two other drawings; if they are the same, then we can be sure that this is the pure schema of the child. But if the child changes from one to another, then we should be sure that this is not the pure schema. The child may even be in the pre-schematic stage. So the test does not always function. It would be better and more objective if it did not rely only upon one drawing.

If we compare this pure schema to the subjective schema [Figure 17], we will see that a child generally uses three kinds of deviations to express an experience. Let's find out what the three kinds of deviations are. How did he express searching? He elongated the arm; he exaggerated the arm. What else?

Student: The legs, the body.

Lowenfeld: He elongated the neck; then, he made the body shorter, and he made the legs apparently shorter. By comparing the two, we will find out.

He stuck to almost the same concept of a head, except that it's a little bit larger. Now let's interpret it with our visual means which we have in art education, without drawing any inferences or psychological interpretations. We would simply say that shorter means less important and longer means more important, according to things which we know from art where larger always means more important because it covers a larger area and smaller means less important. So the hands are more important when he searches. Yes, indeed, when he searches and discovers his body feeling while he is searching, then the arms become more important to him. We can then say the first deviation is exaggeration of important parts. Diminution or even omission is another deviation. You may omit or you may diminish certain parts if they are less important or, also, if they are repressed. That means the child doesn't want them. You see, they are repressed. So diminution or omission is also a sign of the expression of an experience. Experience may be indicated by importance or repression. Repression, in a way, is also important here, because those things which we repress are important to us.

What else can we see? What is the third kind of deviation the child uses? Now look at the hands, the searching hand. Is it the same as in the pure schema?

Student: No.

Lowenfeld: No, he changed the symbol, didn't he? He used an altogether different kind of symbol.

So the third deviation which a child uses to express an experience is a change of the symbol. Whenever a child changes a symbol, whenever a child exaggerates a part, or whenever a child diminishes a part in size or omits a part, we can be sure that the child expresses an experience, consciously or subconsciously. That means that often the child is not aware of such an expression. *Most often* the child is not aware of such an expression. For instance, this child although he was searching, was not aware that he drew a part elongated. For the child, this is not an elongation. For the child, this is merely an expression of an important feeling of which the child is not even consciously aware, because none of these feelings become really conscious to the child. It is a part of the total feeling of the child. But we, as adults, translate this feeling of elongation or exaggeration as meaning importance; for us, it is an exaggeration. For the child, it isn't even an exaggeration. For the child, it is merely a right proportion, depending on what you call right.

You remember when we talked about our basic philosophy?—and this is very important. When we talked about basic philosophy, we said that there are visual proportions and emotional proportions. What is more important in your life? It all depends on whether you depend more on what you see or what you feel. If you depend more on what you see, then exaggerations may be disturbing to you. But if you depend more on what you feel, you are used to feelings which are in contrast to what you see. As I told you, if some relative of yours, some close relative of yours, were to have an accident far away in Korea, he would loom large in your mind. None of us could ever assume the size in your mind of this relative who has had an accident. It doesn't mean that he has grown in proportion. He still is actually the same size, but in your mind he has grown because of the accident. So emotional proportion is different from visual proportion.

For the child, emotional feelings are more important than visual experiences because he depends much more on the self and the reactions which he has to himself and to the environment. An exaggeration for him is not an exaggeration but actually an indication of his subjective relationship. Manuel Barkan, who is head of the Art Education Department at Ohio State University, made me aware of this factor: that we may make a wrong statement in saying that children exaggerate things. They don't. Only *we* see them in an exaggerated way. That's why, in the book, I made this statement, quoting from Manuel Barkan. I said, "It should be understood that exaggeration and neglect refer to size only; whereas the change of symbols refers to their shapes. It is needless to say that all these characteristics refer to the way *we* see them. Indeed, Barkan is right when he says, 'Children do not overstate; rather they create size relationships which are real to them.' " Do you see? They are real to them and are not over-statements or exaggerations. Now, knowing that children have a rather limited way of expressing their experiences, we will look at children's drawings differently. We will not then say exaggeration is out of proportion. We rather will look for an experience which the child expresses.

Indeed, this is not foreign to those who have looked at primitive art, because for a long time man has expressed important feelings through exaggerations. Even far, far back in prehistoric times man expressed running by exaggeration of the legs, by long legs. Previously, the interpretation was that apparently the people of this time must have had long legs. This is not true at all, because these people during the Neolithic time did not express their proportions by visual perceiving but actually according to mental concepts. So their feeling for running was expressed by long legs, and the variation which accounts for the different lengths apparently had something to do with the significance of the legs for their motions.

We have also discovered in this drawing that the child not only expressed one incident, but he also expressed several incidents: searching, finding the pencil, putting it in the pocket. He expressed several time phases in one drawing or in one space; therefore, we can say this is a space-time representation. Why? Because several time-phases are expressed in one space as we see it. All of a sudden, the child included the base line, as you can see. He was not quite confident, because in one instance he removed himself slightly from the base line. Now, let's find out what experience was behind it. Apparently, the pencil fell on the floor so this made him aware that the pencil was on the floor and he was on the floor. This made him introduce a base line. An emotional experience was responsible here for the inclusion of the base line. When he showed himself standing upright, he was clearly standing on a base line; but when he showed himself bending down, apparently it was more important for him that the hands were on the base line when searching for the pencil than that the legs were.

Now, go through this experience yourself and search. You almost forget where the legs are. Even in your adult feeling, when you, yourself, go through the feeling and concentrate on searching for something, the legs no longer are attached to the floor as definitely as are the hands when you concentrate on the feeling that you are touching the floor and searching for something. This apparently was the feeling of the child, unconsciously or subconsciously. The child was searching for the pencil; therefore, the hands were definitely connected with the floor and, thus, with the base line. Only when he got up, did he get the feeling of standing on the floor again, and therefore expressed it by means of attaching himself to the base line—even giving the feet a double line, which also is a slight change in symbol, to

Fig. 18. "Fruit Harvest"; "I Am Picking Apples" (7-year-old gifted child). The picture is divided into two sections.

signify apparently that he was standing on the ground. Yet, when he put the pencil in the pocket, you can see that there are no fingers any longer necessary for that action, because the fingers have somewhat shriveled; and the arm which had no function was diminished in size. We would say it's a stump, but it isn't. You see, that would be a visual concept. For the child, this arm had no significance as related to the other arm, so he scarcely felt this arm and expressed this in terms of a proportion. Now, when a child introduces the base line and becomes aware that several things are standing on the ground, he may signify this in different ways. And the ways by which he signifies it are fascinating.

Look at Figure [18]. Here the child expressed a fruit harvest. Actually, I should have the colored reproduction of it here to show you that the lines— the two lines in the middle of the picture—one is blue and the other is brown. The child expressed here, also, two phases. He drew a base line here at the bottom, drew trees with apples on them on the base line, and said: "I'm standing here, picking an apple. I am standing here at the bottom picking an apple." Then he said: "Above me is the sky; and far back on another ground there is Dad; there is another tree. Dad is going home with a load of apples." So he drew the wagon on another base line, as you can see, and the horse attached to it. He actually expressed his space in two sections, because this top section also has a sky.

Now, if you would really like to understand this drawing, you have to cut it in two and fold it over. I'll draw you a perspective view of this. Can you all see the drawing as a perspective view? In both drawings you have the sky above, the ground below. Do you see?

Student: This, then, is the child's representation of perspective?

Lowenfeld: This is the child's representation of his space or, as you say, perspective; but it's a different kind of perspective than we have. Actually, the child expressed two different spaces here: one is the foreground; the other, the background. "Here am I, picking the apple; there is Dad, carrying the load home."

This is not an unusual expression. As a matter of fact, historically, we know of this type of expression. Egyptian artists have long ago shown that drawing in sections is a form of space representation. And the child shows it to us again and again. If a child introduces two base lines, it simply means that he signifies that the section above is behind and not above. He has not yet visually discovered distance and the quality that distant objects apparently diminish in size. They are the same size and, therefore, he treats them the same in size. Now, if you look at Figure [18], you may then see the schema of trees. This child has found a concept and assures himself that he can draw a tree by repeating this drawing of a tree—the schema. The large apples are red, while the small leaves are green. You cannot see it because it's not reproduced in color. So the child's schema for tree is this: a tree has a trunk, a tree has branches, a tree has leaves and apples. What did the child not conceive of?

Student: Twigs?

Lowenfeld: Twigs. There are no twigs in the schema of this child although, apparently, he had much to do with trees by being the child of an apple picker. This was a Negro child who lived in Norfolk. He said he picked and put the apples into the basket. Why have the apples now become so small when he puts them into the basket? Just put yourself in the place of this child. What happened?

Well, you know, you always long for those things more which you can't have. Isn't it so? The apple on the tree is always more significant in your mind; it looms larger on the tree than the apples which you have in the basket. So this is a very poetic form of expression. You could make a poem out of this. Those things for which you long, those things which are not obtainable, are always looming larger in your mind, you know—an unfulfilled love, also; yes, indeed. And those things for which you are longing—if you were to long for freedom, then you would know how large it looms in your mind. And if you have it, you don't treasure it any longer in your mind. You see, this is a deep point.

I would just like to point out the implications which such a thing has; it's beautiful! Just get the feeling of the beauty of it. This is a tremendous concept which the child gives us here, not knowingly, of course, but this is a beautiful thing. When I said in the very beginning that so many artists long for the freshness of children's expression, when I quoted Brahms, who longs for the way back to children's land—well, this is it. Look how beautiful such a thing is! There the apples are so large. Oh, could I have them? And when I have them, I don't treasure them any longer. This is the expression here. They even become smaller when they are in the wagon. Loaded up, the apples lose their significance, but not those which he has left behind. Look at them! Those which are still on the tree are large. And this is very, very beautiful.

Now you may be interested in a remark which I got when I asked the child, "What's the bird doing?" I was surprised myself at how quickly the child answered: "You know, we have to sort the apples. Those which are picked by birds we cannot ship in crates. We have to sort them out because they are spoiled." The birds played an important role, so he included them. Think of the harmonious organization in this painting. This is truly a poem. In this drawing you scarcely can omit anything which does not function and contribute to the meaning—that does not function and does not serve a purpose. He wanted to say, "There is an orchard." Therefore, he was not satisfied by merely drawing one tree; he drew several trees because only several trees make an orchard. "The apples on the tree are the most beautiful ones because I want them. But I have picked some and put them into the basket. I'm now picking one. Those in the basket are no longer single apples. There are already dozens of apples which I have picked. Daddy is carrying them to town. He is going away. Therefore, he is in the distance. Birds are picking on the apples. We don't want the birds."

All this gives you the story of the whole feeling of the child. Now you can see how the child related himself actively to the environment: he is on the ground; the baskets are on the ground; apples are in the basket; the trees are on the ground; the wagon is on the ground, but further away; the horse is on the ground; the bird is in the air; the sky is above. There is a very definite spatial order introduced, a consciousness which signifies the child's understanding not only of himself but also of the significance which the environment has for him. It is the awakening of a mass consciousness.

LECTURE 19

The Schematic Stage: Space Schema, Color Schema, Design Concepts, Evaluation of Intellectual and Emotional Growth

---

The child's personal and individual body feelings are unconsciously or sub-consciously expressed in the schema. So don't feel that children's schemata should express reality. They don't. In fact, schemata consist of representative symbols. These symbols, when separated from the whole, lose their identity. We discussed that previously. So the schematic stage is still a stage in which the child does not refer to realistic lines (lines which, when separated, retain their meaning) but rather to geometric lines (lines which, when separated, lose their identity) as seen in representative symbols.

Yesterday we discussed the norm of what the child should actually achieve in terms of a human figure. We were about to discuss what we expect in terms of spatial relationships. Indeed, we expect the child to discover himself as being a part of a larger whole; that means, the child establishes a definite concept of space. This we call the child's space schema. See, we call one the figure schema; this we call the space schema. Actually, the vehicle of the space schema is the base line. This is the most important thing, and the variety in which children use the base line is amazing. But let me say this, the poorer the child is in his mental concept, the less variety will he apply to his base line concept. The simplest base line concept is when he uses the edge of the paper as a base line.

Then, when he introduces one base line and places everything on the base, his thinking is: "I'm standing on the ground; the tree is on the ground; the house is on the ground; we all are on the ground; above is the sky; and in the middle is air." So he never draws the sky coming down as we would see it visually. The sky only comes down as an optical illusion, you under-stand? The child is more correct in his space concept than we are as adults, because the sky never meets the ground, as you all know, since there is air between the ground and what we see or visually obtain as a sky concept. Actually, there is no sky. It's only the accumulation of air on top of a dark background. You could produce an artificial sky by putting masses of air in front of a dark background; or if you have black paper and get some slightly opaque sheets of paper in front of it, it turns also slightly blue. Of course, this all depends on the reflective quality of the papers. But if we think of the sky as being above, then we know that in the middle is air, and on the bottom is the ground. Never correct such a concept. It would be against our basic philosophy if we were to correct a child's concept according to our adult understanding. The concept that above is the sky and below is the ground is a very valid concept, at least as valid as our adult concept that the sky and ground meet. Both are illusions, because, actually, we cannot speak of a sky as such.

Now, when the child still has a great feeling for expression and a great desire to express space concepts, he will introduce not one base line, but two base lines, as we saw yesterday in Figure [18], and he signifies with that that there is not only one but there are sections of spaces as we go back into the distance. For the child, distance does not mean diminishing quality of distant objects. The child has the same space concept that blind people have, namely, a tree in the distance is just as large as a tree close to you. For the child, too, a tree in the distance does not change in size. It is just as large as a tree close to you. This is a more realistic concept than ours, because ours is an illusion. So, again, it would be foolish to impose our illusion upon a concept which for the child is, indeed, real. Philosophically, surely it's real also to us, because a tree in the distance isn't smaller. It is the same size. Only in our optical illusion does it grow smaller and diminish in size. The child goes through quite intricate kinds of understandings in using the base line. Here, I would again refer to your poetic understanding. It's very difficult to explain the poetic feeling which the child puts into his drawings, because it lies in the nature of poetry in that it cannot be explained in the same way as art cannot be explained. It is here where the intuitive quality of a teacher must come in in order to get really the full enjoyment out of children's drawings.

Just as I told you yesterday—by means of this one drawing, you are given a little understanding of what it may mean when we look at a child's drawing. How beautiful it is that a deep philosophy may be expressed in it in a very simple manner; for instance, in this drawing we have a philosophy that sizes grow with the longing for something. This can be applied almost to all human longings, including freedom and everything actually that we would like to have. The less we can have something, the more our desire for it grows in intensity. All this is expressed in a child's drawing as we have seen it.

If this is meaningful to you, then you will feel there is something very powerful in children's drawings, something very inspirational. If you can find this inspiration in children's drawings, your teaching will be richer and you, yourself, as a person, as a human being, will become richer. This comes from the enjoyment of teaching. May I say here that there are scarcely any other professions which allow this enjoyment. So I hope you gain from this course not only knowledge but also happiness in your classrooms. For this is, I believe, one of our lost arts—that we gain happiness in our jobs. I hope that some of this will come back to you and you will feel that it's not merely the material reward which you are working for, but the enrichment of your lives. You understand what I refer to? Indeed, we have lost much of this individual feeling which we gain from the satisfaction of teaching or which we gain from the satisfaction of any job. As a matter of fact, there shouldn't be any job on this earth which does not help man. Whatever we do and wherever we do it, we should gain the feeling that we are helping man in some aspect. Whether it is in the kitchen or whether it is in doing some handicraft to make our apartments or our homes more beautiful, you help man. If every individual thinks in these terms of helping man, of course, we not only help our immediate environment but we also help the whole world to recuperate from a mental breakdown—which help, I feel, is needed for today. But I am not pessimistic in this respect. On the contrary, I'm very optimistic that we are moving towards a much better time when our difficulties will be resolved—and they will. There is a great tendency in the world of today to see that these difficulties are resolved, a much greater tendency than we have probably seen in the last century. If you want me to elaborate on it, I shall occasionally. There are signs which are very encouraging in spite of all that goes on in the Cold War between our hemisphere and, let us say, Russia, on the other hand.

When the child uses his base line concepts in quite a variety of ways, he arrives at some concepts which are so completely different from ours that we have difficulty accepting them. And then the danger is great that we could interfere with the child's own concepts. For such a concept, I want you to open your book and look at Figure [19].

Obviously, we would immediately say, "Well, this child isn't quite normal because he draws upside down." Now, I shall introduce you to this concept of upside down, and you will immediately get a lot of fun out of it. It isn't upside down. Indeed, what the child did was this: he was drawing on the floor—or on the desk, if you want. This child was painting on the floor as we do in our children's art classes. Now what he said was this: "I am saying goodbye to Mommy. She is leaving on the boat for Norfolk. Norfolk is on the other side." This was painted in the Hampton Road vicinity. "We are on the one side, and Mother is going to work. She leaves for the other side." The child knew exactly how the other side looked because he had accompanied Mother before. He was quite confident of his knowledge of both sides; that means, confident of his mental concepts. So what he actually said is this. He stood and said, "Now I am painting the side of Norfolk." So he painted the side you see with the factory where Mother is working and the house where the boat, the ferry, will land. You see even the word "ferry" there. And, of course, in front of him is also the boat. He saw this all in front of him and translated this into his mental concepts, and painted them. And then he said, "Well, I am turning around to draw my side because here is a fence and everything else." So the child turned around and drew the other side.

This is actually what we do, don't we? If I were to draw this room, I would say, "Well, here on this side are four windows." I paint them. "On the other side there are also four windows." I paint them, too. We actually turn around if we look at both sides. And this is what the child does. So, actually it is a very valid concept when the child wants to draw both sides simultaneously, because both sides have significance for his concepts, not for his percepts. For his percepts, he couldn't perceive both sides simultaneously. If I look in this direction, I only know that there is something behind me; I don't perceive it, but I conceive of it. I know it is there. In order to do justice to his concept, of course, he turned around.

Fig. 19. "Norfolk Ferry" (8 years old). Space is expressed by "folding over" one shore line. Both sides of the creek are related to the middle.

Fig. 20. "On the Seesaw" (9-year-old boy). Subjective expression of the experience of going up and down.

Now you can see why I believe that easels are not conducive to the forming of concepts, because they take away much of the poetry of the child's concepts in his paintings or drawings. You see, if a child were to draw this on an easel, the child couldn't walk around the easel. He would have to stand on his head and somehow be suspended in the air. This is impossible, so the child reverts to a one-line base line concept on the easel, or possibly two base lines. But never would he express himself on an easel as he wants to by going around his drawing. Did I make myself clear?

This is an excellent spatial concept. If you really would like to get the feeling for it, fold the page in your book along the base lines. And then you will see there is the river in the middle, and on both sides you have the houses going straight up. It's almost a model. Do you see? This is the concept of the child: "I'm looking at one side; I'm looking at the other side." If you wanted, you could cut out the boat and also fold it up. Then it would be the perfect spatial model, much more perfect than our perspective could ever be. This concept of folding over is only for our feelings, not for the child's feelings. Folding over is only our terminology, you understand. It is not the child's terminology. The child invents a spatial concept here which is very valid. It expresses more of the true spatial relationships than perspective does.

A similar concept you have on the next page, Figure [20], where the children are playing on the seesaw, going up and down. Of course, the children face each other, and they know they face each other. If you were to cut it out and fold it on the base line up where the children sit, they would face each other, and this is also a true expression. What happened here was that the child painted the boy. The boy is way up in the sky. You can see him. And now she puts herself into the place of the boy, who is now looking at the girl. She is way down at the grass. Of course, she had to go around and paint the girl from the other side. Or, most likely, it was painted by the boy because he was feeling exalted by being up high; and, therefore, he painted himself much larger. Such concepts are not rare. You should appreciate them and their poetic quality rather than feel that there is something wrong. It always means putting ourselves sensitively into the place of children and then the door will open, the door into children's land. You know, it's a privilege which only we have in a way.

All of these belong to space-time representations. Why do these examples of folding over belong to space-time representations? I said it if you were listening. You remember how we defined them? We said space-time representations are representations in which several phases, time phases, are represented in one space. How does this definition apply to folding over? Well, the child couldn't look both to the front and to the rear at the same time. These are two different time phases. You cannot simultaneously see the front and the rear of a room. You have to turn around. So there are two different time phases expressed within one space. Therefore, folding over is also one of the space-time representations. Now, we have two kinds of space-time representations. In one, several time phases are actually represented, such as picking up a pencil and putting it in the pocket. These are two different time phases. And now we see that folding over is another time-space representation.

We have a third one which is expressed in Figure [21]. This child is the child of a miner. "Coal Mine" was her picture, and she said: "See, we are living in one of these company houses." This is on the slope of a hill as you can see it at the right of the drawing. "And Daddy always goes everyday into the mine. It's a coal mine. See the coal?" And she pointed at these lumps of coal, you know; they come already made! In the mine, you see that the workers are working with their wagons to bring them to the center. There a wagon is lifted up and carried to whatever place it is supposed to be carried. Here, two temporal phases are expressed, inside and outside. You cannot perceive of the inside. You cannot see the inside and the outside at the same time. You can only conceive of it. So two temporal phases—inside and outside—are expressed in one space. This is usually referred to as an X-ray picture, because it is similar to the X-ray—sees right through—which we get. Actually, these drawings are referred to in the literature as X-ray representations.

Student: If the child in the sixth grade has an X-ray picture. . . .

Lowenfeld: If a child in the sixth grade still draws X-ray pictures, that means he's still concerned with the inside and the outside concept and not with the percept. We will see that this is done by children who are very self-centered, because they still regard the world *not* as something to look at or as something of which they are outside, but just as something to be included. We will also see that children who are repeatedly concerned with being in the center and who use the concept of folding over are ego-centered children, because they always regard the world only from their own point of view. "I'm looking in this direction. I'm the center. I'm still the center, although I'm expressing environment. I'm the center." We have found that there is a significant correlation between the ego-centered feeling of children, more than normal, and continuous folding over. From the point of view of emotional growth, continuous folding over is not desirable. You understand, we accept the child on the level on which he is; but if we see that the child continuously uses the concept of folding over, we like to motivate him so that he not only sees the world from his own point of view but also experiences the world from the point of view of others, too. How we should motivate that, we will hear today.

Fig. 21. "Coal Mine" (9 years old). Subjective space representation shows also the inside of the mountain (X-ray picture). Space-time concept.

234

Fig. 22. "Saying Good-bye." Different time sequences are expressed in one drawing. X-ray picture shows inside of compartment. Space is "filled" according to importance.

Now, you have a drawing here [Figure 22] of the same boy saying goodbye—the same boy who put the pencil into his pocket. This expresses various temporal phases. His father is drawn inside the train and also outside of the train waving with his hand. The boy is sitting in the train. He has even two concepts for stairs: stairs going up are the broken ascending lines, and stairs going down are the parallel lines. I show this drawing only to show the variability of concepts during the schematic stage. You all would recognize that this is the same boy, because the drawing has the same characteristics of the schema that we found in Figure [17]. Now, just to summarize, we have three different kinds of space-time concepts. The one involves different temporal phases which are actually represented within one space, such as searching for the pencil, finding the pencil, and putting the pencil into his pocket. These various temporal phases are actually represented. The second is the concept of folding over. Several views are represented within one space which could not be done simultaneously. Then the third is a representation of the inside and the outside simultaneously, or what we call X-ray.

What does a color schema mean? Do not confuse it with a color scheme; a color scheme is the matching of several colors. But a color schema refers to something different. It's the color concept which the child establishes during the schematic stage. He discovers that there is a relationship between color and object. He discovers the sky is blue, the grass is green, the tree is green, the water is blue. Such simple color relationships to objects tend to remain fixed. There's an interesting story behind this. When children once have established such color relationships to objects, they usually don't change them. For instance, the sky is blue; the sun is yellow. Even when it rains the sky remains blue, but the rain is superimposed, such as we see it in the one colored reproduction which we have signifying the schematic stage, Figure [23]. In this drawing the child drew first the green ground, the base, the blue sky; but then thunder and rain started. Of course, you can still see the blue sky and the brown clouds put over it. Sometimes you can even see the sun included in such a concept. So the child begins usually with his color concept and changes it as he goes along. The more the child approximates the next stage of development, the less the child sticks to such previously conceived color schemata. But, in the beginning, the child almost rigidly adheres to it. Even in winter, the child may

Fig. 23. "Lightning and Rain" (7 years old). Color is related to objects. The color-object relationship often becomes rigid. Notice that the sky retains its color-object relationship of "blue" although it is raining. This is characteristic for a color schema. (Schematic Stage) [*Note:* For color, see Lowenfeld, op.cit., Plate 4.]

draw a green ground, then put the snow on top of it, because the once established color schema was, "The ground is green; the sky is blue." Now it snows, so he introduces the changes. He deviates from his color schema and introduces the experience which is important to him. Yes, please?

Student: Can you help a child speed up by giving him different colors of paper or might that confuse him?

Lowenfeld: This is a very interesting question. We often actually use different colored papers to make a child more flexible. Yes, it may be confusing; but we feel that this confusion has also a very positive meaning, namely, the adjustment to something new. You see, it is not our intent during the schematic stage not to disturb the child in his established color schema. On the contrary, a schema is, to a certain degree, an indication of rigidity. While the child needs this rigidity for his confidence, as we said— for his self-assurance—we do want even in our children's art classes to introduce, now and then, colored papers. All of a sudden the child is forced to establish a new concept, and that brings him away from a certain stiffness. So we shall see that we use that as a motivational means in making his concepts more flexible.

Student: A personal experience would change the concept?

Lowenfeld: A personal experience would change the concept, yes. In fact, we would *like* to introduce such personal experiences to make the child's concept change. For instance, the child has established a color concept: the ground is green, the sky is blue, the trees are green and have brown trunks. But in the fall, we would like to motivate children very strongly towards differences in color. We collect various leaves and make the child aware of the different colors. "What color is this leaf? Oh, look! Let's find out what other colors we can find. Now let's find out," we would say to the children, "what colored leaves you have found. Mary, what colors did you find? Well, we'll remember that when we make a painting, won't we?" You see? We motivate the children toward greater sensitivity to color, but we should not be shocked if a child reverts to the color schema which he has established. This, indeed, is our goal: to enrich the schema and keep it flexible as much as we can.

With regard to design and design concepts, we see that for the first time the child introduces here what we may assume to be a more conscious relationship toward the meaning of design. If you think of the schema as a repetition of a concept, we have at this stage one characteristic which is a very important natural characteristic of a design concept, namely, rhythm or repetition. As you understand, rhythm is nothing else but a variation of repetitive statements. Rhythms which are monotonous, like the fan which goes on and on, we don't hear any more. Have you ever heard the ticking of a clock in your room? And after some time you don't hear the ticking any more because it is a monotonous noise which you are no longer conscious of. If you are for a long time in an airplane and you hear the buzzing, well, you forget that it is buzzing. You just hear no noise; you become adjusted to it. So a monotonous noise no longer is significant for establishing a rhythm.

Only when we slightly deviate from the rhythmic quality, do we get the real feeling for rhythm. And that is used throughout in art, you see. When Beethoven established a theme—dit dit dit da; you all know the "Fifth"—he immediately made it more significant by saying, "Dit dit dit da." But he didn't remain with it. He said, "Dit dit dit da, dit dit dit da, dit dit dit da." Do you see? He varied the rhythm and made it more exciting. But he came back again: "Dit dit dit da! Da! Da!" and then he went on again. It's a repetition of the same theme, but under various circumstances. These various circumstances contribute very much to our richness of concepts, including the theme of Beethoven.

Actually, if you think of it philosophically, we all are themes. You may think of the human race as the total theme; we are individual themes. I am a different theme and you are a different theme, although we have the same rhythm. The rhythm may be a result of our internal qualities and our external qualities. But the difference in themes is what we have inside and probably the little variations we have externally. But, you see, if we would really like to become interested in the theme, we must get acquainted with each other, and then we discover that there are various reactions which are entirely different among human beings; and these are the variations. The longer we become acquainted with an individual, the more do we discover the variations in him, and the richer is the individual to us. While in the beginning we all may seem alike, after getting acquainted with each other, we discover the different themes within ourselves. That makes human relations richer and richer and richer until we really can predict reactions. Then we are very rich, because we no longer remain ourselves. We include in ourselves all the richness that we gain from our friends. This makes life very rich then. This includes in our theme the theme of others. Do you see? This is actually the basis for rhythm, for the quality of art, because in one work of art we feel that there is the repetition of one theme. But this repetition also takes in the influences of traditions and various other themes which have occurred during various periods of time and enriches the work of art to us, as such. Yes, indeed, the meaning of rhythm is one which has eternal meaning, for we meet it in every phase of life, including art.

If we look at a piece of sculpture, there, too, we can say the theme of the sculpture is expressed as we see it. But as we walk around the sculpture, we learn to know the sculpture as we learn to know a human species. We make friends from all different angles. We see overlappings. We see different characteristics. We see different spirits which the artist put into it. And then we come and shake hands again when we are standing in front of it, for we now know that the sculpture is a theme which consists of many other themes which make it complex to us.

The same is true with the child who discovers a concept and uses this concept over and over again but not in the very same way. Oh, no! He invents various kinds of rhythmic variations. Do you remember how the child treated the various trees in the orchard? They consisted basically of the same theme; but he varied them rhythmically by placing the apples in different places, making them larger or smaller, and thus introduced a new variation of a theme. This desire for new variations is a natural desire at this stage, because repetition is a natural desire. Repetition is a result of the desire for self-assurance. Variation is the desire to express with self-assurance the various kinds of experiences which one has. You can see that we arrive here, quite naturally, at a concept of aesthetics which is basic to any art form. Therefore, we should feel that the child has arrived here at the natural desire for design—design used as a harmonious organization of items which are repetitious, probably, in their own form but which express new things. So you can see that rhythm is a natural form of growth during this period.

How do we use it? Well, in various forms. For instance, ask children to draw a forest. What would the child do in conceiving a forest? A forest is nothing but the repetition of the same concept of a tree; but probably one is small, one is large, one is a baby, one is dead, you know. So we can, of course, personify various kinds of trees; and if you would like to, you can even put it into a stencil, or into a linoleum print or a potato print, and say, "Now, children, we are making a forest." A child would then print the same concept again and again; and if he has two—a variety of two different sizes—for him this is quite naturally a forest, although it is the repetition of one schema. Do you see? So this repetition can be used now for what we may call decorative purposes. And it comes about naturally. We can really say the child is an innate designer, in a way, because all this grows out of his own innate feelings.

We have discussed generally all aspects, and now I would like to go a little bit into individual aspects and see how the child expresses himself according to the various growth components. That leads us to evaluation. Before we do so, let me add just one more aspect, and that is the aspect of three-dimensional expression in clay. We discussed the formation of various concepts during the pre-schematic stage, when children express themselves either synthetically or analytically in clay, and we now know what these different approaches mean. May I say at this time again that these concepts are overlapping; some children use the synthetic approach and the analytic approach at the same time. We also know what these mean, and it makes us more sensitive to children if we know what they mean. Never forget that we learn all this only to become more sensitive to children. During the sche-

Characteristics	Human Figure	Space	Color	Design	Stimulation Topics	Technique
Discovery of a definite concept of man and environment. Self-assurance through repetition of form symbols: "schema." In pure schema no intentional experience is expressed, only the thing itself: "the man," "the tree," and so forth. Experiences are expressed by deviations from schema. Use of geometric lines.	Definite concept of figure depending on active knowledge and personality through repetition: "schema." Deviations expressing experiences can be seen in: (1) Exaggeration of important parts. (2) Neglect or omission of unimportant parts. (3) Change of symbols.	First definite space concept: "base line." Discovery of being a part of environment: assumption for cooperation and correlation. Base line expresses: (1) Base (2) Terrain Deviations from base line express experiences: subjective space: (1) Folding over (egocentric). (2) Mix forms of plan and elevation. (3) X-ray pictures. (4) Space-time representations.	Discovery of relationship between color and object, through repetition: "color schema." Same color for same object. Deviation of color schema shows emotional experience.	No conscious approach. Design forms received through repetitions, subconsciously.	Best stimulation concentrates on action, characterized by "we" (I, John, tree) "action," "where" (characterization of terrain). Topics referring to: (1) Time sequences (journeys, traveling stories). (2) X-ray pictures (inside and outside is emphasized), factory, coal mine, and so forth.	Colored crayons. Colored chalks. Powder paint (tempera, poster paint). Large paper. Hair brushes. Clay: (1) Synthetic. (2) Analytic.

EVALUATION CHART
Schematic Stage

		None	Some	Much
Intellectual Growth	Has the child developed concepts for things familiar to him? Are his concepts clearly expressed? Has he a tendency to differentiate his schemata? (Hands with fingers, eyes with eyebrows, etc.) Does the child relate colors to objects?			
Emotional Growth	Does the child use his schemata flexibly? Does the child vary the sizes according to the significance of the represented objects? Does the drawing show deviations from the schema by exaggerating, omitting, or even changing meaningful parts? Does the child use his lines or brush strokes in a determined fashion? Is there a lack of continuous "folding over"? Is there a lack of continued over-exaggeration?			
Social Growth	Does he identify himself with his own experience? Has the child established spatial correlations? Does the child use base lines? Does the child characterize his environment? Does the child show awareness of his social environment in identifying himself with others?			
Perceptual Growth	Does the child mostly draw with continued uninterrupted lines, expressing kinesthetic sensations? Is the child aware of differences in texture? Does the child depart from the use of mere geometric lines? Does the child show visual awareness by drawing distant objects smaller? Does the child differentiate his color-object relationships? (Does he use different greens for different plants and trees?) Does the child model analytically?			
Physical Growth	Does the child show body actions in his drawings? Does the child show the absence of continuous exaggerations of the same body parts? Does the child show other signs which indicate his sensitivity toward the use of his body? (Joints, special details.) Does the child guide his brush strokes so that he remains within the predetermined area?			
Aesthetic Growth	Does the child unconsciously utilize his drive for repetition for design purposes? Does the child distribute his work over the whole sheet? Does the child think in terms of the whole drawing when he draws—not in terms of single details only? Does the child use decorative patterns?			
Creative Growth	Does the child create his own representative symbols (concepts)? Does the child vary his schemata? Does the child frequently change his symbols for eyes, nose, mouth, etc.? Does the child invent his own topics?			

matic stage, the child also develops his definite concepts in clay. He will, through repetition, assure himself that "I know how to model a man" and, therefore, the difference in concepts shows itself much more clearly than during the pre-schematic stage. Therefore, we have fewer intermediate stages between synthetic and analytic but have a clearer indication of synthetic or analytic modeling.

And now let us look at the Evaluation Chart, Schematic Stage, and at one of the drawings which we have here. Let's choose Figure [24] as the drawing which we will evaluate. Or would it be better to choose another one? No, I'll give you as homework the evaluation of the colored drawing which we have in the book. If you would like to obtain a drawing from your own children, it would be more interesting for you to evaluate it. But knowing that you may not have any with you or can't obtain any, evaluate the drawing, "Lightning and Rain" [Figure 23] as homework.

Now, let us look at the drawing "Playing Checkers" [Figure 24], for our evaluation. Keep your finger there so we can look at it repeatedly. "Has the child developed concepts for things familiar to him?" Usually we can only say that if we see more than one drawing; but in this drawing, we can give an answer. Why? Because we have two figures represented, and we can see in both of them a definite concept. What would we call a definite concept? The schema. If we were to define it, we would say that the child uses the same characteristic symbols for the same body parts—if he uses for legs the same symbol, for feet the same symbol, and essentially the same symbol for eyes, nose, and mouth. Since we see the same characteristics applied to both figures, we can then definitely say that the child has established definite concepts. "None," "Some," or "Much"? Who is for "None"? Who is for "Some"? Who is for "Much"? Well, you see, we all agree.

"Are his concepts clearly expressed?" "None," "Some," "Much"? Yes, we all agree. They are clearly expressed. We have not yet said whether they are richly expressed.

"Has he a tendency to differentiate his schemata?—hands with fingers, eyes with eyebrows, etc." "Some." Hands are with fingers, but eyes are not with eyebrows. Nose is not with nostrils. Mouth is not with upper lip and lower lip or lips at all. So we can say, "Some".

"Does the child relate colors to objects?" We do not know that. But may I say, it is also an aspect of intelligence if children relate colors to objects. I know this drawing of the child. The child does not yet relate colors to objects in this drawing. So we have an equal number of "Much" and an equal number of "Some" and "None".

As a whole, what would we then say? The child is seven years old, so he is at the beginning of the schematic stage. We would say the child is intellectually average or fair. Yes?

Student: How would you classify the elimination of the eyes?

Fig. 24. "Playing Checkers" (7-year-old boy). The checkerboard is "folded over" because of its significance.

Lowenfeld: Omission?

Student: Yes.

Lowenfeld: Well, I would say that omission does not belong to intellectual concepts, except if it is a part of the differentiation of the concepts. But if a child once draws it and another time does not draw it, then we would say this is the result of an emotional factor, as we shall see. The child includes it when it is important, omits it when it is unimportant or when he represses it. Yes, good.

Let's go on to the next growth component, emotional growth. We see that we have here a number of questions, more than for intellectual growth. It seems, therefore, that emotional growth is very important during this stage of development. Why? Well, we know there is a tendency toward stiffness, toward repetition and rigidity, during this stage; and we have to be careful that the child does not fall victim to his desire for reassurance. This is one thing which we have to remember.

So we ask as the first question, "Does the child use his schemata flexibly?" Let's find out: "None," "Some," "Much"? I don't want to explain it;

I would just like to get your spontaneous reaction at this time. "Does the child use his schemata flexibly?" "None," "Some," "Much"? Well, I would agree with "Some," but we do not have, actually, reassurance of expressiveness unless we were to see three drawings. Having two figures in one drawing allows us to make a certain judgment. We see that he has somewhat used the arms flexibly, but this is the only point on which we can base our judgment that he has changed. I beg your pardon. . . .

Student: He colored in one ear.

Lowenfeld: That's right. This is the second part. He changed his ears; but eyes, nose, mouth, body—well, he elongated the one body a little bit more, but otherwise the symbols remain almost the same.

Student: He does try to get them onto the chair.

Lowenfeld: Yes, yes, but this is a space relationship, not the flexible use of concepts. You see, the flexible use of concepts would be expressed in the flexiblity of the concept itself. Yes?

Student: Does the circle above the table have anything to do with it?

Lowenfeld: The circle above the table means light.

Student: Light?

Lowenfeld: Light. It's probably a light fixture or something of this sort. I asked the child. It was a light.

Now, let's go on. "Does the child vary the sizes according to the significance of represented objects?" Well, we'll say "Yes, he does." Would we say "None," "Some," or "Much"? I would say between "Some" and "Much." If I were to judge it, I would put my check mark on the line between "Some" and "Much." If you put it on "Some," it wouldn't matter; or on "Much," it wouldn't matter. One-half point up or down does not change our sensitivity; but we have become more sensitive toward it, and this is most important.

Student: Would you say that the elongated fingers are most important?

Lowenfeld: Yes. Fingers are most important because he uses them for playing checkers; and, therefore, he may have exaggerated them for this purpose. What about the sharpness of the other figure? I don't think that we can make a differentiation concerning the sharpness of one or the other on the basis of a black and white drawing. Some colors reproduce better than others.

"Does the drawing show deviations from the schema by exaggerating, omitting, or even changing meaningful parts?" It would be best if we were to have several drawings for this purpose; but we can say that the drawing shows deviations from the schema, because we have two schemas of the man and we see that both are slightly different and do show deviations.

"Does the child use his lines or brush strokes in a determined fashion?" "Much," yes.

"Is there a lack of continuous 'folding over'?" Well, we don't know. We would have to see several drawings in order to show this. What has he folded over?

Student: The checkerboard.

Lowenfeld: The checkerboard. Right.

See how you have become sensitive! Almost all said the checkerboard immediately. Your sensitivity toward children's drawings is really wonderful. Wonderful. I'm quite proud of you, you know, seeing those things now as folding over after we just talked about it. Whether the child uses this continuously, we could not say. We only would be able to say it if we were to see several drawings. Why do we say, "Is there a lack of continuous 'folding over'?" Why do we say it negatively? Why did I state the question negatively? If there is much lack, it's good. Do you see? I did not say, "Is there continuous folding over?" If you were to say there is much continuous folding over and if we were to place our check mark on the "Much," it would indicate for us that it's good. Do you see? But it's not good. So I said, "Is there a lack of continuous folding over?" Because if there is much, it's always good. You see, this is used throughout the book: "Much is good, and little is not good."

Now the question is, "Is there a lack of continued over-exaggeration?" Why is that bad? If a child continuously over-exaggerates, then he is not stable emotionally. He becomes so much bound up with one part that he forgets the rest. And this is not good either.

Student: That means one part of the body, doesn't it? I mean, if he exaggerates the arms in one and then the legs in another . . . .

Lowenfeld: Yes. However, if he continuously exaggerates more than the arms or the legs and to such an extent that he loses contact with the rest—as in the one drawing, "Playing Tag" [see Figure 14]—it is not good. I said that he wants to catch him, wants to catch him, wants to catch him, and makes the arm longer and longer and longer, and all of a sudden he's even out of paper and has forgotten that this is the arm of this child. He becomes bound up so much with one part only that he forgets the rest; and this is emotionally, of course, not healthy. The child should always retain the feeling for the whole because this is a part of his expression, and he should not lose the feeling for the rest. We had such a drawing made in our children's art classes, you know. Some days ago, a child had to add and had to add and had to add paper after paper until he reached the wall. This was a lack of organization, of an ability to see the total or the whole. He had no control of his feelings but grew only as his feelings grew. If this is continuously done, then we deal with an unstable child who just cannot deal with his emotions and cannot judge himself, as it were, and cannot put himself into relationship with something else. Yes, please?

Student: In regard to that folding over question—"Is there a lack of continuous folding over?" You say it's good if there is a lack of it. Well, if it's good, why don't we discourage it then, instead of putting paper on the floor for kids to draw all the way around it? Why not let them draw on an easel if we're trying to discourage it?

Lowenfeld: Well, I don't think it would be a good motivation because it would force the child to— we rather think of experiential motivations which are meaningful to the child and change the child's inner understandings or concepts. This would be forcing the child by external means, you see? I would not think it to be a good motivation for a child who continuously puts folding over into the drawing to make him draw at an easel. It would frustrate him. Yes?

Student: What about easels for a sixth-grade child?

Lowenfeld: For a sixth-grade child, fine. Whenever the child goes away from these concepts, it's fine. But may I say, there is no necessity for it; because, for instance, the technical, material thing of color running on the vertical is always greater than on the horizontal. Of course, at some point, it is good if a child learns to control running. And an easel certainly contributes to the color running.

LECTURE 20

The Schematic Stage: Space and Time Representation; Evaluation of Social, Perceptual, Physical, Aesthetic, and Creative Growth; Motivation; and Art Materials

I have here a note from one of the class members: "Under the heading, 'Space and Time Representations,' describing the two approaches in the 'different episodes represented by different pictures in one sequence of drawings,' and in the 'other spatially distinct impressions,' the text implies a peak psychological implication. Will you please clarify the psychological aspect of this? I detect a deeper meaning than I am able to understand. The two types of pictures, pictures in sequence and X-ray pictures, are the means of the child's representation, but I missed the deeper psychological aspect."

I am sorry that I did not emphasize it enough. The psychological aspect of the inability to differentiate between time sequences, the putting of various time sequences into one space, is that the child at this age does not yet differentiate between experiences that happen at various times. Therefore, the meaning of yesterday and tomorrow—that means, various time aspects—are not yet a part of the child's definite concept. In other words, space and time for the child of seven or eight years are not yet distinct matters as they are with us. Just think about the role that space and time play for us as adults. You know that time is almost the essence of life as we go through it. And, of course, space is distance which separates us in the same way. For the child, apparently, space and time have not yet become distinct features. So the child of seven or eight may mix up space and time; he signifies so in his space-time concepts. Those things may be simultaneous to him in his mind, while actually they are separated—both in time and space. So the significant or deeper psychological meaning is that the child has not yet arrived at a distinct understanding of what time is and what space is. Therefore, we will frequently find in children at this level of development a mixing up of yesterday and tomorrow; and two days or three days or four days is like a week, and a week is like a month, and a month is

246

almost infinite. You see, a month is beyond any concept of the child at this age and developmental level. Now this is the deeper meaning of the mixing up of space and time in children's drawings.

I'm sorry that I did not emphasize this enough yesterday; but you should always know, whenever there are indications in children's drawings which so clearly point toward a trend, that this is part of the child's make-up and is intrinsic. We learn again through such an understanding to become more sensitive to children. We will not be upset at children who do not understand what it means if we refer to "three days ahead," or "next week you will—," you know. For the child, this may be entirely out of his realm of understanding. Now, let's continue.

There is still another note: "In what way could you help a child toward emotional stability when the child continually exaggerates parts and loses contact with the whole? In what way could you motivate the child?" We will discuss such motivations today. Indeed, such motivations would refer more to size relationships. And size relationships should refer, actually, to experiences which refer to your own body as related to other things. For instance, let's pull down the shade; let's pull the shade here in the room. You see, a child who continuously exaggerates the arm would draw himself pulling the shade and would be limited to a certain point. The shade is only that high, and the child would have to stretch his arm only to this point. So such experiences which give the child a limited reach and an understanding of limited size relationships would be the ones which motivate best for such continuous exaggerations, because they give the child the feeling of a limit. Do you see? Now, the same would be so if you were to ask the child to reach for the doll which is on his chest or to reach for some object which is well known to the child. Select an experience that the child has gone through time and again and knows that it is *not* unlimited, an experience that the child can well conceive of in advance of his drawing. Such would be the motivations for a child who continuously exaggerates or elongates sizes. You can invent all kinds of topics which are close to the child, but you should have in mind that the child should, from the beginning of his drawings, know the limitations of his body reach and other body capabilities.

Now, let's go on with our evaluation because we did not conclude it yesterday. We would like to conclude our evaluation today and then talk about motivation and bring to an end our discussion of the schematic stage. Look at the Evaluation Chart, Schematic Stage. I believe we'll start with social growth. We again look at the one drawing [Figure 24], which we have reproduced in the book. Whenever we evaluate for the first time, I would like for us to use drawings from the book for the reason that all of you can refer to them.

Now, again as we have heard previously, one of the most important beginnings of social growth is the ability to identify one's self with one's own work. So, "Does the child identify himself with his own experience?" Well, indeed he does. The checker players. "Does he identify himself with his own experience?—None, Some, or Much?" "Much." We all would say "Much" because he is concerned with the checker player. Would you say "Very much"? No, there we disagree. You have not yet learned to look sensitively at the drawings, you see. I would be more inclined to say between "Some" and "Much" than "Very Much." "Much" would not be wrong, because, yes, the child does identify. But where does the child not identify himself with the experience?

Student: He is not looking at the checkerboard.

Lowenfeld: Yes, he is not looking at the checkerboard. Did that occur to you? If the child is playing checkers, he is very much concerned with playing checkers, but the checker-playing motivation was not strong enough to make the child deviate from his schema. His schema, of course—as we can see—is the head with a dot for the nose and a stroke for the mouth. We have that as his schema.

An experience is represented or expressed by children in the schematic stage usually by three kinds of deviations, you remember: exaggeration of important parts, omission or diminution of unimportant parts or suppressed parts, and change of symbols. A change of symbol here would be a profile, which would occur if the child were to get the feeling that he has to look at the checkerboard. Apparently the motivation of the checkerboard was not strong enough to introduce this change. We can also say vice versa: the child was not emotionally flexible enough to become diverted in his schematic representation. This only minimizes it a little bit, but I would never say "Very Much." We know that the child identifies himself with this experience quite well. He puts himself close to the chair, indicating that he may be sitting on it. The child even folded over his checkerboard to show where the checkers are. The child paints his arms and fingers to show that he uses the checkers. And here comes the only weak spot in the self-identification: the child did not deviate from his schema by instituting a profile representation so as to look at the checkerboard.

"Has the child established spatial correlations?—None, Some, Much?" The majority is for "Much," but there is a clear indication that it may be between "Some" and "Much." I would do the same. I would say it's between "Some" and "Much," but on what do you base your evaluation? Why do you say "Much"?

Student: The people are in relation to the table. The chairs are in relation to the table. The window seems to be on the wall away from the table. The light is in relation to the people and the checkerboard.

Lowenfeld: But why didn't you then say "Much"? Why did some of you say "Some" and others "Much"? Apparently there is, then, the common consent that we would say between "Some" and "Much." Why do we not say "Much"? Do you know? Well, we should not make any judgment on the basis of one drawing.

Student: He doesn't have anything else in the room except the window, the little window.

Lowenfeld: That would not be an indication that he did not achieve good spatial correlations, because we only can judge by what we have.

Student: The arm on one of the boys is longer—.

Lowenfeld: That doesn't deal with spatial correlation. If the child elongates one arm, it only means importance, and that does not deal with spatial correlation.

Student: Well, the figures could fit on the chairs better. They could have their legs bent.

Lowenfeld: Well, correct. This is one instance which I think has some significance: that the child did not put himself into a better relationship with the chairs. But there is another indication, the one which we just mentioned. Is there a spatial relationship between the face of the child and the checker playing? You see? This is the very same instance which we just mentioned. See this is also a spatial relationship: if I, for instance, were to reach for an apple here but I reach out there and look away, I may stretch out my arm, but this is not a good spatial relationship. My intent is to relate myself spatially—that means, in space—to an outside object. My intent is also part of the spatial relationship. So, if we identify with the child, he was sticking to his schema. A man has two eyes, a nose, a mouth; and at that time, he went on and brought in his close relationship to the chair but not to the checker playing.

Student: Could a child be influenced by someone who takes photographs? For instance, they always say, "Look at the camera," and the child thinks, "Well, in the picture you have to look forward."

Lowenfeld: Well, anything in the child's experience may influence him, but a child who is flexible and identifies closely with his experience should also remain flexible during the motivation.

Student: In other words, he should relate himself to the experience rather that to the picture.

Lowenfeld: Correct; yes—that means he should be intensely concerned, just as he is with his arm, also with his face, in facing the checker player. And that is probably why we said between "Some" and "Much." Now, may I say, it doesn't make any difference whether you say "Much" or whether you say "Some."

But you know what is the difference? The difference is that now you do look at it. You see, this is the difference: that through such questions we become more sensitive to the child's needs. This is the difference. Previously, you may not have looked at all at such things in children's drawings; but now, all of a sudden, we become aware of so many detailed aspects that we don't know where to start when we look at a child and his drawings. It is this sensitivity which you may have gained in this course which is of main importance to me. As far as I am concerned, you may forget all the evaluation charts—after the course is over, you know—but I hope you will never forget how deeply we can look into children's drawings. I hope this will be a lasting experience even if you do not get immediately into the meaning. I hope that especially those who deal with children's drawings or art will get the meaning; but even if those who deal with children's drawings do not derive the meaning immediately when they look at children's drawings but only are aware of the personality characteristics, the growth characteristics of a child, the course will have fulfilled its purpose. We all have become more sensitive toward children through their drawings and all of a sudden see that this is a whole new world with so many questions to ask. Even when we have answered all of these questions, we only know a fraction of what there is to know about the child. This should always be in our minds.

Student: The checkerboard fold-up—would that be an aspect of spatial relationships?

Lowenfeld: Yes, this is a spatial relationship which is part of the child's developmental stage. It means that the child wanted to show you what is on the checkerboard, so he folded it up. You see? This is a good spatial relationship, because the child put the checkerboard in relationship to the table. Of course, there would have been another opportunity for the child. When the child folded up the checkerboard, he lost the relationship to the table top. Another better spatial relationship would have been to have the checkerboard on the table top, but apparently the child's emotional sensitivity—which we found is very well developed—is stronger than his social responsibility. Social responsibility would require that the checkerboard be on the table. Do you see those relationships of the one to the other?

How I relate myself to the outside or how I see things related to one another is always responsible for social growth. Do you understand the deeper meaning of this in teaching? It means that a person is more developed in social growth if, for example, the instruments which he uses in the kitchen are in the right place. Yes, indeed. When you go to a kitchen and say, "Where is the can opener? Where is the can opener? I just used it"—if you have no relationship to the things that you need in your kitchen concerning the places where you will find them, this is part of your make-up. There are people who constantly seek for their things and never find them. They have no places established for them. Go into a workshop and you will see how the carpenter puts his tools with which he works in certain places so that he can save time. Saving time is part of his social make-up, his social responsibility. You know, there are all kinds of things related to it, but it starts here.

The child's emotional sensitivity told him, "Checkerboard, yes, checkerboard, I have to show the checkerboard." This is subconsciously done by the child, so he folded it over; but in folding it over, he did not relate the checkerboard to the table top. This is an important thing which we have to realize, this social relationship of object to object. Let us say that with the order in your workshop begins the social awareness that one thing belongs to the other. I hope I made it clear that this is not an isolated part of an interpretation, but it is actually the beginning of the whole social make-up, continuing from the child up to the adult. Now, "Has the child established spatial correlations?" We were then right when we said between "Some" and "Much"—but not "Much."

"Does the child use base lines?" Yes. "None," "Some," "Much"? "Some," I would say. Why not "Much"? Of course, in this drawing we only see one base line, but we could have seen several base lines. For instance, if the child had wanted to introduce more space in the room, the wall space could have been another base line. The child introduced one base line and was satisfied in placing everything on this base line. Now we would be better able to judge if we were to have more drawings of this child.

Student: Isn't that a second base line at the top of the picture itself?

Lowenfeld: The top of the picture is not a base line. It may be that the child wanted to indicate that feeling, but I doubt it, because there is not even a full circle. There is no indication that he really experienced the feeling for ceiling, but he has the feeling for ground and that the chair is on the floor, that the boy is on the floor, and that the table is on the floor. He even has the feeling that the checkerboard is on the table top, because this is also a base line. He folded it over from the base line. So we could say between "Some" and "Much." Now, let's go on. Our time runs short.

"Does the child characterize his environment?" By characterization of an environment, we mean the inclusion of those things which are important for the environment. What is the environment here? The environment is a room. What is important for a room? Well, the things which make a room a room, such as a door, windows, and also furniture. Now, "Does the child characterize his environment?" Somewhat. Yes, he included the window. He did not include anything else but the window and the light, but this we would consider a characterization.

"Does the child show awareness of his social environment in identifying himself with others?" In a way, yes, because he plays checkers with the other fellow and identifies himself, because he not only plays checkers, but he also puts himself into the other's place and stretches out the arm; so he does identify himself. I would say again not "Much" but between "Some" and "Much," because he didn't even identify himself with his own experience by looking at the checkerboard. He preferred his old experience (his front view schema) to that of another. We would have to see several drawings in order to answer this question better.

Student: Under social growth evaluation, you evaluated this picture [Figure 24] in the book (on page 175, the last paragraph, last two sentences). There, you have a check mark for this last question under social growth, as well as the former question, under the column "None."

Lowenfeld: It says here, "However, for a more accurate answer we would have to see several drawings by this child." Now I give here this reason: "In Figure [24], the child drew only the objects which are of immediate significance for his experience of playing checkers. The only characterization of his environment, outside of his experience, is the window. But even that might have been his source of light for playing. The child gave us no indication in what room he lives by adding some more characterizations. Since the child did not even characterize his own home environment, it is not expected that he would be aware of his social environment in which he would identify himself with the social group in which he lives. However, for a more accurate answer we would have to see several drawings by this child. The check mark for this as well as the former question would have to be put in the column 'None.' That means that the child is not conscious of his social environment."

We could put it in the "Some" column but never any higher, because I see no indication of anything else. However, as I said, there isn't even a door where he can walk in and there isn't even a chest or any indication in which room this took place. It's just the bare necessities of a place for playing checkers. A mark down or up should never disturb us. Indeed, we would be better off if we were to have more drawings for this evaluation.

Now, if we look at all of our answers, we see that the child is quite emotionally sensitive, that he is socially aware or socially conscious of his environment. In none of the social questions did we go above "Some," and in some even below. We see that he is socially probably average and only concerned with himself and not yet with others. So this may be indicative of the child. We thought that intellectually he is probably average; emotionally he is very sensitive; but socially, we thought that he may not be very aware of his social responsibilities.

Let us move to perceptual growth. "Does the child mostly draw with continuous uninterrupted lines, expressing kinesthetic sensations?—None, Some, or Much?" "Much." Well, we all feel that there are very few interrupted lines, that the child has great confidence and also apparently uses uninterrupted lines.

"Is the child aware of differences in texture?" No, we cannot see any textural effects in the drawing.

"Does the child depart from the use of mere geometric lines?" Not even in the hands; because if we separate the hands from the whole, they are just lines. Would you say this is a hand if I separate it? You see, it has no relationship to a hand as such. It still is a geometric line.

"Does the child show visual awareness by drawing distant objects smaller?" We don't have any indication with regard to that. We would have to see several drawings in order to judge whether the window, for instance, was drawn smaller because of distance; but we have no indication of that in this one drawing.

"Does the child differentiate his color-object relationships?" By color differentiation, I mean: Does he signify this as a dark red, this as a light red, and so forth? We don't know because we have no color reproduction. Here it says, "Does he use different greens for different plants and trees?" That would be differentiating color-object relationships.

"Does the child model analytically?" We don't know because we have no modeling. What would you say then, in general, how the child is developed perceptually?

Student: Dull.

Lowenfeld: Fairly dull, and that really fits with the picture. Can you already see how the personality of this child evolves out of that which we have found? He is of average intelligence, but emotionally tied up with the things he does, sensitive; he is socially not quite yet developed and aware of his environment or himself as a part of it; perceptually, he doesn't see; he is just concerned with his own self. So, the most outstanding quality of the child is that he is an emotionally sensitive child, but otherwise he is average.

Now, let's find out about physical growth. We should always pursue this question with great care. Our contribution to this area is relatively meager. "Does the child show body actions in his drawings?" "Some," because he stretches out the arms; but, otherwise, there is none.

"Does the child show the absence of continuous exaggerations of the same body parts?" We don't know, but we must be cautious concerning one thing. What? The ears. Actually, I know that this child has frequent earaches. I know that this child not only has earaches but also some inflammation of the middle ear.

"Does the child show other signs which indicate his sensitivity toward the use of his body, such as joints or special details?" "None."

"Does the child guide his brush strokes so that he remains within the predetermined area?" "Much." Yes, we don't see uncontrolled strokes. This would show us his motor coordination, an indication of physical growth. Well, this he has mastered. So, in general, we would say that we have a child who is well built, probably strong, definite in his actions, enjoys running, enjoys kinesthetic motions, but, otherwise, we haven't any other indications.

Now, let's look at aesthetic growth. "Does the child unconsciously utilize his drive for repetition for design purposes?" We cannot see that in his drawing, so we would not even check it. We don't know it.

"Does the child distribute his work over the whole sheet?" Beautifully, very beautifully. Now look at what he has done. Actually, he was very much concerned with this kind of organization. The table is very beautifully placed in the center, and the chairs and all the spaces are very well distributed.

"Does the child think in terms of the whole drawing when he draws, and not in terms of single details only?" Indeed, you see he has put the window there where he put the smaller child, and he thought of the whole drawing and not only of details.

"Does the child use decorative patterns?" "None." A slight indication of it might be the checkerboard, but we would not say that the child is very much aware of that. In general, however, we would say the child's emotional sensitivity and his aesthetic growth are the two components of his growth which are the most developed.

And now, his creative growth. "Does the child create his own representative symbols, his own concepts?" Most likely he does although we have no way of saying so unless we see several drawings of this child and are present while he is drawing to see whether he has confidence in using his own representative symbols.

"Does the child vary his schemata?" Apparently very little, because even the motivation of the checkerboard, playing checkers, wasn't strong enough to make him vary his schema for a head. We would have to look at more drawings for this answer, but we would rather say that the child does not. We would rather say between "None" and "Some."

"Does the child frequently change his symbols for eyes, nose, mouth, etc?" No, we cannot see any frequent changes. Look at the legs; look at the arms—probably "Some" in the exaggeration of the hands. We would have to see several drawings, but we would say between "None" and "Some."

"Does the child invent his own topics?" We don't know whether this was a motivational topic, but we assume that it is the child's own topic.

Now, again, after such a detailed analysis, let's shake all our data very hard so that none of them remain isolated, so that we actually see how we think all these details fit into the whole personality of the individual. We can best do that if we again forget those single details and have a total impression of the painting as it is, and give our intuitive feeling in addition to our knowledge of the child. Then we would say that the child actually is not a very bright child. We can feel, however, that he is sensitive and that he is emotionally concerned with the things he does, but not beyond the things. He may not be very socially inclined in doing things in the house, because he isn't even aware of what there is in the house. There is nothing beyond his immediate needs which he feels is of significance, so he is only emotionally concerned with the ego. But socially, he probably needs some motivation in order to become a member of a larger family or society later on. We also know that this child has great aesthetic feelings, because the distribution on the paper is very well organized. We should remember that this child may have a very, very wonderful ability for organization, and we should use it.

Of course, any talent which we discover in children, in whatever direction it may lead, should be motivated. Often, children's drawings will give us an important lead. We know that this child may not be very inventive. That goes hand in hand, probably, with his average intellect and also with other aspects of his drawing. If he had been very creative, changing his symbols frequently, and being as aesthetic as he is, we would probably have here what we call a talented child. In the talented child, the creative aspects and the aesthetic aspects go hand in hand. We don't have a child who spontaneously and forcefully expresses himself, because he doesn't have the means for it. Neither does he have the flexibility to shift from one to another, nor does he probably have the ability to invent and discover things. Therefore, we get an interesting feeling about this child. He is not a bright child, but he is emotionally quite sensitive in one aspect, bound up with the self, in a way. Of course, you know that not all emotional aspects are positive. We have to watch a tendency toward a stereotype. If the child doesn't change his schema and remains with the same things, this is a kind of rigidity; and we have to watch that, too. So, as a whole, we probably have an average child with high distinction in aesthetic growth.

Now we come to the last part of our discussion with regard to the schematic stage and that is this: How should we use all this knowledge for good motivations? Out of this comes the question, "What materials should we give our children?" I shall repeat this again and again: no motivation is good if it doesn't relate to the child. Therefore, it is the very first thing and the most important thing: we should always know the needs in order to find the right motivation.

We have discovered the child's needs. What are they? The child's one and most outstanding need is to discover himself as part of a larger environment, that means, the need to get away from the egocentric feelings which we previously discovered in the pre-schematic child. The child discovers that he is not alone in this world, that others are in the same space. This is a very important need; therefore, we will have to include this need in every motivation which we give to the child of this developmental stage. While we call the pre-schematic stage probably the "I" and "my" stage, we can call this the "we" stage, because the child now has discovered the "we"—the "we all are." This is very important. All motivations, which we now use even with topics, should no longer be "I" am playing with "my," or "I and my," but "we" are doing this and this. So we have already one important need which should be seen in the choice of a topic. What is another need? Well, another need is really an educational need which actually counteracts some of the tendencies of the child. I will explain this a little bit.

As we enter this stage, the child discovers his concepts. He needs, of course, to be reassured of his concepts, but we should watch the child very closely so that this reassurance does not result in a stereotype. You see, the lazy child will say, "I can draw a tree, I can draw a tree," and will repeat the same tree again and again. All of a sudden the tree becomes a stereotype. He can no longer deviate from it, and the same may be true for the figure. We will see that retarded children via this reassurance get stuck and become stereotyped easily in their drawing.

This is the developmental stage when children easily develop a stereotype. We all know that from our own homes if we have children who are seven and eight years old. These are years in which children are difficult to handle. They discover their own will power; they have discovered it before, but now they discover it consciously. They want to do this, and they want to do that. They have their own way of doing things. A child who does not remain easily flexible may search for escape mechanisms such as stereotypes, the repetition of the same thing. We will have to counteract that if we discover such. Therefore, it will not hurt if every motivation has somewhere in it a part which points toward the flexibility of using the schema, and every action included in the motivation should point toward this flexibility. So, we should frequently use action motivations during this developmental stage. Now, we already have the "we," and we have "action" as a part of the motivation.

The child also discovers the terrain, the ground on which he stands, whether it is a hill or whether it is a plane or whether it is the floor. This is for him the base; therefore, we shall include in our motivation environmental factors, that is, the "where." We should then keep in our minds that if we choose a topic which serves the child's needs, it should have three things in it: the "we," an "action" which motivates flexibility, and the "where" which introduces environment. If we were to say, "Johnny and I are playing tag on the school ground," this would be a topic which includes the "we." "Playing tag," is the "action." "On the school ground" is then the environmental factor. But, indeed, it would be not a good motivation if we were just to tell the child, "Today we are playing tag on the school ground, and we want to draw that." This would not activate any of the feelings of the child.

We should keep in mind what we said before—that every motivation should have an introduction, a point of culmination, and a concluding summary statement. So, when we introduce a motivation such as "We are playing on the school ground," we should begin with an introductory statement. "When do you play? Well, at home? Yes, when? And do you also play at school? When? During intermission. Oh, I see. When? During lunch hour? Are you allowed to go out during lunch hour? Where do you play? And what do you play?"

Then the child will recall the different play activites. One may be playing tag. Then we would go into it and say, "Now, when you play tag, how do you play this game? How do you play it? Do you run? How do you run?

Do you run by standing straight? Let's see. How does it look when you run this way? Oh, you have to bend forward when you run. Why do you bend forward when you run? Oh, if you run fast, you will fall back unless you put your weight forward. Let's try to play tag and run. The children—did you see how they run?"

The children should put themselves into the place of the running child. They should get the feeling very much. "Now if you bend forward and you stoop over too much when you are running hard, what happens? Do you fall? You know, when I was a child, I fell very hard. Even some of the gravel got stuck in my knee; it was all bloody. Yes, it hurt. Now don't bend forward too much. What? You also had a bloody knee? Oh, I see. Well, there is nothing wrong in having bloody knees, but you know you shouldn't lean forward too much. What will happen if you don't bend at all? You can't play tag, and what else? You will fall backward. Sure, this also happens to children, and then they rub their heads; so it's better to run forward because it is better to rub your knee." You give the child all possibilities for running so that the child really gets the feeling of running.

Now and then you will have a child in the group who will just draw a figure with no motion in it. The child will have no feeling in it. Now, you could even ask, "Do you have both legs in front at the same time? Oh, no, that only can be done by a rabbit. Yes, he jumps like this; but we are not jumping rabbits. Try it. Can you run this way?" Have fun when you motivate the children. And now we would suggest the feeling that one leg is ahead and the other is in the air. "Try to run. Try to run hard. Can you have both legs on the ground at the same time? Johnny, try it. No, you would walk fast; you wouldn't run. What happens when you run? Oh, one leg is in the air. Isn't that funny? One leg is in the air. Did you ever think of that?"

You see, after having made the child aware of his own actions, you activate for the flexibility of the schema. The child may have a schema like the example of the child playing checkers. This was not well motivated, or maybe the reaction was not very good. The child was stiff in his reaction. In the motivation, I would have given the child the feeling of how it is when you sit down and play checkers, and how it feels when you sit down and when you get up. I would have given the child a very intense feeling of it so the child actually would feel his legs and his feet on the ground, and so forth. The motivation may have been good, but the child may not have reacted to it; and this is signified partly in his stiffness, emotional stiffness. Yes?

Student: Concerning motivation, say you have a child in the class who can't run, has trouble walking, or something—what do you do about that?

Lowenfeld: This child will even make a much stronger drawing. We consider such questions in another course, which deals with therapeutical

257

aspects. We have made experiments, for instance, and a crippled child became very much motivated. It is very healthy for a crippled child to engage mentally in running, because it is part of his outlet. This is used as a part of the therapeutical aspect of art—that the child fictitiously goes through some activity through which he actually cannot go.

Student: I was wondering, you know, if it is good.

Lowenfeld: It is good, yes. It is not good to confine the child to his handicap. If the child cannot run, the child may mentally run and may even run more than others do.

Now, we'll just point out some differences regarding materials used by children. We use essentially the same materials for the schematic stage that we use during the pre-schematic stage. We still use selected colors. It is not necessary to give your children a wide range of colors, because they won't use them and they even become confused by them. It is, however, important that you give your children paint now and not merely crayons, because with paint they can more forcefully express their own concepts. But if you don't have paint and if you have large classes, don't feel badly because crayons are a good means. I am not as religious in those restrictions as I have read in some books. Some writers have discouraged many teachers who do not have the opportunity to use paint because the classes are too large and probably also because the supply of paint is not adequate. If you can use paint, it is better to use paint than crayons. And if you use paint, you may gradually use a thinner paint, not as thick as during the pre-schematic stage. ·

It is good if you use brushes of various sizes: a large brush, let us say, of a half-an-inch; and another brush, probably of a quarter-of-an-inch, so that the child may draw details and may also have an opportunity to fill in spaces with greater ease. Still use absorbent paper because it prevents running. But you can occasionally use easel paper which is not absorbent—or not as absorbent as newsprint—because the child must now develop a better control of his material. You see, this is also a part of our educational intent. It is good if the child gets three-dimensional material such as clay for expressing himself. It is, indeed, very good if the child is given a variety of materials so that he can use different textures and different materials. That leads to a discussion of the meaning of the importance of crafts. Of course, crafts are a very, very important part of any art educational program, but we discuss this in another course.

Student: Would you enhance the three-dimensional aspect if you were to introduce the use of tools?

Lowenfeld: I would not introduce the use of tools in modeling, because the child can gain greater confidence by using his fingers directly.

Student: What about the use of cut or torn paper and paste?

Lowenfeld: It is very good, but don't use it too often at this stage because we will see that a material is best used at a time when we can make the best usage of it. At this time paper cutting or paper tearing, while it gives additional understanding, leads to the understanding of overlapping for which the child is not yet ready. For instance, if a child cuts a mountain or several mountains, one mountain may overlap the other mountain accidentally and the child may not really make use of this and may not understand it.

Student: I have two questions. One is regarding clay. If you mix the media—for example, buttons, quart cans, sticks, etc.—would that force the synthetic type of modeling?

Lowenfeld: To a certain extent it would force the synthetic kind of modeling. Mixtures of materials such as clay, toothpicks, and buttons, do not allow an analytic kind of modeling or an analytic kind of treatment. However, the child would not be thwarted; because whenever the child has a feeling and the need for analytical modeling, he would simply reject those materials. You should not force him to use these materials.

Student: What about wire?

Lowenfeld: The same is true with wire, but the child may get a concept in wire and use analytical modeling rather than putting things together.

LECTURE 21

The Schematic Stage: Color Motivation; The Stage of Dawning Realism: Gangs, Sexual Awareness, Characterization, Group Work, and Cooperation

---

The question is: "If it is desirable that a child differentiates his color-object relationships—that means, uses different greens for different plants and trees—would it not be better to give a child in the schematic stage a twelve- or sixteen-color choice of crayons rather than an eight-color choice?"

I am always in favor of a limited number of colors on all levels, actually, because a limited number of crayons or colors encourages the child to creatively mix colors himself. Good crayons can be mixed. A child who actively has the desire to show different greens, will, for instance, put over one green a yellow and make it yellowish, and over another green a brown and make it brownish, and over another green a blue and make it bluish. This desire to invent his own colors and actively to mix them is a creative desire. So I would say it is much better to let the child do his own mixing than to provide him with ready-mixed or ready-made colors. This is much more true for poster paint than for crayons.

If you give children a limited scale of colors, you encourage them to invent their own colors if they feel the desire. If they don't feel the desire, it's of no use to give them a large range of colors; because they won't use them out of their own feelings, but only as a matter of using the different choices which they have. It's like choosing in a multiple-choice test item, you see. You have four choices—well, let's take this one. It is then the choice of the child, instead of really actively engaging in a desire which reaches for fulfillment. A desire which reaches for fulfillment is always more desirable than something which the child only passively accepts.

Student: Can you or should you motivate this use of color?

Lowenfeld: Yes, you should motivate for any sensitivity, as I told you in the beginning of this course. You remember when I made the comparison between children's personalities and vases, when we poured in a motivation? You see, you may pour in the motivation of a greater sensitivity to color on almost any level that you want to. If the child is not capable of holding it, it will spill over and it will not be visible in the child's work, but it will not hurt. No sensitivity ever hurts. It will not fall on fertile soil, though, if the child isn't ready. So there should not be any misunderstanding.

May I also stress that a sensitivity towards environment should not be confused with a difference in concept towards environment. A sensitivity is something which is here in nature and must be discovered. Do you see? In our environment, or even in human relationships, this is what we call sensitivity—to discover what is already here, not to introduce something new. I will give you an example. It would hurt the child of seven or eight if you were to talk to him about perspective. Perspective is not in nature, and to discover one's sensitivity towards perspective would be confusing if we were to call it sensitivity. Perspective is a new concept which takes place in our mind.

But it is something different if you ask a child: "Have you ever looked at the plants? How different they are?" If you were to pick and bring in a bunch of flowers, in this way you might explain differences in greens. Even if you go out with a group and say, "Now, children, we'd like to find out how many greens we can discover in nature," and you collect leaves, that would probably get their attention more readily to a color-object relationship of a more sensitive nature. Now, you would relate a motivation to this, and some of the children may discover for themselves that there is a great subtlety among the greens. But others will stick to green as it comes from the jar and will not change it, because all the motivation which you have poured in spilled over. They couldn't hold it. Their ability for sensitivity has not grown to that point as yet.

However, if you would tell children: "Now, children, let's look into the distance. Do you see how things diminish in size?" the child would think: "Well, a tree is a tree. What does he mean?" You see? This is nothing to discover in nature. This is to discover in your mental concept. There should not be any confusion about sensitivity and differences in concept. We frustrate individuals if we introduce differences in concept, but we never frustrate individuals if we make them more sensitive to existing things. Another frustration would be if you were to ask a child who scribbles, "Can't you draw a house?" A house is something for the child which is inconceivable as a drawing concept, because he still thinks in terms of motions and not in terms of mental pictures. So you introduce a new mental concept which is inconceivable to the individual.

Whenever we introduce things which are inconceivable to the child at his stage of development, we frustrate him in the same way as if I were to give you a very exciting lecture today, but in German. Do you see? You would say, "I know that he was bound up with it, but I couldn't understand a word." And you would want to know what I was talking about. It is incomprehensible to you. But German is not a sensitivity which you have not discovered; it's a mental concept that you have learned—a new language. So you may encourage any kind of sensitivity on any level. We should never leave it out.

Even when I go through the fields with Robin, I pick out a flower and show him a drop of dew on it. How lovely it is! I turn it around; and when the sun mirrors itself in it, he laughs. These are things which we should point out time and again. We cannot start early enough in childhood. May I again repeat, sensitivities are not new mental concepts, but they are increased and intensified relationships to existing things. As we said previously, they are detailed relationships, when we discover the details which are in them—such as the details of the differences in color, the details in a plant, the details in shades—and these things are already existing.

But still I would not suggest giving the child a big set of poster paint, a big set of many colors, because the child should discover his own ability to invent colors. You discovered that probably by yourself when your children for the first time discovered mixing. I remember very distinctly when my son discovered mixing. He was five years old, and he introduced a new word for each new color. That means he was not only inventive in mixing the color, but he also saw a new color there, just by accident, and invented a new word for the color, too.

I also have here a note which says: "Will you please discuss Exercise [1], Schematic Stage, in the book?" Relate an objective to the term given on the left side—that means, relate "geometric lines" to any one of the "personality characteristics" on the right side. Now, I think this will take quite a long time, and we will take away from our new subject matter, but I would like simply to go over it briefly with you. We know that no child during the schematic stage expresses himself realistically. Therefore, what we call geometric lines would simply relate to the average child. Do you see? So I would draw an arrow to the average child. Does it relate to something else? Well, not as I see it.

Student: Would this child be inclined to be subjective?

Lowenfeld: No, not definitely. Every child draws by means of representative symbols when he is between seven and nine years of age, and, therefore, we would not really designate him as a subjective child. However, he may also be subjective, you know. He certainly isn't objective. Now, for "realistic lines," we would say the child is "visual" and more "objective" if he does use them. Then for the "base line"—well, we would say a base line would point toward what? Awareness toward the environment, and therefore toward a mass consciousness, and therefore toward "cooperation." They most probably relate to one another. "No base line" would indicate that the child has not yet discovered himself as a part of the environment, and therefore it would indicate that the child has not yet discovered active

SCHEMATIC STAGE/DAWNING REALISM

Exercise 1. Schematic Stage

Analyze a child's drawing in using the following scheme (check the correct part).

Drawing Characteristics	Personality Characteristics
Geometric lines	Subjective
Realistic lines	Visual, objective
Base line	Cooperative
No base line	Noncooperative
Rich schemata	Intelligent
Normal schemata	Average
Poor schemata	Dull
Folding over	Egocentric
Frequent exaggeration	Emotional
Too much exaggeration	Emotionally unstable
No emphasis on particular parts	Dull
Frequent use of bright colors	Joyous
Frequent use of dull colors	Sad
Space-time representation	Subjective
Stereotyped repetitions	Emotional maladjustment
X-ray pictures	Subjective
Good organization	Well integrated and balanced

cooperation. "Rich schemata" would mean that the child draws many details, and therefore it would indicate that the child is of a higher "intelligence" than others, also of a higher alertness than others.

Student: Dr. Lowenfeld, that was my question, and you've answered it very well now—thank you. I know that you did discuss it yesterday, but I didn't quite understand. Someone said that these columns were of no relationship to each other.

Lowenfeld: Of course they are in relationship. We just relate those attributes which belong to each other.

Now, we have discussed the child who has found his concept. The concept, which we consider as a real discovery, is one which the child has found himself as a part of the environment. As we have seen, the child notes this by saying: "I am on the ground. The tree is on the ground. Dad is on the ground. We all share a common ground," which is signified by the base line.

But this child now moves and grows older, and the next stage into which he grows utilizes this new discovery. This is always very wonderful in nature. On the one hand, he had a rest pause (let us say) intellectually, because he did not add to his concept. But on the other hand, he actually discovered it socially, because he now no longer draws in a fashion as we saw it previously

263

when he said: "There is an ambulance. There is a plane. There am I." He now relates the things to each other. He says: "I am on the ground. The sky is above." He brings a definite order into his relationships, and out of this definite order grow new discoveries—first of all, the discovery that he is not alone in this world. As he discovers that, of course, he also discovers the characteristics of those things with which he is not alone. For instance, he discovers that he can better associate with boys, that there are boys and girls, and that he finds friends with whom he can better cooperate in play, which we usually call the "gangs." Therefore, we will call this stage the "gang age" because children associate with groups.

Actually, I should not have called it the gang age, because we have a bitter aftertaste when we say "gang." This bitter aftertaste is probably due to the inconveniences which are caused to adults by the gangs. You know, children want to associate with each other, and thereby form a gang. Instead of being glad when we see children associate with each other, discovering that they are as a group more powerful than alone, discovering their belongingness—instead of being glad, we feel there is something detrimental in it. And so we call them "gangs" with a bitter aftertaste. This is not good. Indeed, we must correct our relationships with groups of this age. If we only think that during this stage, for the first time, the child develops the active desire to share with others of his own age in his play, joys, activities, all things—the major portion of his life, actually—and if we think of it as something positive, namely, that the child is sharing, then we no longer will look at a gang with a bitter aftertaste.

Because of our attitude toward gangs, we find them most often inconvenient. For instance, "Mother, may I go and sleep with Pauli out-of-doors? Look, Pauli may sleep out-of-doors, may I, too? May I do it, too? And Joe joins us, too. We all could sleep out-of-doors in a tent." "No, you mustn't do that, you are too young to do that." You see, we interfere with children and with their own independent longing for group life. Whenever such children come to you as parents or teachers, please do your utmost to fulfill their longings; because if you don't, this longing will be fulfilled anyway behind the bushes or elsewhere and you no longer will be a part of it.

There was a marvelous film last year, or two years ago. It was a French film, and I forget the title. It showed what happened to a gang. The gang had as its friend a teacher, and the teacher shared with this gang all its secrets. But the gang was not liked in town. Whenever the gang came, people pointed at them and said: "Now this is that destructive gang which comes. They throw stones at windows." Well, that's the usual connotation which we have. We immediately have a hostile feeling toward such groups because they are different than we are. It is our task, as teachers, to contribute to the life of gangs and to make a group life possible for them, a conducive group life.

I remember back to my childhood. If I can remember back to this stage, then it must have made a very distinct and important impression upon me. It must even have influenced me very positively. I remember very distinctly how we converted a little island into a wonderland when I was a child. We were in a gang, a wonderful gang. We built a secret bridge. I am quite sure it was not larger than this; but when we went over this bridge, it appeared to us as if it were miles long. Going over the bridge and entering our land about which no one knew—this was fascinating. We were making a building there at the highest point—there was a little hill, you know. We made our own money, of course. We collected the money for entrance to our island, and we counted it. I still remember when we had our pockets full of paper money which we ourselves had printed.

We found there the bones of a dead animal, and we made a little sign there saying, "These are the bones of an animal from 2000 years ago that we discovered," and we really looked at them. They were put there in a certain order, and this was something magical to us. And another place was the snake point, where we had spread out a dead snake that we found. When we went there, we really got goose pimples. This was the snake point—"Let's go to the snake point!" Then, we collected gravel and built little paths. These were real paths, you know. We had a hide-out, and when it rained we covered it. So this island was really something magical.

Now imagine the possibilities if we were to promote those things in school—if we would promote group life. This is creative, you see, even when it deals with what we can invent in a certain environment. We can even use our classrooms for the purpose of promoting group activities in a positive sense. How we can do this, especially in art, we will discuss later. Then, we would help the child in his desire to discover his own relationships to his own group and share with him experiences of an important nature. Only when this group life is frustrated, only when adults are against it and do not permit the child to engage in it, will the group turn against adults.

Experiments which have been made in England with regard to that are very revealing. There were schools in which children of this developmental level were given the freedom to conduct their own lives, even their own discipline. And they did marvelously. The outcome of these children was splendid with regard to their behavior and with regard to their group contribution. Their learning was on a higher level than those in the control group, in which children were opposed in their group life and discipline was imposed upon them by adult standards. And the outcome of these two groups was quite different.

We should know that all we can do for children during this level is to help them, because this may be the very starting point for either their friendly relationship to people or their hostile relationship to people. Actually, there is no more wonderful means than art education to do it, for we can discover in the art work the relationships which people have. We can help them through group work to make their activity important. However, we have to be very careful with the means which we use, because group work may be frustrating or it may be motivating.

Group work is frustrating when the individual feels he could have done better alone than in the group—when the group interfered with individual differences. I will give you an example. You come back from vacation to your class and are very inspired to do some group work. You say: "Now, children, we are going to paint a mural. We, all together, will paint a mural. I know you have all had a wonderful vacation, so we will paint this mural of our summer vacation." You see, when you do that, Joe may have been to the sea, while Mary was in the mountains; and one child was with Grandpa, and another child was in a camp. So one will start painting this, and the other will interfere with it. Individual experiences which are focused on an individual's life are not appropriate topics or themes for cooperative projects. Here the individual child will say, "Well, I can do that better myself!" He will feel this inside. He will feel that someone else is interfering with his project rather than helping him.

Group projects are only positive in their effect when the single individual has the feeling that he alone could not have accomplished what the whole group has accomplished. I will give you an example of this. For instance, you have your class on the shore and you say: "Now, children, have you ever thought what would happen if the boats would not have a common place where they can harbor? What would happen? How would it be if each of you were to have his own boat? What kind of a boat would you like to have? Now, each of you children select the boat which you like best."

Now we come to the second point. Cooperative projects can only be done well if you use a material which lends itself to such projects, usually a material that is appropriate for assembling or putting things together. In this instance, I might give the children construction paper. "Cut out the boat which you like best." Each child then has the freedom to develop his relationship to a boat after he has been motivated. One may cut out a sailboat. The other may cut out a rowboat and put himself or other friends in it. Another may want to cut out a P.T. boat or destroyer or aircraft carrier, and so forth. Then we have a marvelous opportunity to assemble them in a harbor. If you have a class of thirty, we will have thirty boats. And each child, while pasting the boat on a common ground which may be blue water or whatever you have there, will have the feeling that he has made his contribution to a common harbor. This common feeling which he has is part of our intentions; namely, to fortify his feeling for group life, his feeling for cooperation. In the end, every child will have the feeling: "There is my boat. There is my boat. There is my boat." But all of the children will have the feeling, "This is *our* harbor," and no one has interfered with the other's boat. You have here an example, then, where group work has the desired effect of bringing satisfaction with cooperation.

So, may I repeat again, group work may be frustrating or motivating, depending on how it is used. We may interfere with the group if we interfere with individual differences, that is, if our topic is not geared toward group work and the individual has the feeling that he could have accomplished more if he were left alone rather than working with the group. Group work is conducive to cooperation and group methods of working if the single individual has the feeling that he could never have accomplished what the whole group has accomplished. Therefore, we have motivated the sensitivity in children towards the desirability of contributing to a group effort. You can see, then, that we can make a very important contribution in art education, since we can use our classrooms for the motivation of group enterprises.

Now, may we begin discussing the single characteristics which we expect from children in their paintings or in their art work as they grow. First of all, we know that children discover their own strength as groups—in our society, usually as separated groups. There are some mixed gangs, however. You know that there are some girls who participate usually in boys' gangs, but the sexes normally are separated. The real cause of this separation is the influence of society. There is nothing, I believe, inherent in this separation, because in other cultures we know that groups are completely coeducational. But, in our society, the interests which develop in boys are so different from the interests which develop in girls that boys are called sissies if they engage in things which girls do, and vice versa. We see some boyish girls participating in gangs, but this is an exception. Whether this separation is good or not is questionable.

I don't know whether any one of you recently read—it was, I believe, three or four weeks ago—a review in the *New York Times* of a book which is called *Why Men Don't Cry,* a very, very interesting review which greatly criticizes our society. It says that children, and boys in particular, are geared from the very beginning toward the behavior which covers up emotions rather than displays them. "In this way," the author says, "we may only contribute to greater tensions in our society." He says that experiments which have been made in various kinds of societies have shown that in societies in which men display their emotions as readily as women do—that means, in which men cry on the shoulders of women and women on the shoulders of men equally readily—the ratio of heart diseases, especially coronary diseases, is about equal or lower for men than in societies like ours in which even boys are considered sissies when they cry and are discouraged from displaying their emotions and have a tendency to keep their emotions inside, developing tensions. The author says that he believes that part of this social pattern is responsible for our large number of coronary diseases. I have no judgment in it, for I know too little about it. But there may be some truth in it, especially if it is experimentally proved that, in societies in which men also display their emotional, overt expressions, there is not such a ratio as we have here.

Educationally, we should by no means start at a level at which the child isn't even conscious of his emotions to restrict him in the expression of his emotions. If we would like for people to withhold their emotions, we should rather start at a time when people become obviously conscious of them, *not* when the laughter of a child is still the free laughter and *not* when the cry of the child is still the free crying so that we inhibit these emotions. I would like to say, at this point, that we should wait with our criticisms of sissies, and so forth. Since this is the age when "sissy" is usually applied to a boy who cannot hold back his emotions because they are overflowing, I think we should be careful with such statements as teachers and educators, because we are not doing anything good for the child.

We know from psychology that emotions which are displayed are mentally healthier than emotions which are withheld. I do not say that this is true for adults, because as adults we are living in a certain social structure. But as long as we can control things with our intellect, they are never as harmful as at a time when things are not controlled by intellect but are simply an expression of the being of a person.

So, I would not feel good if any one of you were to get into this group conformist attitude by saying, "Don't be a sissy." This is nothing which will help the child. You will only frustrate him. You haven't done anything for a child if you mark him a sissy. Solving his difficulties is our task rather than marking him with another brand, and we have many brands available. One brand with which we mark children is called I.Q.; let's not add anything more. Let's also not group them as creative and non-creative people. Let's accept the child as he is, and try to make him more sensitive toward his own life and his environment. This is our task, and we use art as a means to this end.

So if we have children who now discover that they are boys and others are girls, who discover this difference on the basis of the social structure, then you can readily see that lines which are merely geometric lines will not serve the purpose of characterizing boys and girls. This is actually the main reason why children discover the drive in themselves to change from geometric lines. A girl wears a skirt, hair, red lips. These are characteristics which have now become meaningful to the youngster, and so he includes them. But whenever the child includes them, even at a low level, then the child has already discovered the difference between boys and girls and has moved to a stage of characterization. Now may I say that there is a stage in between when we clearly see that the child still expresses himself by means of representative symbols.

Developmental stages do not occur all of a sudden, but gradually. The child moves gradually from the schematic stage into the stage in which he discovers himself in a group, discovers there are boys and there are girls. He moves into a stage when he develops the desire to characterize. You may see quite a number of different kinds of schemata. Some are rich; others are poor; and most of them are somewhat isolated and not related to one another.

Now let's find out what may be the reason for it. Then, we will talk further about space relationships. You may have an obvious impression in a drawing that girls and boys are playing with one another. You see, the one may be standing here. One may be standing there. The other may be standing here. Another may be standing there. They may all seem to be isolated in a way. Experiments which I made a long time ago, and which were confirmed by Dr. Mattil in his dissertation and by others, have shown that children who are frustrated in their group relationships—who have not had the opportunity to cooperate—have a tendency in their drawings to become stiff and to separate their figures from one another.

I made an experiment, with 400 children participating, in which I presented the following theme or topic. I said: "You are standing under an apple tree. You look at the apple tree, and you see on one of the lower branches an especially beautiful apple. You stretch out your hand because you would like to reach the apple. But you are just a little bit too short, so you have to get on your tiptoes to reach the apple. And now you reach it, grab it, and enjoy it." This was the topic stimulation which I gave to the school children. The topic was chosen for the following reasons: I wanted to know, first of all, to what degree children relate themselves to outside experiences—grabbing an apple. What is the size relationship to an especially beautiful apple and probably to the other apples? What is the size relationship between themselves and the apple tree? How do they express body experiences such as getting on their tiptoes, and so forth?

Now, when I gave this topic—and I have in your book some illustrations which refer to it—the largest number of children who did not establish any spatial relationship between themselves and the apple tree was found during the gang age—that is, between nine and eleven years—but particularly at eleven years. I was then a little bit curious about why it appeared that children revert to kind of stiff representations. Figure [25] shows you one of the figures which had not achieved spatial relationships. The child is simply standing there and the apple tree is there, and no relationship between picking and the apple has been achieved.

I found out—and this has since been confirmed by other studies—that this is an indication of children who have been frustrated in their cooperation. For this child [in Figure 25], it would be just as easy to place the figure a little bit farther to the left and a little bit higher in order to reach the

Fig. 25. "Picking Apples from a Tree" (10 years old). Inability to establish a correlation between the figure and the tree is caused by egocentric attitude. Emphasis on apples. (Stage of Dawning Realism)

apple. So it is not a technical disability, because it is just as easy or as difficult to do it the other way. It is apparently a sign of frustration—no desire to establish a relationship with the outside. This we found is true, especially in groups in which we have no cooperation or frustrated cooperation. Since then, we have related this study and other studies to the ability of children in their social relationships, their ability to work in groups, and have found that children who work readily in groups and are very cooperative show this cooperation also in their desire to establish relationships in their drawings.

Our society counteracts this very much. It is a common thing to see children in our schools who have not been motivated or stimulated in their group activity. This is sad—indeed, very sad—that we, who are all for limited freedom and democracy, have not discovered this very important meaning of cooperation. It is terrible if we think that education should just be the education of the mind but not the education of the soul and the education of our hands. So what do we do about it? You are all teachers who have had past experiences with children. You have had a training background in teaching. Did you hear anything about it in your training? No, you heard the subject matter which you should cover in arithmetic and in reading and in writing, but you have not heard anything about this very important matter of how to get along with people. And this, of course, is the foundation which is laid right here—when the child begins his desire to share with others. Instead of taking it into our own hands and finding the means by which we can promote this desire to cooperate, we are still concerned with the fact that Johnny can't read, as you have heard, which is a falsification also. So it is very important to us, then.

What can we do about children who feel themselves as being isolated rather than a part of a group or who feel that their group life has been frustrated and they have to go behind the bushes or outside to satisfy their group life without the adults, and thus become hostile towards adults? You know, that is the reason for hostility towards adults. Group life has been interfered with by adults. What can we do? We will talk about that when we talk in detail about motivations and the meaning of motivations in the classroom. We have an important means in our hands for motivating group activities through art, because here the child not only engages in group work but, while he is engaging creatively in his work, he also identifies himself with what he does. And this self-identification—to put himself in the place of another—is one of the most important foundations for cooperation.

I have partly, without even saying so, covered what the child should be able to express during this stage. First of all, in his figure drawing, we assume that the child should move from mere geometric lines to lines which characterize boys as boys and girls as girls. This is not a matter of skills, please. Whether you characterize it well or not so well may be a matter of aesthetic experience and sensitivity. But characterization and the desire to characterize is a matter of mental development. If a child of thirteen years has still no awakening in himself that these are girls and these are boys and draws them all by means of the same concepts, then he has not become mentally alert to his environment; and that is not a factor of skills but a factor of his mind. I hope this is clearly understood, and I emphasize it here as I have emphasized it in the past. We expect to see these differences.

Children of this level of development should include hair in their drawings as an important characteristic of figure drawing. They should include eyebrows and, usually, the details which are around features, especially those details which characterize differences such as cheeks, lips, and so forth. They should relate the color, too. Children should, indeed, draw pants and so forth for boys, and, for girls, skirts and their outfits. The more they differentiate in them, the more they are aware of the differences. Again, the ability to differentiate is not a matter of aesthetic experience. To differentiate them adequately and well in their drawing may be a matter of aesthetic experience, but to differentiate them can be done by primitive means on a continuum from, let us say, no aesthetic sensitivity to great and intense aesthetic sensitivity.

Now, we would like to get still a better understanding of what we mean by characterizing lines. One of the most simple ways of differentiating lines which characterize from lines which are realistic is one line which most definitely functions as such a characterization and which we have found from comparing hundreds and thousands of drawings—and that is the hemline in skirts. This has a more and deeper psychological meaning. Whenever children merely use a skirt to characterize, the hemline will be straight. Whenever children discover their visual percept, their visual sensitivity, they also discover the changing effects in nature.

Under these changing effects in nature, we have three categories: changing caused by motion; changing caused by light, that is, illumination; and changing caused by distance, that is, that distant things appear smaller. The changing caused by motion immediately introduces a hemline which is no longer straight but is probably jagged and irregular. Whenever the child introduces or becomes aware of this changing hemline, we no longer deal with characterization. We are then further ahead in our sensitivity towards the child; namely, we have discovered that the child already sees things and perceives things carefully in detail. Now, you understand that this hemline has a deeper meaning than merely straight or in motion. It means whether the child still thinks: "This child has a skirt; it is a girl," or whether he thinks, "This skirt has this attribute—it moves when the child runs." Do you see? The one is still a mental concept; the other is a visual percept, as we discussed it previously.

LECTURE 22

The Stage of Dawning Realism: Visual Perception; Color; Sincerity in Design; Evaluation of Intellectual, Emotional, Social, and Perceptual Growth

During the gang age the child perceives space and his environment, and also goes through certain changes. During the schematic stage, the most important discovery, probably, was the discovery of an order—to bring an order into space by the introduction of the base line as a vehicle of spatial experiences and expression. Now the child has discovered his hide-outs, the meaning of his hide-outs, and so forth. He is no longer interested merely in the concept that we all are on the same ground. Oh, no! He moves around on this same ground, and in his characterization of the environment, the base line is no longer sufficient for characterizing the ground. Because he moves around on the ground, he discovers the plane—first, by introducing several base lines, and, then, by refraining from the use of base lines. This refraining from the use of base lines introduces him to meaningful space; that means he then discovers the plane. He moves on the plane, and the plane is now part of his whole experience. So we go a step further, as we shall see. Whether or not the child already includes perceptual space in his drawings can best be seen if he introduces the changing effects which refer to the environment. What would they be?

Student: Light?

Lowenfeld: Well, light would still be more a part of the object.

The first introduction usually is distance. The introduction of the horizon line—a horizontal line—is the first. You can imagine a child having a base line and then feeling that he should go into space by introducing one base line here and another base line there, usually above the first one. He then gradually refrains from using base lines and feels, "Oh, the sky goes all the way down." That makes him draw the sky all the way down probably to this horizontal line which, in the beginning, may be not the horizon line but another base line. But it gradually assumes the significance of the horizon line. So the horizon line would be the first indication of perceptual space when the child relies not on his knowledge but rather on his observation. We will see that this introduction of the horizon line is a significant change. Sometimes children arrive at the meaningfulness of the sky as such during the schematic stage, and we should not be misled. It may be due to the fact that the child has been told that the sky is not merely on top but goes all the way down; but it still remains a mental concept. It only becomes a percept if the child includes the diminishing size of objects as they move into the distance, that means, whenever the child includes changing effects in nature. This is something wonderful.

It was a great inspiration to me when I discovered that this is so simple. You know, it sounds so very simple. I wish you would have been with me when I discovered that the changing effects in nature signify the percept. It's wonderful, as all simple things are wonderful. They sound so simple, you know, but when you arrive—after reading all this literature which has been written on art—at such a simple concept, then you feel good. So I felt very good. And also I feel good to be able to tell you that such a simple matter as the characteristics of the movement from a concept to a percept is something very tangible. You know, it doesn't take away from our intuitive feelings. On the contrary, it enriches them. So, when looking at a child's drawings from now on, we will be able to determine how much of a percept the child is using—that means, how much he is actually using his eyes immediately for his expression, not merely as an intermediary.

I told you that all concepts are also based on percepts. Yes, indeed. The basis of any concept must be seeing, touching, or something involving the senses. That is obvious because a child who has not yet come in contact with his senses has no concept whatsoever and is completely cut off from any growth. We understand that. But when I speak of a visual percept, then I mean that the eyes are immediately responsible for the kind of expression which the child uses. This we call a percept.

We call it a concept when the mind forms what we gain through the eyes, for instance, the child says, "A man has two eyes, a nose, a mouth, and so forth." Now I am looking at the changing of the eyes, the changing forms and shapes of the eyes, according to individual differences. I'm looking at the light and shadow in a face. I'm looking at the motions through which a skirt goes. I'm looking at even the motion of hair when someone is running or when the wind blows through it. I'm looking at the diminishing sizes of objects as they move into the distance. These are things which are directly derived from seeing. So the most significant factor in space representation, again, is the changing quality. Whenever this changing quality is introduced, we deal with a departing from a mere conceptual space to a perceptual space.

Now, let us look at how children deal with color during this period. You see that there is a great unity in the changes. Also in color, the child moves from mere rigid color-object relationships to characterizations of color. Characterizations already include the mixing of colors—that means, one sweater is more bluish-red; the other sweater is more yellowish-red. This characterizes the sweater. But it is not yet a perception of the sweater. Why?

Student: Because it's the color he wants.

Lowenfeld: Sure. He does not indicate the changing effects of color in light and shadow as a result of illumination or the changing effects of color as a result of being in the atmosphere. These changes are not included. Isn't that wonderful? It goes all the way through the child's art. So this is a criterion which we should not forget and which we should incorporate into our active knowledge, not only in the knowledge which we know but do not use. So, you see, if I say "Your blouse is yellow," is this a concept or a percept?

Student: Concept.

Lowenfeld: At this time, it is a concept. If I say your blouse is slightly greenish-yellow?

Student: Still a concept.

Lowenfeld: Still a concept. Your blouse is lemon-yellow in the light and greenish in the shadow.

Student: Percept.

Lowenfeld: See, the color changes from the light to the shadow. The most beautiful color percepts were produced during the Impressionist Era, in which painters actually lived in perceptions. This was a very basic inspiration—the refined perception during the era of French Impressionism, when people even analyzed the differences in colors in light and shadow. They even put down dots as brushstrokes. Those who know this era know what I mean. It's not necessary that you know what I mean, although it's good if we become interested in our cultural past and know what has been produced. I believe it belongs to the basic background of every cultured person.

So, in color, the child between nine and eleven years will not yet introduce a percept but will gradually move from a mere conceptual stage of color or color-object relationship to a characterizing of colors—that is, the shade of this tree is different from the shade of another tree, or the sky has a different blue than the river or the lake, and so forth. He will see different shades and should discover them. If a child, during the gang age, still uses rigid color-object relationships, the child is backward, not because he does not use new colors—you understand that this would be a very superficial answer—but because in his perception he has not yet refined his gain of seeing differences in the shades; for instance, that this shrub is darker than the lawn.

You may say, "Is this important?" Yes, it is. I say, "It is." And I would like to underline it ten times, because we have been conditioned too much to the idea that those things are only important which either contribute to the accumulation of our knowledge or to our pocket. Indeed, a refined and better ability to recognize things which surround us adds to the richness of our lives and finally will lead to a refined perception. Without a refined perception, we will pass by the beauties in life—like animals—not recognizing them, as we are used to doing and as is fostered even by our education of today.

We still do not recognize that the things which are not immediately contributing to our pocket are of significance. We have a long way to go to recognize the meaningfulness of spiritual values. But you are the ones, like I am, who have the deep responsibility for promoting them in your schools. If you once have committed yourself to a deep feeling for spiritual values—not just on Sunday when you go to church, but every day—then you have a deep responsibility for promoting these spiritual values in your classroom. One of them is to discover the riches in life—not the richness; that means, your pockets. Basic to this is also that we discover the riches which are in our work, that we enjoy what we do and gain a lift from it instead of going into our classes and thinking of them as just a chore that we have to do in order to live. You know, this is awful. I do not have to stress that I am for higher salaries, but this is an entirely different question. I feel that, as long as we are not inspired as teachers, we have no right even to ask for higher salaries because we may be spoiling children instead of giving them the education which they deserve.

Now let me speak about the meaning of design during this period, because this is really an awakening period. The meaning of design—that means, the harmonious relationship, especially in our environment—plays a very important role during this period. With regard to his environment, the child is awakening. Indeed he discovers that boys are different from girls, but he also discovers the meaning of various products which he finds in nature as these can serve him for his hide-out or for beautifying his little environment. We did it when I was a child, as I told you, and all of you have gone through similar stages, I hope. You may have missed a lot if you didn't, you know. Don't take away those beautiful things from your children, because they are precious and will remain with them for many, many years, probably to the ends of their lives. If children have them, they enrich their lives. As children discover the meaningfulness of their environment and relate it to themselves, I believe it becomes most important for education to give them a feeling for what is sincere and for what is insincere in their environment. This, I believe, is the most important function of an education for design and for harmonious relationships at this particular stage.

With regard to sincerity and insincerity, it is important that we engage children in the thinking and discovery which relates to the beauty of materials as they are found unspoiled—that means, give them a feeling for differences of shapes and forms in rocks and pebbles which they may find on beaches, shells which they can pick up, bark and moss which we can find in nature. Have them make collections. They are right at the stage of collecting things. They love to collect. Use it for developing their sensitivity. How many different kinds of pebbles can we collect in our environment? Make displays of pebbles; make displays of rocks of different shapes and colors. If you are on the shore, have displays of shells of various shapes and forms and colors. Go on excursions and discover different kinds of bark and moss. Discover the various characteristics of scrap materials. These also have some beauty.

Even the mold which develops on various objects when they are hidden in moisture has beauty. You get to see mold and look at it with fresh eyes, not with eyes that see mold as mold, but with eyes that see that mold may be beautiful. You may discover a different kind of sincerity. We are conditioned, of course, in regard to that by what is good for us, that means, what helps us. Mold is something which we feel is destroying some of our things, especially when we discover it on our clothes. So we get conditioned negatively towards mold. But mold may be beautiful. It may be a patina on various materials, and we may enjoy it if we find it in the woods and recondition our thinking and redefine the value of mold. We will have to redefine many values as we discover them with all the sincerity which we can muster. So, the sincerity of beauty as found in materials of nature should be encouraged, but we should relate it also to things which we find in our environment.

That brings me back to the discussion of the meaningfulness of materials as found in architecture. In the very beginning when I spoke about the relationship of art and society, I said that we should try to discover the type of environment which fits our society and satisfies our needs of today, and we should not long for something which belongs to the past and is no longer meaningful to our present. Such longing only represents our inability to create a spirit that can create a glorification which fits our needs today. As you remember, when we talked about this, we talked about a chapel, the shell of which had to be borrowed from the past. Why? Why is that necessary? Make your children discover such discrepancies which are insincere. We, ourselves, must go through a re-education if we have not yet felt, deep inside, the discrepancy between sincerity and the borrowing of things from the past. We cannot change our being and our birthdate. We are here to live in this time. Whatever you do, you are not able to change that. So we have to start where we are. Do you remember when I said that this is one of the most important educational principles—that we have to start on the level of the individual; that is, where they are? And for us, this is also true. We are living at the present time. We are not living in the past. So we have to start here, where we are, and re-educate ourselves as to where we are. In this we have to discover the spirit of our time, the sincerity in it and also the lies in it.

So, when we go and look around on excursions with our children, we should encourage them to go and knock on a column to see if it is really supporting something or if it is there only presuming to be something—to fool us, as it were. We find out that it's hollow, but it is painted like marble. "This is a lie. Look, it isn't here to support something; it is only supposed to be something which it no longer is." Children should learn during this stage to differentiate truth, sincere from insincere buildings, because it is here where man has most of all created an expression of his culture. Throughout the history of time, architecture always has been an expression of the culture in which we live.

If we look back to periods long gone, not a single man is remembered because of the money which he made. Did you ever think of that? We don't know of one. There were very, very rich people during the Renaissance who accumulated lots and lots of money. Do you know of a single name? Not a single name is known to us of all those rich people who lived during the Renaissance, but we know a lot of poor people who contributed through their culture, through their art, through their paintings. We know actually all of them who have made a major contribution. You see, man documents himself for posterity through his cultural contributions. That should give us something to think about.

So, we expose our children to the cultural contributions of this present day and we lead them on excursions to the understanding of what is sincere and what is insincere. This should now be known to all of you. Stone is stone and brick is brick and glass is glass; and a wall is a wall; and a column, if it doesn't support something, is without any value. A tower, if it is not meaningful for something, is merely an insincere decoration. You see, in past times, this may have been different. A tower was here to express—to reach for God, and then it had expressive qualities. All of the architecture was designed toward this reaching for God. But if a tower is put on a dining hall, as it is here, with no purpose whatsoever but just as a piece of decoration (which it isn't), then you should ask yourself, "Where is the sincerity?" There is no purpose behind it other than to conform to a pseudo-style. When we stick a wreath which has leaves and foliage around a window, like over there, then we ask ourselves, "What is it for?" Well, some would say it's a decoration. What does it decorate? What does it glorify? The attic? What a glorification! Do you understand? Now, this is not only wrongly used, but entirely without any sincerity.

I can still better understand if you glorify, let us say, the windows for someone who has contributed much to society, and, therefore, you would like to stress this window and surround it by marble. Then at least it would be in some relationship to the spirit, namely, you would like to glorify this person by giving him a specific window frame. But to glorify an attic into which no one can go—because it isn't even an attic; it's all closed up—by surrounding it with a wreath and by making it pretentious is such a lie that I've never heard a greater one. If you experience it this way, yourself, then we will live in a more truthful society. But since we are conditioned to accept those things as they have been done, we simply pass them by and have them influence us; because all environmental aspects influence us unconsciously, even if we don't want them to. And we go on living in an insincere environment. So may I ask, for yourself, that you question yourself as you go around with regard to the sincerity of things. Why are these columns there? They don't support anything. They are unnecessary. If you knock at them, they are hollow. They are not even carriers. They are only here to conform to a past style. To make children discover this is essential, because they will be the citizens of the future and they may be sincere or insincere. Now, do you see?

Please, don't misunderstand. I'm distinguishing between a sincerity and an insincerity for which an individual is responsible, and a sincerity and an insincerity for which a culture is responsible. You understand what I mean by that? For instance, we are not responsible for this insincerity here as an individual. Not even the architect is responsible, because he, too, is a victim of his culture. I would not say that President Eisenhower is responsible as an insincere person because he built in the colonial style when he remodeled his estate in Gettysburg or when he makes remarks about contemporary artists' works being non-fitting to the dignity of governmental buildings. Indeed, he is also a victim of his culture. You see, if you look at it now from another point of view, the point of view of what the culture means to the growth of a society, then we should feel that we as teachers have a special responsibility because it reflects upon the sincerity of people. You wanted to say something?

Student: I wanted to ask how this fits in with functionalism. Are you referring this in any way to that?

Lowenfeld: Yes, I am.

Student: How do you distinguish, then, between sincerity and the function of—?

Lowenfeld: Inasmuch as the function is part of it. Indeed, a column— or, let us say, a stone wall which is a stone wall should not pretend to be a wall which is painted over and where you no longer can see the stone as such. Or a wood wall should not pretend to be a stone wall by painting stones on it. Inasmuch as this refers to the function, it is also part of functionalism. May I say, it becomes most important during this period that we make the child aware of the relationship between the material, the function or the purpose, and its design—what it serves. There must be a harmonious relationship between the three in order to create a sincerity. For

Stage	Characteristics	Human Figure	Space	Color	Design	Stimulation Topics	Technique
Gang age. Preado-lescent crisis. Dawning realism.	(1) Removal from geometric lines (schema). (2) Lack of co-operation with adults. (3) Gang age. (4) Greater aware-ness of the self with regard to sex (boys and girls).	(1) Emphasis on clothes (dresses, uniforms), empha-sizing difference between girls and boys. (2) Greater stiff-ness as result of egocentric attitude, and the emphasis on details, as clothes, hair, and so forth. Tendency toward realistic lines. Removal from schema.	(1) Removal from base-line expression. (2) Overlapping. (3) Sky comes down to base line. (4) Discovery of plane. (5) Filling in space between base lines. (6) Difficulties in spatial correlations as result of egocen-tric attitude and lack of cooperation.	Removal from objective stage of color. Emphasis on emotional ap-proach to color. Subjective stage of color. Color is used with regard to subjective ex-perience.	First conscious approach toward decora-tion. Use in connec-tion with mate-rial. (1) Reproduc-ing techniques, emphasizing repetition. (2) Emotional design using the meaning of repetition. Acquaintance with materials and their func-tion.	Self-awareness stimulated by char-acterization of dif-ferent dresses and suits (professions). Cooperation and overlapping through group work. Subjective coopera-tion through type of topic: "We are building a house." Objective coopera-tion through work-ing method.	Paper cutting. No crayons from now on because of re-moval from linear expres-sion. Poster paint. Flat colored chalk. Clay. Papier-mâché. Linoleum cut. Wood. Metal.

EVALUATION CHART
Gang Age

		None	Some	Much
Intellectual Growth	Is the child beginning to use details to characterize the self and environment? Does the child depart from the use of schemata? Does the child depart from the use of geometric lines? Do details retain their meanings when separated from the whole? Does the child characterize boys as boys and girls as girls? Does the child depart from base lines? Does the child express the plane?			
Emotional Growth	Does the child identify himself with the drawing? Does the drawing lack stiffness? Are brush strokes or lines used freely? Does the child still use exaggerations? Does the child's drawing show accumulations of details on those parts which are emo-tionally significant?			
Social Growth	Does the child in his work identify himself with the group? Does he correlate figures to each other? Does he coordinate figures with space? (Environment.) Is the child socially conscious of his environment? Does he cooperate in group work by subordinating his work to the whole?			
Perceptual Growth	Does the child include the horizontal line? Has the child become aware of overlapping? Is distance expressed by the diminishing size of distant objects? Has the child become aware of the changing effects of light and motion? Does color indicate more than characterization? Has the space between base lines been filled in? Are textural qualities expressed?			
Physical Growth	Does the drawing indicate a distinction between sexes? Is there emphasis on secondary sex characteristics (moustache, hair, etc.)? Does the child's drawing show body action? Does the child retain flexibility in body movements?			
Aesthetic Growth	Does the child use decorative patterns on clothes or elsewhere? Does the child relate material to design and purpose? (Or does he look only for func-tion?) Does the child relate details to the whole? (Or does he become bound up with them?) Does the child relate colors to each other?			
Creative Growth	Does the child choose his own subject? Does the child experiment with different mediums? Does the child invent his own forms? Is the child inventive in using materials for new purposes?			

instance, if only one is lacking—let us say, the relationship between material and purpose is here—we cannot yet say it is sincere if we do not ask "What does it serve?" Does it serve as a part of a church—some spiritual aspect? Does it serve as some practical part of an engine? And so forth. The relationship of the three must be always here in order to be sincere.

Student: Is decoration a function?

Lowenfeld: Decoration, if it serves a spirit, is a function—yes, indeed—because the spirit is part of it. That's why I include what it serves as one of the criteria. For instance, let us say you build a cross for a church. A cross doesn't serve any material function; it serves a spiritual function. But you still would like to have a cross—if it is iron, to look like iron; if it is brass, to look like brass, you know; and to be deprived of any insincere decorations. Whenever we go into details, just ask yourself the question: "What is it for? What is it for?" Now, you may discover, let us say, that there is a foot on a little cross. The foot is actually formed like the paws of a lion. Then you ask yourself, "Has it a function?" It serves as a foot—but, a paw is a paw, and a paw isn't made out of brass. So it is insincere not to put there probably a geometric form in lieu of the imitation of something which it pretends to be—a paw. Do I make myself clear about it?

In this category belong also flowers. For instance, if you put some flowers in your hair, they're beautiful if you pick them and you feel like doing that. But if I go closer and see that the flowers are artificial, then I shudder because you fooled me. You really fooled me. I was thinking that these are real flowers. So, it is insincere. Do you see? That goes deeply into our lives, indeed. Imitation for imitation's sake isn't good, as you know, when I transfer the real flower into something man-made. Indeed, all of our inspirations stem from nature in some way, but then they are digested and transferred into a concept. To pick them up and imitate them so that we are disturbed by their imitation, or actually fooled by their imitation, is something which I consider insincere.

To this category belong also all of those enameled corsages which almost look like flowers; but if you go closer, they are not flowers. You can use flowers as an inspiration and do something with them so that you will not be fooled, and your spirit may still be derived from the inspiration of flowers. That would lead us really into a design course, and I would love to stay here for a length of time and go into details. However, since we can't do that, I would like to stress for this group that it would be most conducive if you were to go with your children and discover beauty in materials—an old stone house, for instance, if you have one in your community. Stress with your children how stone is used as stone and remains and keeps the beauty of stone. Then you may go to another house in which the stone has been painted over and the stone no longer is visible in its beauty. You would say, then: "Oh, the stone suffocates underneath. It is deprived of its beauty."

Fig. 26. "Our Family" (11 years old). Color now characterizes and often gives meaning to objects. Notice the blue puddles on the shaded ground. Parts when separated from the whole retain their meanings. (Gang Age) (Teacher: Jean Holland, Duke of York School, Toronto) [*Note:* For color, see Lowenfeld, op.cit., Plate 6.]

Student: What about the use of wood?

Lowenfeld: Well, the same thing. Use the beauty of the wood, the grain of the wood, and paint only such wood which has no grain or no beauty in its grain or when you have no other protective means for the wood. For instance, I would never paint over redwood; but I would paint over, let us say, second-grade pine which I cannot stain because the stain would not bring out any beauty in the wood and because it needs protection in order to remain over the years. So I would not hesitate to paint it. I would not paint over walnut where the grain of the walnut is something which I would like to protect and bring out. Well, that means always identifying with the single case of wood; we cannot generalize. There may be situations in which I would like to do away with the busyness of wood and make it more plain. But these involve intricacies with which we should not have to deal in this particular class.

Now, let's open our books. I think we have discussed all matters pertaining to the various forms of expression. We would like now to find what differences are responsible for individual children; and after that, we will discuss motivation—how effective group motivations are and how we should deal with motivations in general. Find the Evaluation Chart, Gang Age, in the book. I would like that we, at the same time, look at one of the paintings of the gang age. Maybe you would like to look at the painting in

Figure [26]. May I say, this is a painting by a rather gifted child. Not all paintings at this age will be like that. You could look, for instance, at Figure [27], where you find a painting not by a gifted child but by an average child. I tried to include in the book a variety of paintings in a range from average or below average to gifted children—that means, those who express themselves richly.

Now, in looking at the painting in Figure [26], let's answer all of these questions. "Is the child beginning to use details to characterize the self and environment?" Who would say, "None?" "Some?" "Much?" You see, we all agree it's "Much." Of course, I said in the beginning that he's gifted, so most of the things will come out under the column "Much." Why is this responsible for intellectual growth and not for another form of growth? To discover what relates to characterization is a mental act; to discover details in things is a mental act. Details, however, during the gang age, are expressed in terms of characterizations, so this is a mental act.

"Does the child depart from the use of schemata?" Well, does he depart "Not at all," "Somewhat," or "Much"?

Student: "Somewhat."

Fig. 27. "Man with Umbrella" (10-year-old boy). Awareness of clothes. Stiffness due to emphasis on visual experience.

Lowenfeld: We would probably say between "Some" and "Much," no? He has quite a variety of deviations here, although in the face he uses the same kind of symbol, especially for nose. However, the nose on the figure to the left is different from the noses on the other central figures. So, I would say between "Some" and "Much," or "Much."

"Does the child depart from the use of geometric lines?" Yes, he clearly uses lines which characterize, especially in the puddles where he even uses changing effects. If you look carefully, you can even see some shadings in there, some darker and lighter parts.

"Do details retain their meanings when separated from the whole?" Yes, the mouth remains a mouth. Don't you think you would recognize this as a mouth even if you isolate it from the fact?

Student: What about the shoes?

Lowenfeld: Well, the shoes you would recognize as shoes, no? Some of the clothes we would recognize as clothes. Some of the umbrellas or the hands you probably would not recognize when isolated from the whole, but he departs quite a lot. So we would say that details retain their meaning when separated from the whole—probably between "Some" and "Much," if not "Much."

"Does the child characterize boys as boys and girls as girls?" Yes, he does. We would have to see several drawings in order to find out to what extent he characterizes boys and girls. But, yes, he does. Raincoats, and so forth.

"Does the child depart from base lines?"

Student: Yes.

Lowenfeld: "Does the child express the plane?" Yes, he uses the plane in between; so, as a whole, does the child express the plane? Yes, he does. He fills in even by shading. This child is eleven years, so we would say his intellectual growth is very highly developed. He is on the upper line of eleven or even beyond.

Concerning emotional growth: "Does the child identify himself with the drawing?" How can we know that? How can we know whether he identifies with the drawing?

Student: Perhaps because the one figure with the heavy pants has a bigger head?

Lowenfeld: Well, we can see it. Don't you remember the stages of identification which we noted? What is the lowest stage of identification? Stereotypes. Do you see any stereotypes? No. Generalization was the next step. Do you remember? Does the child generalize? Are all figures alike? All houses alike? All things alike? No. Then we said the next step would be. . . .

Student: Characterization.

Lowenfeld: Characterization. Does the child characterize? Yes. Quite a lot. So he probably would be in this stage. The last stage was: "Does the child include himself in his drawing, directly or indirectly?" I think he does. You see, otherwise, he would not be able to say: "I'm carrying the umbrella. Dad is carrying no umbrella. I am protected by the umbrella," as the child is. So the child does identify himself very closely with the drawing. Remember these stages which we have noted here; otherwise, these stages will not be meaningful if we do not use them. So, as a whole, we can now say the child identifies himself with the drawing "Much."

"Does the drawing lack stiffness?"

Student: Between "None" and "Some."

Lowenfeld: There is some stiffness in it. What stiffness is it? There is no interrelationship between the figures. Not one child, for instance, tries to approach another figure. Is there one place?

Student: It looks as though the little boy with the red coat might.

Lowenfeld: The person in the red coat may be reaching for the hand.

Student: For the one in the blue coat.

Lowenfeld: Yes, this is possible.

Student: And blue and yellow are overlapping there.

Lowenfeld: Yes.

Student: The hands.

Lowenfeld: So there is some indication. There is still more indication than in the example in Figure [28]. There, you have another drawing which is from the gang or late-schematic stage. Look how stiff the figures are. There's not a single approach except in the circle where they touch hands. But look, for instance, at Figure [29]. See how different this is? This child is much more relaxed in her emotional relationship than the other child. Do you know why? Look, wherever she can make some contact, she does. Look at the boys to the left. The one is even voluntarily holding the other's shoulder while there isn't any need for it. Do you see it? And look at the girl holding her carriage and at the two boys sawing the tree.

Student: Also, you have a feeling of the turning of the heads of the spectators there towards the object.

Lowenfeld: Right. You have all this flexibility. Do you see?

The more you look at drawings, the more you will be able to differentiate. Much comes, of course, with your now newly won ability to look at drawings differently. I don't want to offend those who had already the sensitivity, but I said we deal in this course as if we all started anew. I know that many of you had this sensitivity before. I know that. But with this additional knowledge that we have now, we may look at children's drawings differently. Well, emotional flexibility is probably not as much established here [in Figure 26]. We could draw some conclusions from that, you know. You may feel that the child hasn't been exposed very much to group or gang experiences. Do you see?

Fig. 28. "We Are Playing on the Playground" (8 years old). Rigid color schemata and form concepts most often go hand in hand. They are usually signs of emotional inflexibility. The child cannot adjust to a new situation, and therefore repeats the same schema again and again. Notice the tendency in this drawing to express "running," "watching," or "standing" with the same stereotyped concept. [*Note:* For color, see Lowenfeld, op.cit., Plate 5.]

Now, the next question is, "Are brush strokes or lines used freely?" Yes, quite freely. We would say between "Some" and "Much" or "Much." Why? Why not so outspoken about the "Much"?

Student: Many of them are similar.

Lowenfeld: Yes, you see the child was a little bit compulsive—in what?

Student: In the vertical.

Lowenfeld: Look how the child always outlines every drawing. Around every drawing, there is a black outline. This is compulsive. A flexible child would put an outline where he needs it and no outline where he doesn't need it. But this child put an outline around everything, even around the puddles. So, there is a certain stiffness or sameness here. The brush strokes or lines are not entirely free, so I would say between "Some" and "Much."

"Does the child still use exaggerations?"

Student: Yes.

Lowenfeld: Yes, the child still uses some exaggeration.

"Does the child's drawing show accumulations of details on those parts which are emotionally significant?" We haven't discussed that, so I would like to do it now. Gradually, exaggerations are overtaken by an accumulation of details; that means, children who previously had no other means but to exaggerate that part which was important to them now have an additional means, namely, they can accumulate more details in those parts which are meaningful than in those parts which are meaningless. For instance, if a child is very much drawn to houses, he will accumulate much detail in houses because they are emotionally meaningful to him. Or if a child draws several houses but one of the houses is his house, he will draw more details on his house than on the rest of the houses. Instead of exaggerating it, he may draw more details on it. More details in one part than in another means more emotional emphasis. So, we see that, as a whole, the child is emotionally flexible, more than average, but we see some indications of stiffness.

Now, the next category is social growth. "Does the child in his work identify himself with the group?"

Student: Much.

Fig. 29. "Cutting a Tree" (11-year-old girl). Painted after a hurricane had felled a tree near her house. Notice exaggeration of tree. Awakening of visual awareness.

Lowenfeld: Well, quite a lot. He feels small; the children are small; adults are tall. He makes differences in the sizes of the children, so he identifies quite a lot with the group.

"Does he correlate figures to each other?" Only "Some," not "Much." As we said previously, the child conceived of all children as standing straight and only turned one child slightly to the other.

"Does he coordinate figures with space?" Somewhat, yes, but not too richly. For instance, all of them are nicely holding the umbrellas. Some of them are standing in puddles. So he does relate the figures to space, but not as much as the ones who are cutting the tree [Figure 29], who have a direct relationship to the space. We would have to see more than one drawing in order to answer this question correctly.

"Is the child socially conscious of his environment?" Yes, quite a lot— the puddles, the rain shoes. You know, the overshoes are indicative that the child was aware of his relationship to the environment—his relationship to rain, to a rainy day.

"Does he cooperate in group work by subordinating his work to the whole?" We don't know. We would have to be present while the child works.

Now, let's move to perceptual growth. "Does the child include the horizontal line?" We believe that he would, but we have no indication in this drawing that he has done it. We would have to see several drawings that would account for visual perception.

"Has the child become aware of overlapping?"

Student: Yes.

Lowenfeld: Yes, very much so. The child apparently is high in perceptual growth.

"Is distance expressed by the diminishing size of distant objects.?"

Student: Yes.

Lowenfeld: Yes, the houses are much smaller than the figures.

"Has the child become aware of the changing effects of light and motion?" "Some." Where?

Student: Not motion.

Lowenfeld: Not motion, but shadows. We see that the space is darker where the people are standing than where they are not standing. We still see the straight hemline. Do you see it?

Student: Now that you mention the hemline, I would say that it would indicate a lack of motion.

Lowenfeld: That's correct, but we would have to find out whether this is the straight hemline which is only created by standing still or whether the child probably draws a different hemline in other drawings. In Figure [29], the hemlines are also straight to a great extent, although we see some indication of movement. Yes, we would have to see more drawings than the one.

"Does color indicate more than characterization?" I would say only in the puddles; otherwise, it's mere characterization.

"Has the space between base lines been filled in?" Yes, very much.

"Are textural qualities expressed?"

Student: No.

Lowenfeld: "Some." I would even say between "Some" and "Much." Look at the puddles, the shading. Even in the clothes, there is some textural quality expressed.

Lecture 23

The Stage of Dawning Realism: Review of Space and Time Representations; Evaluation of Perceptual, Physical, Aesthetic, and Creative Growth; and Motivation for Cooperation

Whenever we see in one drawing both the side view and the top view simultaneously expressed, we have a drawing in which plane and elevation are visible. Top-view and side-view drawings are part of a space-time concept. For instance, in the drawing of the checkerboard, [Figure 24, Lecture 19], you remember the table is expressed in side view while the checkerboard is expressed in top view. That means the child mixed side view with top view. This is often done in children's drawings whenever the child feels, in one instance, that the side view would be more indicative of his concept of the object, such as a table, and the top view is chosen whenever the top view is more indicative of the child's experience with that part of the object—and thus his concept.

In this instance, the child wanted to show us the checkerboard. Since the child is always used to looking upon the checkered part as the important part of the checkerboard, and the child also is used to showing the action which takes place while moving the checkers, he felt the need of showing the checkerboard in top view, while in his mind the concept of the table was in side view, in elevation. Therefore, he put elevation and plane into one drawing. Since both views cannot really function in one drawing simultaneously, they are only perceived in different time sequences. I see the side view of the table and I see the top view of the checkerboard in different time sequences. Therefore, we call this mixing in time of side or elevation and of top or plane a space-time representation. Yes?

Student: What would happen if a person would show three sides of a house? Wouldn't that be the same thing?

Lowenfeld: It's the same thing, yes. We see several sides simultaneously which we otherwise would not be able to see. If the child shows three sides, you know what this refers to? It's a folding over. See, the sides are folded over just to show us that the house has two sides. So it also involves the principle of space-time representation. We had another space-time representation of the mixing of plane and elevation. You remember in one drawing [Figure 10, Lecture 14], where Mother is in the flower garden? Is there an item there which refers to the mixing of side and top view?

Student: The pond.

Lowenfeld: The pond, correct. The pond was drawn in top view, while everything else was drawn in side view. So we have here, also, a mixing of plane and elevation. This is an instance when the child is more conscious of the top view. You see, he knows the pond is a certain area in the backyard. He has the area in his mind, probably from stepping into the pond. This would not have been expressed as well by a concept expressing the side view, because the side view would be merely a base line. Do you see? So he introduced the top view.

Student: In the plane drawing of the table [Figure 24], why didn't the child put on the legs? He drew the plane; and then on the lower end of the plane, on the bottom of the paper, he drew the two legs, but he didn't draw the other two legs.

Lowenfeld: Well, there was no necessity. If he folded it over and he drew the two legs, then this would mean that his concept is that the table has a top and two legs; and the top is a certain surface on which he wants to place something. Therefore, this surface is merely an indication of the top, which is actually his concept. But there are children who may also fold over the legs, fold them over this way as you often see them—standing out, as it were. But, of course, it's both a concept of folding over as well as the concept that a table has four legs. So you have a great variety of concepts in children's drawings: side view only, side and top view mixed—indicated with two legs, four legs, standing, spreading out in all four directions, and so forth. Let's remain flexible and think that the individual child will express his concept according to his own needs. Always.

Student: Would the ambulance [in Figure 8, Lecture 14], be the same thing?

Lowenfeld: Correct. The ambulance is also a mixture of side and top view. You know how the side and top views are indicated? The child made the four wheels, you see, and then folded it over and actually used the top view. As I remember, it's this way. Here is the cross, and here are the two wheels. Here is the side view. But then he had the concept "an ambulance has four wheels," and he added the two wheels there. For some time in his mind, this was the top view. But then, since it served his concept better, he again resorted to drawing it as a side view.

You will all experience wonders when you look at children's drawings and see the great variety with which children express themselves. You now can penetrate into this variety and have fun as a result of understanding the sources which lead to this type of expression. Still, you will be puzzled, and it is wonderful that we are puzzled in life. If all questions were answered, life would not be half as interesting as it is. So don't be eager to solve all problems and questions, but try to penetrate as sensitively as you can into those areas which you can penetrate. As I said once with the words of Einstein, "The more we know, the more we know what we don't know." And this is deeply philosophical. Do you see? The more you penetrate into something, the more you find out what you don't know. So don't be afraid that you will penetrate too far, but penetrate only for your own sensitivity's sake, for understanding children and not for categorizing them, as I have pointed out time and again. Now, let us go ahead.

Student: May I ask one question?

Lowenfeld: Yes.

Student: The horizontal line, the term as expressed in our book, does that always refer to the skyline?

Lowenfeld: Yes, horizon or horizontal line refers to where the sky apparently meets the ground.

Student: It doesn't replace the base line, does it?

Lowenfeld: In the beginning, it may serve as both. When the child first discovers that the sky drops all the way down and is not only above with air in the middle, then he may still stick to the base line concept and use the horizon line as another base line. But whether the horizon line is not another base line can only be seen by the fact that the child introduces changing sizes with regard to drawing things large in the foreground and in diminishing size in the background.

Let us continue. We covered all growth components except physical growth, aesthetic growth, and creative growth. Under physical growth—we know that one of the growth factors during the gang age is that children will become aware of their own qualities in regard to belonging to different sexes. So the question is: "Does the drawing indicate a distinction between sexes?" Awareness towards sex characteristics is also a matter of physical growth. If we look at our drawing [Figure 26], we would say: "Yes, the child has become aware of differences in the sexes."

"Is there emphasis on secondary sex characteristics?" Under secondary sex characteristics, we understand those which are not directly related to genitals but are only related to hair and more social aspects, such as red lips and a moustache, you know. Yet, we can see here that the only person who has no red lips is the man in the center in the blue jeans who looks a little bit like a woman.

Student: The others have eyelashes.

Lowenfeld: The others have eyelashes, too—yes. So the child is somewhat aware of the differences in the sexes as shown by secondary sex characteristics.

"Does the child's drawing show body action?" Not much, but somewhat, as shown by raising the arms back and holding the umbrellas; otherwise, the figures are stiff and do not show body action. So we would say "Some," probably even less than "Some." We do not see much body action.

"Does the child retain flexibility in body movements?" Less than "Some," probably. His physical qualities are least developed in comparison to other qualities which we have seen. We would not think that this is a very robust child.

Student: Don't you think that in this picture you should take into consideration the fact that on rainy days people are stiffer because they have on raincoats?

Lowenfeld: It could be, but there is no indication in this one drawing that the child really wants to draw movement. You may also run in the rain, you know. You may have the desire to move because it's raining hard, so you go fast. But they are standing still in spite of the rain. You could look at it from all points of view, but I would say the only valid evaluation you could make would be from looking at several drawings. I would never look at only one drawing. I've emphasized that time and again. We are doing all the time something which we should not do by looking at only one drawing.

Student: Don't you think it looks like they're standing on a sidewalk and that line right below their feet is the curb?

Lowenfeld: Yes, it may be that they are standing on the sidewalk and even waiting for a policeman to give them the crossing sign or waiting for the green light. We are entirely wrong by looking at only one drawing. This also indicates the need for looking at more than one drawing in order to validly answer this question.

Now, we have found out that we cannot adequately answer the questions on physical growth. It shouldn't bother us at all if we cannot adequately answer any question. Don't be bothered by it. Our aim is fulfilled, in a way, in that we have become more sensitive to certain considerations to which we probably previously would not have looked. So, in this way, the questions have fulfilled the purpose even if we have not gained an answer. See, we're looking for these things: Are there secondary sex characteristics? Is there action? . . . and so forth. We have become more sensitive to the drawings, and, of course, relate this to the child. So whether we obtain an answer, a valid answer or no valid answer, the purpose is fulfilled; namely, we have become more sensitive inasmuch as we now look no longer at the whole but also at details.

And, now, with regard to aesthetic growth, one of the important considerations during this period is whether or not the child develops a desire to do something beyond the necessary things, such as becoming aware of the patterns on clothes and colors in clothes and relating these to one another. So one of the questions which appears here is, "Does the child use decorative patterns on clothes or elsewhere?" Yes, we see quite an awareness toward pattern in the umbrella. There the child does use it. So what would you say? "Some," or between "Some" and "Much"? Between "Some" and "Much," probably, because the child also has become aware of a nice distribution of colors.

"Does the child relate the material to design and purpose, or does he look only for function?" We would not be able to say that here in this drawing, because we can better judge this in craft work and in work in three-dimensional things when the child has different materials. But we can say that he used the crayon very wisely and brought the material (crayon) into a very beautiful functional relationship by using it full, shaded, and in many different ways. We have the feeling that we deal with one who makes much use of the material which he has at his disposal.

"Does the child relate details to the whole, or does he become bound up with them without relating them to the whole?" We would say that the child has a wonderful feeling for relating the details to the whole, because I would say that the details, the patterns on the umbrellas, are merely a part of the whole pattern in the drawing, just like the puddles on the ground are also characteristics which are related to the whole.

"Does the child relate colors to each other?" This is a subjective question which can only be answered by asking ourselves: "Is the red only on one side? Does the red stand out so that it is in the way of our feeling for it being balanced?" This was a question which least significantly related to a general judgment; but we can say here that he probably did relate colors—blues and reds to each other, and so forth. We'll say that he is aesthetically highly developed.

Creative growth: "Does the child choose his own subject?" We don't know. We don't know if this drawing was motivated by the teacher, so we cannot answer it.

"Does the child experiment with different mediums?" We also don't know this, because it was a crayon drawing and we have no indication of experimentation with other mediums. During the gang age, the child should want to experiment, because it is at this age when he goes out for discoveries. My, how we did experiment with different materials even in building our hide-outs, do you see? So the desire here should come from the child, especially if the child is creative.

"Does the child invent his own forms?" Obviously he does. We can say that, because we see a great variety of raincoats, a great variety of differences in clothes, even in the umbrellas. So we can answer this positively.

"Is the child inventive in using materials for new purposes?" That we do not know. It would be obvious if we were to look more at the crafts.

Now let's mix all of these components. We can then say that the child is very high in almost all growth components. Therefore, we would call such a child, who is high in all growth components, a gifted child. Do you see? There you have a definition of gifted, namely, that gifted is *not* just one-sidely expressed—that means, when the child is only emotionally sensitive and cannot harmoniously bring this emotional sensitivity into relationship with his other sensitivities. Actually, this gift in art, in child art, shows itself when the intellect, the feeling, and the perceiving are brought into a harmonious relationship and are expressed that way.

We still have one of the most important parts to discuss and that is the practical application of all that we have learned about the gang age. How should we motivate children? What kind of topic should we select for them? How should we obtain a classroom atmosphere which is conducive to the growth of children? What is the first thing that we should discuss now? You should know now. What?

Student: Teacher-student relations?

Lowenfeld: No. What should we now discuss? Who said it? You did. Yes, indeed, *the child's needs*—because we always said in the past that a motivation which doesn't reach the child and doesn't serve the child's needs is not a good motivation. You see, there is something which objectively we can call a good motivation. A good motivation in the gang age would be a poor motivation in the scribbling stage, or in the pre-schematic stage, or even in the schematic stage when the child is not ready for group work. So a good motivation must serve the child's needs. We should then discuss, become again more sensitive, and find out what the child's needs are. As you remember, the main need of the child during the gang age is cooperation among his own team, his own group; and out of this cooperation may result a more cooperative attitude towards adults. We know that when cooperation does *not* come about among the group, children will develop hostile attitudes towards adults. This is the reason why, according to statistics, juvenile delinquency—reaching its peak during the gang age—is highest during the late gang age. Eleven is the year which is usually pointed out as the age when delinquency reaches its peak.

Do you know why juvenile delinquency is so dangerous during the gang age? Do you know why? Well, I'll tell you a story and then you can tell me. I believe it was three years ago, not far from here, in a mining town—and it was here, too, about half a year ago when they started with the construction work. They found in the mining town a hide-out of a gang of children between nine and eleven, just the stage that we are discussing. I looked at the ages. One child was twelve, and one was thirteen, and all of the others were between nine and eleven—ten and eleven, mainly. In this hide-out they discovered a collection of dynamite capsules which was large enough to blow up the whole town. The children went into the mining areas and stole them. When the police discovered this, they asked the children why they collected the capsules. The children said they wanted to dynamite the school because they didn't like their teacher. Imagine what could have happened—not only the school and the teacher but all the children and probably the whole town could have been blown up. Now, what is your answer? Why do you think this juvenile delinquency is almost more dangerous than any delinquency in adults?

Student: It's uninhibited by the adult feeling of responsibility and the feeling of what will come later.

Lowenfeld: Right. You see, when a gangster is planning something, he's planning it carefully, step by step; and he is aware of the final action. If he wants to kill this bank director and get the money, then he goes step by step and knows what he wants to do to obtain the money. He knows he's not going to dynamite the whole street and the people who are not concerned with it. He goes step by step in planning it.

With the child, it is different. The child has no feeling for the final product, neither in art nor in his actions. You remember when we said the process is the more important part? This is true for his games, play, and for all of his actions. So the child only has in mind "Let's collect dynamite capsules" or "Let's dynamite the school"; but, in most instances, this is not ever done. In this case, collecting the dynamite capsules was the result of a kind of romantic feeling of the children, their feeling for power—that they could engage in doing it if they wanted. They had it in their hands. Do you see? There is still a step necessary in order really to put the dynamite in the right places in the school. Most likely, if it ever would have come to it, they would not have placed the dynamite capsules where they would be effective so as really to dynamite and blow up the school. Maybe they would have placed the dynamite in the open, under a table, or somewhere, but not planned according to where the dynamite would be most harmful. However, we can learn from this that juvenile delinquency is harmful because it is uncontrolled in its final results. It is only carried on by the emotional desire of children to counteract the restrictions which they have experienced as a group. We should learn that the child needs to live a happy group life.

Don't feel that I'm optimistic in thinking that only you, as teachers, are responsible for that. Indeed, in the upbringing of children, parents have to contribute tremendously in order to make our work possible. But we should never give up, even in school, if we deal with children who have no home in which they are encouraged to work together as children and with adults. We should never give up inspiring children to cooperate with each other and to have a happy life, even if it is only in the school. So the greatest needs of children during this period are to find themselves, their own power, and their relationship within their own group. These are so outstanding, above all other needs, that we shall discuss them as the main needs.

Second to these needs is the child's discovery of his own sincere relationship to his environment and, in this way, to objects and materials which we have already discussed. So both of these groups of needs will determine our motivations. Now, see how logical it is if you really build it up from the very beginning, from scribbling up to the highest levels of art education. The one logically follows the other. So if we want to inspire children in their cooperation and in their sincere relationships to environment, we must find topics which inspire those things.

Topics with regard to cooperation may be topics which subjectively inspire the child with regard to cooperation by identifying himself with the situation. We call this the subjective form of motivation of group work or cooperation—that is, through the topic. Such topics would include: "We are gathered around a campfire"; "We are collecting wood for the fireplace"; "We are cooking out of doors"; "We are helping the flood victims"; "We are engaging in the Red Cross drive"; and so on. Whenever the child can identify himself with a larger undertaking which he feels cannot be successful without the group, then such a topic will inspire cooperation. Of course, whenever we use topics of this sort, it is important that we give an introduction, a point of culmination, and discuss the conclusion as we have previously always done.

The introduction for group work is no longer the "when and where," which we used in previous stages, but is more concerned with the social implications of group work. So in "Helping the flood victims," we would first discuss in detail the social implications of what it would mean if you, yourself, were a flood victim. "On the other side of town all the houses are under water. Whose houses are also underwater? Whose house is underwater? Now, let's imagine that we are living there, and we are watching how the water rises and rises." That means self-identification—putting one's self into the place of those for whom we do the group work. This is most important in effectively motivating cooperation. You remember when I said, in the very beginning, "Without self-identification there is no cooperation." You remember that? Now we are here at the main stage in which we should teach it. Without identifying ourselves with other people, we cannot feel like other people do, and that includes our neighbors.

We may identify ourselves with a slum area. "How would it be if we were all to wake up in the morning but we would not wake up in a house well-cared for, where we can take a bath, where we have breakfast in the dining room, where we have a clean environment, and where we have a backyard? Well, let's see how these people live. Let's open the window." Let's live it, you see; and here you go into great detail, as many as you can encounter in your own mind and in your own feeling, in making the children relive this particular area or this particular group of people which you are discussing.

Student: Don't you think that in doing something like that you'll run into prejudices that have been built up within the children's minds by adults?

Lowenfeld: Yes, indeed, you will run into prejudices, probably in all these matters, but it is part of our educational aim to break them down.

Student: What would you do if in your classroom—let's say, in a suburb—you ran into this from the very wealthy class on down to what you would consider poor whites?

Lowenfeld: Well, I would identify with both situations.

Student: In other words, separate motivations?

Lowenfeld: Yes—well, one after the other. I believe that in such a situation as we are discussing now, the children who live in a slum area will have no difficulty accepting what I say because this is their environment. It will only be difficult for the others. And another time we will say: "Now, children, this time let's wake up and we are in a wonderful environment— you know, where you all have backyards and beautiful houses. Everything is repaired; the shutters are in order; and everything is fine. Now we are in a well-to-do area because our father has——, you know, and now let's iden- tify with this group." You would then go into great detail here, too. The children who are in slum areas will probably gain a little understanding for, let's say, a cleaner environment. You would say: "Now, look. It's not the money alone. To have it be clean in one's environment does not depend on money alone. But, of course, it's very difficult to keep things clean if the paint is peeling off the houses, and so forth. You can easily keep things clean if you have newly painted houses. So let's paint a slum area this time and a well-to-do area another time. Then we can even compare the two." And you would also say: "Let's look at the colors. What colors did we use here? What colors did we use there? What characteristics did we use here?"

We may even discuss one drawing and say, "Mary has put herself in the place beautifully because she has included this and this and this." We should not say. "Now let's look at Mary's drawing and compare it with Johnny's." Never compare one work with another, you remember; but we can say, "Let's look at Mary's drawing." Then we can say; "Now look at yours. What have you been able to include? Did you include something else Mary did not include? Who did? Joe? What did you include?" The discussion about the child's creative work is a part of revitalizing creativeness in chil- dren and should not be overlooked. So this method, the "subjective method," uses a topic to motivate cooperation.

The more effective method probably is the "objective method"—that is, the method of group work as such. I call the one "subjective" and the other "objective," because in the subjective method the topic is usually digested by the individual himself, and therefore completely relates to the subject of cooperation. In group work, the topic is of a general or objective quality, such as, "We are building a circus." Everyone is making an animal, and we are building the cages, and so forth; and the whole thing will become a circus. We often do it in our children's art classes and in our elementary education classes when everyone contributes, and the outcome is a cooperative work in which every individual has the feeling that he alone could not have done it as well as the whole group. This is the meaning of cooperation.

Now, I would like to discuss with you in great detail how we should deal with motivation of group work, because many technicalities are related to it which may motivate, promote, and also spoil group work. First of all, let's have foremost in our minds that, when the children cooperate in group work, it is the children who cooperate in group work and not the teacher who makes them cooperate. Don't fool yourself. When you distribute the chores so closely and watch what the children have to do, then it's dictated group work. You may feel that they are then all working, but you fool yourself into thinking that they are doing group work when actually it is dictated group work. So you should have foremost in your mind that the teacher must remain, as much as she can, in the background and should be only the catalyst. Do you know what a catalyst is? In chemistry, a catalyst is that element which makes others function or combine. But the catalyst is not a part of the combining elements. It still remains a part outside; it is the stimulating part. Without the catalyst, however, the elements cannot merge into a new combination. So the teacher should be a catalyst in the process of cooperation. She should give some stimulating factors. Here we get our democracy in action, of course. While children are still children, there is nothing wrong if we introduce democratic forms. For instance, we say, "Now, children, we all are building a city." Probably it would be better motivation if you were to say: "Our city has an anniversary, as you know, and everyone is very eager to decorate one's own house for this, because during the anniversary we'll have a big carnival. Everyone would like to participate in it." So you create the feeling, "This is our city." This is, then, the general topic.

Now, what materials would you use? Only those materials which serve the needs of the child—that is, the need of working for himself and, finally, enjoying the group project—are good. Usually, during the gang age, materials which lend themselves for assembling purposes are the best materials— construction paper, clay for modeling, and also materials for the building of models. Actually, the building of models now almost replaces modeling as such. Only in the subjective kind of motivation will modeling in the previously mentioned form have any meaning. For instance, if we were to say, "We are sitting around the campfire," well, each of the children could model himself showing how he lingers or how he sits or how he kneels or how he lies on his tummy and watches the campfire. He will model himself.

We should probably have a board as big as a table, and all the children's modelings would be placed on it. A group might want to start a little fire in the center so that the children are now motivated by their own subjective feelings in modeling. Or you could model, "We are cutting wood." You see, there is some cooperation necessary in cutting wood. But in objective cooperation, as expressed in group work where children actually cooperate in groups, it might be even better if we used the technique of model making. "We are making an Indian village, a Pueblo village, and everyone is contributing his part." Here we use all kinds of materials, such as clay, wood, little pieces of gravel, textured materials for roofs, straw, and anything we may find. So don't stick by force to clay if other materials serve your needs better. Let us choose, for instance, construction paper, which could be a very important material here.

Some time ago, I remember that one of you asked me if it is good to give children construction paper and let them cut it out. I said, at that time, that it isn't bad to give it to them, but we certainly have a stage in the development of children at which time construction paper is really glorified, when the child can do with it what he wants to do. This is that stage. During this time all kinds of questions which will now be appreciated will develop while you are motivating the children. Previously they may not have been appreciated by the children.

First of all, the assembling. Indeed, before you start with your motivation, you should have your materials ready. Then you probably will distribute the material—but to whom? Well, you don't know yet. It is always good if you discuss the topic first. For instance, you say, "Now, children, what districts do we have in our city?" You take your chalk into your hands—don't ever let those ideas simply go—and write them down. It's always good to have those things written down which you have discussed at this stage. For instance, one child may say, "We have a living area." "Yes. What do you call it?" "The residential district." You write it down—"residential district."

"What other districts or areas do we have? What? Would you like to have a factory built in your residential area? Would you? No. You would like to have what? A factory in a district by itself. What would we call it?" "The industrial area." Put it down—"industrial area."

"What other districts do we have? Do you want to have your stores right there where you have your backyard? Now what else?" "The shopping area." "Shopping area. Let's write down shopping area."

"What other districts do we have? Well, if you want to have fun on a Sunday or after work, where do you go and play?" "Playgrounds, the recreation areas." "Fine."

So we have now four areas. Let us say, to simplify matters, that we have a class of forty children. Let's put each of these areas under one leader. "Who would like to serve as the chairman for——?" Now, you may do it this way, or you may do it by election. You may now introduce an election in your class. Without any doubt, the leaders will come out. Do you see? And then you have four people. The one will be in charge of the residential, another the shopping, another the industrial, and another the recreation area. But we always need a fifth group. This fifth group is in charge of grounds. Yes, indeed. And we need a chairman for this, too.

Now, this has to be prepared in your mind. You no longer can simply go into the class and spontaneously say, "Now, what am I going to do?" No, you have to prepare it. This is important, because you have to know what areas you have, what groups you should deal with for certain topics—as, for example, in a fair. "Now, what does a fair consist of? What kinds of different stands do we have?" and so forth. You would again subdivide it and put people in charge of the different areas. Concerning "Our City," we now have five groups of eight. One group leader is with seven children. As much as possible, you try to divide your space, your classroom, into areas where the seven can be together with their leader.

But, before you do that, now comes the motivation. "I want the leaders especially to listen." If you say that, everyone will listen; because everyone identifies with the leader quite logically. You would say, "Now, children, I want every leader to think as hard as possible about what we have in these different areas." For instance, you could say: "A shopping area does not just consist of stores. What do you have there? Well, you have little stores. You have department stores. You have movies. Well, I don't want to continue this. It's the job of the leaders; they should do that." You see? You then should leave. You may motivate a little bit but should leave the rest to the leaders. "Now in the residential areas, we can't say we just have houses there. We have different kinds of houses. What? Well, yes, you are sure to have small and large. But you also have what else? Churches? I don't want to continue, you all have——," and so forth. They should now make their decisions.

"And, now, I have something important to tell the whole group. If we do not bring our houses into some relationship, one person will make them very large, another very small, and so forth. You all have construction paper. The group leaders each have an assorted pack of paper." You know, you get the assorted little packs which aren't very expensive. "Now this is a special size; it is as large as this. I want you to know—especially the group leaders, who should watch this—that the largest building in town may be the size of the whole paper. You should relate all the rest of the buildings to the largest building. For instance, if you want to cut out a big church or cathedral, which will probably be the largest building in town, then you may use the whole sheet of paper. But if you only want a one-family house, then it will not be as large as a factory. So now you know. You just use as much paper as you now think you need for your building." This should be enough of a suggestion to have sizes related. Do you see? Then we would say: "Now, let's go ahead. You may decorate your house as you want it because this is our anniversary." The children would then cut out buildings. But in the meantime, the grounds committee would be working. They would be providing the ground for our city. "Would you like to have a city on a lake surrounded by mountains with a river going through it, or what?" You suggest this, you see, and they decide.

Now comes a very important part, and that is what we call organic growth. We would have first the ground, the sky, probably a mountain cut out or torn out of construction paper, and the river going straight through. This can already be looked upon as a finished product. So the city grows. And now we would say: "Children, where will we have our industrial area? Maybe we should put it far away on the other side of the river. Where is the industrial group? Will you come forth with all your products?" And they would paste their own products on it. Now we have on this side of the river all factories, smoke stacks, and whatever you have there. Even when it is as far along as that, it can be considered a finished product. That we call organic growth—that you can look at the product at every stage of its development and it looks finished, do you see?

But another question may occur. Johnny will say, "But he has pasted his house right in front of my house, and I don't want him to cover my house!" This is when Johnny has not yet discovered the meaning of overlapping. This gives you a fine opportunity to explain organic development and the meaning of visual overlapping, especially at the time when overlapping becomes meaningful. You know what I mean by visual overlapping? Then we can also refer it to social customs, and you could say, "Now, when you go to a movie and you look at the screen, right in front of you comes a lady with a big hat and sits down. Now you can see nothing. Is that nice? No. Well, let's say this. You sit in a movie and right in front of you comes a boy and sits, and you see wonderfully. Your legs are covered by the boy, but that doesn't matter. He may even cover you up to here. Everyone will still recognize you as Joe Smith. You see? Now, overlapping is fine, but you should not completely cover up the other person's work. As long as you can see that this is the church, it's fine. A part may be covered. That's always true in life. You cannot be always in the foreground and be visible as a whole, you see." This is a very important part.

After everything has been assembled, every individual—every child in this class—should have the feeling, "I could not have accomplished alone what the whole group has done." This is the main meaning of cooperation.

LECTURE 24

The Stage Preceding Adolescence: A Preparation, Meaning of Adolescence, Unconscious to Conscious Development, Three Approaches to Teaching Adolescent Art, Individuality versus Conformity

Student: Is characterization still a concept, or is it a percept?

Lowenfeld: Characterization is still a concept as long as it does not contain the changing qualities of which we spoke. It should be clear in our minds that characterization represents a transition to the percept. We may sometimes see in characterizations signs of changing effects, for instance, the changing effect of distant objects appearing smaller. Then the child is between the concept and percept. As we've learned throughout this course, developmental stages are not confined to absolute age levels, chronological age levels, and do not change abruptly; but rather we see that they change gradually from one level to the other. We always have stages of transition, even stages between the gang age and the stage which we are now to discuss. There are intermediate stages, but they are not defined as clearly as the ones we have discussed. They are transitions and, gradually—as we shall see—the child moves from the concept to the recognition that what he sees, what he touches, and what he feels should be directly translated into his art.

Now, our time has gone awfully fast, much too fast for my feeling. So, in our discussion during these last two classes—two class periods of eighty minutes—I'll try to combine a consideration of adolescent art and the stage which immediately precedes adolescence. In fact, I should do this all the time, because the stage preceding adolescence can scarcely be understood unless we understand the meaning of adolescence, especially the effect which adolescence has on the creativeness of children and on the art expression of individuals in general.

Here I would like to develop some understanding of the changes which adolescence brings about. As I said previously, the changes are so great between children's understanding of the world and their imagery and actions, and adults' understanding and their imagery and actions, that we would consider an adult insane if he were to act like a child—for instance, if I were to stand at the door and make a sound, "dat, dat dat," like children do. Even when they hold nothing in their hands but simply imagine some invisible gun and relate it to their actions—well, with children we would find it quite natural and see nothing wrong whatsoever, because these pretend-to-be games are all accepted by us. If the child makes "pfereee" and falls down, you know, this is quite obvious to us, and we don't get excited about it; but, if we see the same actions in adults, we would consider the adults to be insane. Such is the difference between the imagery of children before they go through the stage which we call adolescence and the imagery which finally results in adulthood.

We often forget that changes of such an abrupt nature occur. Of course, they do not occur suddenly. They occur gradually, but not as gradually as we may think, because who of you have not had the experience in your own classroom—before vacation and after the summer—of seeing the innocently laughing Johnny running around doing his pretend-to-be games and coming back after vacation with a half-changed voice and stepping from one foot to the other when you say to him, "My, John, you have changed!" He answers merely with a, "Yes, ma'am," and doesn't know how to move. He has become conscious of his own body; he has become conscious of his relationship to environment. As part of this consciousness, he also has become conscious of his own imagery and with it, of course, of the products which he produces, especially in creative art. This is, indeed, a great change.

Remember when I pointed out at the beginning—or nearly at the beginning—of our classes, the *two* changes which influence most of our growth? Then, I said they were the changes which occurred (1) during the stage when the child starts to name his scribbling, when his imagery relates to outside experiences and no longer to kinesthesis, and (2) during adolescence, when the imagery changes from the unconscious to the conscious, and adult awareness approaches. For the child, a pencil may be an airplane; it may be a gun; it may be almost anything. For the adult, a pencil is a pencil for writing. These are the changes at which we have to look. And we have to investigate and find out what accompanies these changes. Only when we find out under which circumstances these changes occur will we learn to understand adolescence, the meaning of adolescence. We will learn to understand also the meaning of the stage which immediately precedes adolescence.

Indeed, we all know that these changes occur. They affect the individual. If these changes occur without any difficulty, we simply call them growth. Change which occurs with difficulty, however, we call a crisis. So the question now is up to us whether or not we conceive of the changes which occur from childhood to adulthood (during adolescence) as changes which result from growing up and which are part of natural growth and without difficulty in adjustment, or as changes which occur under great difficulty. If we feel that these changes occur under great difficulty, then we can readily speak of the crisis of adolescence. Now, indeed, those who are acquainted with children—and especially with children who are going through these changes of adolescence—know that Johnny doesn't step from one foot to another just merely out of pleasure. The ability to recognize his own actions and control them—this awareness—does not come about just from one day to another.

I'll give you an example of this from my own family. When Johnny, my son, was in the stage before adolescence, he was a member of a gang. He had his fun; he had his group of children—his gang. At this time we lived on South Atherton Street. He was always tall and a little bit out of proportion to the other children, but he didn't even recognize that; he didn't see it. He associated with younger children, who were not as tall, and he had his wooden gun or wooden stick or his little bow with him and freely played with them. But there came a time when I came home from work—from the university, from my office—when I saw, as I approached the house, that he somewhat tried to hide the gun. I said, "Why don't you play with them?" And he said, "Oh, I think—isn't it silly?"

I said, "No, it's not silly at all. Why don't you play with them? It's fun, isn't it?" You know, they love it—they love it.

When I went into the house, he went on engaging in his pretend-to-be games—that means, he again felt that he was not being observed and not being controlled. Since the smaller children accepted him in the group, in the gang, he freely continued his game. But these interruptions became more frequent as he grew older. At one time, then, later on, I could only see him with his wooden gun or sticks, self-fabricated, standing there and watching them playing pretend-to-be games, now and then participating or giving orders, but already standing outside. Until one day, he was in the basement, putting away his wooden gun which he had so carefully whittled; but still he could not part with it. Sometimes he went downstairs and tried to improve it. But he no longer associated with the group; he just watched them. So there was a stage in between when he felt torn—when the children, the gang, were no longer part of his desires, but when the older children did not yet accept him. He felt torn between childish reactions and an adult awareness.

Any stage in which you feel torn in two directions is not a stage which contributes to mental health. On the contrary, it contributes to a state of confusion if we are unable to help those children gain confidence in their own stage, the one in which they find themselves. So it is important that we recognize this back-and-forth shifting to and from childhood experiences and from childhood experiences to an awareness in games, in art work, and in life in general. This is the transition from childhood to adolescence. As one continues into the adolescent stage, this shift gradually peters out and a higher degree of awareness develops. You wanted to say something?

Student: Is that the eleven-to-thirteen age?

Lowenfeld: No, this is the eleven-and-beyond stage. You see, it begins probably at, let us say, twelve or thirteen. With girls, it may begin at eleven or twelve. Actually, it begins when menstruation starts, that means, when physical changes occur. With boys, it begins when pubescence starts, that means, when physical changes start. Physical changes bring about a greater awareness for which most of our children are physically unprepared, but mentally even more unprepared. We will have to discuss that in greater detail.

Now, may I insert a parallel so that we'll understand our function as art teachers and also understand the significance of art teaching in relation to this change which takes place in children when they move from childhood to adulthood. Concerning physical changes, we are well aware of the importance of a crisis. If we know that we will move into a crisis situation, into a physical crisis, we will do everything possible to move under the best conditions into this crisis so that we will have the utmost chance of overcoming it.

As an example, if you are to have an operation and you go to a physician and you are run down, the physician will say immediately: "Well, I think you will have to get in better shape. We cannot operate on you now. I think we'll wait two weeks. When your health and your physical stamina have improved, then we will have a better chance of your recovering early." This is the logical answer which every physician will give you. He knows that the change which the body has to go through during and following surgery is great. The body has to adjust from one stage to another. Let us say, one kidney has been infected and has to be removed, and you are run down. Well, he will tell you that you have to rest; you have to eat; and you have to take it easy before you go through the operation—if the operation, of course, is not an emergency case, and then he takes the risk. But if he has a chance to suggest to you that you should be put into better condition, you will do so. Then, of course, the kidney should be removed.

And what happens is this: the body will have to adjust to working with one kidney only; that means, the one kidney has to process the waste products of the two kidneys. All of the little channels now have to be redirected into this one kidney, but some may go into the blood. And you know when waste products go into the blood, they cause infections and difficulty. So, after the operation has been performed, when you ask the physician, "How is the patient?" he will still tell you: "I don't know. The operation has been performed well, but we will have to wait until the crisis is over. The crisis," he says, "is that stage at which the body definitely will have to adjust to the new situation."

Only after the temperature goes down, after many ups and downs in your fever curve, will he say, "Well, we are over the hump; we are over the hump." Then you will breathe easier, and you will say, "Well, so has he

STAGE PRECEDING ADOLESCENCE

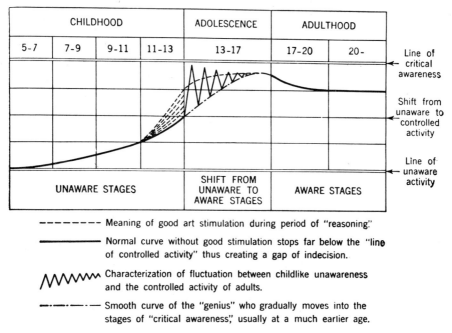

CHILDHOOD				ADOLESCENCE	ADULTHOOD	
5-7	7-9	9-11	11-13	13-17	17-20	20-

Line of ← critical awareness

Shift from unaware to ← controlled activity

Line of ← unaware activity

UNAWARE STAGES — SHIFT FROM UNAWARE TO AWARE STAGES — AWARE STAGES

- - - - - - - - Meaning of good art stimulation during period of "reasoning".

————————— Normal curve without good stimulation stops far below the "line of controlled activity" thus creating a gap of indecision.

⋀⋀⋁⋁⋀⋁ Characterization of fluctuation between childlike unawareness and the controlled activity of adults.

—·—·—·— Smooth curve of the "genius" who gradually moves into the stages of "critical awareness", usually at a much earlier age.

Shift from Unaware to Aware Stages

adjusted or recovered?" "Well, he is on his way. His temperature has gone down, and it is most likely that the patient will recover." We know that the patient has much more probability of recovering if he is in good condition before. And from this, we should learn.

If we know that our children are going to move through these changes which will affect them to such a degree that, like most people in general, they will lose their confidence in their own creative activities—well, that is serious. We know that children in general engage freely in creative activities, while adolescents or adults usually say "I can't draw" or "I can't paint" or "I'm not skillful enough." Why? Because they have become aware of the final product. Now that is a serious affliction. If we can save the free creative expression of childhood during adolescence and into adulthood, we may be able to save a great deal of creative potentialities.

The question is: Can we do it, and under what circumstances do we have the best chance? For this, let me draw for you a little graph. You have this graph [Shift from Unaware to Aware Stages] in the book. Let's call this stage childhood, and let's call this stage adulthood. Then, in between is the change, and this change from childhood to adulthood, we call adolescence. If we attach approximate chronological ages—and I would not like to be rigid

307

here—adolescence starts whenever the physical changes occur, and this varies greatly. It varies not only among boys and girls in our culture, but it varies even from culture to culture. As you know, maturity occurs in Oriental cultures earlier than in our northern states for some reason which we don't know.

Now, let us begin with the last stage of childhood. This would be the last stage to discuss, the stage between eleven and thirteen. We would, then, call this the stage immediately preceding adolescence. This is the stage which we have not yet discussed but which we will discuss simultaneously with the stage of adolescence. Before this stage is the gang age, as we know. And before the gang age, we have the schematic stage. And before that, we have the pre-schematic stage. And before that, let us say, from ages two to four or two to five, we have scribbling. Now, after the stage immediately preceding adolescence, we have ages thirteen to seventeen which we usually call the stage of adolescence. We also have here ages seventeen to nineteen or twenty, usually considered post adolescence, and twenty on up is considered adulthood.

Now, let's draw a bottom line, and let's confine the adolescent stage by drawing a somewhat darker line so that we know that this is adolescence. Let's arbitrarily consider this bottom line as the line at which creativeness occurs under the least external influences, that means, when creative activity is done unconsciously or is uncontrolled. We would call this line the line of unconscious activity—unconscious, creative activities. We'll then call this line on the top the line of critical awareness—in contrast to unconscious activity. I'm critically aware of all things which I do. I even don't know how to move my body. Because I'm aware, I don't know where my limbs belong at this time, so I'm moving them in a somewhat wooden fashion—a characteristic of the beginning of adolescence. So, we have critical awareness here at the top, and in between we have a line which characterizes the shift from one to the other. This is in the middle.

If we draw a curve showing how the child develops from the beginning, we would say that, as long as the child isn't even aware of his motions in his scribbling—when the child simply scribbles, often not even looking at his scribbling—this is the most unconscious activity. Even when the child discovers that there is a relationship between his line and the motion, as in longitudinal scribbling, this unconscious activity already moves the line up a little bit towards consciousness. But the whole activity here is still more unconscious than conscious. It reaches the level of complete unconsciousness here in the beginning of scribbling. Up to now, do you all understand it? This is very important, because if you do not understand what we have discussed now, you will not understand the rest. At this point, I would like to encourage those who want to question our graph to do it now. Don't be modest. I told you, you fool yourself if you are modest. I hope I explained it, but I may not have explained everything clearly. Do you understand these lines?

This is the line of completely unconscious actions in creative activity, such as when the child scribbles and doesn't even look at his scribbling. When the child names his scribbling, when he is about four, he has already acquired some consciousness that there is a relationship between his thinking and the outside world. But this relationship is still more unconscious than conscious, although we have moved up. And, as we know, when the child moves up during the pre-schematic stage, he develops more conscious relationships. He develops, for instance, the ability to recognize in his drawing a relationship between what he draws and the environment: "My dad has a head and two legs; my drawing has a head and two legs." This is a higher stage of recognition; therefore, the curve will move up.

The awareness curve may not move up as much during the schematic stage, when the concept remains (the active knowledge probably remains the same in general), but there is another new consciousness which comes into action. That is the consciousness of being a part of the environment; you remember, the beginning of a social consciousness, as it were. So we will draw the curve still further up, maybe not as much; but if you were to draw it up just as much, it would not matter. At any rate, we move into a higher consciousness. And, indeed, during the gang age, when the child discovers his own power within his own group, the consciousness moves up still further. We have a steadily rising curve until we come to the stage which we are now to discuss. During this stage, immediately preceding the crisis of adolescence, the consciousness grows even more.

As we know, children have already started to reason. They know exactly what goes on in the world. In their play, however, they are still childish, so there is sometimes a discrepancy between their high degree of thinking, intellect, and reasoning, and their naiveté in their games and play, but they still move up. Just when we arrive at puberty, at the physical changes, we are here. This is exactly the point where the shift occurs from an unconscious to a more conscious activity. From now on, the child becomes conscious of himself, aware of himself; and he also becomes aware of his environment. As a matter of fact, he becomes very critically aware during this time. Who does not remember the shock which we all experienced during our first physical changes? We suppress these shocks. And, as you know—especially those who have been engaged in psychoanalysis or psychoanalytic thinking—many of our traumatic experiences have their bases right here when the physical changes occur.

Parents do not prepare their children, girls and boys alike; but usually girls are less prepared than boys. The shock is great when the first menstruation occurs; and the child is completely unaware of what has happened. So, indeed, we need to prepare our children—at home and, I hope, also at school—so that they don't have to get knowledge secretly behind the bushes and in a wrong way. Even if they are prepared for what will come, the shock is almost unavoidable. It is here, then, that the girl looks around, and she probably feels very important now because everyone should know that she is a mature girl. Of course, nobody does.

But you see, this is another consideration. The subjective feeling is the important thing. She has become aware of it, and now she emphasizes this awareness within her own self. And the critical awareness goes up steeply, because this is a definite point. It's not a transition. It's not a gradual setting-in which occurs, but it is a point in time—a day in your life. This is important for us. Because it occurs so suddenly, we may be exposed to a serious or a not so serious shock, depending on the preparation which we have; but, mentally, we have to adjust to it. We may have played quite unconsciously with our dolls or with a wooden gun; but here, all of a sudden, I know the gun is a wooden gun and I must not play with it. Soon afterwards, I may have adjusted to this, to the physical change, and I go back and love to play with a doll and a wooden gun. But all of a sudden, I realize I should not play. Then I go back and love to play, and this up and down goes on during puberty until it gradually peters out and we adjust to what we are.

Now, here comes something which I want you to understand, and I need your full attention because a whole philosophy may depend on your understanding of this. In this back-and-forth movement—being thrown in one direction and then the other—you may retain some of your naiveté, your unconscious feeling, or you may get rid of most of it and try to solve everything by means of your intellect. Have you noticed that? This is the stage when some of the boys would like to clarify everything. The problems of the whole world can be solved simply by reasoning. Others engage in the romantic—maybe go out alone into the fields and whistle and are all by themselves in a unity probably with God or someone in the world.

So you have here a certain fluctuation; but where you land—whether you land from this fluctuation here, here, or here—may determine the amount of conscious attitude toward your life which, from now on, will be yours and part and parcel of your own personality. Someone with a more naive behavior, especially those who engage in art, will go through this fluctuation and may land right here. They are closer to childhood and to naive behavior, to an unconscious type of behavior. Others who engage in intellectual contemplation and like to reason out everything may go up high and end up more on the level of awareness. So this curve has to be conceived of as being very flexible, depending on the personality which finally evolves out of this struggle.

Student: In your graph line there, in that first sudden upper drive, right there—I realize that's a sudden upward drive; but when you get to the top

310

there, shouldn't that be a stretch of suddenly downward again, or is that a sort of projected curve there first and then down?

Lowenfeld: You never go as far down as the previous point, because one experience influences another experience, and this influences this, and so on. That's why you have this petering out. Do I make myself clear?

Student: Well, my question wasn't clear. I meant at the top peak you have a sudden, abrupt change, and then back downward again. I was wondering if it is that way, or do they come to a realization gradually or somewhat gradually?

Lowenfeld: I'll explain this abrupt change. This occurs when the individual feels himself observed, such as when I came back from the office and Johnny all of a sudden said, "There's Dad, and it's silly that I play." That was a high point of consciousness—here. But when I went into the house, he went on playing. That was a return to unconscious activity and may be here. In a school situation, we see these trends also.

In general, in the United States and elsewhere, we see three tendencies today with regard to the recognition of the adolescent and his problems, especially in relationship to art. The one tendency is that of, let us say, so-called progressive teachers, often artists, who see in child art a great challenge and who love the intuitive character of child art. They would like to prolong childhood beyond childhood and thus retain an atmosphere of childish unconsciousness in their art rooms. I could mention to you some of our very fine art educators who are very happy if they can show you the freshness of child art produced by an adolescent. Then, adult art work looks almost like child art work. They stimulate for free behavior in their classrooms, encourage free expression of adolescent youths or anyone beyond thirteen, and are very happy if they can retain this freshness. As a matter of principle, they are happy if they can retain this freshness, because it is something which appears precious to them. And, indeed, it is.

But, in the same way that we would not like to impose adult standards on children, we don't want to impose children's standards on adults, or growing adults. So there is something wrong. The result usually is this: if those youths, with their products, are exposed to a free environment, they are usually ashamed to show their own products outside of the classroom because they are no longer experiencing the protection and encouragement—you know, the environmental encouragement—of the teacher. They feel deprived of this encouragement and then realize suddenly that their's are childish drawings. "This is not *I*. I should draw differently, and I should paint differently, and I should act differently." This is the group plainly built on the satisfaction which we—as art teachers, artists, or individuals—derive from the unconscious and fresh approach of children.

The second group includes those who are satisfied with nothing but perfection. This is indeed shocking. You should have seen the Carnegie

Exhibition of Scholastic Art last year and the wonderful craft products and design products which were produced by high school kids and which could have been displayed in the showroom of any Fifth Avenue shop or even gallery. We may have admiration for the perfection, but I cannot help saying that these youths have lost their youth and have been driven into perfection at a time when they should still be youths. So this drive for perfection not only deprives the youth of his youth but also deprives us, as art teachers, of the great opportunity which we have in influencing not only the selected few but all in their creative growth. Obviously, only a few can arrive at such a high degree of professional competence and the rest cannot; therefore, they have no opportunity to participate.

Student: Isn't it so that adolescents do push for perfection? I mean, their own standards are standards of perfection.

Lowenfeld: Yes, that is perfectly expressed. Of course, they push for perfection; but we have to recognize what is *their* perfection, or their feeling for perfection. And if we recognize their feeling for perfection, we will arrive at a different basis of perfection than that imposed upon them by adult perfection. We shall discuss in greater detail what we mean by their kind of perfection. Their perfection is quite different from adult perfection, but they do have a drive for perfection, without any doubt. In this drive, a shift takes place from emphasis on the working process to emphasis on the final product. This is, without any doubt, one of the important attributes of adolescence.

Student: Is it because of their drive for perfection that psychologists say that this stage—the age of 16, let's say—is the stage in a human being's life when he is more capable of learning than at any other stage?

Lowenfeld: Well, I would challenge that greatly—what you have said. I would not feel that this is that stage; but it, indeed, is the stage in which individuals are discovering their capabilities with greater awareness. This has nothing to do with their ability to learn, because I believe that we never learn again as much as we learn in the first three years of our lives. You learn to master a whole language. You learn to recognize the meaning of things in your environment. A child of three years, my, what he knows! It's simply incredible! We will never be able to catch up with the degree of learning which takes place in the first years. But during adolescence, the individual discovers his capabilities, and that is something different. You see, the child doesn't do that. The child learns but does not discover critically, or with awareness, his own capabilities. This is the stage when he does discover his own capabilities.

Now we will discuss the third group; and this group is, indeed, the one which recognizes the adolescent as an adolescent and, therefore, bases motivations on the restrictions and on the capabilities of the adolescent—may I add, of the *individual* adolescent, for at no age level and at no developmental stage does individuality play the important role that it plays during adolescence. One of our doctoral students, Dr. Robert Burkhart, has made a study on the individuality of creative expression during adolescence. And, indeed, his study resulted in this important statement: "At no time is individuality as important as it is during adolescence." Therefore, we can't speak of adolescence as a general developmental stage without considering the significance which the individual has during this stage and the drive which he has to find his own individualities and his own role as an individual in this society. These are all drives which we have to recognize; and these drives are somewhat contradicting another drive. This other drive is, of course, a drive which we all know. It is different in different cultures but is especially strong in the culture in which we live here in the United States—the drive for conformity. You know, individuality and conformity go hand-in-hand here at a time when the individual, for the first time, has really become aware of his own contribution.

I would like to give you an example of this conformity. Just look at the way adolescents dress, including their hair, their shoes, certain behavior mannerisms. You see, the peers always play a leading part. To be accepted is a very important and crucial consideration at this stage—you know, to be accepted by others. And you know the role which this plays among adolescents. They will do anything to be accepted, even to the extent of conforming to the rest of the group. May I say that this is especially great, or even outstanding, here in the United States. The reason for it is probably because customs are also very distinct here with regard to, let us say, even lovemaking. The stages which you have here—the steps of dating, and then petting, or whatever the stages are called—there is no other society in the whole world which has defined the stages more than we have here in America. Because of this certain conformity to a certain behavior, the uniformity of behavior—the drive for conformity—is very great. I personally do not believe that this is healthy. Indeed, to the contrary, I believe it takes away from the individual's experience.

I know that some of you are still close to this stage. You may not agree with me; but those things which are, indeed, personal in nature actually belong way deep in everybody's individual heart. One of the most important experiences in everybody's life—love—is almost put on a level of a spectatorship where people just look and display with a kind of an exhibitionism. These display cases of adolescent behavior we scarcely see in any other culture or in any other civilization, let's say. So I do not think this is a healthy direction, but one which we have to recognize, indeed. We have to take individuals where they are and move on from there. I would love to engage in a discussion with you in regard to that, because I feel that it is a very, very important criticism which I make here of our society in general. I say this because much of our later life depends on the influence which these experiences have made on us: whether we grow up as people who have gone through deep experiences which were meaningful to us, or whether we grow up as people who have gone through an experience which should have deeply affected us but affected us only in a rather superficial way. Everything is relative, you understand.

Even here in this country, in spite of this conformity, we have a deep, deep urge for individuality, as our studies have shown. So you have here a contradiction. This contradiction probably also causes difficulty in an individual torn between his own individualistic approaches, his search for individualism, and the compliance to conformity. These are opposing things, don't forget. Opposing things are never healthy in a society. We have and we will resolve this. One of the results of all this—. What is the name of that singer? Yes, Elvis. There you have an example. Tom may grow sideburns. That's a conformity, indeed. Everyone sacrifices his own self to it, but deep inside he feels himself to be an individual; and the striving for individuality is very great. I do not just talk of subjective attitudes; this is based upon research. You have these contrasting feelings where people just hang on to the Elvises, you know, and at the same time consider themselves as individuals. This only contributes to a stronger crisis in adolescence.

This is not true elsewhere, in other countries, and especially not—well, I'm referring now to Europe. Two years ago when the sideburns really burned, we had a group of singers here from Europe, the Academy Choir. Those who were at Penn State visited with us. They were shocked by this behavior which they encountered. "How is it possible that people can go for this?" they asked. They also were adolescents; and they were shocked that this is possible. So you have here contrasting social behaviors, which, we have to recognize, are determined by societies. While we are very much against conformity, we are merely lending to this our lip service. We have not yet really engaged in digging into the nature of it.

Student: Now, with what possible type of therapy can we approach our adolescents?

Lowenfeld: We will talk next time about the practical implications which all this has. Because I have this graph drawn on the blackboard, I would like to finish discussing it.

Since we can contribute through art to an individual's behavior, our best contribution would be to minimize this curve and this shock. Based upon research and experimentation, we can do it. We can do it during this stage, this very important stage, if we do the very same thing that the physician does. If we condition the individual more concerning what he can expect, if we prepare him not only in his physical aspects but also in his mental aspects—that is, if we can raise this curve higher and arrive during childhood at a better and clearer understanding and awareness of what he can expect during adolescence—then he will probably land up here towards a higher consciousness. And the fluctuation will be much less. Even if it goes up that high, the distance between here (unaware) and here (critically aware) is not as great. How can we make the child more aware of himself and his environment? This is, then, the practical question and implication of this theory.

LECTURE 25

The Stage Preceding Adolescence: Conditioning for Awareness, Subject Matter, Motivation, and Visual and Haptic Characteristics

One of the greatest problems during this stage of development is to raise the level of awareness at a time when the level of awareness is still on the unconscious level of childhood. As we said before, the change from childhood to puberty is rather abrupt. It is not like the other stages of growth as we usually see them, gradually evolving one out of the other. It is the physical change, the actual physical maturation in girls and boys, which causes the initial shock. The initial shock may be greater in girls than in boys, because we are always more shocked when we see blood. We are afraid that maybe we are hurt or that something serious may have happened if this change occurs unexpectedly. But for bòth girls and boys, the shock is great. The greater the shock, the less it is conditioned.

This shock brings about a change in attitude, a change in self-awareness, and a change in the awareness to environment. If we consider all that, then we may find that this change is as great as is the change from sanity to insanity, as I mentioned yesterday. If we were to play with an airplane and stand at the door, zooming up and down with a pencil, we would be considered insane; that means, if we were to act uncontrolled like children do. Indeed, this is only possible at political conventions or if we are drunk, but then we consider the special circumstances. In our normal lives, this is, indeed, not possible.

If we consider this great difference, we know the importance of conditioning children to this difference. And if we also know and have in our minds that most of us have lost our free ability to express ourselves creatively at this time, especially in the visual arts, we would know that for art education this is one of the most crucial points in one's development. If we then could condition children into accepting their aware stages, we would indeed have done something great for mankind, not only for art education but for man as a whole. Now let us find out what we can do in order to condition children for what will come.

I remind you of the graph which we developed [see Lecture 24]; and I shall briefly, without going into details, repeat it. This top line, as we said, is the line of critical awareness, and this bottom line is the line of greatest uncontrolled activity. I'm simply repeating what we said the last time. This middle line represents what we call the "shift." We then developed this curve, the line beginning in the unaware stages of childhood and continuing to the aware stages of adulthood. We have here, between childhood and adulthood, the stage of adolescence; and immediately preceding, we have the stage which we are now to discuss—ages eleven to thirteen (adolescence being ages thirteen to seventeen).

We have seen that the child begins with very, very uncontrolled activities, such as his scribbling, when he isn't even aware that he scribbles but simply makes motions until he learns to control them. We said that when the child comes to puberty he is usually right in the middle between the unaware and the aware stages. We then said that all of a sudden the child becomes *critically* aware of himself, not just aware.

You see, we as adults are also aware; but we can shift our awareness, depending on how we live. If you are highly intellectually inclined and control yourself at all times—this is also a social factor—then you are aware at every minute and you wouldn't do anything out of your emotional drives. You would hold yourself back and control yourself. Then you would be way up here somewhere. You will have some times when you don't control yourself, so I wouldn't put you up all the way. But you may also be one who lives as though his emotions dictate to him and who doesn't care much for society. He says: "I'm I, and I'm not a conformist. I express myself as I want to express myself. I don't care what Joe Smith says." Then you would be rather low—down there.

You know, artists usually are not conformists and are closer to childhood than anyone else. The longing for seeing things as freshly as children do, as I said before, is an internal longing of artists of every category. We can understand, then, that artists express their emotions much more readily than people who control themselves. But somewhere in between is every one of us. If we go down below that, what happens?

Student: The person is permanently retarded?

Lowenfeld: Well, more than that.

Student: Institutionalized.

Lowenfeld: Yes, indeed, the person may be schizophrenic. His control of his social interactions disintegrates, and he acts like a child. This is what happens if we go below the level of aware stages. Then, like children, we are no longer aware of what we do, and that is the reason why schizophrenic individuals often react like children. Especially in their drawings, they are completely uninhibited. Do you understand?

I told you that this is a whole philosophy—this weighing of the status of the outcome of what happens here. You see, here we are all at this stage before adolescence. What happens from here on? The adolescent individual is just not as aware as you are. He is more aware at certain times, especially after the physical change has occurred; then, he is critically aware of himself. At all times he thinks of this change. This is something which now dominates his life for a certain time. You may have forgotten, but what happens is that his consciousness immediately goes way up high to a kind of critical awareness, and the child is unable even to control himself and, therefore, the way he reacts. He is aware of his limbs, aware of his motions, aware of how he talks, and aware of almost everything including his creative activity. Out of this critical awareness results the inability to master it. Now, as he begins to adjust, his awareness indeed goes down; then it fluctuates until he reaches some level, depending on what puberty and heredity have done to him. I say heredity because the mental capacities of an individual and his emotional set are never only determined by environmental conditions. But, thank God, we cannot and will not control heredity, although we do influence environment by education.

If we can raise this curve of consciousness before adolescence, it would mean that we condition the individual to a less abrupt critical awareness. The question is, "How can we do this?" I'll erase this curve for a moment and show you what happens if we raise the level of awareness before puberty, during the stage of reasoning which precedes it. If, at least through reasoning, the child can become aware of what will happen to him, this will result in a greater control. The fluctuation thus will no longer be so great. You see, it never goes further down than to the level which we have just left. So we do not retrogress, but we go back and forth from the level where we presently are to the level which we have just left, until finally the curve peters out and we become individuals adjusted to the social environment and our inherent abilities and trends.

Student: You said before that the artist was closer to the shift line than the regular adult. According to this, then, if we do raise the level of awareness, wouldn't that destroy a lot of possible artists?

Lowenfeld: I wouldn't say it would destroy, but it is doing some harm to the intuitive, the purely intuitive, approaches. But, as always, we have the choice. We are not focusing our education, especially art education, at the few who may become artists; but we are focusing art education at all people, raising their ability to create spontaneously. We are focusing our attention not towards the selected few, but towards the masses. This is important. We may do harm in developing awareness for a few people who would lose some of their spontaneity. I shall discuss that later.

Student: Why can't you be an individual—a non-conformist, I mean—to a degree and yet be critically aware? I figure you can be aware of what's going on around you and—.

318

Lowenfeld: Your question has absolutely nothing to do with the problem which we now discuss. You may be involved as an individual who is critically aware, you see, and be a non-conformist, but critical awareness and emotional freedom do not go hand in hand. You see, these are contrasts. You may be a non-conformist with all your critical awareness and even be a non-conformist out of conviction; but you lose your spontaneity whenever you are critically aware, in a way.

Now, let us discuss what we can do to condition our children during the ages from eleven to thirteen. In order to condition individuals, we have to know towards what we should condition them. We should know how the imaginations of individuals work in order to condition them to what will come. How their thinking works, how their feeling works, how their perceiving works—these all are presumed. Otherwise, we may condition an individual but may not meet his needs; we may condition him for something entirely wrong. Therefore, it is important that we should know what goes on here so that we know what techniques we can use to condition individuals.

Let me discuss very briefly some of the characteristics which we shall encounter, especially in the visual arts, with individuals who move towards adolescence [see Summary and Evaluation Charts for Stage of Reasoning]. In the visual arts, one of the basic changes which occurs is the change in imagery: the unconscious imagery as expressed in children's art and the aware imagery, controlled imagery, as expressed in the art of adults, artists, or adolescents. What is the nature of this more aware art? One of the basic difficulties which we have had is that we did not know the subject matter, as well as the type of stimulations, to which our adolescent individuals are most sensitive. First, I have to say that whatever I say now is focused on our western civilization, because all attributes of awareness in adolescents are greatly concerned with social changes.

As we heard yesterday, the adolescent is a very peculiar species, a mixture of the highest degree of individuality, in which every individual would like to be considered as an individual, and conformity. This is a very strange mixture. Conformity as expressed by—well, everyone would like to wear sideburns and be Elvis; and, at another time, everyone would like to wear blue jeans and have them as tight as possible; and at still another time, another fashion arises and the adolescent again is apt to come close to his peers. These are things which we have to consider, indeed; but, on the other hand, we also know that the drive for individualism is greatest during adolescence, as our research has shown—not only ours, but the research of others, too. So we have to meet both of these.

The subject matter, then, has to be concerned very much with the awakening of the awareness to the self: how do I feel—my emotions and various environments, especially the social environment. It is also important that the subject matter deals very greatly with the kinds of activities adoles-

Characteristics	Human Figure	Space	Color	Design	Stimulation Topics	Techniques
Developed intelligence, yet unawareness.	Introduction of joints.	Three-dimensional space expressed by diminishing sizes of distant objects.	Changes of color in nature with regard to distance and mood (visually minded).	Personification of color. Conscious approach to stylizing of industrial products (symbols for professions).	Figures in dramatic environment. Actions from imagination and posing model (with meaning).	Water color. Mixed technique (water color and tempera).
Realistic approach (unconscious).	Visual attention to changes introduced through motion or atmosphere (visually minded).	Horizon line (visually minded).			Relation of proportion of figures to environment.	Poster paint.
Tendency toward visual- or non-visual-mindedness.	Proportion.	Retrogression of non-visually minded to base lines or expression of environment only when significant.	Emotional reaction to color of non-visually minded (not related to nature).	Function of different materials, and simple designs related to them.	Color moods. Color expression through personification. Illustrations of dramatic stories.	Bristle brush. Hair brush. Linoleum.
Love for action and dramatization.	Emphasis on expression of non-visually minded.				Murals ("from–to"). See design.	Clay. Materials for design (wood, metal, stone).

EVALUATION CHART
Stage of Reasoning

		None	Some	Much
Intellectual Growth	Does the work indicate a complete absence of schemata? Is there a tendency toward a more conscious approach of subject matter? Does the child give attention to meaningful details? Does the child's work indicate an alertness either toward expressive details or differentiated appearance? Has the child become aware of the use of techniques?			
Emotional Growth	Does the child identify himself not only with his experience but also with his environment? Is intensity of experience expressed either by exaggerations, or by differentiation of objects in distance? Does color serve as a means of expression either by using it symbolically or by referring it to mood? Is the child losing some of the stiffness of figures characteristic of the gang age? Does the child freely project either his emotions or his environment? Is the child experimental in his mode of expression? (Style.)			
Social Growth	Has the child become aware of his social environment in his creative work? Does the child characterize environment or figures? Are spatial relationships obtained? Does the child identify himself with others in his work?			
Perceptual Growth	Visual: Has the child become aware of his visual environment? Does the child express depth in his drawings?			
Perceptual Growth	Does the child include the horizontal line? Does the child include lights and shadows? Does the child observe wrinkles and folds in clothes when in motion? Does the child change intensity of line, color, and shades in distant objects? Has the child completely departed from base lines?			
	Non-Visual: Has the child become aware of his own subjective relationships to his environment? Does the child express kinesthetic sensations? (Linear representations or movements?) Does the child express tactile or textural experiences? Does the child express body feelings? Does the child contrast darks and lights as means of expression? Does the child retrogress to base lines?			
Physical Growth	Has the child become aware of the use of joints in his drawing of figures? Does the child clearly distinguish between the representation of boys and girls? Are characterizations according to differences in size and age visible?			
Aesthetic Growth	Does the child distribute the parts of his creative work in a meaningful way? Does the child relate design characteristics to the meaning of the work? Is the technique used to its best advantage? Are colors related to each other? Is there a relationship among design, material, and purpose?			
Creative Growth	Does the child's growing critical awareness keep him free from inhibitions? Does the child create without intellectual interferences? Is the child uninfluenced by his classmates? Can one easily distinguish this child's work from that of others?			

320

cents engage in. It would take me too long to discuss in detail the subject matter. I undertook a study in which I tried to find out what the subject matters are. In the new edition of the book, I divided them into various categories which make up the greatest extension of the older edition. But I shall discuss with you the nature of motivation which we should apply to the subject matter in which the individual becomes now interested. Here, we also have failed by focusing our motivations merely at the awakening of our visual awareness. We are not only becoming visually aware, but we are also becoming emotionally and socially aware. We have neglected this type of awareness in the visual arts—probably misled by the title, visual arts.

So, may I say that during this stage two attitudes toward experience evolve. While these two attitudes are on a continuum, we occasionally see extreme types of both of these attitudes. I'm speaking here of extremes only for the sake of convenience in order to be able to explain it to you more adequately. Although the difference in individuals may not be, in general, as great as I'm pointing them out now, you can usually see that the tendency or the trend towards the one or the other is present. We see individuals who develop an intense awareness towards visual factors, who would like to draw things as they are with realistic lines—lines which, when isolated, do not lose their meaning. You remember, we defined realistic lines, as such, previously. This means that our sensitivities are now more and more focusing on what we can see and the desire to transfer what we see into creative expression.

We should remember at all times, however, that art is not the representation of things but the representation of experiences which we have with things. So, in the visual arts—that means, in the tendency to express visual experiences—art is our individual experience with visual sensations and not merely a representation of what we see. In this instance, it is the experience which we have when looking at things. So, one individual will concentrate mainly on visual experiences [see Figure 30].

At the other extreme an individual will become aware in another way [see Figure 31]. His awareness is that more of his own emotions, of his own body, of his own ego, and the expression which evolves out of this subjective form of experience.

While our present art trend emphasizes the subjective relationship, in our secondary schools we still see the emphasis on perfection with regard to visual expression. There we lag somewhat in our ability to comprehend what goes on in the arts and still concentrate more on what we see, still thinking of our past experiences and academic standards where visual experiences were the basis for any art form of expression. And this, indeed, is a nonsense. We think that an artist has to go through a visual training before he can arrive at a method which expresses his emotional feelings. May I say that the one has little to do with the other. What we see may even be in our way if we want to express what we feel. In extreme instances, it is indeed a

321

hindrance if we know visual factors rather than an awareness of our feelings and emotions. In the same way that the visual artist does not first need to undergo a training of what it means to express himself emotionally, vice versa: the emotional artist who depends on his emotions—on his ego evaluations—does not have to go through a training which is based on visual factors. Both would be a kind of academism.

Now let us look at what we can do in order to find out the motivations which are appropriate for individuals belonging to these two different categories. We will take a little time in which we can find out for ourselves. I would not encourage those who have gone through this test to go through it again. However, I think the majority of you have not gone through it. Would you like to find out about yourself and your own reactions? Then please tear out a sheet of paper; any size will do, but it should be blank on both sides. No one will see it but you. It's self-testing. Indeed, it is not conclusive; but it gives you some guidance and some idea with regard to your own reactions, and thus will help you in your teaching, inasmuch as it

Fig. 30. "Parade" (13 years old). The visually minded child feels as a spectator, watching the parade. He uses color in its changing effects, mixing it freely to express atmosphere and depth. Notice the glaring effect of atmosphere achieved by "dissolving" the color surfaces. [*Note:* For color, see Lowenfeld, op.cit., Plate 7.]

Fig. 31. "My Barber" (14 years old). The haptically minded child uses color for expressing his subjective relationships to the environment. Color is often used purely symbolically with no visual reference to the object. The child does not feel as a spectator but is subjectively bound up with his experience. He often uses plain color, as in this painting. He is not interested in depicting depth or atmosphere. [*Note:* For color, see Lowenfeld, op.cit., Plate 8.]

will show you what you should know about yourself. As a teacher, you should have an understanding of both types of individuals: the child who is visually oriented and the child who is evaluating his experiences completely out of his ego involvement.

Do not draw unless I tell you to draw. In this test, whether you draw well or whether you draw poorly does not make any difference, because it is a psychological test and not one in which we test drawing ability. In fact, it will work more objectively with those who have had no drawing experience, and it will not work with those who have been conditioned in their drawing experience concerning how to draw things. In order to eliminate this conditioning effect, I shall rush you through the test as fast as I can. This may eliminate, even in those who have had art training, referring back associatively to past experiences with regard to drawing. So I shall rush you through as fast as I can with your drawing of the items. Now, listen.

On top of a table, there is a glass of water. Draw it fast: a glass of water on the top of a table; draw it! Are you through? All right, now as a second drawing, you copy what I do on the blackboard. This is supposed to be the gable end of a house. Will you please copy it? Now, listen. On the left side of the gable, there's a chimney. Draw the chimney! Fast! You through? Turn the page. Now, listen. On the top of a table, there is a checkerboard. Draw it fast! A checkerboard on the top of a table—draw it fast! Are you through? Good. Now, compare the last drawing with your first drawing.

We will have in this group three kinds of reactions. There is one group of students here who drew the table for the first and the last drawing alike. The table is a perspective view, and they put the glass somewhere and the checkerboard somewhere. If the tables are alike in perspective in the first and last drawing, you are likely to be visually inclined, that is, you put yourself outside and observe how the table would look. Whether there is a glass on the table or whether there is a checkerboard on the table will not change the table.

If you, however, are subjectively inclined and disregard visual experiences and depend more on your subjective attitude, the table changes according to what is placed on it. Then, the view of the table in the beginning may be like this, a perspective view; or it may be this, a side view (elevation). But the second view of the table has changed when the checkerboard is on it and you see only the top of the table, that is, you are no longer outside the table looking at the table and thinking whether the glass is on it or the checkerboard is on it. The table remains the table, but you evaluate the table according to what is on it and, therefore, have become subjectively involved in what you draw.

There is a third group who have omitted the table completely and only drew either the checkerboard or the glass. Thus, they have indicated that only the object has meaning. They are the conceptual people—those who think not of a view, not of a relationship, but of the thing itself. This most likely then is a group which does not relate itself to either perception—that is, to a perception which is ego-involved or to a visual perception—but think of the thing itself, the concept of the thing; and, therefore, they are the people in between. In an average population, the distribution is the following: among four people, you have two people who express themselves visually; one individual who expresses himself subjectively or, as I call it later on in my book, haptically—*haptikos* is a Greek word which means being able to hold, to lay hold of, to touch, and to refer it to one's self; and one person, one individual among the four, evaluates his art or his experiences according to the significance they have for himself—and this one is in between. So we have the distribution of two, one, one.

Could we check? For those who are visually inclined, the table (in perspective) does not change. Raise your hands. Twenty-nine. Those who have changed the view, raise your hands. Twenty-two. Twenty-nine and twenty-two. This is not a normal distribution. Those who have drawn the object only, raise your hands. Well, we have only four. I think some have not raised their hands.

We have almost the correct number, I believe, of visually inclined individuals, just half of the class. Probably, not everyone is here; I do see some empty seats. Since we have seventy-two in this class, the ideal number would be thirty-six. We have twenty-nine. But we have twenty-two who are non-visually inclined. The reason for this may be due to the fact that we have a large number of art education people here. People in art education are greatly influenced by the trends of art in this period, in this era. The trends in art are subjective, possibly even to the point that we do injustice to visual representation or expression. Because of this suppression of visualization, of visualizers, we may have a larger number of non-visually minded individuals here than we usually have in an average population. The average has been obtained from non-art people—that is, on Air Force bases where the tests were used—and not from a group of art specialists, you know. You wanted to ask something?

Student: What's the possibility of our being conditioned by the drawing of the checkerboard in the book?

Lowenfeld: You know, it's a great possibility.

Student: That's the first thing that entered my mind when you mentioned checkerboard.

Lowenfeld: Yes, there's a great possibility that there are some conditioned by the drawing, and, therefore, are continuing what they have seen. It may be responsible for the larger number of non-visually minded individuals than we usually have. Now, let me draw a conclusion from what we have said. We have to become aware of motivations which are focused in the direction of visual thinking, as well as of motivations which are directed towards non-visual thinking. In order to be able to focus a motivation, we have to know the attributes.

Let's go very quickly through some of the attributes so that we shall know them. With regard to figure and space and color, the visually minded individual will have a tendency to transfer his visual impressions to his drawings, and therefore, he will become aware of the implications of transferring a three-dimensional impression in nature into a three-dimensional expression in his art. This involves, of course, the understanding by a teacher of perspective, which is the art of transferring three-dimensional forms onto a two-dimensional surface. A teacher who does not know how perspective functions would be greatly handicapped in a secondary school class. On the other hand, it would be quite out of place to teach perspective because perspective—the ability to express a three-dimensional space in two-dimensions—is only one of the necessary tools for one group. You may remember how you reacted to perspective when you first heard about it. Some of you may have welcomed it as a tool which helped you to express yourselves visually, while others may have been confused by perspective and it may have always been a puzzle—whether the lines should meet, or whether the lines should go apart, and when they should go apart. Some of you may even have mechanized this feeling of when they should go apart and when they should meet, when they should be divergent and when they should be convergent. So to teach perspective in art is, indeed, a nonsense.

Perspective should only be taught whenever there is a need for it by particular individuals. In the same way, anatomy should only be taught to those who would like to use it in their art, because anatomy, as you know, is a science. And geology should only be taught to those who want to use it when they would like to know what's going on underneath a landscape. That's the same as for those who would like to know what goes on underneath the skin, and that is anatomy. We also believe that emotional factors should only be motivated for those who would like to use them.

For the visualizers, expression of the three-dimensional is the most important thing, and that refers to the changing effects in nature, all the changing effects—that is, changes caused by motion; changes caused by light and illumination, as we have discussed them; and changes caused by distance. These are the three major changes. Changes caused by motion refer to the qualities that a part of the body or part of our dress has when it changes while we are in motion, or the qualities which a tree has as it changes when the tree is in motion, or the water has as it changes when the water is in motion. All things change when they are in motion. To hold onto these changes is one of the greatest qualities of impressionistic art. Impressionistic art is the art of appearances, how things appear to us visually. Therefore, impressionistic art is the art which refers to the visualizers. So, when we would like to motivate these changing conditions, we should start here somewhere to instill in children the sensitivity to see the changing effects caused by motion—by a storm, let us say, when a storm moves the trees, when a storm moves the clouds, when we see the ripples on the water, when we see the waves. These sensitivities must be motivated. And the changing effects caused by illumination, by the differences in light—how light changes color. In sunshine a lawn looks different than it does in the shade. Color changes completely on the illuminated side and on the reflected side. These changing effects caused by illumination are then the sensitivities which we should motivate in children who are visualizers.

The changing effects which are caused by distance, however, may be the most important ones. They involve a knowledge of perspective, the diminishing quality of distant objects, and the laws which refer to this diminishing quality. I believe that even in the art of the visualizers we should not refer to construction procedures but always refer to our fresh reaction to what we see. So, these are the qualities of the visualizers.

Now, let's shift to the qualities of those who are haptically inclined (subjectively inclined). As we have said previously, they evaluate a thing according to the significance it has for them. So, indeed, we shall recognize that their proportion will be a proportion of value. Their feeling for outlines will only be a feeling which relates to kinesthetic sensations of going with a line around the body; and, therefore, their lines will have a different character than the lines which are drawn by visualizers.

The lines by the visualizers are mainly concerned with the mental pictures which we have of the thing and, therefore, will presuppose or presume much which goes on in our minds. The haptically inclined individual will not depend on closure and on the image which takes place in the mind. For instance, a visualizer may use a very sketchy line, such as this. Now, I exaggerate. You see, in our minds we close these broken lines into an image. We think, indeed, that lines are present which are not there. There are lots of lines to be closed here in our minds. The visualizer depends much on this closing, because he only gives us a brief impression of the changing effects. A tree, to a visualizer, may look very sketchy, like this. In this, we close many things in our minds. Actually, the appearance is created here in your mind, not there in the picture. These lines are all loose and not interconnected. So the visualizer depends much on closure. That's the expression in psychology, closure. This has nothing to do with a line which creates in us a kinesthetic sensation.

An example of a kinesthetic sensation would be if you were to move your finger across your body. There is no interruption. Do I make myself clear? If you do this, you see, you get a line which is caused by kinesthetic sensation. You go with your hand around the outline. Therefore, in non-visualizers, we will see many more closed lines than open lines. The non-visualizer will express his kinesthetic sensations while drawing a line. He would not be satisfied with a sketchy figure running like this, but probably like Picasso or many other non-visualizers, he would try to go with great care into kinesthetic sensations, making a continuous line without much of an interruption and drawing the feeling which he has when running. Do you see?

Now these are the differences. Here we have a kinesthetic sensation, and there we have a sensation of appearance. A haptically inclined individual would not be satisfied with a sketchy tree like this. If he tries to draw a tree, he would either draw it so that he gets a feeling for the details of the tree and even of the hanging of the leaves on it or he would try to circumscribe it with one line. This is no longer the appearance in which the mind closes the picture, but it is the sensation of the doing. You may get some insight into your own art from this. Of course, it's rather superficially treated in this short amount of time, but it gives you some insight.

The last question with which I would like to deal is "How, then, can we raise this curve?" Well, you know, when I said proportional value, this almost covers everything. It says with regard to the figure: "I'll depend on my subjective experiences rather than on what I see and evaluate the meaningfulness of the parts in relationship to the significance which they have for me. In space, I'll disregard the three-dimensional space altogether. It has no meaning for me because, if something is distant or close, it has only visual meaning. Something which is distant may be more emotionally affective, may more emotionally influence me than something which is close." If something happens to my brother away in the distance—probably now he is in Oslo—this would tremendously affect me and I'll do right here in my mind almost everything that happens. So distance, in emotional terms, is wiped out completely and probably means only that the longing grows with the distance, you know, or with the unobtainable things. Here we come to a philosophical discussion of space rather than to a perceptual discussion: therefore, space in haptic art, or in expressive art, has meaning only by philosophical evaluation and should only be regarded as such.

You can see readily how perspective space may hinder children who are now gradually becoming aware of the significance of their emotional relationship to themselves. It would be a hindrance to their expression rather than a promotion. Therefore, never teach perspective to a whole group. If a child, a single individual, feels that he did not express depth as he wanted it, give him an experience which leads to it and do not discuss it with the whole group. How does this look in a classroom situation? It looks rather simple. At this point, when children still create like children and when we would like to create in them a higher awareness, all the implications of these experiences which I discuss now are boiled down into a very, very simple classroom procedure; and that is the wonderful thing about it. You approach the child, who is right here, before he is aware and interrupt him for a minute and say: "How did you get this? How did you get this?" In the child's drawing, we always start on the level where the child is. If the child intends to paint and paints distance, you would say: "How did you get this tree that distant?" Obviously, the child in the unaware stage would say: "Oh, it just happened. I don't know."

Then you would try to bring it into the consciousness, the awareness, of the child, and you would say: "Now, don't you know? Look at the tree which you have drawn here and the tree which you have drawn there—what is the difference between the two trees?" Let the child discover his own achievements. May I repeat that loudly so that you will get the real meaning of it, "Let the child discover his own achievements." But in this discovery you have to be the promoter. You have a very, very important job, namely, the one of helping the child in this discovery. Now you can see readily that this discovery may thwart some of the spontaneity of children. Yes, indeed, it may. But since it is the child's own work which you have discovered for him, it may merely make him more self-aware at a stage when it doesn't hurt, when the physical changes have not yet occurred, when the child is not yet so critically aware that he needs to come to perfection as a result of some kind of developmental attitude. Yet, if we ask the child: "How did you get this stormy sky? What colors did you mix?"

"Oh, I don't know. It just happened."

Then we would say, "Now, look." You take the child from an accidental achievement to an achievement which the child can gradually learn to control. This transition from an accidental achievement to a controlled achievement is at the crux and one of the most important things which we should stress at this critical stage; because whenever the child achieves something but cannot repeat it, he becomes discouraged. So if you ask the child: "How did you get this sky? Now, let's find out—what did you do? What? How did this flowing quality develop? You must have painted into wet colors. Didn't you?"

"Yes. I painted into wet colors."

"But what else did you do? Now let's find out what happened when you painted into wet colors."

Let the child answer. Whenever it is possible, let the child give the answer so the child will discover his own achievements and you are only the helper in this discovery, the catalyst, as I said before. This is very important. If you do this continually in your teaching during this critical stage, the child will gradually move from a stage of lesser awareness to a stage of greater awareness in which he learns to control his own achievements. Do I make myself clear? The classroom procedure is very simple. If I see that a child has exaggerated one part which is very significant to him, then I would say: "Now, let me see, how did you get this expression? You probably felt your hands more strongly when you did this motion." So you move his feelings towards his own emotions and into a greater awareness. Size relationships become, then, expressions of value and of significant emotional experience rather than of distance. If we are now aware of the distinct details which signify the various personality trends and also discover those children who are in between, we can then, in our motivations, help all children in discovering themselves.

The critically aware child shies away from doing things which are immediate expressions of the self, because they appear to him too primitive. I'll give you an example of this. We have seen that, when children in our children's art classes make a drawing which involves themselves, they would like to destroy it in the end because they feel what they have done is inadequate, especially if they have not gone through this conditioning effect. They're ashamed of their own product because it does not meet their own critical evaluation. If the child draws a horse, the horse is too plump. It doesn't look like the horse that he wants to draw. But we have experienced that whenever this horse, or whatever he draws, is translated into a technical medium—that means, when some technique has been inserted which removes the direct expression from the child and brings a translation of this direct expression closer to himself—then he accepts it.

In reality it looks like this—if the child draws a horse and he is not at all happy with it, he says: "I just don't like it. It doesn't look like a horse. It doesn't look like a horse." You give the child a piece of celluloid and tell the child, "Now put it on your drawing and engrave the horse into the celluloid." The child takes a needle and engraves the horse into the celluloid, and you make a print from it by putting some ink on it, like an etching, and you print it. All of a sudden, the child accepts the printing. We have done that in experiments. And you know that these transitions are very healthy transitions. Or if you take the same drawing and you have the child emboss the horse in copper, as we have done in the children's art classes, all of a sudden the child is delighted by the very same naive quality of the horse which he had expressed in his pencil drawing or crayon drawing. Why? Well, because the technical involvement with the material in engraving it, in cutting it out, or in embossing it has removed the handwriting from the child—the direct emotional experience—and has inserted a technical procedure. As the child has become involved in this technical procedure, he now can accept his own drawing, his own projection. As you can readily see, technical transference from one medium to another plays an important role during the oncoming stage of adolescence.

In crafts, this always takes place. Craft work is not as direct in its expression as painting or drawing or modeling are. Because of its lack of directness, craft work plays a very important role during this stage of transition, especially for children who have not gone through this conditioning effect and who are all of a sudden here and lose confidence in their own creative impulse and expression. Therefore, crafts will play a most important role during the stage of adolescence. Whenever we have not been able to have these craft classes during this stage, it has been difficult. While direct projection plays a lesser role in the crafts, yet I would like to point out that the crafts will never be able to replace the visual forms of art such as painting, drawing, and sculpture; because, in these forms of art, we have an opportunity to relate ourselves directly to our experiences without this translation of which I spoke. Facing one's self is always more important than escaping it. Since crafts do not give the child, or anyone else, this direct opportunity to face one's self but only an indirect opportunity, the crafts shall not replace those forms of art which allow individuals to express themselves directly.

Our class has come to an abrupt end, and I wish we could continue it. I hope this information has been meaningful to you. I would not be happy if you would now go back and look at this just as a pleasant experience. I hope that you all feel now as missionaries when you go into your classrooms. Do not keep things secret to yourselves, but engage the teachers with whom you work in discussions and open their eyes as I have tried to open yours, so far as they had not been opened already. I hope that you will use your knowledge and apply it with your children. Much luck to you.

SECTION II
Art and the Adolescent

LECTURE 26

Secondary Art Education: Philosophic Considerations—
Art in Art Education, Material Values versus Personal
Values (Creativity, Aesthetic Experience, Sensitivity to
One's Sensory Experience, Needs of Others),
Responsibilities of the Art Teacher; Methods (Media,
Procedures, Technique); and Visual–Haptic Types

Art education should not involve using a theory of education which emphasizes our standard of living, no matter how high it may be. We should look at our standard of living from a different angle. Our standard of living is what we get out of life, and this is something entirely different, independent of the material wealth and value with which we surround ourselves. We may have our pockets full of money, or we may be as poor as the monks. We may not see the riches of life which are offered to us. One of the most important things which art education should do for man is to make him sensitive—sensitive to his own problems and sensitive to his environment.

What means do we have here to make him more sensitive? That includes, of course, questions of basic philosophy; but it also includes questions which are very important in regard to practices. I am discussing this in one of the last hours of your class, but I hope it is something that will remain with you for your whole life. Teaching must include developing our sensitivities, especially our sensitivities towards values, and that means values which are neglected in the rest of the education that we have in our schools. An art education which does not promote these sensitivities is not an art education. It just makes sure again that someone is promoting materialistic values, which, indeed, is against everything in our philosophy. So try to combat this, and, by means of aesthetic experiences, emphasize the values which are important in life.

Now I would like to express some of them—at least this is one of them. We have recently been defining values which relate to creativity, as such. I don't want to conceal from you that we are living in a time which is probably more exciting to art education than *any* previous time in history. Recently, when I addressed the Pennsylvania Art Education Association, I had the opportunity to emphasize this. The thing of which you and many of the professional people in art education are not aware is that we are right in the midst of a period in which something is happening which never has happened before in the whole history of man, namely, that our philosophy—the philosophy which we are promoting which tries to unfold the creative potentialities in people—is now preached not only by educators in general but also by businessmen and scientists, and now you can read about it everywhere.

Almost everywhere you hear the word "creativeness." This was a very rare word a few years ago, a very rare word. If you said "creativity" to someone in education (whatever area of education it may have been) or in the sciences or in the social sciences, he would have thought this word to be synonymous with art. You know, creative education is only what belongs to art. Now, we hear it coming from everywhere, even from the business people. The last convention of the Association of Commerce Clubs had as its title, "Having Creativeness." Imagine! Can you imagine that? It's a terrific change which has taken place, but I don't think it would have taken place—first, without the terrific changes to which we have been exposed in industry and in science, and, second, without the preparation of society which we in art education have done. Don't forget that. People will never admit, probably, this latter part of my story; but, indeed, people would not now think of creative education if we would not have prepared the ground for it. Indeed, we have; just think of it.

When I started here at The Pennsylvania State University some twelve years ago, there was no Department of Art Education. At that time, we simply started some courses. The first year, we didn't have a text. My students asked me when I talked, "To whom can we teach that? Who will believe us?" I was teaching that we should not copy or trace patterns. I said that we have something much more important to give, namely, to give man an opportunity to unfold *his* creative abilities according to his own individual differences. From that time twelve years ago to the present time is just a very brief period, as we have seen, but our era has changed.

Not long ago—it was in April—I attended a meeting in Washington. This meeting was set to lay down plans for the next White House Conference which will be in 1960. You know, every ten years the President of the United States calls in educators from all over the country to discuss the future plans of education in general. There were twenty members on the advisory board of educators, who were called in from all over the country and who will prepare the larger conference. I was very surprised that I received an invitation, because twenty members is a very small number from the whole United States. I was thinking also, "I was invited in an era of science when Sputniks were circling around the globe, in addition to the American who had circled the globe."

At any rate, when I arrived there and we attacked the problem, you would think it would have been a problem of how to produce more scientists. Well, no, the word "science" was scarcely heard. People were mainly concerned with how we can promote human values in our schools and how we can promote the unfolding of the creative potentiality in people. This was quite a change, even from the last White House Conference held in 1950 in which I also participated. So, you see, changes take place, and apparently they are in the direction of our thinking in art education.

Yesterday in my mail I received an invitation to be on one of the planning boards. You may have heard the report of James Conant, the former President of Harvard University. He is the chairman. He was in charge of redesigning the secondary school curriculum and will give suggestions, acting in an advisory capacity. One of the other people is Dr. Kelly from the Science Foundation, and another is the Dean of the Graduate School of Harvard University. They all are now concerned with how the secondary programs, the curricula, can change to serve better the needs of society. We are presently in an era of big changes, and the one that's most gratifying is that the changes are moving in our direction. Whether art education will be directly affected, I don't know. It all depends on us, I believe, and the people who are in charge of art education. If we are foolish enough to promote something which is outside the thinking of people today, then we have worked very hard up to this point but have lost leadership. Do you see?

There are, indeed, indications of this. I'm very much disturbed by some relatively little movements which go on in some areas of art education in which people want to emphasize at this time the "art" in art education. I'm all in favor of emphasizing the aesthetic experience in it; but I don't think it is the time now to promote it officially, because people will think that we have become subject-matter-centered, as it were. It would be the same as if we were to emphasize the "science" in science education. But, we are not emphasizing today the science in science education. On the contrary, you may have heard that M.I.T. is requiring their graduates to take art courses—scientists taking art courses as a requirement just to broaden their understanding of creativeness! Now, when science is requiring art courses, we should withdraw and say, "Oh, no, art only, and put the art in art education"? Now that would be foolish.

We should have in our minds that we should never falter—nor can we afford to—in our demands for higher standards in aesthetic experiences. Do not misunderstand me. I think that the kinds of products which we receive from our students depend on how we teach, on the quality of our teaching. Certainly, we should be very, very much alert to the fact that an aesthetic education, such as art education, has as its aim the highest standards for aesthetic products. But we're not focusing on that. The products are an outcome of what we do with the students. If this product is high and the student still is stereotyped or is inflexible in his pursuit of creative solutions, I think we have not fulfilled our ultimate purpose. I would like to see the product in equilibrium or commensurate with the abilities of the student. We should never aim too high so that we get out of the reach of the student. This is very important. We always have to start on the level of the student and extend his abilities, do you see?

I have often been asked, "What should we do when we get into a very stiff situation?" If, when you go out student teaching, you're in an environment in which your teacher still comes from a school of not quite copying, but almost—that means, distributing samples and asking students to copy or draw from these samples—what should you do? Well, first of all, may I tell you that during student teaching I hope you will not get into such an environment. But in student teaching, you're not there to reform the teacher. You are coming into a ready-made situation; you can only start from there and go on.

If you have a class, for instance, and this class has been conditioned by your predecessor by stereotyped means—that is to say, she has been doing nothing with the girls but copying from fashion magazines and preparing them for fashion drawing, and the boys have been doing, let's say, model work which is mainly based on pure technical approaches and not on the approach of unfolding their own creative abilities—don't ever tell the student: "Now, this is silly. Put it away. We are starting something entirely different." You can't break a conditioned individual; he depends on what he has learned up to this time. You can only lead him away from it. By taking away the very basis of his background, you may surely frustrate him by giving him something too new and different.

So if a girl has been, let's say, copying fashion magazines, I would do everything possible to continue what the student has been doing but have in mind leading her gradually towards something which is more alive. In other words, I would relate the fashion drawing to something alive. I would say: "Well, you have been making dresses for parties. Now, let's create the experience of a party. Let's take off from there and invent or create a composition where you may think of the fashion drawings which you have made, but let's put them in some way together so that we get the feeling of festivity." This would be a fashion drawing for evening, a dance or something. If it were a fashion which would be used for another occasion—let us say, for hiking—well, let's create the atmosphere of woods around it and thus lead the individual from there on to something more creative. Do not frustrate the individual by saying, "Well, that's not so good; this is bad," and so forth. It always creates a better atmosphere by giving the student something better, not by tearing down or by criticizing, but by doing things better. Do I make myself clear?

So it would not be fair if you were to say, "This is copy work you have done up to this time; now that you are with me, you are going to do something entirely different because I don't think that this copying is right." Or, you know, "I think this wrong." For that, let the student make his own decision. Don't take the decision away. But at some time, you will be very gratified when a student gets up and says: "My, this is altogether different. I think that what we have been doing was wrong, because we were always copying." See, the student has discovered it is wrong, and you would have taken this discovery from him. And this is not good. We are human beings and we fail, but whatever we discover for ourselves is the thing which is most meaningful to us. The discovery is something which we should promote at all levels. Perhaps I told you, if we do not now take into our hands what society actually provides for us—namely, the opportunity to promote creativeness in our students—I believe we have failed in our own profession. So, we may promote the aesthetic experience; indeed, we should now be very, very active in telling and showing the world how, by means of aesthetic experience, we can help to unfold creativeness in general.

As you should know, we have been conducting some experiments here.[10] These activities have allowed us to determine or partly determine that creativeness, whether it's applied in the arts or in the sciences, has common attributes. That puts us in the strongest position we have ever been in in art education. If we are not promoting this and if we are not underlining this whenever we can, well, then I believe we have failed in promoting one of the most important aspects. The question is now, "How should we promote it in our classrooms?" As I told you, one of the first things is to make our students sensitive. But as long as we remain with generalities with regard to sensitivity, we will not know how to tackle it. So let's become more specific about what we mean by sensitivities. If you have any questions, interrupt me, please.

There are all kinds of sensitivities, and I'll enumerate them now. The most important sensitivity, I believe, is the sensitivity towards one's own needs. Many of us bury this sensitivity and surround ourselves with meaningless other things. By that I mean that we invent means to divert us from ourselves. We escape and don't really want to be confined with our own problems—emotional and other problems. So we invent all kinds of things. Some things which we invent are very pleasant, such as parties; other things are pleasant probably in a superficial sense, such as drinking, but the outcome may not be so very pleasant. There are all kinds of things escapists invent which we do. Another thing, of course, is sitting in front of the television set and doing nothing but taking in what others say or going to movies and just being diverted.

10. See Lectures 5 and 6.

I think you should be aware of the fact that we should have always some time in the day when we can contemplate by ourselves. I'm not against movies; I also go to see them. I'm not against drinking; I also enjoy a good drink. I'm not against any of these, because I'm not an extremist, you know. But we do not recognize that it is probably necessary every day to think about one's own self, one's own problems, and to confront one's self with whatever injustice has been done to us. Let's find out how we can resolve it. Not by escaping it, not by simply counteracting, but by analyzing a situation, we may find often in the injustice some justice. So it is very important.

Another means of escape is that we look mainly to our jobs for purpose or value in our own living. This is another diversion. Then there are people who go from one meeting to another and think they are doing very important things. I, myself, would be included. I don't go home and think that this was all nonsense but try to separate the things which were very important from those which were time-killing. We need to underline the importance of things; well, we would be fools not to. But we should always take time for our own selves. This is very important.

Always consider what is important in the work which you are doing as future teachers. It is important that the child learns and gains in this process. If he does not gain from the process, well, what does the process bring about? What does the child learn when he goes through the process? I hope, in the evenings after you have been teaching, you may often think of this. Fortunately, we are among those fortunate people who can contemplate in solitude. In all things which we do, the child should learn to think for himself. He learns to solve a problem independently for himself. See, that's a grand thing. Here, a child has some pieces of glass and some pieces of tile. And now he puts them together in a fashion which he's never seen before. Out comes a mosaic. Tremendous! Man has shaped his own spirit. See, no one else can see it as he does. He has nothing and comes out with something. He has redefined the meaning of glass; and he has redefined the meaning of pieces of tile; and he has created a unity, his own universe, as it were. He has brought order out of chaos. These are all things which you have to rethink every day when you teach.

However, if this does not take place, you can only go home and say: "I have taught a child how to do things step by step." You have deprived him of his own opportunity for problem solving. You have taken away this great experience to form out of chaos a harmonious organization—his own universe, as it were. You have not allowed him the freedom to create, out of his own independent will, what he wants to do. You have put a straitjacket around him and have told him how to do things. This you have to think out for yourself. But often you will discover that you have loosened the straitjacket.

After teaching, I want you to rethink, and then I want you to be like

Christ and say, "God, be kind, it was my fault." We always should do that time and again—say "It was my fault."

We as teachers should always think it was our fault when something did not work that we tried to do. Unfortunately, many of our colleagues don't do it. They think that they can fail half of a class, well, half of a class is gone. Instead, they should evaluate themselves. They should say, "I have not been able to submit the knowledge. It was my fault." Look at yourselves in a mirror; then we will have better teachers. Don't ever blame anyone else, even if someone else could be blamed. It's still better to blame one's own self because you're better off. I'm telling you, you're better off always, even if you find no solution for it, because you, yourself, remain sincere to yourself. That is one of the greatest assumptions for good teaching. Also, to be sensitive towards one's own self is one of the most important things in teaching.

There are many other sensitivities which are more or less extrinsic and which more or less do not belong so intimately bound up with one's own self, although they may be part of it—for instance, our sensitivity towards our sensory experiences. By sensory experiences, I mean the senses which we have been given by God. We must use them so that we learn to refine them in their usage. Psychologists say, and rightly so, that without the use of our sensory experiences there is no learning. You've heard that probably in psychology, too. There's absolutely no learning without our sensory experiences. If you could not use your eyes, if you could not use your ability to move—we call it kinesthetic experience, if you could not use your sense of touch or your sense of smell or your sense of hearing, if you were deprived of all your senses, there would be no learning. None! Absolutely none!

Fortunately, we have our senses. But wouldn't you think that education would draw its conclusions from that important statement?—that it would say, "Well, wouldn't it be logical then to refine our sensory experiences so that we can learn better?" You see? But we don't do it. So, actually, we miss a very important part of education that is especially important on the secondary level; because, here, youth becomes *aware* of the use of sensory experiences, sensory perception. We should try to develop sensory perception as much as we can, and that depends on our own open-mindedness and sensitivity, you know. We should try to make the individual see things—things which he has never seen before.

There was a wonderful experience which I once had, probably like you or like anyone else. Do you remember Miss Emerson? She was teaching here, of course. I went with Miss Emerson down the hallway and there on the floor they had just brought in somehing from the courtyard—burlap sacks. These burlap sacks had deteriorated. The material had been out in the courtyard for a long time, and all kinds of molds had collected around the burlap. It looked black and green and yellow and mulchy, really. And she said, "Oh, look at the beautiful pieces." She sat down and lifted up this piece of deteriorated burlap and looked at the tiny little molds and little stems—white, partly green, partly black, partly brown—you know. She said, "Look at it!" She was holding it like a jewel, as a jeweler would hold a diamond. This sensitivity towards things which we have probably never experienced before, we should always preserve. We should develop an openness towards sensory experiences so that we may encounter things in our lives every second, or minute, which may fascinate us. It is fascinating to see new things and look at them with new eyes and listen to sounds with new ears.

Most of our inspirations will come from nature. There's no doubt about it. Science is only a servant of nature. You always have to come back to the greatest of experiences, and that is nature. So keep your eyes open and your ears open and try to create an enthusiasm in your students to see new things and to use them as a basis for their creations. Please don't take a mobile and use Calder as your example. Calder created the mobile, of course. But let's go back to nature again, and let's observe how things move: how a blowing wind makes the dust move, how the paper starts flying in the air, and how the New York pine trees overlap when the breeze goes through them and creates a constant feeling of pattern. Let's observe those most intimate things in nature, and out of this get our inspirations. It is those things to which you should direct your students.

Sensitivity to a sensory experience we call sensory perception. And to me, sensory perception means perception also towards environment, especially nature. Most of our inspirational stimulations should be directed there. Of course, you can sometimes have secondhand experiences, and there's nothing wrong with them. But, basically, we should never lose our relationship to nature. We should not learn love from Hollywood pictures. We should have a basic experience involving it, and I don't have to preach that, I hope. You will understand, then, that one who has never been in love will never understand what love means. You can explain it to him by means of secondhand experiences in a movie or a story, but if he, himself, has never felt what love means, how could he ever have a meaningful experience when he sees a secondhand experience. Do I make myself clear? If you never have been shaken by love, a story won't do it for you—nor will a movie. You have to have firsthand experiences. I'm very grateful to Dr. Mattil for conducting the children's art classes, because without them you wouldn't have a real grasp of what to expect in schools when you go out to teach. Then you'll really know whether you have learned something here or whether we have gypped you. You'll really feel it when you go out and teach, because those things you learned may come to life there. If they don't, then go back and study again.

There are other sensitivities besides the ones which I have mentioned.

These are social sensitivities—the sensitivities which we should develop concerning the needs of others—which also come very, very strongly into the teaching situation. Unless you can identify with your students on the secondary level, you will not be able to serve them well; and you will be all wrong, especially in developing a secondary school curriculum. Do you know what we usually find in our secondary schools? Students are put before a still life, and the teacher says, "Draw it; eat it up." You know, the student has no relationship to it whatsoever, and it is entirely of no significance to him. Because most of our students are anxious to do art, we confront them with a collection of things and say, "Do it," instead of finding out what is important to them. This is a very important problem on the secondary level. We need to know that things are important to them which pertain to social activities—yes, to their awakened feelings for the other sex. You are still in it, and I hope you never grow out of it. But these are important things, and to by-pass them would be silly. I don't know why we should not also include in our subject matter, on which we base our motivations, experiences which pertain to the very essential things which are taught, promoting topics which deal with them. How we deal with them is left again to the student.

We know that the secondary student, the adolescent, is very much concerned with experimentation and technical processes, isn't he? Yes, indeed, we know it. He is not satisfied unless he is confronted, unless he sees the final outcome as something he can appreciate. Therefore, we should help him in this desire. See, we have done experiments in our art classes in which our students have used topics which were very much related to themselves. In drawing, for instance, they were very unhappy, even with their own topics. Even if they used romantic topics or they used dramatic topics, the students were very unhappy because the end product reminded them very much of primitive and naive drawings which they could not accept. Their drawings were too childlike. Do you see? So we made the following experiment. We said, "Take a piece of celluloid and put it over your drawing and make an engraving out of this." You know to what I refer? An etching or engraving. They did so. And then they inked it and printed it. All of a sudden the very same drawing which appeared naive and primitive to them was something they appreciated. That's marvelous. That's marvelous! You know why? Because they used a technical process, and this technical process removed the very intimate feeling and also the naive feeling of the drawing and transferred or transfigured it into something finished, as it were.

The same would happen if you were to say, "Use this for a mosaic." The drawing, they wouldn't like it; but the mosaic, they would most likely accept. Or, "Use the drawing for repoussé in copper." They would use the same drawing and would engrave it in copper, like you have it there, and all of a sudden they would be most pleased. They would work hard to achieve this procedure, yet it is still related to them and only to them. Therefore, we should provide our students with various means with which they can identify which take them beyond the mere acceptance of the immediate and provide for very creative projection.

Here I would also like to give you something to think about. You should always differentiate between procedure and technique, and I make this distinction. Procedure is something we should and must develop. Procedure can be taught. Technique is individual and personal. It is the way each individual develops his procedure according to his own technique. I'll give you an example of this. Let us say you would like to do an etching or an engraving using the plate of celluloid. The procedure would be telling the students or your children what they should do with the materials. You would tell them: "Here you have a transparent sheet. You can put it on top of your drawing and take your needle and engrave it. But don't be a slave to your own drawing," you would say. "Don't be a slave. I know that, while you're engraving, many other things will come to your mind; and you may redefine what you have done. So take your engraving needle, and now engrave what you have done. You know what we are going to do then? We'll take the celluloid, and we will rub some printer's ink over it. Then, we'll remove the printer's ink from the smooth surface—we can immediately remove it—but the ink will remain in the engraved parts. You will see it. It will remain dark. And then we'll use some paper which we have previously moistened, and we'll pull it through the press. The moistened paper will pull out the ink from the engraved lines, and that we call an etching." Or you could say it's called a needle etching if you would like to be specific.

However, you would not tell the student how he should use his needle. One may use it linearly; another may try to create a black-and-white pattern; a third may be interested in creating some three-dimensional effects. All of them will do it differently. This personal and individual way of using the procedure we call technique. Techniques are not taught. They are developed by each individual. Do I make clear this difference? Whenever we develop a procedure, we try to make the individual feel the medium—feel what it is to have a copper plate, what a copper plate can do, what different behaviors a copper plate may have, how it reacts to various pushing in or pulling out and so forth, how flexible it is, and how far you can go. Of course, you have to find this out for yourself. But, you have to teach for this experimental approach.

This is another way we can identify with materials, with media. Of course, we have to. Unless we become very sensitive to what various media can do or what materials can do, we're not good friends with them. For instance, if you take this reed and continue working with it trying to work it in—could you do it? Why? Do you think you could take a piece of reed and just continue weaving it around as we have it here? Would it be good? Yes or no?

Student: No.

Lowenfeld: Why? It's too brittle. It is too stiff. It would break, you see. You have already learned with that an understanding of a reaction of a medium: a reed. When you become very sensitive in your brain, then you can almost predict this reaction. Two people who are in love almost react like one, because they are so sensitive to one another. They feel each other so much. It's not the same when you look into a landscape alone, and when you look into a landscape and feel the other person with you. You feel it in the same way that you develop a sensitivity toward materials. We feel the materials. We feel the reaction of the material. It would break. Oh, I shudder when I think that it would break. You should enjoy going around and should have fun shaking hands with the other reeds. It goes around until it is finished and glorified and a wonderful part.

You see, you should always try to get the feeling of personification in all which you do. Let's put the reed in its best position so it can do the best it can do. Make it wet, soak it; now the reed will certainly go around fine and can do what reeds can do. What can wood do? What can wire do? What can copper do? And what can pieces of tile do? Shake hands. Love each other. One piece of tile can look to the other and say "It's so good now in this environment." And this one is saying it there, right now. It felt very neglected when it was in the pile of useless, broken-up pieces. Now it has found a place for itself, you see? Think in these terms and become much more sensitive towards media. Identify with them, as it were, and then you won't combat the spirit of any medium because you will immediately feel it. But don't forget—try to give your students an understanding of procedures. It is procedure to soak it. It shows you what the material can do. But to invent a basket for himself should be the student's activity. We should come out with different baskets, not all with similar baskets.

The same is true if you go to the ceramics room. You know yourself, if you are doing some pottery, what a brilliant experience it is to see what clay can do when you draw it up. When you go too far, it starts wobbling and feeling, oh, just like an upset stomach. All of a sudden it wobbles, and it breaks. You can always identify the feeling of clay (or the feeling of any media) and how glorious it feels when it is developed into a beautiful shape. And when a glaze is put around it and makes it permanent, this is a wonderful feeling, a glorification of clay as a medium.

This one consideration is one of the important meanings that you teach. If we lose sight of what developing this awareness does to people, we have failed. We have become product-centered and that doesn't develop this sensitivity. If you develop this sensitivity, you will become an artist. An artist is one who has developed sensitivity to such a great extent that he

Fig. 32. "Street Scene" (painted by a visually minded 16-year-old adolescent youth). Light and shadow, atmosphere, and visual proportions (determined by the law of perspective) govern this representation.

cannot do other than bring things into harmonious relationships with each other. The aesthetic product is really an outcome of the great sensitivities which we develop. Then to emphasize art in art education would be to me like beginning on the top and working down to the bottom. We should develop the sensitivities, and the art in art education will be an outcome, a necessary outcome, without which we cannot even exist. Do you get what I mean? You should always keep this in mind.

I know you have lots of questions. I could go on indefinitely. I would like to give you also some aspect which may have developed from the book, and this is the sensitivity towards different kinds of experiences, such as visual experiences and haptic experiences. Have you engaged in this? I'd like to tell you a little about it because it's very essential, I think, for finding the needs of students. One student may have predominantly a need for visual experiences [see Figure 32]—he's very much excited by what he sees; while another student's needs may be focused around himself [see Figure 33]. But may I warn you that you will not find these two different types in their extremes. They are only developing in their basic attributes. However, you can differentiate between these two types and stimulate them. In your classroom you will find that most students are in between somewhere, but usually with a preference for the one or the other type of experience. You'll generally find a preference for experiences.

Student: This is an important consideration, I think, but we've discussed it before—haptic and visual children and this preference—and we got into quite a disagreement trying to identify which way a child conceives things when he puts them down on paper. We know the criteria and know the scientific rationale, but we cannot seem to apply it.

Lowenfeld: Yes, now let me clarify, first of all, one misunderstanding which I already derive from what you said. You spoke of children. What do you mean by children? How old?

Fig. 33. "Lying on the Bed" (painted by a haptically minded 17-year-old adolescent girl). Everything is focused around the self. Color has a subjective meaning; so have lights and darks.

343

Student: There were several age groups we tried it on.

Lowenfeld: Tell me the age groups.

Student: I think they were all secondary, beginning with the twelve-year-olds.

Lowenfeld: Well, you see, when we move up to the secondary level, we do not differentiate between ages. However, all children develop their creative activity, especially their picture making, from their own concepts and not from visual experiences or haptic experiences.

LECTURE 27

Secondary Art Education: Meaning of Visual and Haptic Types for Teaching Methods; Realistic/Abstract Art and Artists; Judging Art—Conviction and Sincerity; and Art of Our Time

Now, look at this. This could reflect a visual influence. First, you can see that the artist in this drawing felt more like a spectator. He looked at things. He was especially concerned in drawing a landscape in the lower part. Here we see some of the changing visual conditions: first, their application to perspective. You can see how the house goes into the distance by the diminishing sizes of the windows. This is a changing condition. We also see light and shadows as changing conditions. The house is in the light, it is different in the sunshine from the way it is in the shade. We even see motion—the motion expressed in the trees and in the foliage. You see a certain kind of movement, a clock-spring effect. Here we see another changing condition. So I would say that this is clearly visual. In the other part, in the upper painting, we can no longer see it as clearly. Although we can still say that the individual looks at his world as a spectator, we see a certain involvement, a personal interpretation of what he does in it. But we still have the feeling that the predominant inspiration in the painting is a cold light and the reflection of it on the roofs. You know, these are reflecting colors. Do you see how they change in the light and how they are different in darkness? You can still see some of the changing effects. So the upper part is less visual, although it is still visual.

But may I tell you that I would be perfectly happy in not evaluating drawings as to whether they belong to visual or whether they belong to haptic types. This is merely putting them into a cubbyhole, and I could be accused of teaching you to put people into cubbyholes! So what if I cannot evaluate drawings according to visual or haptic? It doesn't matter. This is not the ultimate reason why I've discussed the two types. I've discussed them in order that we may be able to reach students better through our motivations. Previously, the only motivation which was given in schools was

345

visual. All had to copy nature or to learn perspective and to orient themselves towards seeing, giving a visual presentation, and imitating nature. Because I wanted to break down this tendency, I showed that not all people react visually towards their environment. So, even if you cannot detect the basic experience in a final product, I don't mind. Please don't become compulsive about it.

So what if you are not able to detect it? You are not able to detect all kinds of things in man. Why should you detect visual and haptic? They are only a fraction of our personality. You meet me, and you don't detect whether I'm musical or I'm not musical; but I think my love for music is a very important part of my personality. Can you see it when you look at me? No? So what? But I think I would suffer very greatly if you were to put me into an environment which is without music. If you were to deprive me of any musical experience, you would deprive me of one of my important needs although you can't see it. So I don't give a damn, really, whether you can see that this is visual and this is not visual or haptic—whether or not you can detect visual or haptic tendencies. Of course, you know, when you look at Picasso's "Guitar Player," you will get much more the feeling of being involved and self-centered, not as a spectator but as a participant in the experience. Well, so what? Why should we know what it is? I just don't want to deprive the youngster of the experience of coming to grips with himself, of expressing his real self. I would divert him by saying, "Well, now we are painting a beautiful perspective" or, let's say, "You can see the light and the shadows on the houses." Well, the person may feel frustrated if I were to say that.

We had a student here some years ago who earned his doctorate, Dr. Biggers. You can see his murals at the entrance, left and right, of Burrowes Building. I had him as a student when I taught at Hampton Institute, where I instigated some evening classes. Biggers came to me and said: "I have an urge. I want to paint." I said: "Have you ever done anything before?" He said: "No, I haven't done anything worthwhile—I copied a picture of Lincoln." He pulled out a half-creased copy of a pencil drawing of Abraham Lincoln. But he added immediately—he knew what he wanted: "I don't want to draw landscapes or flowers. I want to draw people. People are close to me." You see, he is one of the few people who knew from the very beginning what inspired him and what he wanted. But ninety-nine percent of our high school population don't know. They are waiting for your inspiration. And if you push the wrong button, you may frustrate them. If I were to have told Biggers, "You are going to paint landscapes," it would have been terrible. Do you see, then, the meaning? It's not that in the final paintings you can detect that he is haptic or he is visual—this is insignificant. It would just mean putting people into another cubbyhole. We have enough cubbyholes—I.Q.'s and I don't know what all—by which we are classified.

So let's forget this kind of evaluation, and let's only think of ways that we can reach people.

Some are reached better by stimulating them concerning their own experiences, their own emotions, their own movements (including actions), and their own feelings which they have when they put the paint on, getting much satisfaction out of the relationship between their ego and what they do. Others are very much inspired by what they see. Some are in between. But we have to reach them all. Therefore, we have always to ask ourselves if we are including both when we motivate our students in high school.

Never place, in the high school situation, a posing model in front of the class and say, "Now we are going to draw it exactly as we see it." That would be bad. Some may have quite a lot of fun in just trying to find out the lights and darks and outlines in developing sensitiveness as you want them to grasp it and get the visual character of it, but the others may be entirely frustrated. You may use a posing model, a posing figure, but give the student the freedom to develop other things that he wants. For instance, you can say: "Well, what does this posing figure suggest to you? For those students who have no ideas of your own, you can get your feeling out of the pose; but I would like us all to think of something. I'm curious to see what this suggests. You may develop your drawing or your sculpture or painting just as you like it; however, you may get your inspiration from here. The final art work doesn't have to look like the pose at all. Take that part which appeals to you most. You may think only of the hands, or you may even think of what this person is thinking about. You may not relate to it at all, or you may get some feeling of openness or ecstasy and put this into an abstract, and this pose only serves as an initial inspiration. Or you may want to draw the posing figure as you see it." They need this wide variety of suggestions. Then guide your pupils according to their own unfolding of creativeness.

You should expect to be attacked on this. Some people will say you are much too vague in what you teach. You should teach step-by-step procedures. Be prepared for such criticism. How would you respond? What would your answer be? Let me take the role of someone who attacks you. I would say: "You know, with your method, students don't learn anything. They don't learn how to draw! They don't even learn proportion. How will we ever get them to draw a human figure with your method?"

Student: Could I say in return?

Lowenfeld: You say what you want to say. Don't ask me. You say what you want to say and what comes to your mind. Don't hold back with anything.

Student: I'd say the students are developing what they know and are most familiar with. They're going on from a point of their own.

Lowenfeld: But don't you see? You're an art teacher; you should teach them how to draw figures.

Student: Art is nothing unless it is interpreted by the artist himself.

Lowenfeld: But if he has no means by which he can interpret it. . . . He should learn to draw the muscles and the figure, then he will know how to interpret something.

Student: His kinesthetic experience of identifying himself with it is more vital to him than his copying it.

Lowenfeld: I don't think he needs to copy if he does something from nature. There's a figure, and I think you should teach him figure drawing.

Student: That's anatomy.

Lowenfeld: That's a part of it. I really believe that you should teach that.

Student: Part of what?

Lowenfeld: Anatomy as part of figure drawing. Why shouldn't he have a little bit of anatomy?

Student: Ah, but . . .

Lowenfeld: He's in high school. He should develop an ability to draw figures.

Student: But then should we take physics also and go into color theories?

Lowenfeld: Well, I don't know about physics. I don't know anything about physics, and I don't think you know anything about physics. So let's remain within our field. I think that you're not teaching him the necessary subject matter. For me, the subject matter is that he should draw; you should teach him perspective, and he should learn to draw figures. With your method he will never learn even the right proportions.

Student: If he cannot see the right proportions, then what difference would it make if he can draw them?

Lowenfeld: You can teach them to him, can't you? Can't you say the head is a sixth of the whole figure and he can measure it? Can't you do that? That's a classical measure which they have used for as far back as we can think—well, let's say probably to the Renaissance, at least. Do you think that was all wrong—what they did? (See, I'm getting the message now.)

Student: To them, it was vital and reassuring that they could reproduce exactly what they saw.

Lowenfeld: Don't you think that it's important for our students today— that they learn to draw figures, that they learn to draw things correctly?

Student: Well, we have the camera now.

Lowenfeld: The camera is something, but that's not free-hand drawing.

Student: Well, then, we could take a picture and project it and copy it. You know what I mean?

Lowenfeld: Well, probably that would be a good thing. I think your students should be able to do that.

Student: It is easier to do it that way.

Lowenfeld: Yes, I really think your students should do that.

Student: But what advantage would it be for them—a mere copying?

Lowenfeld: Well, they would develop some skill, which they don't do in your school with your method. That's what I'm saying.

Student: Oh, yes. Whew! Help me out!

Lowenfeld: You see, I'm doing this on purpose, because I feel that you should learn to defend yourself, your own beliefs. Now, may I answer all questions about my attack, or would someone volunteer? All right.

Second Student: Why should you try to represent something that a camera can do?

First Student: That's what I tried to say.

Second Student: Times have changed. The idea you mentioned of a long time ago about Michelangelo—and they thought that he drew things perfectly.

Lowenfeld: Now may I tell you something which is very basic for any argument? Don't ever put yourself into the defensive position. Don't come forth with negative things. Come forth with positive things. For instance, you should say: "Well, I would have nothing against him drawing the figure; but, you see, if you look at the history of art, you are very narrow. You are focusing on just one period of art in this area of figure drawing—the Renaissance—when people were concerned with realism. Why don't you look at Egyptian art? Or Syrian art? Why don't you look at, let us say, the art of India? Or why don't you look at Gothic art? Why don't you look at the other periods of art? Rembrandt drew a figure entirely differently from Leonardo da Vinci. Leonardo da Vinci drew a figure entirely differently from the Egyptians. The Egyptians drew a figure entirely differently from contemporary artists. Don't you know, exactly as I do, that even van Gogh didn't draw a figure in correct proportions, not even correct perspective for a roof, and he's a great artist. With all the money you have in your pockets you couldn't buy a single van Gogh. So art, apparently, is somewhat different from what you have in your mind. I have given you, now, several examples. So in order that our students develop their own interpretation, I shall not ask them to do it in one fashion only or in a fashion which is not in agreement with their thinking." Do you see? This is how I would answer them.

I would also say: "Now, look how differently people have treated, let us say, flowers. Have you ever seen a flower in an Egyptian mosaic? It doesn't look like a real flower at all. It's more of an ornament. Have you ever seen how van Gogh painted his flower pieces—the sun flowers? Have you seen the sweet way the Dutch painters painted flowers? These are three different concepts, and no one would be able to say which is the greater concept in art. But you want to say it! Do you think you know so much about art that you really can say it?" See, I put myself into the offensive position now. Then I would draw the conclusion. It's this point which I want to develop:

"Art never has been the representation of things. It always has been the representation of experiences which we have with things, and these experiences may change in different periods or epochs. But today we live in a time when I believe it is very essential for democratic thinking that we develop the individual and his own creative potentiality."

Student: In other words, you're saying that, regardless of whatever happens, anytime we're put on the defensive with regard to art, we can always go back to basic principles we believe regarding our philosophy. If we have a philosophy that's strong enough, it stands up in any kind of discussion.

Lowenfeld: It must! Otherwise, it wouldn't be! You see, I believe that there is, in all things which have happened, what we may call a basic truth and this stands up throughout time. Otherwise, it would be long dead, you see? And, of course, we should always base our ideas and actions on those basic truths.

Student: Dr. Lowenfeld, is it not true that a lot of people who would like to draw realistically draw abstractly because they cannot draw a figure realistically?

Lowenfeld: It may be, but it would be the same thing to say: "Is it not true that generally people don't steal because they would be punished when they steal?" Most of the people really would steal? See, you presume that people basically are culprits, that means, they draw abstractly because they can't draw realistically. This is what you presume.

Student: Yes, sir.

Lowenfeld: It's a wrong presumption. Why do you do that?

Student: I've spoken to many people who feel this way.

Lowenfeld: Yes, but probably not artists.

Student: Well, then, what is an artist? Is he a technician or an artist?

Lowenfeld: No, an artist is not a technician. An artist is someone who has the urge to express his relationship to experiences in some medium. On whatever level this may be, it is sincere and truthful; but these are characteristics which we cannot evaluate. No one ever could. May I say this, too. You know that only time screens the truth and sincerity from the untruth and insincerity. I'm referring here to those people who put themselves on a pedestal and say, "Well, this is true art, this is falsification, and so forth." I don't believe it. The older I get, the more I know I'm also subject to wrong judgments.

Student: What is an artist?

Lowenfeld: Look, I'm not interested in evaluating people and grouping people into cubbyholes—into artists and non-artists. It's meaningless to me. The greatest punishment for an individual is that he knows that he's insincere. There is no greater punishment for him. And if one betrays himself by painting abstractly because he wants to get into a pattern of doing it, he knows it better than anyone else knows it. And it will be on his conscience for his whole life if he doesn't change. Do you see? So this is basic. We recently had in a graduate class a very similar discussion in which someone in our class complained when someone else was making a statement about where we stand in art education historically. It was a class in the history of basic philosophies in art education. She was arguing the premise that we still have not developed our philosophy so that it penetrates to the grass roots. She said: "We are really without power because look at the valley. They are still copying and tracing there." And I said: "Do you know that we have a lot of power? The power you have is not in relationship to the effect which you have in the valley. The power depends on how great is your conviction, your own conviction. This is the greatest power. And you know, when your conviction is wobbly and when you are faltering, you break yourself down. Then, you are weak. But your strength is in the inner strength of your philosophy or morality or whatever you have. This is the greatest power you can ever have, and it cannot be defeated by any external force." Do you see my point of view?

Student: Yes, I do, but . . .

Lowenfeld: And that is the same thing for an artist. If he has a conviction to express what he has to express, then he must express it. This is his power. And if it is not true, it will falter, you know, when challenged by any external influences.

Student: What sets up the criteria of a good painting?

Lowenfeld: I'm not interested in that.

Student: Well, then, of all these paintings that were exhibited or put in the exhibit, why were certain ones chosen?

Lowenfeld: Because certain people who have experience in the field of art felt that some artists expressed themselves with greater sincerity than others expressed.

May I say, to begin with, that these people may be entirely wrong, even if it is Edith Harper. That is nothing against Edith Harper. I like her very much, you know, but I want to say this: I also have great respect for the great German poet, Goethe. Have you ever heard of him? I hope you have. In Germany, he is regarded as probably the greatest spirit that has been created, not only a genius in words but also a genius in many other things— a great philosopher, indeed. You know what he said about Gothic art? He said, "Gothic art is barbaric." Do you know why? Because Goethe lived during a period when the spirit of classicism abounded. He got so involved in the beauty of the Renaissance, in Greek art, that he found Gothic art to be crude and barbaric, deprived of the beautiful setting, of Romantic form; because in the Gothic period, pure expressionism came forth and ugly, barbaric forms developed—the Isenheim Altar by Grunewald, for example. Do you know Grunewald, the very expressive German painter? Now that's Goethe, not Edith Harper. And Schubert sent to Goethe the great song, the

Erlkönig. And Goethe returned it with a few words saying, "Oh, I don't find this composition worthwhile for acceptance"—or something of a similar nature. He was wrong in many things, and so were many others. Why should I not be wrong? And why should the judges not be wrong? I'm against judging, personally. I'm for exhibiting, but when we have such a mass of products that we cannot show everything, we have to make a crude selection. Do you see what I mean?

Basically, we all have the right to create. And whether one is on this level or on another level is no one's business. I have to come to grips with myself, and the highest reward which I can get for that is to be in equilibrium with what I do, to feel that this is mine and I'm here—a unity in what I do. Whether the world, after I'm dead, will consider this as ultimate or as something which is worthwhile to remain is not my concern. I'm doing what I can do. And in light of this, all judging really becomes a superficial act or just a by-product. We know van Gogh couldn't sell a single painting while he was alive. Imagine! There were judges then, too, judges like Edith Harper, you know. Poor van Gogh couldn't get a single painting sold—the desperate letters he wrote—and he still believed in what he did with such a vehemence that he makes us still believe today and probably for a hundred and even five hundred years after.

So this is the point, and it is also applicable to teaching. When every one of you can develop some of this conviction, it will be felt by your students. But if you have none, you will have no influence. This is the basic issue. You see, there is a wide range of sensitivity to these problems. So free yourself from established patterns. Judging art work is an established pattern, and we attach too much significance to it, indeed. One can be way up there and may still not be seen and felt. But the most important thing is to believe in one's own self and what one does. See, this is of a very, very deep spiritual nature. Do you have any other questions?

Student: Why is it that the more creative a person seems to be, the more he turns away from nature and becomes abstract?

Lowenfeld: This is not necessarily so. Let us not be one-sided. You see, there is a great danger in every period which is strong in its forms of expression that an academy will be created, a cliché or a sameness of expression. Presently in art life, the so-called action painting is the strong form of expression. You know what action painting is? It's a form of abstract painting in which the artist feels guided by a brush stroke and the action which he produces. One brush stroke follows another brush stroke as a logical consequence. It doesn't need to be a brush stroke. It can just as well be the finger, or it can be the dripping, or it can be the sponge, or any approach. A logic is created by the way one interweaves with the other into a kind of action.

Some other painters are not satisfied with just this interweaving of patterns—that one brush stroke logically develops out of the other—but have the urge also to hold onto some emotion in this kind of sequence. For instance, as you know, I believe the paintings of Dr. Pappas are great paintings of subjective feelings because they affect me very much. To the naked eye, let us say—to one who is probably not very much acquainted with them and not quite sensitized to them—they may look like action paintings; that means, he just paints and develops a pattern out of his brush strokes. This is not quite true, because Dr. Pappas, according to what he says, is always bound up with a certain feeling towards a certain sensation—whether this sensation is the atmosphere, let's say, of religious symbols which you have in a church environment, or the atmosphere which you have in spring—and out of this he develops vigor, emotions, color, and the relationship of shapes to each other, although they have no similarity to the shapes or forms which are contained either in church or in spring.

But, to answer your question, often a period of time develops a certain preference—a fashion, may I say—for a certain type of painting. Then, a feeling is created, especially in young people, in those who are affected by this art, that they also have to be in the avant-garde—that is, thinking within the framework of the very latest creations. Then, some kind of an adherence to it occurs, but not an adherence from the inside. I personally believe that any sincere relationship which you may establish with nature, whether expressed through action or abstract or symbolic or realistic painting, will always have its place. And we should not remain one-sided.

I believe one of the great advantages in the period of our time is that, actually, we are very unique. The art world has never been as tolerant as it is today. If you go to the Museum of Modern Art, you will see abstract, symbolic, stylized, realistic, surrealistic—all kinds of paintings—on one wall. You could not do this during the Renaissance. You would have seen on the wall maybe fifty paintings, and you would have had difficulty in differentiating which painting belonged to whom. They were all Florentine or from so-and-so's school. Well, today we accept them all, even the naive and primitive ones. They also have their place, and this is great.

SECTION III
Art Education Therapy

LECTURE 28
Therapeutic Aspects of Art Education: Psychotic-Neurotic Considerations

---

The definition of a neurosis depends upon one's background and the school which one has attended. It has also changed during these past years, so I'll give you various definitions, referring to where they come from and to what is involved.

Today, with our knowledge in the area of psychology, we no longer differentiate clearly between a neurosis and a psychosis. We simply say that a psychosis is a severe neurosis; that means, a neurosis and a psychosis are on a continuum. The school which I attended in Vienna many years back very clearly differentiated between a neurosis and a psychosis, calling a neurosis a functional disturbance while calling a psychosis an organic disturbance. In a way, I like this differentiation—if it were true, you know. But the more we learn, the more we also know that there is no real distinction. However, we may ultimately come out with a statement that all of these disturbances are chemical. You know what I mean by chemical? It means that apparently something in the brain lacks certain nourishment, that there are certain imbalances of, maybe, nutrition (in a wider, a broader, sense of nature), and this imbalance causes disturbances.

However, the school that I attended, which was close to the Freudian school, taught that a neurosis usually is caused by some childhood trauma, a traumatic experience. A traumatic experience is an emotional experience of a severe nature which not only disturbs the proper functioning of your reactions but, indeed, becomes traumatic, especially when one's consciousness is no longer able to deal with it. It becomes buried in the subconscious and then goes on in the mind, something like a disturbance. I referred to it last time or sometime ago as a disturbance in the sequence of the development of an individual—let's say, one's emotional development, which is very different and separate from one's mental development. Let me explain it to you. This should not be considered as the only explanation, because there are various explanations; but it may be the most plausible explanation. In view of the fact that Freud considered psychoanalytic treatment possible

355

only with neurotic cases and not with psychotic cases, he, too, made the very same distinction between a neurosis and a psychosis. You see, if there were no distinction whatsoever, then we could apply the same treatment all the way through—let us say, a more intense treatment with the severe cases and a less intense treatment for less severe cases—if this continuum theory were true. You understand? Nevertheless, I believe our schools throughout the United States today believe in this continuum.

Some time ago—I believe two or three years ago—there was quite a discussion in *Life* magazine about the various definitions of a neurosis.[11] The various schools of thought came out; and it was rather unclear (especially in view of the letters to the editor) as to which definition was actually the correct one because there were psychiatrists of great reputation who disagreed with *Life*'s interpretation of neurosis. There were others who agreed with the article and who counterattacked some of the letters to the editor. I don't know whether you remember this or whether you followed it through.

At any rate, let me explain it as I would according to my own experiences and background. Think of human development, let's say, as a kind of architecture, a building, childhood being the base (probably somewhat like the bottom of a pyramid) with little that is on top. When you consider the intensity and degree of development that takes place in human beings, and since the intensity of this development is greatest in early childhood, childhood would therefore be the broadest part of this structure. You see, we learn most in the very early stages, we are most flexible in the very early stages, and the very early stages are certainly concerned with developing attitudes and character formation much more so than later on. It's here that the subconscious and the conscious are much more unified than later on. Our reactions are more direct in early childhood, not being carried out by reason or by intellectualization. Our reactions are also most definite and intense at this age. The degree of learning, the factor of learning, is also greatest in the early stages. During the first three years, the child learns to master a language almost completely. He learns to know reactions; he learns how to reason; he learns how to handle himself and how to react to outside experiences—to his environment. This all takes place in three years. Imagine what trouble you would go through in mastering a foreign language if you were just now to start learning it. If you were to have three years, you would never come as far as a child would in three years in the complete mastering and understanding of the language. This is quite apart from the fact that the child, in addition to the mastering of the language, actually develops from a completely isolated human being to one who relates himself

11. "Return to Sanity in 12 Weeks," *Life*, 15 October 1956, pp. 149–156; "New Avenues to Sick Minds," *Life*, 22 October 1956, pp. 119–124; Eric Hodgins, "The Search Has Only Started," *Life*, 22 October 1956, pp. 126–142.

to his environment. So the most fundamental changes take place in the very early beginning. That's why I say I consider childhood as the broadest base.

As we go up—it's like a pyramid, you see—as we go more towards senility, which is late and which varies according to individuals, the amount of new knowledge which we take in grows slimmer and slimmer, until in the end we may not be able to accumulate new knowledge at all and are satisfied merely to digest what we already have. So let's consider this as a certain part or stage of our life.

Now what happens, you remember, is that a traumatic experience occurs. Some of the foundation is not ours; that means, some of our reasoning and some of our experience no longer is based upon anything because it is deprived by a traumatic experience—a shock which has occurred at some time. It does not allow the child now to build upon this foundation and develop his intellect and his emotional relationships in a normal manner. So we have a hole here somehow. The child continues to grow, but still there is a hole there; and as the child grows, of course, the outer appearance remains the same. That means the appearance is there, but there is a hole in the center. And this hole may cause difficulty at some point. If all this additional growth and development becomes too heavy, if emotions and intellect are too intense, the likelihood for a neurosis is greater than if you live a naive life, where the pyramid (one's development) is very slim to begin with.

As the child develops and if this development is heavy, the structure may crumble because there is a hole in it. Then the neurosis starts. Yet, we don't know what makes it crumble and what causes this. The nature of the psychoanalytic treatment popularly expressed would be to go back and find out where the hole exists and fill it in. Actually, this is the nature of any psychoanalytic treatment. That means, you start with the present experiences of the individual (of the patient) in a relaxed situation, as you know, and the analyst tries now to use all his knowledge and understanding of psychoanalytic theory to trace farther and farther back to certain connections which existed and which may have brought about a traumatic experience, and possibly to see if there might not have been certain relationships involving the child which made the traumatic experience possible. Do I make myself clear in that?

A traumatic experience does not take place out in the open air. It only is possible when there already exists some kind of a shaken confidence, a shaken personality. Such a shaken personality may exist as a result of a fatherly relationship or feelings toward mother or all kinds of very intricate relationships which did not permit the child to develop securely. Let's say, in a certain period of insecurity, a shock occurred, created by some type of an experience which may have been an accident or a bad dream at night or awakening after a dream with which the child could not deal and when the child was still in a state of fear and had no one who could help him to realize the situation. Such a traumatic experience is in addition to—and I would like to emphasize that—*is in addition to* the feeling of insecurity. Never is a traumatic experience created without this feeling of insecurity or the readiness for it.

Well, a vacuum was created, let us say, in the past; and so the psychoanalyst now tries to trace back through some configuration the relationships between mother and father or brothers or other things, and, of course, sexual relationships or sexual traumata which may have occurred in early childhood. He finds this, and now he brings it into the consciousness of the individual. You see, we cannot deal with the subconscious because the subconscious, by its very nature, is something out of our reach. The psychoanalyst brings us back and confronts us with these experiences in terms of realistic occurrences and happenings, explaining the relationships within ourselves and to our environment. Thus, he fills in all this which has probably been damaged or omitted in our structure. Now we can build upon a firm foundation which previously did not exist.

This is called a functional disturbance, because we can never in a neurosis find any organic damage to the brain or any organic damage to anything which relates to the brain. So, we consider this merely as a functional disturbance, because our everyday function is disturbed. You might be afraid to go out on the street, or you might be afraid to deal with certain situations. You would feel insecure; and, therefore, you could not engage in certain things. You would be suffering from certain characteristics which would be in the way of your development. That is why a neurosis is called a functional disorder. Now I correct myself. Now we have discovered that there are no discernible organic defects in some psychoses, do you see? We know, for instance, that according to an encephalogram and all of our analyses that we cannot find anything in certain schizophrenic (which we certainly consider psychotic) patients. So the theory of functional and organic disturbances has fallen to pieces on the basis that we haven't been able to find any evidence of organic disturbance.

Now, I happen to disagree with this, and I may be open to all kinds of criticism. I will simply say that I do not believe that what we now know is the final evidence. I really believe that in the future we will be able to trace some chemical disturbances, organic disturbances, in psychotic patients. We just have not yet the means by which we can trace them. I base everything on my many experiences, you know. I have probably attended as many lectures on psychosis at the university as anyone with a degree, but I have not engaged in it professionally, you understand. I am intensely interested, of course, on the basis of my direct contacts and relationships, and I was very happy when I saw in the last congressional report about the convention of psychiatrists—an international convention in Zurich—that this attitude has been expressed generally by psychiatrists: they expect to be able to find some chemical changes in psychotic disturbances. This again would lead us back to our previous notion of a division into functional and organic diseases or disturbances. But we have no proof, as yet.

Would you like to ask some questions? Would you like to engage in some discussion at this point? I would be very glad to do so, especially with the people from the psychology department who probably have something to say about it.

Student: I was wondering how you arrived at that—some sort of faith, or what?

Lowenfeld: No, it's not purely on faith. It is based on the entirely different types of reactions which psychotic individuals and neurotic individuals have. A neurotic individual reacts completely normal, except that certain emotional tendencies or reactions are exaggerated. The reaction of fear may be exaggerated. The reaction of inferiority may be exaggerated. Normal reactions are simply exaggerated and get in the way of further development. Now, in psychotic individuals, you do not have normal reactions exaggerated. You have odd reactions introduced which we would not find in normal individuals.

Student: Such as?

Lowenfeld: The inability, as we shall discuss it later, to distinguish between reality and fantasy or the inability to—well, an odd body image— the inability to distinguish or to predict a certain behavior when going through body motions; for example, the experiment which Angyal made with schizophrenics.[12] The experiment he made involved exposing schizophrenic individuals to certain actions. He found that the predicted behavior—to predict a certain weight, let us say, which we certainly would always know—was completely absent in schizophrenic individuals. What happens to us when we see there is a heavy stone? We lift the heavy stone, and as we lift it, we already contract our muscles in prediction of what will happen; that means, we extend our body image to the heavy load which we are predicting to lift. Now, as we lift, we lift with the expectation of a heavy load. In the schizophrenic individual, the predictive behavior of body movement is generally absent or is significantly absent; that is, the schizophrenic individual does not project himself towards the outside. He cannot even differentiate between his own self and his body, his muscles. You see his inability to reason.

The schizophrenic's logic is usually called, or is referred to as, paleologic. Do you know the term? You know what Paleolithic means? Paleolithic is the first culture which we had during the Stone Age—very primitive persons. An expression of paleologic is then a very primitive logic which is like this: Switzerland loves freedom. I love freedom. I am Switzerland.

12. Andreas Angyal, "The Experience of the Body–Self in Schizophrenia," *Archives of Neurology and Psychiatry*, May 1956.

LECTURE 29
Therapeutic Aspects of Art Education: A Case Study of Virginia, a Neurotic Child

The child was seven years old. She was probably institutionalized at this time because the mother could no longer handle her. The child was just reacting oddly. She was throwing herself on the bed, crying for no reason, going into tantrums, and displaying behavior with which the mother could no longer deal. The child did not follow orders, but was usually too frightened to follow orders. She didn't want to go out on the street and was generally afraid. Such symptoms made Mother bring the child to the institution.

The child first was observed at the institution. Later the psychiatrist there tried to give her hypnotic treatments to try to find out whether, in a hypnotic state of mind, she might react differently so that he could get certain clues which might lead him to some of the causes of the child's strange behavior. The child was also given some shock treatments later on. At that time shock treatments were still considered dangerous because they were administered by metal bars, or the child was given insulin which was introduced intravenously. The shock was a severe one. Control of the mind was also something which was not as well controlled as, usually, shock treatments are today. This child did not really react to them—oh, a very little, and only for a short time—and so the shock treatments were interrupted and not continued.

Psychoanalytic treatment was also tried with the child, but, as you know, with children psychoanalytic treatment is a very difficult thing, very difficult, because the reactions of the children are not like the reactions of adults. The child doesn't differentiate between reasoning and fantasy. The normal child has some characteristics which usually can be found in schizophrenic individuals, such as being unable to differentiate between fantasy or dream and reality. This is often quite a normal sign of childhood.

When I first saw Virginia, her reactions were queer; and, may I say, they were not typical for any neurotic patient, because neurotic patients usually have no really overt behavioral reactions which we would immediately distinguish as untempered or odd. But Virginia had them, and still was

360

VIRGINIA (NEUROTIC)

considered a neurotic patient. When Virginia was left alone, she read; she was a very intelligent child. She learned to read. She was good looking and normal looking in her behavior. She was just sitting always by herself and did not want to be disturbed.

She had one peculiarity. She liked her dresses very much and was overly careful with them. Her dresses always looked very, very neat. Wrinkles in her dresses disturbed her. She liked dresses very much and was very much interested in them. When a new child came, she approached the child, with dresses in mind, and said, "Where did you get it?" or "It is a pretty dress," and was very much fascinated with dresses. This I say because it has some bearing upon her problem later on.

When Virginia was surprised by some kind of order or demand, she reacted queerly. For instance, when you said, "Virginia, can you blow your nose?" Virginia would become somewhat frightened, because, for her, blowing her nose meant a complete change in her present situation. It would mean: "Where do I have my handkerchief? Where can I get it? Shall I blow my nose?" Or, "I can't find it." She was confused about this whole situation, so she was certainly not reacting normally.

If we said, for instance, "Virginia, could you bring me a glass of water?" She would reply: "A glass of water? Why? Why should I bring a glass of water? Why? No, I can't; I can't; I can't," and that was the end of it. But if you were to sit close to Virginia and say: "Oh, I'm so hot today and I'm so thirsty. I really would like to have a glass of water. I feel so dry. Outside, to the left of the door, there's a faucet. You just have to turn it on. There is a glass there, too. I would love to have a glass of water. Oh, Virginia could bring me a glass of water, I'm sure. Oh, Virginia, could you bring me a glass of water?" Virginia would say "Yes" and would go. This is not typical of neurotic behavior, not at all, because it's a kind of an odd, overt behavior. But, as we shall see later on, Virginia was still classified as a neurotic case, a severe neurotic case.

This means that, whenever she was brought out of her present balance, she had to adjust to a number of new situations. Adjustment to new situations was probably her greatest trouble, because there she was blocked. If you told her, "Virginia, blow your nose," she would say: "Why? Why should I blow my nose? Why doesn't John blow his nose? No, I can't blow my nose." She would respond like this and would stop. Then you would say: "Sniff, sniff, I have to blow my nose. When we have a nose cold, we just have to blow our nose. In my pocket I have a handkerchief—in my pocket. Virginia has a handkerchief also, in her pocketbook, but probably Virginia just hasn't taken her handkerchief out of her pocketbook and she has to blow her nose. Virginia, couldn't you blow your nose?" "Yes," she would say. You see, it was a kind of conditioning that was necessary, a gradual conditioning that was needed, for the acceptance of a new situation. This acceptance of a new situation was leading to an adjustment to the new situation, and that was the desired effect.

Actually, for those who are in art education, we always do some of this conditioning in our art motivations with normal children. We try to put the child into a situation and make him or her identify with the situation so intensely that the child goes through the experience and accepts the experience and then portrays the experience out of a feeling of self-identification. Some children—even normal children—just cannot immediately identify with a situation and, therefore, are blocked when you ask them to express a certain experience.

Virginia was blocked even in a normal situation so that we no longer can speak of her as normally adjusted. We speak of the abnormal adjustment which was necessary for her. In a way, then, her behavioral reaction was similar to a tantrum. Do you see? A tantrum, then, should also be considered as an overt behavioral reaction. Therefore, we should correct a little bit our notion that neuroses are not physical and are not shown in overt behavior, as we usually read in our textbooks, because children who cannot accept new situations and thus withdraw into a tantrum also use an escape mechanism as a means to show their inability to face new situations.

We call a mechanism which is always inserted whenever we cannot face the present situation or adjust to a new situation an escape mechanism. For instance, if a child who is peacefully at play with her doll is told, "Now, Mary, you have to go to bed; put your doll away; you have to go to bed; quickly! quickly!" the child all of a sudden has to adjust from playing with the doll, and being intensely occupied with the doll, to going to bed. Well, this means quite a serious adjustment. The child, who is much more intensely concerned with this obligation, cannot reason why she has to go to bed now, and therefore escapes into a kind of mechanism which does not meet the new situation but which is only inserted out of a lack of adjustment. That is a tantrum. Mary may go into a tantrum and may start crying and may not face the situation of going to bed and of not being able to continue playing with her doll. So, you see, we call this an escape mechanism.

Well, with Virginia, it was similar. When Virginia was told, "Go and get a glass of water," she could not immediately adjust to the new situation, which is a normal situation but which called for her to get up and move. "Where? To the door? Where then? Where's the faucet? A glass of water? No, I can't, I can't." Do you see? This is a complex situation of adjustment for an individual who is very much wrapped up in her own thoughts. Therefore, she escaped by using a mechanism which could also have been a tantrum for her, but she just established another kind of escape mechanism: "Why? Why? Why?" This was her escape mechanism which she inserted until she came to a reaction—reaction meaning usually for her to come to a standstill, namely, that she could not go on. So, in this way, Virginia's adjustment was blocked. However, sometimes she said "Yes," when she could face the situation.

In her drawings, this inability to adjust to new situations was clearly shown. Oh, she loved to draw, by the way. You didn't have to encourage her very much; in fact, she doodled a lot. Whenever she drew, her drawings were repetitions of stereotypes such as you can see here [Figure 34a]. These are not five girls. These are repetitions of the same figure. You understand when I say these are not five girls? It means that Virginia did not establish any relationship among the five girls when she drew them. On the contrary, she simply filled the page with the five girls. This is only one of the pages which Virginia drew. She, indeed, drew pages and pages with the same thing that you see here. This doesn't mean many girls. It simply means the repetition of the same figure which she drew again and again. This is only a cutout of a large sheet, which simply shows how repetitious she got. You can also see here that she repeated the same kind of symbols, namely, a triangle for the body with some belt-like symbol in the center, the same kind of head with the same kind of symbols for eyes, nose, and mouth in all of the figures, a few strokes for hair, and the same kind of legs and feet representations.

Since it is always a sign of flexibility when an individual can adjust to new situations in his drawings, we try then to start from the level of the individual; namely, to make the stereotype alive. It is then our task as teachers, or we may call them clinicians, to take this stereotype, which is clearly expressed as a desire by the child, by Virginia, to escape from certain experiences, and to make this stereotype alive. How can we make it alive? Well, we'll have to find out. First, we have to observe Virginia's behavior and reactions. Of course, you have to study her case history and know some of her past from that. Then you study her reactions by following her and seeing how she reacts—how she sits in the garden or whatever she does.

Virginia loved to sit in the garden, and she always chose the same spot, namely, on the bench under a tree in the institution's garden. So the story with which I tried to motivate her was, "Virginia is sitting on a bench under a tree." How would you do it? How would you motivate? Well, this is not simple; and, may I say, she did not draw anything in response to the motivation after the first time, but you just have to do it again and again. So I sat many times with Virginia before I even suggested that she draw something. The motivation was such that I talked to myself, "May I sit here?" To talk in the third person often is very conducive to the adjustment of a neurotic patient, inasmuch as the first person or the second person easily shocks him when you approach the individual directly. So I said: "Oh, I love to sit on a bench. I just love to sit in the shade of the tree. All the benches are under the tree. I know Virginia loves to sit on a bench under the tree. I know Virginia always likes to sit on this spot. I know Virginia likes to sit on the bench. I know Virginia loves to sit on the bench in the shade under the tree,

Fig. 34. Drawings by an emotionally maladjusted 11-year-old girl.

(*a*) Inflexible schematic repetitions.
(*b*) "Sitting Under a Tree." No spatial correlations.
(*c*) "Picking Strawberries." First correlation with environment.
(*d*) "Picking Strawberries." Second phase of direct connection of arm to berry.
(*e*) "Swinging on Rings." Greater awareness of body action.
(*f*) "Picnic Out of Doors." Profile is introduced.

VIRGINIA (NEUROTIC)

(g) "Family." Freedom of action and spatial correlation show adjustive effect.
(h) "Dancing Around a Flagpole." Notice spatial conflict between group and pole.
(i) "Our House Burns." Spontaneous expression of oppressing past experience, with the effect of final release.
(j) "My Best Sunday Dress."
(k) "Dancing Around a Tree." Correct spatial correlations of the completely adjusted child.

365

because it's cooler here. I love it here, too. I know Virginia loves it, too, because it's cooler on the bench under the tree." You may feel that this is very silly, but it is the way an individual can easily become conditioned to a situation and accept the situation. Well, then I said, "Good-bye," and left. And Virginia remained there all by herself.

Another time I did the very same thing until I was recognized by her— "I'm the person who comes here and loves to sit on the bench under the tree"—and I could easily present to her a tablet of paper and say: "I know Virginia also loves to draw. Virginia would love to sit and to draw how she sits on a bench under the tree." This was the drawing Virginia did [see Figure 34b].

As you can readily see, this drawing is approximately from the stage which we would call the pre-schematic stage; because here we have a dispersion of objects in space—things are not related to one another. Virginia was thinking in these terms: "There is a tree; there is a bench; and there am I." But neither is Virginia sitting on the bench, nor is the bench under the tree. These spatial relationships are not yet conceived of because they represent a higher level of adjustment. They would indicate the awareness of Virginia as being a part of a larger whole which at that time had not yet occurred to her. She was still too much bound up with her own self. Encouraged by my suggestion, Virginia loved the bench. The bench and the trees and Virginia— now there are three items which clearly occurred to her; and the fourth, the representation, shows this. May I say, there might be all kinds of other interpretations of this drawing; but as I said in the very beginning, we only draw our conclusions from the configurations which are directly and visually perceivable. So we would say there is a tree schema which is not much different from that of a five-and-a-half-year-old child, a five-year-old child, or a six-year-old child. And there is a bench schema which is not much different from that of a six-year-old child. There is a drawing of a figure which is not much different from that of a six-year-old child. Here, in Virginia's drawing, we have clearly the drawing schema of a five-year-old child; as you notice, it's a very nice schema. After Virginia reacted to such a complex situation, I tried to go really more into details; because this complex situation would not lend itself to a further realization of the ego, an extension of the ego to the environment, which is mainly needed for Virginia.

So, first of all, you have to establish a certain security within one's own self. And you have to find out about the child's frame of reference which you can extend. A frame of reference was easily established because Virginia loved food. She loved to go into the institution's garden and pick strawberries. So in the same way as I found her sitting on the bench under a tree, I found her also picking strawberries. You often can introduce a greater consciousness of an action by withholding the action or by trying to delay the action of the individual—to inhibit the action or to put a stumbling block in the way of the individual to make this action more conscious to the individual. This was done when Virginia was bending down picking a strawberry. I was holding her back a little bit, saying: "Oh, there is a beautiful one. Could you pick this one? This is beautiful. Oh, Virginia would love to have the strawberry. There is a big one." I actually was holding her a little bit so that she had to stretch out her arms. As a result, she made this drawing [see Figure 34c]. You can see several things here by comparing this drawing with the first one. I would like for you to try to find out what happened here. What do you see first?

Student: First, there is the arm with a joint or something like a joint—anyway, a downward extension of the arm.

Lowenfeld: Well, first of all, you have the extension of the arm. May I say that this extension was only introduced later on, not immediately. When I gave a pad to Virginia, which was the same as with Camilla [see Lecture 31], it was the sign that she now should draw. Virginia drew the figure without the arms. But what is most interesting is that she introduced a dress here; or, in other words, she changed her schema. In children's drawings, a child's concept formation is called a schema, which, by repetition, is used time and again. Here she completely deviated from her schema, departing from her previous schema. This is often done on the basis of an experience and also on the basis of a disturbance. Virginia was very much disturbed here, and therefore she was thrown off her usual escape mechanism which served her as a balance. She was irritated, and this irritation was clearly expressed in the change of her schema which we know from past drawing experiences. Visually, it is clearly discernible by the change of the schema of her dress. Everything else in her schema remained as it was.

When I saw her disturbance, I said: "Oh, if Virginia cannot pick the strawberry, we'll just have to go home." This meant another disturbance, and at that time Virginia made this elongated arm which is actually another attached arm, you understand? This is no elbow. It's simply an attached arm which is leading down with some kind of a disturbed motion, down to the berry. The berries were drawn previously. This was a great triumph. First of all, Virginia could deviate from her previously stereotyped schemata. As soon as an individual can change his stereotypes, we see the first sign in a neurotic individual for a successful therapy; because we see that the child is able to adjust to external stimuli. The more difficult this adjustment is, then the longer it will probably take in order to arrive at some success.

At that time, I still was concerned mainly with the establishment of greater flexibility within the individual. It must be noted that any neurotic behavior results in a greater inflexibility toward external stimuli caused by, let's say, a question mark. We didn't know what it was, and we didn't want to engage in any inferences at this point and say what it might have been. We didn't know what it was, and the case history didn't really point out anything of real significance. We had to find out if this greater flexibility would lead to other things, to other forms of expression, and to greater freedom and a greater acceptance of certain situations which we may call external stimuli. Now, what would you do after this? Simply as an art teacher, what would you do?

Student: I would motivate her for a growing awareness towards some of the things she has eliminated, such as maybe motivating her for something where she uses her hands.

Lowenfeld: Right, correct. I would certainly increase in her the feeling of extension, of picking up something with the use of her arms. It is very good to remain with one topic over a period of time and not to shift from one to another abruptly.

Well, I went again with her several times. By the way, I don't have all of her drawings. I will show you only the main steps. I went with her again into the institution's garden, but this time I said, "Well, we'll take a basket along." Do you know why? Because I wanted to make her feel that she was carrying something. I said at that time, "Virginia is going to put the berries into the basket, because in the evening we will get cream." She loved cream and berries, so that was a great stimulus. I said, "We will now pick the most beautiful berries, and in the evening we will eat them with cream." The drawing which Virginia did was this one [see Figure 34d]. You see, this is probably in one way a regression and in another way a progression. Can you find out why we call it a regression?

Student: For instance, the hair, the feet, and . . .

Lowenfeld: Yes. Well, let's say she has gone back to the belt idea. She again has established her stereotyped schema, but even her stereotyped schema is lacking something, mainly the feet and the hair.

And how do you see progress in this? Because she brought the basket in relationship to her action, to her arm; and, most of all, from the very beginning there's now attachment. She was thinking that the arm has to come from the shoulder and has to pick up the berry right from the beginning.

You see, this caused in her so much excitement to begin with that she went right back to the previous schema, because now she only had on her mind, from the beginning, how to get her arm down to the berry. Even here you can see a line at the end of the arm like a pincer, which almost looks like the grasping of a berry—although of this we are not quite sure. At any rate, there is some kind of intention here which shows that there is a disturbance, as indicated by the one line which holds the berry. The feet are likely forgotten because the child reacted not to standing but rather to picking. The feet no longer appear as part of the schema. And the hair most probably is omitted because the child just wanted to get to the arm and get over with the experience, the faster the better.

That's a naive explanation, but this is the explanation in which we should engage and not in anything else. Do you understand now why I'm so much against any inferences? Because there are art teachers who get a drawing into their hands and say: "This child is——," or "This is a sign of——," or "This child is sexually this and that." They draw inferences which are completely based on dilettantish knowledge. I think we should not engage in anything of that kind. That's why I emphasize time and again that we think of our therapeutic approach as basically an extension of our teaching. Therefore, I call it art education therapy, because it is an extension of art teaching. Now, Virginia went through the experience of picking the berry in which she related herself to the ground as you can see here. Picking up a berry also meant that she had to come down to the ground with her arm.

I went through all kind of pains to catch her in certain situations which she loved to do, until I decided that it would be better if we remained with normal exercises which she loved to do on the apparatus—such as the swings, the rings, the slides, and so forth—which we had on the grounds of the institution. At that time, I believe Virginia liked me already; that means, she was not at all disturbed by me. On the contrary—when I was standing around the apparatus on the grounds of the institution, she came there and simply, without saying anything, put herself on the swings and, even more so, on the rings. Once when she was swinging on the rings, I did the same. I was swinging on the rings, but I made the rings higher than they usually are. You see, the rings are usually lower. I adjusted the rings higher because I wanted to make it more difficult for Virginia to swing; it meant pulling herself up on the rings. It meant also putting a little stumbling block in her way. This resulted in a very interesting drawing, as you can see here [see Figure 34e]. Basically, you can see that Virginia still has the schema which she had in the beginning. It is the triangular shape of the dress, only she now uses maybe a little greater care, especially in the sleeves. But the important thing is that in this drawing, for the very first time, she established an ordinary relationship to the swings; she recognized that she is that far from the ground. Yes?

Student: What's the time perspective of this?

Lowenfeld: The time of this drawing is about six weeks after the first drawing. The whole therapy occurred over a period of a year, over a year. That's a long period, you know, with a session almost every day, but never more than two days apart. So this is a long time, you understand; and it's only possible in an institutionalized situation. But we can learn much from it for application to the normal child.

I said then: "Well, Virginia has to pull herself up this time so that she will be better able to swing. That's hard. I wonder where Virginia feels that most? Will she feel it in her arms or in her legs? Where does she feel it? Oh,

I have to pull myself up, too. It's difficult. I don't have the power. I feel it in my muscles. Now let's swing. OK, let loose now. Let's swing again." These were stimulations that I gave her, always talking more to myself than actually talking directly to Virginia. Then, Virginia made this drawing [Figure 34e].

You can see here a number of things. First, you don't see any regression. You see only some progress; a more detailed concept formation indicates progress. A greater realization of environment is another example of progress. You see that here Virginia actually bent her arms. Now this is not merely an attached other arm as it was in the beginning. You can clearly see it. Out of a feeling of predicted excitement, she drew the arms very long. She elongated them, because she became emotionally involved with the pulling up. Exaggeration is quite acceptable even in normal children. If you look exactingly, you can see fingers—but not the exact number. She drew three fingers, as you can see; but she became aware of holding herself, which was also emphasized in the motivation because I had said: "Oh, I wonder what would happen if I would now all of a sudden let go? I would fall down. Let's hold on to the rings." This was additional motivation. The rings were attached to her. This was a change. She didn't realize the change; but she did realize that there were various links in the chain, which she indicated in her drawing. This was great progress on her part. Otherwise, the schema was kept as it was. We went through many more of these exercises on the apparatus—on the swings.

When I saw that Virginia was reacting to herself so intensely after about three months, I thought: "The time has come when we could introduce a relationship to other people." I thought I would be the best person to whom she could relate. So, I started to bring a ball and play ball with her. Now, again, I motivated her in the usual manner, saying, "It's nice to play ball." I talked also about how to catch a ball and how to throw a ball: I couldn't catch a ball if I had a fist; I couldn't throw a ball if I couldn't stretch out my hands; and so forth. The drawing which resulted from this experience included the biggest change. First of all, Virginia introduced pattern and design in her dress. She represented my pants by a disturbed dress and included buttons, which were also an indication of my clothes. In drawing herself, she basically kept to the same schema—a triangular affair with lines for the belt—but she then put a design into it. This was all on her own. I did not talk of design at all. I did not even mention the word design.

This is an example of good teaching in art education from which we can learn; namely, that *perfection grows with the urge for expression and the freedom for it.* We can often learn from abnormal individuals much more than we can learn from normal ones. Here was a clear indication that, apparently, Virginia felt freer—or had established more freedom in her own handling of her own self—and, therefore, developed a greater urge to put more details into whatever she expressed. Now, she no longer attached the fingers. Although there was only a kind of a zigzag line at the end of the arms, it was a clear indication that she felt there were fingers. The fingers were part of the hand, although not at all clearly delineated. The one hand—the catching hand or, rather, the throwing hand—was stretched out; and the other was in a horizontal position. She differentiated very carefully between the one and the other, which, on her part, showed a great flexibility. It also shows a move from one stage to another.

If you know the normal development of children in their spatial concept, you would also know that she had now moved from the base line concept (which is the simplest spatial concept, that of simply belonging to the ground—I'm on the ground, the tree is on the ground, we are all on the ground) to a concept in which she discovered the plane. She documented this by putting grass on it. She even became sensitive to the texture of grass, which she indicated by little lines. The trees were growing out of the ground. Indeed, she showed them even at different distances by putting a tree far away where she only showed the stump of it. This was great progress and showed that Virginia was gradually growing out of her enclosure and was accepting her world at large.

At another time, about half a year later, the children were washing and cleaning dishes after a party. At that time, she was already participating in such activities as washing dishes, while previously she had always remained isolated. This is her drawing and her concept of washing dishes [see Figure 34f]. You can see another thing here. Virginia became quite aware of how to handle the drawing area, quite apart from the fact that she now used her schema much more flexibly. You see, the elbow clearly has now become quite a part—a very integral part—of her schema, because she uses it on purpose everywhere. She could just as well stretch out the arms and reach the dishes, but she uses the elbows.

She came into conflict when she drew first herself and then the attendant. The attendant is the big lady who stands behind them, with her arms on her hips, watching the children cleaning the dishes. Here again, she shows some of this disturbed concept. You see, she always introduces such a concept when she is, apparently, slightly disturbed. We only can say that because we see it time and again. She had an odd relationship with the attendant, whom she didn't like, and whenever she felt disturbed—for instance, when I forced her to change her concepts, as in the beginning of picking the berries—she introduced this kind of a wavy line. Otherwise, we still have some reminiscence of the triangular shape with some kinds of variation. For the first time, she introduced the profile, as you can see here. She was now aware of a faucet, which was a big problem to her. One of her reactions had been: "Why should I go? Why should I get a glass of water?" Here she reacted much more consistently and, indeed, filled the space quite beautifully. She knew that she couldn't extend the table any farther, because she had to use the space here for the one child, here for the other child. There were four plus the attendant, who were all cleaning dishes.

Student: Did you suggest what to do for a drawing?

Lowenfeld: Yes, but not out of a clear sky, because we had a party. I went to the party and said: "Oh, Virginia is helping. She is helping." I repeated my motivation during the action. Virginia did not do it on the spot, but she came right to my room. I said, "Well, Virginia was helping to clean the dishes." I went that far with suggesting.

Student: At any time during the period of therapy did Virginia have an opportunity to draw anything that she thought of herself rather than drawing from outside suggestions?

Lowenfeld: No, we did not expose her to a drawing pad on purpose, because in the very beginning we had the drawing pad at her disposal all the time. Well, what did she do? She went back and drew repetitions of the same figure.

Student: That's what I was leading up to.

Lowenfeld: You see, because we thought that this continuation of a habit should somewhat be interrupted, we did not expose her to a drawing pad on her own. I worked in very close cooperation with the psychiatrist of the institution. We thought that we should not expose Virginia to any drawing opportunity or creative expression other than what she did during our motivations. So, she did not do anything else in drawing; therefore, a desire, a greater urge, was also created by this withdrawal of her drawing pad.

Sometime later—this was about, I believe, nine months or so—we all participated in a hike to a state park where there were some fireplaces. We cooked quite elaborately and spread out our blankets, and so forth. I, of course, was always very close to Virginia, still talking to myself, but now and then approaching Virginia. Virginia was already used to that and took in very carefully what I suggested. The outcome was a drawing with a fireplace; and there are blankets with people sitting around. To the left is Virginia; to the right is another girl. Virginia said: "I don't like peas, and I don't like tomatoes. I only like scrambled eggs. I only like scrambled eggs." She put on her plate only scrambled eggs, while on the other plate she drew the green peas and a ripe tomato. Then, again, she put the attendant in front. But this time, she made fun of her. The attendant was an elderly woman, by the way, and Virginia made her with a big nose. What she didn't put now into the edge of the dress, she put into the nose. She made this big rugged line around the nose, but she laughed this time and took it very humorously. However, the attendant still has her hands on her hips.

Here Virginia engaged in quite an intricate design; she was a very sensitive girl with regard to textures. She really made, with great perseverance, the fireplace and the smoke which comes out of it. Putting grass where the trees were and surrounding the place with trees and tree stumps and blankets and making the design in her dress interested her very much. She elaborated a little bit more on the hands, although they are not yet clearly expressed. She introduced the knee, which she didn't do previously. She had only introduced the elbows. She had some difficulty reaching the plate with a compulsive elbow, which she still had from the rings and from her muscle feelings. It is quite logical—you know what I mean by compulsive—because she had to elongate the arms so much. She could have done it more simply, but she had to introduce it when holding the plate. On the whole, this drawing showed a surprisingly great flexibility when compared with her previous drawings.

At that time—it was exactly ten months after the first drawing—Virginia came for the first time to me suggesting that she wanted to do something. "I want to draw my family," she said. And this is her family [see Figure 34g]. She was quite verbal when she explained about this drawing: "See, this is my baby sister." She pointed at the baby which Mother is holding in her arms. Notice the very complex relationship of holding the child in her arms—one arm of the mother around her apparently holding her head, and the other arm holding one leg. Then she said, "See, this is I," pointing at the girl to the left. "And this is my brother who always is teasing me," and she pointed at the one who teases her. Do you see how he is pointing to the dress? Apparently, there he is teasing her. "This is father," and she pointed to the legs. If you identify with the child very closely, first of all, you have to put yourself into the situation. What is the situation? Well, she is now twelve years, you know. Apparently, she thinks of herself still as one who is five or six years or even smaller—even four years. That this is true can also be seen in the very big legs, which are usually an expression of children. Children most often begin in their drawings with head/feet representations, because the legs are impressive parts as the child looks at them from below—a kind of perspective we gain when we are low, looking up.

This drawing apparently leads back to some childhood experience and not to an experience which has been lately experienced, although Virginia went home for vacations and was brought back to the institution after vacations. She had her home. This did not portray any experience which she had recently but went back into former stages of childhood. This was very significant to us, because it showed that there was something that had happened during this time which apparently had made a deep impression upon her and because it had been a long time since Virginia had left her home in this condition. She also talked of her baby sister. She had a sister who was about three or three-and-a-half years younger than she was, but her baby sister was now nine, you see. We couldn't really call her a baby sister. So the whole drawing was leading her back to her childhood experiences. Of course, any sensitive art teacher or clinician would immediately try to explore this very situation. Now, all topics which we discussed were leading back to her childhood. I was trying to find out how she had played with her brother, how her brother had teased her—the details which she could remember when he was teasing her. It was mainly pulling her dress and such things, which she had drawn again and again in many drawings.

But one time, and this was about eleven months afterwards—let us say a month after this drawing—she came very excitedly at an odd hour to my office and said she would like to draw how her house had caught fire [see Figure 34i], and how her baby sister was carried out of the burning house, and how her own dress also had caught fire—but nobody cared about it. But Mother saved her best dress! Can you see Mother's dress? Do you know where it is? This is Mother's dress in the upper right section. These are the legs of Mother. This is her best dress. We call it a pathological exaggeration in children's drawings when the individual loses contact with the whole and sacrifices the whole for enlarging a detail. We call this pathological, as contrasted to normal, exaggeration. So it is, let us say, a sickly exaggeration—a pathological exaggeration. Now she drew Mother, saving her best dress. Here you have the house catching on fire; here you have Virginia, her dress also catching on fire—and, as she said, "But nobody cared about it." The baby sister is being carried out of the house—you can see that two are carrying baby sister. Now, indeed, she includes the sky. She includes even the sun in this, and she has the ground as a base line. This is a very interesting drawing. Let's find out what happened.

Indeed, you always have to relate the case history to what has happened. We must be very much alert, of course. We invited Mother, because nothing in the case history pointed towards this experience. Case histories are only complete to the extent that we can get reports. Parents also suppress certain things which they do not want to think about, so these are the reports which we get in case histories and which are mainly collected from parents after questioning. Also, much depends on the conditions of the parents. We cannot always think that we have a complete case history if we have collected all our data only from the parents. We invited again the mother, who at that time was divorced. The father was not here. We asked Mother to tell us something—whether their house had burned. She said that the house hadn't burned: "At that time, I was still married to my husband. We came home from a party, and we saw smoke coming out of the upper floor. I rushed to the upper floor where we had the bedrooms, and there was just some smoke in the bedrooms. We tried to get the children out as quickly as possible." Of course, Virginia in her sleep got up, saw Mother in her best dress, and got just a little impression—you know how you feel when you are suddenly getting out of your sleep and something has happened. The other children were carried out; and then they all probably looked back and saw smoke coming out of the window, maybe some flames. The fire engine came, and there were all kinds of commotion. The children then moved into a motel, as I was told, and the mother said: "Yes, but nothing happened. We were insured, and the house was in order. We moved back; and when the children started talking about it, I said, 'Let's not talk about it because it's all over'."

You see, the mother did exactly what she thought was right, which was exactly contrary to what she should have done. It would have been good if the mother had confronted the children with what had happened. If she had told them: "I was at a party with my husband, and we thought you were all sound asleep. When we came home, we saw smoke coming out; and we rushed and got you out of bed and into the car; and we telephoned the fire department." If she had explained everything in detail and had even confronted the children with the situation, she would have done the right thing.

May I say at this point, this was still quite an experience of which I have spoken. But this experience should not have become a traumatic experience, because Virginia has two sisters and, for them, it was not a traumatic experience. However, for Virginia it was. So, in addition to the fire experience, there must have been something in the family relationship or otherwise which made Virginia, and only Virginia, conducive to having a traumatic experience. Do I make myself clear about that? It was not that Virginia woke up and suddenly saw a fire—the shock situation. Well, you know that's enough, indeed, and that is not conducive to any child's development; but some other condition must have existed beforehand—maybe some jealousy of Mother, an idea that Mother loves Dad, you know. Mother takes her best dress! The dress was apparently the syndrome which developed in Virginia a kind of compulsive idea that the dress is the thing onto which Mother was hanging, because Virginia had no opportunity for rationalizing the whole situation and reasoning it out. So it went on in her mind. Notice that actually what this creative therapy did for Virginia in this case is very similar in nature to a psychoanalytic treatment, although with entirely different meanings and entirely different interpretations. But it surely was leading Virginia back to an experience which she had to face, for without facing it she could not recover.

When Virginia became more flexible—even before she drew her childhood experiences at home—she no longer reacted as queerly or as disturbed in the institutional situation. At this time, she was completely changed. She could face all situations. After she drew the experience of the fire, we dramatized it. We got all details, and we told Virginia it was not Mother who saved her dress, but Mother who went home from a party and discovered that there was some smoke coming out of the window. We made a kind of psychodrama in which Virginia could talk out the situation. We staged the whole situation—two teachers dressed up like parents and came home from a party. We even burned a little hut which we erected on the stage. Then Virginia was carried out in her sleep. We asked Virginia to act very surprised and shocked that someone was waking her up from her sleep. We tried, through questions, to stimulate her to talk: "What do you see? Do you see my dress?" Virginia reacted and talked out a lot of things which we never would have expected her to do within this situation. After that, we tried to fortify the situation by going to town and letting Virginia select and buy the dress which she liked the best.

Here is where Virginia drew herself in her new dress [see Figure 34j]. You can see an almost completely changed concept of herself if you compare this drawing with one of the stereotyped schemata which she used in the very beginning. This is really a very startling comparison and a tremendous recovery to a very complex understanding of herself; because we have to regard that as an understanding of one's self, of a changed relationship to one's self, and not as an improved drawing, indeed not. You see, you can compare Figure [34a] with Figure [34j]; you can now understand what has happened in the meantime. Intellectually, we can say what has happened: she has become aware of herself. Even Goodenough would indicate that we could determine her intelligence by the details which she now includes: eyes with eyeballs and eyelashes, nose with nostrils, cheeks included, mouth with lips, hair, and the neck as a separate symbol. You still see here the shape of the dress. You can still see the belt, but only very slightly. You now see her in the position of the attendant. Do you see? That's how she portrayed herself. She takes care of herself now. You see the sleeves? You see the very complex design which she now uses for her dresses? You see the socks, the feet?

Her last drawing is very important for me now, because I'm working on the problem of a duplicity of styles. Children express themselves differently in different situations. The last drawing deals with a group of children at a party which we gave for Virginia before she left the institution [see Figure 34k]. She studies now in college and makes very high grades—a very fine student. When we gave her the party, she portrayed herself in two ways. The children were dancing around the tree; you see, it was a party. She painted herself, as well as the attendant, dancing. She also portrayed herself standing outside, reverting to her previous concept of her stereotype—the triangular shape exactly as she had drawn it previously. She pointed at this saying, "This is how I was," now actually realizing not only her situation but her conceptual change, also. In other words, she really is now rationalizing. This, of course, would be the stage at which children rationalize—at twelve or twelve-and-a-half years—and this is the age she was at that time. Virginia was a very well-developed girl, as I said, a good-looking girl. This drawing, I would say, does not quite come up to that stage; but later on, if you could see her other drawings—well, they are usually what would be expected from twelve-year-old children. I would say that Virginia has completely recovered from her symptoms and is leading an entirely normal life.

Student: How long after the drawing of the fire did she leave the institution?

Lowenfeld: About three months afterwards. See, there still was a period of adjusting to close relations with others, until she did this drawing of the party.

Student: Since you've completed this and she was completely cured, then would it follow that she wasn't psychotic when you first saw her?

Lowenfeld: Yes. This follows for me and for the psychiatric diagnosis.

LECTURE 30

Therapeutic Aspects of Art Education: A Case Study of Aggie, a Mongoloid Individual

I'll give you a case history of a mongoloid individual just to show you the development of such a person. The most important thing in any such case is the attitude of the clinician or teacher toward the individual. In the case of mongoloid children, the attitude usually is that this is a disease which cannot be cured and, therefore, we cannot help him much, so why should we bother. Usually these individuals are left by themselves, and any work or time spent on them is considered to be wasted. Now, I believe that this is not only educationally wrong, but, first of all, ethically wrong. I do believe that as long as there is a spark of life in a human being, we have to try to claim it. This is a deep ethical responsibility which we have to every human being, without any exception. So whomever we meet, we must try to bring his potential abilities to light. We should always encounter this person, this individual, with the feeling that what we see is only that which functions and not what is potentially available. Very often in the lives of individuals, especially those in institutions, the difference between the potential and functional abilities may very well mean functioning in a society or not functioning in a society (the inability to function in a society).

For instance, in the case of Aggie—the girl to whom I would like to introduce you through her drawings, through her creative work—this difference was great. She was a mongoloid type, twenty-nine years old.[13] When I give her mental age, those who deal with mongoloids know that this will not be an exact figure; because in many instances the individual reacted beyond this age level, and in many instances below this age level. I'll give you an example of this. Her mental age was about five-and-a-half years or between five and six years, according to testing. But, in many instances, she reacted below this age level, such as not going to the bathroom by herself or still having to be reminded to go. This was, of course, a tedious job; and, most often, she was reminded too late. You know? Things happened. This made her a member in an institution who was very difficult to deal with.

13. Age is given as twenty-seven in *Creative and Mental Growth*.

AGGIE (MONGOLOID)

This individual was eating properly, but not as properly as you would expect for a five-and-a-half-year-old child. For instance, a five-and-a-half-year-old child eats very properly, while Aggie ate sloppily, drooling and dropping food out of her mouth in a way that we wouldn't think a five-and-a-half-year-old child would ever do. In other instances, Aggie reacted at a level above that of a five-and-a-half-year-old child. Let us say her sex glands were developed; and, of course, she had lots of motherly feelings toward her doll, which she called her child and treated with the same care as you would a child. In her affection for others, she was overly affectionate—as we often find in mongoloid types. In straight testing, she wasn't reading nor was she writing (probably just beginning); but, overall, she had probably the mental age that was in her record—five-and-a-half years. When she drew or when she was asked to draw, she reacted properly; she reacted to you quite easily, especially if you were nice to her. She became very affectionate. She kissed you, and she embraced you, and she enjoyed herself. She was the more happy type of mongoloid individual. But still, she was never left alone in the institution because she always had to have someone behind her to see that nothing happened. This, of course, is safe for an institution; but may I emphasize that it was not for this reason that we tried to get all potential abilities out of Aggie. It was for ethical reasons that we did it. I would like to implant that very deeply into you, because Aggie is a human being and we should try to go as far with a human being or with any living thing as we can. So, especially in an institution dealing with human beings, we try to bring them up to their potential abilities.

Now, let me give you some indication of Aggie through her drawings. This is a drawing by Aggie [see Figure 35a]. I repeat, Aggie was twenty-nine years of age. She drew head and feet representations which are usually indicative of five-year-old children, although we should not generalize. This is the stage immediately following the stage of the naming of scribbling, when a child discovers that there is a relationship between the outside world and himself. He says, "Mother has a head and two arms and two legs; my drawing has a head and two arms and two legs; therefore, my drawing is Mother." You see, here Aggie said, "I'm going downstairs out of the institution." Also, she said, "Downstairs is indicated by steps one, two, three, four." She could count. That's just about five years old. She could count to four, as you can see here in the steps. The steps appear to be important to her—the steps which led from the institute to the institution's garden; there were four steps. But she did not apply the same concept of counting to her fingers. Do you see? She only made a symbol there for a hand, which indicates that she had a general concept of hands that is much lower than a detailed concept. Her general concept was: "I have an arm; and at the end of my arm, there's a hand. Something sticks out of this hand which I call fingers." But how many did not belong to Aggie's concept.

Fig. 35. Drawings by a mongoloid (27-year-old individual).

(a) "Going Downstairs." Head-feet representation is at the 5-year-old level.
(b) "Stomachache." Stimulation on body creates no deviation of inflexible schema.
(c) "Sitting on a Stone." Drawing showing introduction of body.
(d) "A and Her Child." Drawing showing greater awareness of the self.
(e) "Riding Horseback." Emotional freedom is clearly seen when compared with (a).

380

AGGIE (MONGOLOID)

It is important for us to notice, at this point, that she had no detailed concept of her own self. Apparently, she lacked body feelings and a higher degree of body consciousness, which we can see. She has a head. She was quite conscious of her features, as you can see. This doesn't necessarily mean that she is laughing, because the features indicate a moon face. You know this kind of a face? In it is simply her symbol for a mouth, and to us it appears at the present time as if it is laughing. Don't put your own concept into the concept of others. You have to prove that she really means laughing before we can accept it. She knew that she had two eyes, a nose, and a mouth. She did not differentiate between the symbol of nose and mouth; both are just a stroke, a line. But she did indicate that the eyes are round; she made two little circles.

She was not at all conscious that she had a body. Therefore, she still had a concept typical of five-year-old children. Not being conscious of the body means merely that the body has not yet a specific function or that the function of the body has been suppressed. Psychoanalytically, it may mean that, because she probably was not yet toilet trained, she suppressed the function of the body. But it may also mean that, at such a low stage as children are at five years, the body doesn't play the role in consciousness that the legs and feet play. We just take for granted what we see appearing at the present time and relate it to our concept of art education therapy. There are two lines for legs and two lines for feet. This means that she was conscious of feet—not a differentiated concept, but a general concept. As I said, the four steps were represented by four parallel lines. To the left and to the right of the steps, you see two vertical lines. These two vertical lines are the railings, the left railing and the right railing, because she was conscious that she could hold on to the railings. Therefore, these also appear to give an increased feeling of insecurity, body insecurity, because she emphasized them quite clearly, compulsively almost, putting a line to the left and to the right. You can see that there is a tree—this one line—and you can also see the crown in an irregular line, which is probably a diffused concept of a tree as you may see it around this mental age.

What would you do with a child like this? First, we learn that she has a low concept. You see, her IQ was probably below the concept that related to her age. Well, we better remain with the mental age in such cases of low mental deficiency, because it is very difficult to deal with IQ's. Now, what would you do with her? We know that she could create her own concept. This is already counter to what we usually hear in special education. If she had been given a concept of a dog or a bird to fill in, she wouldn't have had at least this degree of self-identification of going downstairs; and she wouldn't have had the feeling of achievement when she put herself on the base line of the stairs and related herself to some environmental objects.

381

This, I feel, is tremendously important, especially as a beginning step. I'll tell you what I did.

It is important that in such an instance we keep in mind the normal developmental stages of children. We should know that children move from head and feet representations to representations in which they include the body. Therefore, a higher degree of body consciousness might also bring her to a higher degree of understanding of her role within her environment. So any higher degree of differentiation would probably lead her out of this stereotype or low concept of a figure. So what did I do? I tried to stimulate her individual (body) feelings.

The stimulation which I used was not immediately with regard to the body, but it was starting on her own level. Aggie loved to whistle. She whistled every moment when she could, although not very well—kind of a half-blow, like this. She whistled and apparently enjoyed it. I told you a long time ago that we always should start on the level of the individual. So I said, "Well, why don't you draw yourself whistling, a whistling girl." So she made the head and included, in this instance, the eyes. She was already disturbed in her concept, because she now included a nose which was no longer a stroke but something different. This something different for the nose was what we expected for the whistling mouth. The mouth forms a round motion when you whistle; but the nose was formed by the shape which was expected for the mouth. When she came to the mouth, she again made a line in the shape of a ball, a double line which indicated some opening; but then it didn't fit her concept, and she added another mouth. This vertical concept which approximates the concept of the nose was only elongated as the whistling mouth. Everything else was as she had done it previously, except the hands. They are a little bit disturbed. She didn't even draw the third finger. She only drew one horizontal line there for the hand. She concentrated terribly on the figure here, much more than previously. She was disturbed, but this disturbance was very important. She had been brought out of her usual stereotyped representation of a moon face. I saw then that it was possible to motivate her; and this was the major question which we see answered here—that it was possible to motivate her. Her mentality was not so low that she could not react to such motivation. She reacted towards whistling with a kind of disturbance and even a change of symbol.

Then I felt that I could motivate her in regard to her body. Any motivation which was strong enough would serve as a good motivation. For instance, Aggie loved to eat. Eating was her greatest pleasure, but she never knew when to stop. She would eat so much that she would vomit, and then she would start over again. Or, she would start burping terribly, you know. So this time when she stopped, we gave her more to eat—pancakes that morning—and we also gave her a belt which fitted her tightly. Both should have, in some way, motivated her to a greater consciousness of her body.

The result was this drawing [see Figure 35b]. Gretel, my wife, knows exactly how many pancakes she ate. I forget, really—twenty or more, you know. When she really got filled up and was holding her belly, then we started. I said: "Now you have *all* the pancakes that you want. How does it feel?" Well, she said, "Ungh," and she burped. She said she also had eggs. So I said, "Let's get a hotplate." We held a hotplate to her body just to get her motivated in regard to her body.

Then she started to draw, with the upper circle as the head. She drew the body and even the arms holding the body—and the elbow, you see? That means the arms curve, going back to her body, holding it; and then she drew the legs. So I already was triumphant when I saw that she was moving from her previous symbol or concept of a figure—head/feet representation—to something new! This would indicate a greater flexibility and, indeed, a higher stage of awareness. But before she finished, she quickly added the eyes and the nose and the mouth, again in the concept which appeared to her most frequently. She forgot the upper circle and used the body circle as the head. So, again, she stopped with the head/feet representation. Do you see? All this motivation was necessary to make this little change. You have to do it again and again in order to get these individuals out of a feeling of passivity to a feeling of greater alertness. Much work is necessary in order to keep this alertness, and much patience is necessary on your part, too, you know, to continuously motivate the individual.

Because I felt this eating motivation apparently was ineffective, I made the belt a little bit tighter; and I said: "Well, how would it be, now that you have your nice dress on, if we were to take a little walk?" Look at the figure to the right in [Figure 35b]. I now put the emphasis on the dress and the belt because the stomach did not create the right motivation. I don't know if you can see—there is a circle there which indicates the dress; since it is drawn in yellow, you cannot see it clearly. She made her head/feet representation, as you can see here, exactly as in the first drawing, except that she has taken the whistling nose and has now incorporated it into her new schema—into a new concept. This now has apparently become her concept, because we can see it in both figures. She has now adjusted to a new concept for nose, which is a kind of low type of flexibility. She has lost her feeling for the head. She made her head/feet representation; and all the motivation with regard to the "pretty-dressed girl" resulted in her including here a yellow line which she introduced between her legs and her head, indicating that she had some concept, at least, that the dress belonged somewhere in there. So her concept at this time was very vague.

Since all of these body motivations were without success, I tried another concept which often helps. The concept was to introduce another medium. This is a concept which should be flexibly used, especially with mentally retarded individuals, but also with individuals who get stuck in their stereotypes. In this instance, I started again from where Aggie was. I saw her sitting outside on a stone, on a rock, in the garden. I approached her and said: "You are sitting on the rock. You like to sit on the rock, Aggie?" Aggie always laughed very easily and enjoyed herself, and immediately she put her hands around my neck and kissed me and was very affectionate. Well, Aggie was sitting there, and I had brought some clay along. Without any effort, without any difficulty, she introduced a body. Also, she had a much higher concept of her legs and her arms than she previously had in her drawings. This apparently is an indication that here is a duplicity in styles. This is not uncommon. As a matter of fact, I'm now very much concerned with this duplicity of styles.

From research which I'm presently doing, we can see it in normal children who apparently do several things on different levels. The reason for it is not yet known. Herbert Reed also was greatly concerned with this problem of duplicity of styles, and so was the French psychologist, Luquet. There are various hypotheses, which still have to be proved. One is that of Luquet—that different social environments create different types of adjustments. He found that children draw differently at home from what they draw in the classroom, because the classroom adjustment creates a new environmental situation and, therefore, a new reaction. This may be true, but it is to me a superficial explanation. Why should a child go back and forth in his IQ in adjusting to different types of concepts? Accordingly, with the "Draw a Man Test," the child would then have a different IQ in the classroom than he would have at home or on the pavement; because the IQ, according to the "Draw a Man Test," is based on the active knowledge that a child has of the details which the child includes. If the details change that quickly, we would then assume that the IQ, too, changes that quickly, and that cannot be. So there must be other explanations.

The most plausible explanation for me is that different potential abilities are at work in situations of different emotional significance to children. For instance, if a child has been influenced in expressing himself graphically with pencil and he has now, through repetition, been conditioned to this schema or stereotyped concept, then he will remain with this concept as the concept which functions for him. Therefore, his functional IQ is what you can see. But, apparently, the child has been so emotionally insecure that nothing has opened up to give him an opportunity to express more than his mere functional schema or concept. When he is confronted with a new material, such as clay in this instance, it may be that he has to face the world anew, as it were. He has to build up a new concept because he has nothing to rely upon. He has nothing to base his concept upon, nor has he any associative frame of reference to which he can refer anything he has already established previously. So he has to build up a new concept in working with a new material (such as clay), with no frame of reference of a previous nature.

This frees some of his potential abilities, since he again has to dig deeply into areas which he has not touched previously. He cannot refer to something previously established and, therefore, cannot base his concept upon past associations. Do I make myself clear? So he has to establish a new concept with the new medium, using whatever IQ or whatever other possibilities he has—mental or otherwise.

Therefore, when Aggie was faced with clay, she had to work from the very beginning, as it were. What was her beginning? The beginning for work in clay was where she was at the time, and there a duplicity in styles is shown. Her beginning in clay apparently was different from the established concept which she had graphically in drawing. There is, then, a discrepancy; but, for the clinician or teacher, this is a very important indication. As soon as he or she discovers there is a discrepancy in styles, there is a possibility for movement or growth—that means, the child is not in a stage of stagnation where he cannot move. We see that Aggie, in one instance, had grown higher than in another. It is always important to go back to the frame of reference which was previously established in order to create a kind of unity in this person and bring her previous concept—which was stereotyped and, therefore, established—up to the concept which she has now newly established.

The next motivation was that of me holding her. She embraced me as she sat there, and the next drawing which she made was a drawing in which we both were included and in which she had a carry-over from the modeling to the drawing representation [see Figure 35c]. Now, without difficulty, she made the same drawing which she previously did when she ate the pancakes, with the only difference being that she no longer put the face—that means, the eyes, the nose, and the mouth—into her body but really recognized the upper circle as the valid circle for the representative symbol of the head. This is tremendous progress, because it shows that Aggie has now moved from the head and feet representation to a stage higher. Indeed, in her testing, this would show. In her reactions it showed somewhat, too—not too much, you know. You cannot expect drastic changes in a mongoloid individual at twenty-nine years of age, but it showed some change—some higher form of recognition and a greater identification. When she drew me, the figure on the right, she drew herself as still sitting on the stone. She has shown a clear indication of putting my arm around her neck. At the same time, she went one stage higher also in the recognition of an early environment.

Those who have gone through the course in which we discuss the normal development of the child know that Aggie now has moved from spatial representation, which we call one of haphazard distribution of objects dispersed in space with no great recognition for order, into a representation of space in which she clearly indicates that the grass is below, the rock is on the grass, I am sitting on the rock, Mr. Lowenfeld is standing on the grass, the sky is above, the clouds are above, and the trees are on the ground. You see, this is a definite order in space; and this, according to our knowledge, is the concept of a seven-year-old. You see, when we look at this with our understanding of children's drawings, we would say that this space concept is usually found in seven-year-old children, although we would not say that the concept of the human figure is a very rich concept for that age. You wanted to say something?

Student: I was just wondering—how do we know that these are not really conceptions she had before but just didn't know how to draw?

Lowenfeld: Yes, indeed! That's what we call her functional knowledge—her potential knowledge was not developed. Yes, she may have had the concept—the potential for it. But, you see, the skill of drawing is always subordinated to your own concept. You understand what I mean? Her skill has not improved here. Nor has it even been freed, as we can see from the first drawing. You remember the first drawing, in which Aggie just drew herself on the stairway, and later on when she drew only the head? She could have drawn the features also in this upper circle in the very beginning. The skill is just the same, but her intellect was not ready to include the body as an important part of her concept. Do you understand? So it is a mental concept, a mental awakening. See, I would say it is just as easy or difficult a skill to draw the two circles for eyes in the body, and the nose in the body, and the mouth in the body, as it is to draw them in the head. Do you see? But the recognition that this is now a body did not permit her to put the features into the body as she previously did. So it is a higher form of recognition. That the arms come out of the body and not out of the head is a higher form of recognition, a higher mental concept—not skill, but an intellectual concept. It is just as difficult or easy to attach the arms onto the body as it is to attach them onto the head. So it is not a skill factor; it's a factor of greater identification or a higher intellectual and functional ability to recognize one's own body.

Student: How much time has been covered so far in. . . .

Lowenfeld: Well, so far we have covered about six weeks in daily lessons—lessons we call them, or daily contacts.

Student: There was no suggestion of the body from you?

Lowenfeld: No, except for the type of thing I have mentioned. Needless to say, it should be understood that it would be an imposition on your part and you would fool only yourself if you were to say, "Include the body," or give her suggestions that she should include the body. You know why I say you would fool yourself? It wouldn't be an active discovery on the part of the child, but it would be an imposition on your part. "Draw it." Of course, the child might draw it, may be half-confused by drawing it, but you can train a child to do it. So we never would suggest, "Draw a body," but would do everything possible to make the child discover her own body.

You can readily understand that a child with such a low mental age as

Aggie would have enjoyed coloring books or patterns or anything like that, but it would only have encouraged her to greater passivity. You see, she never would have arrived at such mental concentration or even such disturbed qualities as she did those times when she couldn't go on and which eventually resulted in her doing drawings in which she clearly was able to identify with herself and her own experience.

The next work which Aggie did was again taken from a situation in which she was involved at the time. This again was a modeling, and she was holding her doll or, as she said, "I am holding my child." We were now frequently going back and forth from modeling to drawing, because I felt that the establishment of a new concept in modeling helped her very greatly in her flexibility. You see, the greatest difficulty with mentally retarded individuals is the lack of flexibility—the fixation or the holding on to certain concepts, probably out of a feeling for slowness or out of a feeling of insecurity. It is incredible to me how teachers in special education who know of these facts—slowness, lack of flexibility, lack of fluency—will then promote patterns as the means to give retarded children more flexibility or more fluency and more self-confidence. This is simply incredible! You know, when we speak of retarded children in schools, we don't mean Aggies. They are much less retarded and much less deficient than Aggie is. I bring this case to you so that you can draw a parallel with children of lesser degrees of deficiency.

I believe someone is giving a report in our later classes on slow learners. In that report, then, we will deal with retarded children of school age. There you will hear what Gaitskell[14] has to say about this. He is, I believe, quite progressive in his understanding and views.

After Aggie had done the modeling, which she did with very little difficulty, she made this drawing [see Figure 35d]. The glare on the bottom is due to the cellophane which I put over the drawing. Here you can immediately see a much higher concept, but this is after about half a year of continuous drawing and painting—drawing mainly, with crayons or ink. You see what she did? First of all, look at the hands—she counted up to five with regard to her fingers. This means a much higher concept. She returned to the nose concept, and no longer referred to it as the whistling nose. Although the face concept and the features are still the same, she included hair and she introduced the dress. When she first did so, it was very casually, you know, first with a very light line, and then shading it, and then adding the cut around her neck. But now she really is holding her baby, also with a head and a body and the legs. She clearly indicated the bottom and the top. She included the spatial concept and a much higher concept of herself. This is after a half a year.

14. Charles D. and Margaret R. Gaitskell, *Art Education for Slow Learners* (Peoria, Illinois: C. A. Bennett, 1953).

And now, I would like to jump with you over a period of time and show you what Aggie was able to do after a year; and that is approximately where she remained. There is no comparison when you see it, if you compare the first drawing to the last drawing. Aggie was, at this time, almost thirty. You would think that a mongoloid at twenty-nine could not be changed at all, but she did change. Now, when she was playing, she went to the bathroom by herself; and she took care of her own clothes much more meticulously. She could even help in the household—a half a year after she had been drawing. This was done at Lochland Institute in Geneva, New York. They're very progressive there. She was given, with another mongoloid individual whom I had partnered with her, her own apartment or room to take care of. This she did. In other words, she became a socialized individual. She started reading—she read at this time, but very slowly. Of course, her mental age had improved maybe two or three years. There's no doubt about it. Through measuring devices, it was confirmed. There's also no doubt about the fact that it was creative activity which had made this possible, because no other thing had been done or was previously as effective in her whole life as in this instance.

Student: Or was it her relationship with you—that you were interested in her?

Lowenfeld: Oh, yes, this may have been true. It is always difficult to separate, as it also is in any psychoanalytic treatment, you know.

My interest in Aggie, my continuous interest, may have brought her to a higher level of achievement, and this higher level of achievement is also seen in her drawings. But I don't think I would have caused Aggie to achieve so much merely by us being together, without having her draw; because, with this, I had continuously a frame of reference to which I could turn. Drawing and modeling put me in my relationship to her and probably put her in her relationship to me. However it was, the means was creative activity which brought about my relationship with her and her relationship with me.

Therefore, we can include drawing and modeling in creative therapy. It would be very difficult to state whether interest is the cause or the symptom here. But you can surely say that her concept improved tremendously, even if we did not go into great details. Look, for instance, how her concept or her schema of a face has changed [see Figure 35e]. It's now round. The eyes are filled in because she is looking. She is laughing—has her mouth wide open, as you can see. Her tongue (this is her tongue) is even showing; and her teeth are showing—all a contribution of her own. The lips are showing. This is the nose—she includes the nose and puts it here because it's standing out, protruding. There are the two ears. She has a neck. She has a body, she included a dress. She has her feet. Her feet are clearly in the—what do you call them—of the horse?

Student: Stirrups.

Lowenfeld: Stirrups, yes. She has the saddle here. She is holding the horse. She is aware of the relationship of her eyes to the eyes of the horse—both are for seeing. She included the horse's ears here. She said, "The horse is running," and here she included somewhat of a forward motion. She included the ground. She has certainly not arrived at such a different concept for trees as she has for people, but trees are slightly more differentiated as the trunks have now a certain thickness. She has now included the sun, a concept that children include, too.

In many respects, this is the drawing of an eight-year-old child, while, in all respects, the first drawing was a drawing of a five or five-and-a-half-year-old child, according to mental age. Her reactions have improved, but not as much as we would see in an eight-and-a-half-year-old or eight-year-old child. For instance, the reading was far behind that of an eight-year-old child. She could read, but very slowly, and really had not the urge to read or to get the meaning out of reading; but she did read. Her social responsibility was in many ways more highly developed than that of an eight-year-old child. For instance, she made her bed; she cleaned her apartment; she put her dolls—her children, you know; she had two at that time—meticulously into the beds; and she did all kinds of things involving them. So, in many instances, she was higher; in other instances, she was lower. But the most important thing is that you can see in this drawing a certain emotional freedom which is so clearly established and so evident that nothing else could express it more clearly than by comparing it with the stiff, stereotyped, head/feet representation which you saw in the beginning. This somewhat emotionally free expression of a mongoloid occurred after one year of continuous creative therapy.

I have shown you this, not as an unusual example, but because it is almost the rule with mongoloid types that you can bring them to a higher stage of development than you found them. I would like to tell this to everyone who may ever work in an institution with mongoloids, because they are the most neglected individuals within the classification of handicapped or mentally deficient individuals. Everyone thinks that we cannot do anything about them, and therefore we leave them alone because they are mongoloids. I would urge you to work with them. You can enrich their lives, you know. You should do the same for them as you would do for any one of us. Why do we go to school, and why do we learn? We learn to enrich our lives, to become more helpful members in society, to have more fun if you want to in a greatly richer life, and, probably, to have even more happiness. The same is true with a mongoloid. Aggie has a richer life, a greater recognition of her environment, a greater identification with things that she does. She became a more useful member in an institution. All characteristics are found in her that we find in a normal human being. So why should we neglect mongoloids? Only because they are on a lower stage of mental development than we are? This is no reason, and especially not an ethical one—it's a very unethical one! This should serve as an approach to all mentally deficient individuals and can even be used much better with retarded children.

Of course, we will immediately hear from classroom teachers: "But I cannot deal with one child as closely as you have dealt with Aggie." Surely, I was dealing with Aggie as an individual; but this is no excuse, even if we have fifteen—and that is usually the number of retarded children which we have. We don't have such large classes in special education as we have in our regular classrooms. Just have in the back of your mind that you can get them to a higher stage. If you do that, you won't give up. Once you have seen what can be done, you will have the urge to do something with them. If you cannot work as intensively with fifteen as I've done here with a single individual, just keep in mind that you should not be discouraged. By no means degrade them to the mere level of pure imitation or pure filling in. You know, it just came to my mind. Look how Aggie keeps within the outline. Do you see it? She never goes beyond it, even in the trees. She remains within the outline. Well, you don't have to encourage that. This is a result of her own intention and her own urge. Don't let anyone tell you that the exercises which children do involving the filling in of predetermined outlines bring them to a higher degree of body coordination or make them better disciplined.

LECTURE 31

Therapeutic Aspects of Art Education: A Case Study of Camilla, a Deaf-Blind Child

First, I will give you a description of the case of a deaf-blind individual. Her age was eleven when I met her. Let's call her Camilla, which was actually her real name. She had been in the institution for two years, and no attempt to communicate with her had been successful at the time when I met her. People were considering placing her in a mental institution because of her inability to be approached, to communicate, and to participate in learning processes. She was kept in hiding for a long time by her parents, who were farmers in Massachusetts. Her parents had a feeling of guilt because of her handicap; as well-to-do farmers, they didn't want others to know that they had a severely handicapped child. Now and then, the people in the immediate, surrounding area heard shouts like, "Ehun! Ehun!" They reported these noises to the social worker; and, finally, an investigation was conducted. Camilla was found in hiding and was completely, let us say, animal-like. Her eating with hands and her crawling on the floor was not much beyond the first stages of infancy.

Student: You say she was both blind and deaf?

Lowenfeld: She was blind and deaf, and therefore did not communicate, because no effort was made at that time.

She was brought to Perkins Institution for the Blind. I met her at a time when I was there in regard to a grant in which I had a part at the University. I was doing some research, and this case was called to my attention. I thought that the first thing I should do would be to study the case history of Camilla. As a result, I learned what I have just told you. I learned that she had absolutely neutral treatment from her environment; that means, she was given food and nothing else. She was not asked to do anything, but was kept enclosed and sometimes was even led into the court and chained; that means, with a cord attached to her belt. That was all—she was fed; she was led to the bathroom; and she was not taught anything. When she was at Perkin's Institution, communication with her was tried by the usual methods of vibration boards and lip reading. But she behaved in a strange way, inasmuch as she always shouted when someone brought her into the room with Miss Hall, who was the teacher—a very wonderful teacher, by the way—who also taught one of the very great, well-known, blind-deaf individuals, Bridgeman. I don't know if you have heard of her. She is not as famous as Helen Keller, but is also one of the individuals who has advanced from complete isolation to an understanding of the world.

Miss Hall was incapable of getting Camilla to communicate or to have any type of rapport. So when I came, Camilla only had an attendant. The attendant was a very fine teacher, a lady, with whom Camilla apparently had developed some kind of confidence and attachment, because the attendant could go out with Camilla and sit with her. After Camilla was lying on the grass and rolling around on the grass, she sometimes went back to her attendant and touched her and had (as I could see from observation) apparently some kind of affection for her—expressed in a different way, indeed, than we would have expressed affection. I saw Camilla's hand reaching for her attendant's knees or legs and touching and being satisfied after she had touched her and then again rolling on the grass, sometimes shouting or making such sounds as I illustrated previously.

After I had read her case history and observed her very closely, I tried to participate with her in rolling on the grass. For the first week, I was simply sitting close to her attendant, just to be there. I thought it would be better for Camilla to adjust now to two persons and sometimes to feel that other one there. During this time, when Camilla reached her hand for the attendant, I sometimes held or grabbed her hand and tried to give her an expression of patting and feelings of affection, in the belief that affection is an instinct which can be understood by people universally. I did not know if affection for Camilla meant the same as it meant for me; for instance, if I held her hands, the holding of her hands in my hands may mean affection to her or it may mean an attack for other reasons, because she was completely shut off from the environment. Maybe this is simply a conventional way we have learned to express affection, but I didn't know; neither did anyone else.

You see, we hold some symbols so true for ourselves and so universal that we start with them. When I held Camilla, she also stretched her hand out at one point toward me and was touching me and became more and more interested in who I was in the same way that she was touching her attendant. As I was sitting there, she also was beginning to touch my knees—at first, with hesitation, followed by withdrawal; but, now, gradually accepting me as another person sitting there. Now and then we tried to get Camilla to sit between us, between the attendant and me. Her attendant during the two years was also probably used to expressing her affection for Camilla in conventional terms, if you may call it that, by pressing Camilla close to her body or giving her some feeling of closeness. Protection and security is something we all seek even in the womb, and, therefore, we feel it is a kind of a symbol which subconsciously rests within us. I don't want to go into psychoanalytical theory at this point, but I believe there are some universal things upon which we can draw.

After a week, a kind of rapport was established; mainly, Camilla accepted me, and I accepted, of course, the whole environment. We must always, in our therapeutical situations, adjust to the level of each individual, you see. This is a very important function of anyone, teacher or clinician. Well, I was rolling with Camilla on the grass, and she was then accepting me and the attendant and sometimes was shouting, probably in excitement or whatever else she was expressing, which we didn't know. At one point, I thought the time had come—let's say, after a week, although I think it was longer—so I brought Camilla some clay. The medium which we use in art education therapy must be adjusted to the sensory qualities of the individual. For individuals who can mainly communicate with the sense of touch, as in this case, it can almost only be clay. It can be a building process of ready-made cubes, but this does not allow for individual projection. It is something which is already here and would be in the way of establishing contact with one's own self. So I brought her clay.

It is not always easy to get the individual to understand what clay is for, what clay means, and what we should do with clay. First of all, I was merely attempting to give her the feeling of the medium; and this I did by holding the clay in my hands and putting her hands over my hands so that there was a certain participation of commonly holding the clay, which I believe often gives greater security than exposing the individual alone to the situation. This is, I believe, a common thing which we should learn: that a sudden exposure to an unknown always creates feelings of insecurity. A gradual participation is always more advantageous in a therapeutical situation than a sudden exposure. That is why I was kneading the clay with her. I was holding her hands in my hands, and we were trying to find what it means to get the impression of one's own fingers on clay. This was tried out for many days until I really could roll the clay into her hands, and she could, without any hesitation, press the clay and knead the clay and get the feeling for clay all by herself, independent of my participation.

One day, the teacher or clinician should start to wean the individual away from himself and make the individual independent in his experiences. In this, the teacher must be very sensitive. Well, one day I thought the time had come to establish some relationship between what Camilla did and her own self. Very often, especially in such situations in which the individual is completely cut off from environmental experiences, this can better be accomplished by closure—a method in which the teacher or the clinician starts and the individual goes on from there—rather than by completely exposing the individual to his own experience in relation to the art medium.

May I explain the term closure to those who are not familiar with it through Thurstone and his work. I believe he was the one who mainly promoted the term. In any art therapy, we call closure the procedure, the process, in which the teacher or clinician starts an experience which is finally finished (closed) by the subject or the patient. In severe cases, we will often use this phenomenon of closure when the teacher begins an experience and the patient/subject, according to his own individual relationship and personality, closes it. Out of this closure—how he closes it—you may get some insights into the individual. You may start something, but the patient may read something entirely different into it. Tests are built—you know, the TAT, the Thematic Apperception Test—on the basis of this phenomenon of closure. You are exposed to a picture which suggests all kinds of things, and you have to answer as to what you see in it. Out of your answers, we can draw certain conclusions with regard to your own background and with regard to your own security or ability to identify with the situation. As this is usually done on the basis of past experiences and your personality, we can draw certain conclusions.

In the case of Camilla—at that time, Camilla had never communicated consciously in any way. I was forming a coil, a thick coil, and adding to this coil two thin coils, attaching them like the arms. Then I put this into Camilla's hands, touching her body first, very firmly, and then leading her hands around the thick coil, and then touching her arms, also intensely, and then leading her hands over the thin coils. This I did several days without success. She just did not react. She grabbed me and hugged me and reacted in all kinds of ways, but then she grabbed the clay and kneaded it again, as we had done before. There was no reaction, physical reaction, which showed that we communicated at all. Then one day, I had her sitting close to me. I started with the thick coil again. This time I went over her body and then took her hand and let her touch the thick coil. Then I attached the thin coils—not beforehand, but after she touched them—and then I touched her arms and had her touch again this middle, thicker structure and the thinner coils. All of a sudden, she shouted "Eeeeee!" and she grabbed the clay.

For the very first time, I had the feeling that we both had communicated. She added the other two coils which indicated herself sitting. This was the first time she indicated that she also has legs. Afterwards, she also added the neck and the head with the two eyes indented, the nose pulled out, and the mouth also expressed by an indentation. Now, for the very first time, she identified herself with her own model. And, in so doing, she had physically the feeling that she also communicated with me through the medium of clay. This meant that a tremendously thick wall around her was all of a sudden broken. She felt, well, that we both knew the same thing. "This is I. I am sitting here. I have two legs, and I have two arms, and I have a head. And in this head I have two eyes, and a nose, and a mouth." I don't know whether you can imagine what such a step means for a deaf-blind individual; but it is the first, the very first, indication that she has grown out of her completely closed-in self.

Whenever such a situation arises, you have to start on the level where the person is now. Be careful not to go beyond it, for you can only refer to the frame of reference which the individual now has established. Your feeling must be that you have continuously to extend the person's frame of reference by whatever means or methods you can use. May I say, at this point, that there is never one means and there is never one method. The method which I used may have been good for me and my relationship with Camilla, but there are probably a hundred other methods which I could have used to extend her frame of reference. This extension of her frame of reference will also extend her ability to communicate and her ability to communicate will make her more secure and will make her more of a member of a larger environment.

After we had gone through this experience, we did it again; because I believe the feeling of security in repeated experiences, in meaningful experiences, is important on this level. So I came again, and I touched her body again, and she couldn't wait. She got the clay and started again because she knew what was coming; in doing so she was acting triumphantly and, you know, had the feeling. By the way, this was the very first one [see Figure 36a]. The coil on the left broke accidentally; it should have been the same length as the other one. Then she had the feeling that all this was done by herself, and I had no longer a part in it. She had now the feeling that she was sitting all by herself, independently. When she was finished again, she shouted all over the campus. By the way, when she shouted the very first time, people really thought something had happened to her and came from all directions because she had never before shouted in such an excited manner.

About two weeks after this, I thought the time was right to extend her frame of reference, her ability for experience. I was thinking, "How should we do it?" Now, the experiences with normal children came very much to mind. Let's suppose Camilla's a normal individual—how would she unfold from this stage on? Well, we all have two kinds of knowledge—an active knowledge and a passive knowledge. The active knowledge is the knowledge which we have and can use, while passive knowledge is the knowledge which we have and don't use. Much of our education is merely an activation of passive knowledge. Especially in children's drawings or paintings, we extend the activation by giving children experiences to make body parts more meaningful. So, I thought, why shouldn't that be also applicable to Camilla? You see, an art education therapy actually is nothing but a more intensified motivation, and I would like to say this very loudly, especially to the art teachers here. This intensified motivation already had taken place with Camilla in a way, as you can see [in Figure 36a]. If you have children in a kindergarten, you could also start with the body—maybe even by touching the children—because they often perceive more concerning their own bodies.

Now, I thought, the time had come—probably Camilla knows that she has hands, but the hands, as you can see, haven't been activated. They were still in her subconscious while she was creating. As you know, the richer our vocabulary, the greater our ability to express ourselves; and so the tendency here is to improve the vocabulary. So I brought her an apple and had her smell the apple and then had her touch the apple. I put the apple into her hands and closed her hands around the apple. Then I took the apple away and repeated that again, until I left the apple in her hands. I gave her the clay, after having touched her body and her arms again—and, especially, the hands that were holding the apple. I believe it is very helpful in a clinical or therapeutical situation to establish certain signals, or stimulus-response situations, such as withholding the clay until a certain moment has arrived and then giving her the clay—always after the motivation and not before. So I gave her the clay and, as a result, Camilla made this sculpture or this modeling, again after a great deal of excitement [see Figure 36b]. You can see how Camilla responded. First of all, there is a more intensified relationship between arms and body and legs, which was already seen in the last modelings of her pure sitting sensations. You understand there is a gradual continuing from this [a] to this [b]. But, now, for the first time, she put this hollow indentation (her concept formation) into her hands; she still was also holding things with her toes at that time. She loved to do that. She used the feet as she did the hands, probably not as skillfully, but frequently. She applied the same symbol also for the feet. In the hand to her right, you can see the apple. Do you? Now again, when she had finished it, she was tremendously excited. She had communicated with me: "I am holding an apple."

At the same time, very much in the beginning, I was quite aware that I should not remain merely with the modeling, but that I should have a carry-over into life situations. So I tried to stimulate her by putting her hands to my mouth, saying, "Ap-ple, ap-ple," and then giving her the apple, holding it to her nose to let her smell it; but without there being any result. There was no feeling, no response whatsoever, at that time. But I tried to give her some feeling that there are other relationships, at least from my own feeling. I tried to enlarge her frame of reference in many aspects. One I had in mind was language, along with other forms of communication.

After this we made many clay modelings, again through symbolized experiences. I put a stick into her hand. I put a walnut into her hand. I put all kinds of things into her hands for quite some time, and she responded readily now, meaning that, "I am holding a walnut in my hand; I am holding

CAMILLA (DEAF–BLIND)

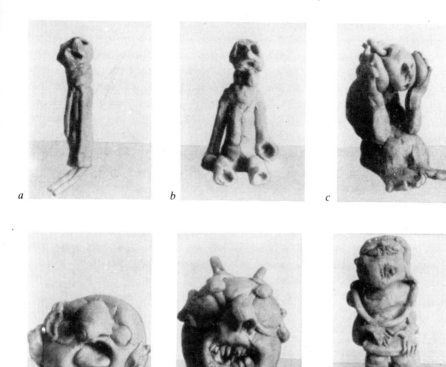

Fig. 36. Modelings by an 11-year-old deaf-blind girl (Perkins Institution for the Blind, Watertown, Mass.).

(*a*) "Sitting."
(*b*) "I put an apple in your hands."
(*c*) "I am very tired, sleepy."

(*d*) "I am yawning."
(*e*) "I am eating candy."
(*f*) "I am reading."

a ball in my hand; I am holding a stick in my hand; I am holding an apple in my hand." You see, this, too—as a repetitive experience—should create a certain security in her and should fortify the feeling of responding independently to a stimulus. Of course, on my part, there was constantly the hope that she, herself, might bring something, some object, which she did not do at this time. You see, I could imagine at this time that one day she would come and bring something to me which she was holding, as her own contribution; but this did not take place until later, as you will see.

One day when I came, there she was. I was a little late. She was very impatient and was sitting there holding her head in her hands—sitting on a little stool which she brought along. She was waiting for me for modeling. We made it a point not to give her clay outside of the work periods, because we believed that the concentration would be greater if she were only exposed to it at a certain time than if she were exposed to it constantly. The excitement also would probably diminish. At that time, when I saw her, I thought that this would be a wonderful situation—to start right off from where she was. So when she felt me coming and I sat close to her and touched her, she wanted to go out of her position, thinking that I was again bringing her something to put into her hands. But, I did not. I held her back. In fact, I put her back into the body position in which she had been by touching her body, touching her arms, touching especially where her elbows were resting on her knees, touching her legs, and her head. Whenever she wanted to go out of this position, I put her back into the position and touched her again and again. It didn't take much time until she understood and again shouted, "Ahhnn, ahmm," and started and modeled this figure [see Figure 36c]. You see, this is probably one of the biggest steps in her progress, although I'll show you one which indicated a still greater change—not for the naked eye, but for the one who has learned to look at these things. I'll point it out later on.

Here, you can see that, basically, her method of approach was still the same. That means, she first attached the legs and bent them. She pulled out the toes for the first time; and as she pulled out the toes, she also pulled out the fingers. At that time, I was trying to give her the feeling of "fin-ger, fin-ger" through lip reading, and was then referring to her fingers, trying again to give her the feeling of the relationship between experience and other forms of communication, such as language. There was no immediate response, although I thought I had found some when she excitedly repeated some of my sounds; but whether they really meant something, we never knew. We still don't know.

Student: Do you think it's good to start out right away with the way you want a person ultimately to communicate—I mean, with symbols such as language? How does this compare with trying to get them to use more simple symbols, like maybe a tap or something like that?

CAMILLA (DEAF–BLIND)

Lowenfeld: I don't know! I don't have an answer for it. I didn't try out any other method. I didn't experiment with methods other than that, probably because I had the feeling that Camilla had a mental level which made it possible for her to do it. Because she'd readily responded to changes, I didn't feel it necessary to do something with tap or other methods, nor had they been practiced in institutions for deaf and blind and still are not practiced. But using a tap as a symbol might be an appropriate approach, I don't know. It might open up new ways, and it might be worthwhile to experiment with it; but to my knowledge, no experiments had been done up to that time, and still haven't been done. So I was trying to use the logical approach of leading her into an environment which later would become useful for adjustment.

Student: I was just thinking that verbal symbolism is really. . . .

Lowenfeld: Terrifically complex, yes.

Student: And I was just wondering how this would compare with the very simplest concept of a symbol.

Lowenfeld: Yes, such as with vowels only in the beginning—to say "ah" is "finger" for example. It would mean, then, a re-learning, and I don't know how complex the re-learning would be later on or, let's say, in comparison to the adjustment needed right in the very beginning. It appears to me always that the most logical thing is to follow the growth of natural things—let us say, how a baby grows. We do not first expose the baby to an artificial language. On the contrary, we deplore such things today; for instance, adults speaking in baby language and not introducing the child to the language which we, ourselves, are speaking. Having grown up with this concept, it simply didn't occur to me.

You can see here, in one instance, that the child changed her method of approach. Holding her head in her hands for the first time made her feel that she has ears. These exaggerated, round symbols, plate-like symbols, are the ears. These ears are not pulled out, but are attached to the head; so is the pin—this is the hair pin. On this day she wore a hair pin on the head. We know this is a different method of approach from that of normal children. The one method of approach in which we start with the whole and deduce the details, we call the analytical method—analysis. The other approach, in which we assemble the details into a whole, we call the synthetical approach to modeling. Here, we have first the parts; and then we assemble them and receive, through synthesis, the whole body, do you see? In this modeling, we see a little shift to a synthetic approach. We know that synthesis means concept formations. This again is an art education interpretation, because it stems from our experimentation with art experiences. Let us say that man consists of a head, the eyes, the ears, the nose, the mouth, the neck, and so forth; and building up concepts for each of these parts means knowing of them, first of all—actively knowing of them. As a child, if I did not know that a man has ears, I would not draw them. Only if the child's experiences are activated to the extent that the ears become an active part of his experiences will the child include the ears in his concept.

On the basis of this, as you know, Goodenough built her intelligence test. She says that the accumulation of details is a response to the intellectual growth of the individual. Yes, indeed, this active knowledge is part of his intelligence. But concept formation in itself is a higher state of consciousness, and so I became aware of the fact that now Camilla was shifting from a purely analytical approach—a diffused perceptual approach which merely refers to the reference of the senses—to an approach which refers more to her knowledge. "I have this and this and this. I am holding my ears; my ears are attached on this part of my head. I have a hair pin; my hair pin is on this side of my head." These are more conscious relationships, more determined relationships, than the pulling out by chance of the legs or the nose or the indentation of the mouth as part of her experience.

Student: I'm not sure I understand this. You say adding the nose as a separate object to a mask would be superior to drawing out the nose?

Lowenfeld: Yes. You see, drawing it out diffusely and leaving it as an undifferentiated symbol means only the nose, "This is a nose." But adding the nose and forming it and putting it exactly where it belongs between the eyes means a higher form of consciousness, not only of the symbol itself as a concept of the nose, but also of its location in relationship to other parts. This is a higher degree of consciousness. And this, of course, also was part of the unfolding process of Camilla.

Student: Just one little detail—did she wear shoes, or was she wearing shoes at the time?

Lowenfeld: She did not wear shoes. She usually went barefoot. It was summertime, and she felt at ease. In fact, she revolted against having her toes together, so later on we gave her sandals. She was an individual whose unfolding and awakening was a little bit untamed in the beginning. That was the reason why the people at Perkins Institution did not consider her as normal—because of her obstructive or unobsequious way of reacting to stimuli.

At this time, I saw that Camilla was closely identifying with these experiences, and this was without any doubt because she now could follow any stimulation, such as the complex shifting from the putting of an object into her hand to modeling herself without doing anything. However, I still was waiting for the time when Camilla would express herself spontaneously, and that had not yet taken place. In psychology, you would still call that guided therapy, as contrasted to any free, spontaneous response, which, in the case of Camilla, was a little bit delayed or was not yet achieved.

Then, I saw Camilla when she was again sitting as she had been before. She was waiting, and apparently she was tired. She was yawning "Ahh"—

like this, you know. I approached her and put her hand over my face and yawned, too, and said, "Yawning, Ahh-ahh, yawning." I put her hand over my face when I yawned, and I put my hand over her face, and she yawned. I said continuously, "Yawning." At that time Miss Hall, the speech teacher, came along and wanted to participate. The attendant was also there. I said, "Yawning," and Camilla, I'm sure, at that time said, "Yawning"—visibly and/or audibly an imitation of the sound which I made, "Yawning." I said, "Tired, tired," and I put my hands into the situation. She tried to imitate some of the sounds which I did which was the first breakthrough towards language teaching. From that time on, I could send for Miss Hall; and Miss Hall could approach her then in her way in promoting the imitation of vowels and sounds and meaningful words.

This was yawning [see Figure 36d]. You can see that this is the first really great step! The other [Figure 36c] may be more impressive because it comes closer to our concept of sitting and holding—it is more complex—but here you have a consistent change in the method of approach. The eyes are no longer merely indentations. She made indentations, but then formed an eyeball and put the eyeball into place. This means a more complex symbol or concept formation. It means, "My eye consists of an eyeball and an eye socket." She made an indentation for the nose, but then formed the nose, including the nostrils. Then she said to herself: "The nose is located between the eyes. I wear a hairpin." You see, at the right side is the hairpin. "I have ears," and now the ears are differentiated. She even added the chin as a separate symbol. Do you see it on the bottom? Because the chin was something separate in her concept, she added it as a separate symbol. This was an enormous unfolding of intellect, identification with her experience, and, of course, communication. It also served as an excellent means for language communication because it offered so many new things. We said, "Eyes, eyes, eyes—ayes, ayes," you know, "nose, nose, nose," and we were holding her nose. She was forming the nose and she said, "Ose, Ose." First, the mere vowels—the consonants were to come later—but all with a great deal of excitement.

What we can learn from this is quite clear. You see that grammar doesn't help us unless we have the urge to use it. In general education, this should be known. We can always learn from the handicapped and refer it to general education. The intensity for expression determines the complexity of your vocabulary use, both in words and in form. So there is no sense in teaching grammar, or how to model a nose, or how to pronounce a word, unless one wants to use it and unless one has an urgency to use it. This urge apparently was never created in Camilla, so speech lessons before were meaningless. Now she knew what she wanted to communicate, and her communication became meaningful. Do you see the difference? From this, we can really deduce general meanings.

After that, as a variation of this experience, I brought her candy. She and I were putting the candy into our mouths. I crushed the candy and also moved her jaw, giving her the feeling that she should crush it, too. And she did. Then I gave her clay, and this was now the established signal for our communication. She used it immediately and with great excitement. The modeling which she did was this [see Figure 36e]. You can see that she extended her frame of reference with regard to symbol formation voluntarily. No one ever told her to include, let us say, the teeth. But the teeth were a part of her experience. She was crushing the candy. You can see the candy in the center. She put the teeth in and did this voluntarily. She had learned "teeth" in her speech lessons. At that time she said, "Deeth, deeth." Teeth were already a part of her; now they were included in her model.

She felt a need to name the parts she already had learned, like "Aye, noe," and those parts by now were a part of her experience which had to come out. For the parts which she didn't know how to name—well, I put her hands to my lips, and I tried to repeat them with her. For instance, she did not know lashes—that which surrounds the eye—but when she was crushing the candy, I saw her pressing her eyes together. She did not refer to it in her language experience. I put her hands to her eyes—she had already modeled her eyeball—and she felt her eye lashes and lids, too. I said, "Lid," and touched her eyelids. Then I pulled on her eyelashes and said, "Lashes!" Well, these she did not get. You can also see the absence of these in her modeling. But, again, her synthetical approach—that means, her concept formation—became much more differentiated. I hope you can see it.

I have omitted quite a number of modelings. What I'm now showing you was done exactly three months after the first approach. But during these three months, three months only, Camilla learned to communicate by language so much so that she was ready to learn to read by Braille. This was, of course, a very exciting experience—to touch something and to know that this is "eye," simple terms which referred again to her own body. For the very first time, she spontaneously modeled something before I was even there. This was the modeling which she did [see Figure 36f]. This is Camilla learning to read Braille. She has the tablet on her knees; you can see her knee caps. Look at the way she differentiated the fingers and the thumb. She pointed to them and said, "Fin-ger, Dumb." This was the day before she had her birthday. I gave her a necklace, and she wanted to show me how she loved the necklace. The coil around her neck is the necklace.

Now there comes something which I have to mention as a very important experience. First of all, the most important experience here is that she spontaneously engaged in documenting herself—in one of her own great experiences. She did not need to be told what to do or even to be stimulated. She herself went ahead in doing it. That means this was the first great experience, this spontaneous desire to go ahead. The other experience, however, which I did not mention before occurs in every situation which we call clinical or creative, or whatever you may call it, in which you come into a closer relationship with your children, subjects, patients, or students. You develop an attachment to them and they to you. This attachment may become very great at some point, especially in serious cases of handicap. Freud calls this attachment "transfer." Let me not confuse matters—I shall call it always attachment. Because I shall not deal with it in a psychoanalytical fashion, I will remain with the very simple way that we deal with it in teaching art to children; therefore, I'll call it simply attachment. It is only logical that, in a situation such as this one with Camilla, there is an attachment which takes place between the individual and you, and I would say also between you and the individual, in a way—only you are conscious of it, while the individual is not conscious of it. At times, a very serious situation may be created, inasmuch as this attachment may grow to such an extent that it may not be possible to dissolve it without serious aftereffects. Knowing that this attachment at one point will set in, we have to think of methods which will dissolve this attachment. In my experience, the best way one can dissolve such an attachment is to transfer this attachment to various situations and various other people.

In the case of Camilla, it was relatively simple; because, as I told you previously, Miss Hall, the speech teacher, was participating, the attendant was participating, the school psychologist was participating, and I was participating. Indeed, Camilla had the greatest attachment to me. Well, she kissed me, she embraced me, she hugged me, and she expressed all kinds of excitement when I came. Previous to this—nothing. But I had already tried, before this modeling, and sometimes afterwards, not to come and to have the attendant or Miss Hall take over my part. Gradually, the intervals between my coming became longer. Camilla continued to express herself spontaneously with Miss Hall and with the others. Speech came in, reading came in, and it was, indeed, a happy situation in which the attachment could be divided among the various individuals until I felt I was no longer that important; and I didn't go at all for a couple of days. Then I came, and Camilla was still very excited as always when I came. The dissolvement of the attachment, the complete dissolvement, was almost impossible. I saw Camilla the last time three years ago. Now Camilla can talk of her experience and knows everything. At that time, she was helping out in the library of the Perkins Institution. I understand that she has now changed her position. She is a mature girl.

I've tried to give you a case history in a rather short time. I hope you see how she used all the details—the lids, the teeth, the nose; and while she was doing each, she verbalized it. I hope you have all experienced with me how the unfolding process through creative activity can be released, how one can stimulate, and how this can be drawn sometimes to a very successful and exciting conclusion. Now, I would not like to be misunderstood. Camilla was not the only case of mine. There were others, and they by no means all responded in this same fashion. Especially as you deal with other cases, you may often have the feeling that you have come to a dead point, and the spontaneous forging ahead of an individual never comes, as it did in Camilla's case. So don't get the feeling that all cases will work out like Camilla's did. I do not want to create a false impression; but in the case of Camilla, it has been shown and demonstrated that art education can become a very wholesome therapeutical means.

Selected Bibliography
of the Writings of
Viktor Lowenfeld

Die Entstehung der Plastik. Brunn: R. M. Rohrer, 1932.
"Teaching the Blind to Model." *The Contemporary Review,* 141, 794 (February 1932): 198–203.
(With Ludwig Munz). *Plastische Arbeiten Blinder.* Brunn: R. M. Rohrer, 1934.
Blindenplastik. Berlin: Blindenjahrbuch, 1937.
"The Experience of Haptic Space and Shape." *Outlook for the Blind,* 33, 4 (October 1939): 118–20.
The Nature of Creative Activity. Trans. by O. A. Oeser. London: Routledge and Kegan Paul Ltd., 1939.
"Sculpture by the Blind." In *Art Education Today,* 88–89. New York: Bureau of Publications, Teachers College, Columbia University, 1939.
"Book Review of *Education of the Handicapped,* I, *History.*" Edited by Merle E. Frampton and Hugh G. Rowell. *Harvard Educational Review,* 10, 2 (March 1940): 250–51.
"The Meaning of Creative Activity in the Education of the Deaf-Blind." *The Teachers Forum* [American Foundation for the Blind], 12, 4 (March 1940): 62–65, 72.
"Visual and Non-visual Expression." *Hampton Institute Extension Bulletin,* 1 (1940).
"Self Adjustment Through Creative Activity." *American Journal of Mental Deficiency,* 45, 3 (January 1941): 173, 366.
"Modelling as a Means of Self-Expression in the Schools for the Blind." *Harvard Educational Review,* 12, 1 (January 1942): 4–6.
"The Blind Make Us See." *Magazine of Art,* 36, 6 (October 1943): 208–11.
"Letters—*Personal Revolution and Picasso* by L. Danz—Similar to *Nature of Creative Activity.*" *Magazine of Art,* 36, 8 (December 1943): 316.
"New Negro Art in America." *Design,* 46, 1 (September 1944): 20–21.
"Negro Art Expression in America." *The Madison Quarterly,* 5, 1 (January 1945): 26–31.
"Tests for Visual and Haptical Aptitudes." *American Journal of Psychology,* 58, 1 (January 1945): 100–111.
"The Meaning of Creative Activity." *Design,* 46, 6 (February 1945): 14–15.
Creative and Mental Growth. New York: Macmillan Co., 1947.
"Psychological Aspects of Creative Activity." In *Art Education in a Free Society,* 83–95. Yearbook of the Eastern Arts Association. Kutztown, Pennsylvania: The Eastern Arts Association, 1947.
"Self-realization Through Creative Activity." *The Playshop* [Division of Dramatics, The Pennsylvania State University], 9, 3 (April 1948): 2–3.
"Self-confidence Through Creative Work." *Progressive Education,* 26, 3 (January 1949): 75–77.
"Technique and Creative Freedom." *Art Education,* 2, 1 (January–February 1949): 1–3.
(And others). *An Integrated Course of Study in Art for Junior and Senior High Schools.* State College, Pennsylvania: The Pennsylvania State University, 1949. (Mimeographed)
"Art and Society—A Dilemma." *School and Society,* 71, 1839 (March 1950): 164–66.
"The Meaning of Integration for Art Education." *Art Education Bulletin* [Research Issue, Eastern Arts Association], 7, 4 (April 1950).

SELECTED BIBLIOGRAPHY

"The Art of the Blind in Its Psycho-Aesthetic Implications." *The American Psychologist*, 5, 7 (July 1950): 242.
"Book Review of *Psychology and Art of the Blind*." *Outlook for the Blind and the Teachers Forum* [American Foundation for the Blind], 44, 9 (November 1950): 268.
Growth Through Art, Midcentury White House Exhibit. Washington, D.C.: The Midcentury White House Conference on Children and Youth, December 3–7, 1950.
"Emotional Freedom for Learning." *Arts in Childhood Bulletin* [Fisk University], Ser. 5, No. 1 (1950): 5–8.
"Must a Teacher Produce Creatively?" In *Art Education Today*, 11–13. New York: Bureau of Publications, Teachers College, Columbia University, 1950.
"Koehler's Tree." *Life Magazine*, January 15, 1951, p. 12.
(With H. Serber). "Decorate Your School with Mural Paintings." *Design*, 52, 6 (March 1951): 23–24.
"Criticisms of 'The Arts in the Integration of the School Program'." *Progressive Education*, 28, 6 (April 1951): 189–90.
"The Meaning of Creative Activity for Personality Growth." *The National Elementary Principal* [NEA Department of Elementary School Principals], 30, 5 (April 1951): 32–35.
"Psycho-Aesthetic Implications of the Art of the Blind." *Journal of Aesthetics and Art Criticism*, 10, 1 (September 1951): 1–9.
Creative and Mental Growth, 2nd ed. New York: Macmillan Co., 1952.
"The Meaning of Art Education in a Democracy." In *This Is Art Education, 1952*, 77–83. Second NAEA Yearbook. Kutztown, Pennsylvania: National Art Education Association, 1952.
The Nature of Creative Activity, 2nd ed. New York: Harcourt, Brace and World, Inc., 1952.
"Competitions and Art Education." *Art Digest*, 27, 9 (February 1953): 21.
"Art Motivations for the Junior High School Child." *Art Education Bulletin* [Research Issue, Eastern Arts Association], 10, 4 (April 1953).
"Understanding Children's Creative Expression." *The Catholic Art Quarterly* [The Catholic Art Association, Buffalo], 17, 1 (December 1953): 5–16.
"Virginia Always Draws the Same Thing." *School Arts*, 53, 5 (January 1954): 7–10.
"Virginia Says, 'I Can't Draw'." *Junior Arts and Activities*, 35, 1 (February 1954).
"The Meaning of Creativity for Art Education." *Art Education Bulletin* [Eastern Arts Association], 11, 3 (March 1954).
"Art Education for Better Understanding." *Art Education Bulletin* [Eastern Arts Association], 11, 5 (May 1954): 2.
"Creative Growth in Child Art." *Design*, 5, 6 (September 1954): 12–13.
"The Place of Techniques in the High School Art Program." In *Art Today in Catholic Secondary Education*. Washington, D.C.: The Catholic University of America Press, 1954.
Your Child and His Art. New York: Macmillan Co., 1954.
"The Significance of Art for Education." *Education*, 75, 6 (February 1955): 374–78.
"The Creative Process and the Handicapped." *School Arts*, 54, 7 (March 1955): 5–8.
"Environment and Education." *Bulletin of the American Institute of Architects*, 9, 4 (July–August 1955): 115–18.
"The Meaning of Aesthetic Growth for Art Education." *Journal of Aesthetics and Art Criticism*, 14, 1 (September 1955): 123–26.
"Leaders in Art Education." *Arts and Activities*, 38, 4 (December 1955).
"The Case of the Gifted Child." *School Arts*, 56, 8 (April 1956): 13–18.
"Therapeutic Aspects of Art Education." *Art Education Bulletin* [Research Issue, Eastern Arts Association], 6, 1 (April 1956): 14–17.
"Values in Children's Drawings." *The Catholic Art Quarterly* [Catholic Art Association, Buffalo], 19, 2 (April 1956): 70–76.
"Children Communicate Through Art." *Childhood Education* [Association for Childhood International], 33, 4 (December 1956): 159–62.
"The Meaning of Creative Expression for the Child." In *Imagination in Education*, 36–46. New York: Bank Street College of Education, 1956.
"Values in Children's Drawings and Paintings." In *Art in Christian Education*. Washington, D.C.: The Catholic University of America Press, 1956.

SELECTED BIBLIOGRAPHY

"Address by Viktor Lowenfeld at SEAA Convention in Atlanta, April 1956." *South Eastern Arts Association Bulletin* (Winter 1957).

"Art for Every Child." *Viewpoint* [Bulletin of the New Zealand Art Teachers Association], (May 1957).

"The Adolescence of Art Education." *Art Education*, 10, 7 (October 1957): 5–12.

"Art and the Preschool Child." *Growing* [Bulletin of the Board of Christian Education of the Presbyterian Church of the United States], 10, 1 (October 1957): 10–11.

Creative and Mental Growth, 3rd ed. New York: Macmillan Co., 1957.

"Creativity and Art Education." In *Art as Language*. Washington, D.C.: The Catholic University of America Press, 1957.

"The Nature of Adolescent Art." In *Art and the Adolescent*, p. 29. Eighth NAEA Yearbook. Kutztown, Pennsylvania: The National Art Education Association, 1957.

"Art for Teacher Education in This Time of Stress." In *Eleventh Yearbook of the American Association of Colleges for Teacher Education*, 77–87. Chicago: American Association of Colleges for Teacher Education, 1958.

"Current Research on Creativity." *NEA Journal*, 47, 8 (November 1958): 538–40.

"Growth in Individual Perfection Through Art." In *Art for Christian Living*. Washington, D.C.: The Catholic University of America Press, 1958.

"The Significance of Art Education in This Time of Stress." In *Sixth Art Teaching Conference* (mimeographed), 1–9. Honolulu: Honolulu Academy of Arts, 1958.

(With Amos J. Shaler and Donald S. Pearson). *An Interdisciplinary Study of Creativity in Art and the Exact and Applied Sciences*. University Park, Pennsylvania: The Pennsylvania State University, 1958.

"A Forward Look in Art Education." *Midlands Schools* [Publication of the Iowa State Education Association], 73, 8 (April 1959): 8–9.

"Art Can Make a Child Happier." *Farm Journal*, 83 (July 1959): 84–85.

"Creativity and Art Education." *School Arts*, 59, 2 (October 1959): 5–15.

"How Can I Evaluate Art Activities?" *The Brooklyn Teacher* [Publication of the Brooklyn Teachers' Association], (October 1959).

"A Commentary." In *Research in Art Education*, 174–77. Ninth NAEA Yearbook. Washington, D.C.: The National Art Education Association, 1959.

"Evaluation of Art Activities." In *Catholic Art Education—New Trends*. Washington, D.C.: The Catholic University of America Press, 1959.

"Is Art Education Missing the Boat?" In *Art Education, The Main Promoter of Creative Thinking*. Sixth Annual PAEA Conference. Harrisburg: Pennsylvania Art Education Association, 1959.

(With Kenneth Beittel). "Interdisciplinary Criteria of Creativity in the Arts and Sciences: A Progress Report." In *Research in Art Education*, 35–44. Ninth NAEA Yearbook. Washington, D.C.: The National Art Education Association, 1959.

"Art for Teacher Education in This Time of Stress." *Perception* [Journal of the British Columbia Art Teachers Association], 1, 1 (Spring 1960).

"How Can I Evaluate Art Activities?" *Rhythm*, 8, 1, (1960).

"Reflections." In *1910–1960, Prospect and Retrospect*, 46–47. Edited by Ruth Ebken. Kutztown, Pennsylvania: The Eastern Arts Association, 1960.

Vom Wesen schopferischen Gestaltens. Frankfurt am Main: Europaische Verlagsanstalt, 1960.

"What is General Education's Responsibility for Creativity in the Language Arts and Higher Education." In *Issues in Higher Education*, 111–12. Chicago: Association for Higher Education, 1960.

"Basic Aspects of Creative Teaching." In *Creativity and Psychological Health*, 129–41. Edited by Michael F. Andrews. Syracuse: Syracuse University Press, 1961.

Viktor Lowenfeld Speaks on Art and Creativity. Edited by W. Lambert Brittain. Washington, D.C.: The National Art Education Association, 1968. (Selections edited from tape recordings of Lowenfeld's speeches.)

Research References

Biggers, J. "The Negro Woman in American Life and Education: A Mural Presentation." Unpublished doctoral dissertation, The Pennsylvania State University, 1954.

Brittain, W. L. "Experiments for a Possible Test to Determine Some Aspects of Creativity in the Visual Arts." Unpublished doctoral dissertation, The Pennsylvania State University, 1952.

Burkhart, R. C. "An Analysis of Individuality of Art Expression at the Senior High School Level." Unpublished doctoral dissertation, The Pennsylvania State University, 1957.

Conant, J. B. *The American High School Today: A First Report to Interested Citizens.* New York: McGraw–Hill, 1958.

Corcoran, A. L. "The Variability of Children's Responses to Color Stimuli." Unpublished doctoral dissertation, The Pennsylvania State University, 1953.

Gesell, A. *Infant Development.* New York: Harper, 1952.

Goodenough, Florence L. *Measurement of Intelligence by Drawings.* Yonkers-on-Hudson, New York: World Book Co., 1926.

Guilford, J. P. "Creativity." *American Psychologist,* 9 (1950):444–45.

Heilman, H. "An Experimental Study of the Effects of Workbooks on the Creative Drawing of Second Grade Children." Unpublished doctoral dissertation, The Pennsylvania State University, 1954.

Lansing, K. M. "The Effect of Class Size and Room Size upon the Creative Drawings of Fifth Grade Children." Unpublished doctoral dissertation, The Pennsylvania State University, 1956.

McVitty, L. F. "An Experimental Study on Various Methods in Art Motivations." Unpublished doctoral dissertation, The Pennsylvania State University, 1954.

Mattil, E. "A Study to Determine the Relationship between the Creative Products of Children and Their Adjustment." Unpublished doctoral dissertation, The Pennsylvania State University, 1953.

Putney, W. "Characteristics of Creative Drawings of Stutterers." Unpublished doctoral dissertation, The Pennsylvania State University, 1955.

Russell, I., and Waugaman, B. "A Study of the Effect of Workbook Copy Experiences on the Creative Concepts of Children." *Research Bulletin,* The Eastern Arts Association, *3,* 1 (1952).

Zawacki, A. "An Experimental Study of Analytic Versus Synthetic Modelings and Drawings of Children." Unpublished doctoral dissertation, The Pennsylvania State University, 1956.